Open Development

Open Development

Networked Innovations in International Development

Edited by Matthew L. Smith and Katherine M. A. Reilly

The MIT Press
Cambridge, Massachusetts
London, England

International Development Research Centre
Ottawa • Cairo • Montevideo • Nairobi • New Delhi

© 2013 International Development Research Centre

Published by the MIT Press. MIT Press books may be purchased at special quantity discounts for business or sales promotional use. For information, please email special_sales@mitpress.mit.edu.

A copublication with
International Development Research Centre
PO Box 8500
Ottawa, ON K1G 3H9
Canada
www.idrc.ca / info@idrc.ca
ISBN 978-1-55250-568-7 (IDRC e-book)

This book was set in Stone Serif and Stone Sans by the MIT Press. Printed and bound in the United States of America.

Library of Congress Cataloging-in-Publication Data
Open development : networked innovations in international development / edited by Matthew L. Smith, and Katherine M.A. Reilly ; foreword by Yochai Benkler.
pages cm
Includes bibliographical references and index.
ISBN 978-0-262-52541-1 (pbk. : alk. paper) 1. Information technology—Developing countries. 2. Economic development—Developing countries. 3. Social networks—Developing countries. I. Smith, Matthew L. editor of compilation. II. Reilly, Katherine M. A., 1974- editor of compilation.
HC59.72.I55O64 2014
303.48'33091724—dc23
2013016541

10   9   8   7   6   5   4   3   2   1

Contents

Foreword

Yochai Benkler

Non-proprietary, self-organizing production has come to play a large role in the construction of the networked environment, networked culture, and the networked social order. Standard setting for both the Internet itself and the World Wide Web is built on non-state, non-proprietary models of organization. The core software utilities that run the World Wide Web rely on free and open source software as do, increasingly, operating systems of servers, smartphones, and embedded computing; enterprise software; and even statistics packages. The basic infrastructure for our synthesized state of knowledge—our age's encyclopedia—is some combination of Wikipedia and the Google search, itself an amalgamation of information produced by both traditional models and new, distributed models. Over the course of the first decade of the twenty-first century, commons-based peer production and social production, more generally, have moved from being ignored, through being mocked, feared, and regarded as an exception or intellectual quirk, to finally becoming a normal and indispensable part of life. By 2012 it seems much too late to ask, *Is this real?* It is now high time to ask, *What does it mean?*

In this volume, authors from diverse backgrounds address head-on one of the major domains of challenge in today's world: how to improve the lives of billions of people who are prevented from flourishing as human beings by significant economic and political constraints. Clearly, open development is not a panacea—nothing would be. But what is new in this broad approach to organizing human affairs?

The Great Recession of 2008 burst the bubble of the post-Soviet, euphoric "market-based everything ideology" that prevailed in the 1990s, although many of its adherents continue to uncritically promote its teachings: lesson learning is difficult. As major American banks and financial actors required hundreds of billions of dollars of government funds to survive, and as General Motors became a state- and worker-owned firm in order to (successfully) save the company (although rapid re-privatization ensued), the ideologues and self-interested parties continued with their free-market rhetoric. The major European countries are undermining their own political stability by trying to impose austerity and limited expenditures in the hope of teasing the confidence fairy out of her deep slumber, as though the markets themselves were functioning well and the problem was only the government side undermining confidence in these markets.

As the glaring imperfections of markets join the equally glaring imperfection of states, non-state, non-market production and practical organization is emerging as an important conceptual and effective alternative to provisioning a range of desiderata, particularly public goods, in networked society. Social intervention is distinctively shaped to approach a problem represented by market or state failure: it seeks to create a workaround that harnesses social production to fulfill the complete function without suffering the same limitations; or it seeks, at a minimum, to create an oversight mechanism or pressure point that forces the relevant market- or state-based practice to moderate the perceived failure.

Much as the ideal of the free market stands as an ideological contrast to bureaucracy, or the state, so too the concept of open models stands in contrast to both these ideal types of social organization. Like the free market, open source development is built on individual, autonomous action, in concert with others, in significant measure outside the state. Unlike the free market, open source at its core rejects the assertion of exclusive control through property, and unlike corporate versions of market organizations, fosters a culture that insists on rejecting hierarchy (as with all ideal types, often honored in the breach, if at all). The point is not that open models really *are* all these things. They are not truly independent of the state more so than free markets, nor are they completely exploitative. Nor is the state, indeed, a monolithic embodiment of either its progressive ideal nor as that of a libertarian dystopia. Like the market, and unlike the state, open models as an ideal rely on non-state action under relatively diffuse power conditions (as in the perfect market ideal). Like the state (particularly in its democratic aspects) and unlike the market, open models consist of non-commodified relations, production, and exchange. (Not necessarily the absence of money per se, but the absence of commodification of the joint product as the organizing principle, and an insistence on not reducing the relations of production and use purely to their commodified, transactional form.)

Therefore, for development in particular, open models provide an important counterweight to the neoliberal Washington Consensus, as well as later efforts to soften it. In particular, open models offer a degree of freedom, in the engineering sense, for designing development-oriented interventions without strong dependencies on either markets or states.

Where a country's telecommunications carrier is too politically powerful, or its government corrupted by promises from a major operating system or enterprise software vendor, open models provide an alternative avenue that builds development goals around such failures. In each of the following cases—whether with community-built Wi-Fi networks in Indonesia that provide broadband at rates people can afford; or in operating systems people can use in South Africa; or in real-time violence monitoring systems in Kenya that, through the collaborative, free, and open-source software development model, become globally available as free software for election and natural disaster monitoring—open models provide a workaround for people of good will to come together and build a solution to the limitations of their market and state systems. In some cases, open models must overcome direct competition or pressure from the state or market they disrupt. In other cases, they can operate to lower the load carried by systems that must be provided by the state, such as education and health, and lower the burden enough to make it bearable for less-than-perfect states and markets.

A new and critical aspect of the globally networked information economy involves the large and growing range of inputs into, and components of, human development that are indeed amenable to being provided or supported by open models of social production. Knowledge, innovation, and the capacity to communicate are core elements of human development and contribute to its improvement. They are also the building blocks and core outputs of the networked environment. The approaches explored in this volume offer a window into a new possibility set, into new ways for people to come together to foster the basic capabilities and facilities necessary to improve the human condition. And, just as industrialization did not completely occupy all domains of life but altered the shape of everything that surrounded it, for good or ill, so too will open, networked social action. It will not be the solution for (or cause of) all aspects of human development. But the new set of effective human action that it makes feasible fundamentally reshapes the problems, solutions, and institutional frameworks of human development.

Preface

We are but one set of curators working among a massive network of people who have collaborated across a number of different plateaus to give rise to myriad ideas. As a friend once said about a conference they were discussing to Katherine Reilly, the coeditor of this book, "we need to think of this not as a single forum, but rather as *mil mini foros* (a million mini forums) that take place through each conversation, each experience, each activity." Similarly, this book is just one expression of a complex conversation; with that in mind, we'd like to use this space to tell you how it came into being.

In 2008, the Information Technology for Development Program Area at the International Development Research Centre (IDRC) did a review of emerging scholarship in the study of information and communication technologies for development (ICT4D). Looking back over the last five years of research in this area, and looking toward the future, they noticed a significant trend. One word best captured it: *openness*.

As IDRC began to expand its work in the area of openness, it developed a working paper titled "Open ICT4D."[1] This led to the publication of "Open ICT Ecosystems Transforming the Developing World" in the journal *Information Technology and International Development* in March 2010. In that work, Matthew Smith and his colleague Laurent Elder hypothesized that open social systems could amplify and transform social activities in ways that would radically alter the impacts of ICTs on development.

"Open ICT4D," however, didn't fully capture the extent of the transformations being hypothesized by Smith and Elder. As further work emerged in this area, it became clear that ICT4D carried too narrow a focus, and that openness was a phenomenon of foundational significance to how we think about development. With this in mind, the IDRC launched a call for papers on open development early in 2009. The goal was to generate critical discussion about the potential of openness in and for development. The workshop, which took place in March 2010, created an interdisciplinary space that included development practitioners, academics, policymakers, and funders from around the world, many of them who had worked with the IDRC over the years.

Around this time, Katherine was defending her PhD dissertation on open networking in Central America, in which she explored the implications of openness for our theoretical assumptions about development. Katherine submitted a paper to the workshop, and eventually began the collaboration with Matthew that led to the production of this volume.

In this book you will find many chapters that had their beginnings at the Open Development workshop, some complementary chapters included to round out the volume, as well as a year's worth of careful thought about Smith and Elder's original hypothesis, its relationship to development theory, and the implications made in the various chapters for its claims. The more we dug into the idea of open development, the more we discussed these ideas within our networks and read the works of others, the more we learned (or unlearned) about development itself. The chapters in this volume individually explore the implications, promises, and challenges of open development within a variety of domains, but together we feel that they form the beginnings of a constructive critique of development practice and theory itself.

As we wrap up the production of this volume, we are impressed to see just how far the idea of open development has come. For example, the September 2012 Open Knowledge Festival in Helsinki, Sweden, created an online platform where people could write from a professional and personal vantage by addressing "What Open Development means to me."[2] The responses posted to the site testify to the power of openness. These responses came from a wide variety of people, and cover a long list of themes including co-creation, sharing and cooperation, bottom-up processes, access to information, mutual learning, dignity, changing aid practices and aid flows, transparency and honesty, transformation, accountability, a focus on processes rather than products, and an attitude of acceptance toward others regardless of status. Clearly the idea has gained momentum, and we look forward to continuing the discussion about the implications of open development as our pursuits in the field move forward.

This book has relied on the dedication and support of many people. We would like to deeply thank all those that have participated and contributed to the development of these ideas and this manuscript, including a long list of IDRC colleagues and anonymous reviewers who provided such great feedback during the workshop, on individual chapters, and to the overall volume. Special thanks to Michael Clarke, Laurent Elder, Heloise Emdon, and Ben Petrazzini, the original progenitors of this process. Katherine would like to thank in particular Ron Deibert for recommending her to the IDRC as an editor for this volume, and to Siavash Rokni for his contributions as a research assistant during the fall 2010 academic semester.

Finally, some personal thanks. Katherine would like to express her love and respect to her wonderful husband Wayne Carrigan, whose support extends well beyond the parameters of any given project and deserves to be acknowledged whenever the opportunity presents itself. Matthew would like to thank his father, who was ahead of the curve on openness; his mother, who taught him how to share, and so much more; and Carolina, for whom everyday he is grateful. He also would like to dedicate this work to his newborn twin daughters: here's hoping they grow up in a world that embraces the values of sharing and cooperation more often than self-interest and competition.

Notes

1. http://web.idrc.ca/uploads/user-S/12271304441Open_ICT4D_Draft.pdf.

2. http://okfnpad.org/okfest-opendev-whatopendevmeanstome.

1 Introduction

Matthew L. Smith and Katherine M. A. Reilly

Rebecca Chiao had already been working in Cairo since 2005 with a local nongovernmental organization (NGO) on the problem of sexual harassment when she became a victim herself.[1] It happened while standing at a busy bus stop in Cairo. Nobody moved to help. Nobody said anything.

In 2009 the majority of NGOs working on the issue of sexual harassment were focused on policy advocacy, trying to create improvements by changing legal frameworks. From Rebecca's perspective, however, the problem was more social than legal; people had to change their ideas of what is acceptable behavior and what is not. This required a different focus, a focus on challenging social norms that created tolerance for sexual intimidation in Egypt.

At around that time she was introduced to Frontline SMS and Ushahidi, two open source software platforms. Frontline SMS is a tool that allows users to send, receive, and manage SMS (text messages) over a mobile network. Ushahidi enables crowdsourcing information using SMS, email, Twitter, and the Web. The combination seemed to Rebecca like a powerful way to better understand and increase public awareness of the prevalence of the problem and to potentially engage with the Egyptian public—especially given a 97 percent mobile penetration rate in Egypt. Her idea was simple: citizens could report, via mobile phone, sexual harassment where it occurs, and display these reports on geo-located pins on a map on the Internet.

Rebecca wrote up the idea and sent it to NGOs, but no one was interested. So Rebecca convinced three Egyptian friends to try the idea themselves. They spent over a year developing a digital reporting system and complemented it with a strong, in-person community-engagement element. If they were to change the culture around harassment, they would have to reach out to as many Egyptians as possible.

With help from the tech company NiJeL, they launched HarassMap in December 2010—and the reports started coming in. Almost immediately, the reports began to break through some of the typical stereotypes regarding harassment. Reports were coming in from disparate parts of Egypt—the desert, the Nile Basin, the Red Sea coast, and places the founders had never heard of—sexual harassment was not something that happened only in the big city of Cairo. Furthermore, the victims weren't just woman dressed in revealing clothes: women dressed in the veil and even the niqab (full-face veil and black cloak) also reported incidents, as did men who were harassed both by other men and by women.

The HarassMap project goes well beyond being a digital reporting system. When someone reports an incident by text message the system auto-responds with a text containing information about free services for victims (including psychological counseling, self-defense classes, and legal aid). The HarassMap team sends a small but dedicated group of trained volunteers into their communities to talk to people with a presence in the neighborhood (such as shop owners or doormen) about sexual harassment and try to convince them to stand and act against it. When community members agree—approximately eight out of ten do by the end of the conversation—the volunteers mark the appropriate place as a safe zone on a map so that people will patronize those shops or move to those areas.

While maintaining the project's core ideas, the HarassMap team has tried hard to be open and responsive in dialogue with the community, often soliciting input and experimenting with new ideas to see what works. As of 2012, they have a series of initiatives including social media campaigns, development of instructional materials, an art exhibition, a video team, police outreach, and research to better understand the validity of the collected data. As Chiao describes it, the way the team works is "a bit free form."[2]

Since the start of HarassMap, teams in sixteen countries have shown interest in the project. At the time of this writing in 2013, six HarassMap clones have been launched in Yemen, Bangladesh, Palestine, Syria, Lebanon, and Pakistan,[3] and others were setting up in Libya, Turkey, South Africa, the United States, Canada, India, Iran, Malaysia, Indonesia, and Japan.

HarassMap illustrates a compelling story of young women taking advantage of openness to tackle a clearly identified social issue. It is a citizen-driven initiative, combining community engagement and a technology-enabled social reporting innovation to reach more Egyptians and break through stereotypes in ways that weren't possible previously. Additionally, thanks to an increasingly open ecosystem of technology and tools, the HarassMap team accomplished all of this for very little money and while holding down day jobs.

Openness: A Challenge to International Development

This book aims to explore new areas and emergent opportunities (such as HarassMap) and to assess their potential in the world of international development. It follows two underlying, interwoven premises: that we inhabit a world rapidly on its way to becoming a network society, which poses significant opportunities and threats for international development; and that international development theory and practice should reflect this new reality. Over the last several decades this burgeoning network society has significantly shifted the conditions shaping development (as well as the means to achieve it). We believe that these changing conditions and new opportunities are becoming increasingly central to development processes.

This volume focuses on one particular source of such opportunities and threats: the emergence of open networked models predicated on digital network technologies. While digital networks have been around since the 1970s, their increasing diffusion, interconnection, and integration across all levels and societies around the world is significantly changing how people can and do organize themselves to accomplish shared goals. This digital diffusion has fostered an emerging set of open network structures and activities through which people and information come together, thus affecting the ways in which we share knowledge, coordinate, organize, collaborate, make decisions, and so on.

Some of these models are widely known, such as the open source software and the Wikipedia collaborative production models. Some are gaining visibility, like open access to scholarly publishing, open educational resources, open government data, and the Ushahidi crowdsourced information platform. Others are less well known, including open access to scientific processes and the private sector's use of open business models. While these models differ in form, content, and outcome, all of them draw on the power of human cooperation and contain some combination of aspects inherent to digitally enabled openness: sharing ideas and knowledge; the ability to reuse, revise, and repurpose content; increasing transparency of processes; expanding participation; and collaborative production.[4]

We refer to the application of these open models and to the logic behind their use in international development as *open development*.[5] Since 2009, when we first began efforts to compile this book, the term *open development* has gained traction. For example: Various international conferences have hosted several open development sessions.[6] The World Bank Institute has applied the term to encapsulate a stream of work they are engaging in[7] (including the Open Development Technology Alliance).[8] The advocacy organization ONE has developed an open development framework that "represents a new vision of what development means, how it comes about and the role that external partners can play."[9] And the African Development Bank writes of a variant—open, smart and inclusive (OSI) development.[10] Of course, it isn't the term that is important, but rather the idea behind the term: harnessing the increased penetration of information and communications technologies to create new organizational forms that improve the lives of people.

This book attempts to engage more comprehensively with the opportunities and challenges that emerge from open development and its implications for international development. The chapters in this volume touch on a wide variety of applications of openness, exploring their potentials, limits, and drawbacks. In chapter 2 the editors offer a theoretical exploration of open development and related terms that lay the foundation for the individually authored chapters to follow. For readers interested in digging into the context, definitions, and concepts involved in open development thinking, chapter 2 is the place to start. For those who prefer to dive into examples of open development, we suggest moving directly to one of three thematic sections. Part I, "Models of Openness," presents various cases in which open models could be (or are) used as a means to address specific development problems. These chapters explore possibilities and ongoing experiments with open models in international development in the areas of health, ethical consumption, biotechnology, and education. Part II, "Openness in Tension," explores the struggles or points of contestation that open models face, such as pressure by incumbents who have a vested interest in the status quo, lack of adequate institutional support, or problems with implementing open policies. Part III, "Constructing Openness," is more conceptual. The three chapters in this section explore, respectively, processes of social construction, knowledge management, and the role of individual intent in shaping the development and outcomes of open models. The last of these three chapters works as a conclusion to the book as a whole, with a consideration of what open development means as a paradigm for development and what is needed to harness the power of open models in a global context dominated by a competing paradigm.

There are many ways we could have organized this volume, each with its own merits and drawbacks. Indeed, given the diversity of domains and cases covered in each chapter, readers will find that the chapters speak to each other, echoing recurring issues or themes, stemming from very different experiences and often very different perspectives. We believe these crosscutting themes and issues make this volume greater than the sum of its contributions. Although it is important to learn lessons from applications within one's area of focus (say, how to implement open government data in resource-constrained settings), it is also possible and beneficial to learn across applications of openness, paying close attention to points of commonality and difference. These applications of openness in different domains may appear quite dissimilar at first blush, but the logic of openness pervades them all.[11]

Crosscutting Themes

In this introduction we briefly discuss some of the themes that emerge from and intersect across the chapters. We do not intend to wrap the chapters in a neat package with a comprehensive list of definitive lessons learned or theoretical insights. Rather, we simply wish to flag what we view as interesting areas of learning and future exploration and, we hope, to stimulate the reader's interest. We see this list as the beginning of a dialogue about important, crosscutting issues that readers will explore and consider as they work through this volume and other open development scholarship.

It's about Development, Not Openness
Most chapters in this volume explore different ways that openness is applied to achieve a particular development goal, be that reduction of HIV in South Africa, improving the educational experiences and opportunities of marginalized communities, or improving government services while maintaining citizens' right to privacy. Openness, in these instances, provides an opportunity to achieve those goals in a manner that has never been done before. That is, openness contributes its own logic—a value added to solving problems. For example, in chapter 5, authors Hassan Masum, Karl Schroeder, Myra Khan, and Abdallah Daar explore the adaptation of the open source software production model to the field of biotechnology production. The hope is that this will improve crop yields or advance medical discoveries in areas of significance to marginalized communities. In chapter 4, Mark Graham and Håvard Haarstad consider the potential use of Wikis and radio frequency identification (RFID) technology (small tracking chips put on products) to make the commodities chain more transparent so that consumers have better information about the labor and environmental impacts of the products they buy. Looking across these chapters, openness offers clear potential benefits in the realization of development objectives.

One question arises from these chapters: How can we gain added value from openness to solve a particular development problem? In particular, the chapters explore how to adapt models of openness to resolve the particular development problem at hand. In other words, there is a strong tendency to start from the development problem and then move to openness and not the other way around. Openness is one means to solving a problem; openness is not the only means, nor is it the end. Of course, openness is conceived of and applied in a variety of ways. This is particularly true given that the idea of development is itself contested terrain, and development issues are themselves highly localized. This doesn't preclude the sharing of lessons learned in local contexts, but it does mean that we need to pay careful attention to working through local contexts when pursuing new open development initiatives.

Openness Is Layered

When considering what value openness brings to the table, it is important to differentiate it from the role of the technology itself. For example, as Marshall S. Smith discusses in chapter 6, there is an important distinction between Open Educational Resources (OERs) and the use of technology in education. Technology used in the classroom, for example, can include OERs but doesn't have to. What makes OERs special is the value added by free access to content, or the ability to remix, reuse, repurpose, and redistribute that content. This is a case of technology *plus* openness.

A larger point here is that open models are layered on top of existing structures, both technological and social; it doesn't emerge ex nihilo. This is not a radical idea, but it is important to point out since open development is best understood as an evolution, not a disjuncture. We can still build on what we have learned; we just have to layer on another level of complexity.

This means we should not abandon the growing set of lessons learned from disciplines such as information and communication technologies for development (ICT4D). There is still a need to deal with fundamental issues like access, capacity, content, meaningful use, and technology policy (although, as we argue in chapter 2, perhaps we need new ways, especially given the growing penetration of ICTs). For example, intellectual property (IP) was never a highly salient policy or research issue in the field of ICT4D, but, as several chapters in this volume illustrate, it is front and center when thinking about open development. Issues of power and inequality aren't dissolved, but rather they are sometimes magnified, sometimes reduced, and yet other times shifted. And where ICT4D might have focused on capacity building, norm setting becomes as important in open development.

Openness Is Disruptive

The study of information systems, a foundational discipline for ICT4D, has illustrated how the implementation of technology results in a series of changes that ripple through the social system. Implementing a technology is never a straightforward *technical* matter, rather it is a social negotiation shaped in part by the technology. For these reasons scholars coined the rather awkward neologism "socio-technical" to refer to information systems: the social and the technical are always intertwined.

Open models, built on information and communication technologies, are also socio-technical systems. Just as implementing technology affects an organization, these new modes of organizing can affect the entire institutional architecture from small ripples of adjustment to more fundamental changes. Indeed, the chapters illustrate how shifts toward more openness drive other institutional changes. Perhaps the most widely known impact is the example of how blogs and online media are challenging the print media industry. These disruptive changes are discussed in more detail in chapter 2.

As the works in this volume illustrate, open models can be disruptive in subtle, but powerful, ways. Two examples that we will mention here appear in chapters throughout the book. First is how organizing around sharing and collaboration forces institutions to rethink metrics for assessments of quality and performance. For instance, in chapter 8, Leslie Chan and Eve Gray show how open access to scholarly publishing challenges the existing, one-size-fits-all system of academic impact assessments and creates a need for new metrics of scholarly production. In particular, research that is relevant to developing countries is undervalued by the current system, but the new metrics of an open access system offer an opportunity to rectify this situation. As Chan and Gray write in chapter 8, "Metrics should serve to support what we value, and not define it." If the saying "you are what you measure" holds true, then the definition of these metrics is hugely important to the type of world we hope to see.

Second are the shifting values that accompany open models. As Yochai Benkler writes in the foreword and Ineke Buskens notes in chapter 13, open models have emerged in a global context dominated by the values of the market and economic theory. Commercial values dominate the publishing and academic systems (see chapter 6), and the West has determined IP regimens. Open models challenge these value systems with a seemingly viable alternative. As Jeremy de Beer and Chidi Oguamanam write in chapter 10, "openness applied to international development bears significant promise for shifting the conceptual paradigms that dominated the latter half of the twentieth century." This is arguably a cultural shift toward the values of sharing and cooperation that run counter to market system based on its model of inherently self-interested people.[12]

What this suggests is that open models can bring about redistribution in the benefits of developmental gains. As a result, open models are inherently political, in that they challenge the incumbents in existing systems and also influence the allocation of resources and, therefore, power. They will also imply new ways of doing politics since they put into place new models of knowledge production that adjust patterns of participation, decision making, or construction of meaning, as Katherine M. A. Reilly explores in chapter 12.

Functional Openness Requires Structure

Harnessing the power of openness does not happen completely by chance; it requires structure. Just as language needs syntax to be intelligible, constructing an open model always requires some degree of its opposite, closedness, to provide the structure to make openness function. Unfettered openness lacks the structure necessary to channel the combined energy of its participants toward meaningful ends. Functional openness balances twin forces: the power that comes from the flexibility of openness and the structure that gives purpose.

The importance of structure for shaping behavior can be seen across the chapters in a variety of forms, such as platforms for biotechnology scientists to collaborate, open access repositories, packaging of OERs into easily digestible and reusable modules, new legal frameworks for intellectual property rights, the need for safe (private) spaces for dialogue, established norms for participation, and even the way data visualizations constructed on top of open data impose a very particular logic on the data itself.

A key dual point here is that this structure is *socially constructed* and done that way *for a purpose*. The contours of open models are formed through the myriad of assumptions and decisions, implicit or explicit, that shape the open space, be they the norms that shape a participation process, the standards for communication, or the procedural means for decision making, to name but a few. Technologies, with their inscribed logic, also shape forms of participation. All of these aspects are the result of decisions or social negotiations that ultimately shape the very nature and possibilities of the open model itself. In other words, they provide both the structure for success and the notion of what that success is (which in turn feeds back into the definition of metrics, as discussed above).

Openness: The Ideal Is Never the Reality

The necessary structure of an open model points to another important aspect: no open model is ever universally and completely open, nor can it ever be. Although ICTs are famous for their ability help overcome the barriers of time and distance, they never do so completely. The constraints of people, existing social systems, and the contours of the open model all provide limitations to who can participate, and how. Time, distance, language, culture, past experiences, and so on, affect individuals' ability to access and participate meaningfully. Similarly, norms, policies, technological infrastructure, incentive structures, and the like provide structure for openness but necessarily close off possibilities and opportunities. In chapter 11, Blane Harvey details how, in setting up a participatory community, "the spaces for achieving openness do not look the same for everyone, and therefore, they accommodate some more easily than others." Openness, according to Harvey, is never open to all, but rather open to certain constituencies. To understand an open model it is necessary not only to see which constituencies it includes, but also how and whom it excludes by its very nature.

Openness Requires a Critical Perspective

The gap between the ideal and reality of openness implies a need for a critical perspective if the model is to achieve its development objectives in a balanced manner. The general appeal of the concept of openness provides an attractive facade that can be used to mask underlying inequity or unintended consequences. As Aaron K. Martin and Carla M. Bonina point out in chapter 9, the desire of governments to improve transparency and accountability through open governance also opens up a series of threats to citizens' privacy. Based on illustrations from government initiatives to engage citizens in online environments, the authors raise awareness of the need for online identity policies that would minimize unnecessary privacy invasions, harmful surveillance, or discrimination.

Parminder Jeet Singh and Anita Gurumurthy, in chapter 7, critically examine the application of openness in a series of domains and illustrate how it covers up, but does not directly address, underlying power asymmetries. For example, they question the benefits and risks of our current reliance on open models based on privately owned platforms like Twitter and pose questions such as, "How open are they really?" and "What risks to openness do we run relying on private companies to manage our open spaces?" Jeet Singh and Gurumurthy argue that the real conditions of openness have to be predicated on what they term "network publics"—an institutional ecology of public institutions, rights, and obligations that support true openness. So while open models may, as Benkler suggests in this volume's foreword, provide an alternative solution to those offered by the market or the public sector, Singh and Gurumurthy argue that openness is dependent upon the public sector and its institutions (much like the market is) to realize its full potential. A key challenge facing open development, in fact, is to analyze and implement new institutional, cultural, and policy frameworks through which open flows can function to enhance (rather than undermine) development outcomes.

Often the forces that shape factors of exclusion are subtle, such as underlying cultural values or assumptions. Buskens, in the concluding chapter, argues that in many cases it is essential to "lift the veil" from different open development initiatives, to see the subtle ways that inclusion in an open model is shaped by the concepts underlying the assumptions that "form us and inform us." Doing so will help us see the internal inconsistency between what is intended (for example, more equal participation) and the reality (the structures of exclusion that are inherent in the process). These concepts are so powerful that if they aren't questioned, the disempowered can actually reinforce their own disempowerment.

Openness Is a Complex Process, Not a State

The concepts of openness and open models described in this book, like all concepts, are always incomplete representations of the reality to which the concepts point. The concepts project the idea of something that is set and static. That something is either open or closed. But the reality of open development is much more fluid and uncertain.

Openness, as discussed in chapter 2, can be thought of as extending in at least three dimensions: openness of content, openness to people, and openness in process. Typically when thinking of open models, we think of openness in terms of content and people. But as an open model becomes more and more open along these dimensions, it also seems to open up along the process dimension. As an increasing diversity of content and people are included, there is an increasing indeterminacy of what is going to happen next because this increasing diversity moves us into a dynamic of social complexity, which by definition consists of nonlinear processes that are unpredictable and unknowable in advance. In other words, as Harvey writes, "openness is perhaps best understood as a collective process that is continuously under development and review."

As in the HarassMap example we discussed at the beginning of this introduction, open models do not just accept this contingency, they embrace and harness it. Development has, of course, always been a socially complex process. The authors of these chapters make clear that trying to work with openness forces this complexity into plain sight. As Melissa Louden and Ulrike Rivett point out in chapter 3, the co-creation of collaborative research is based on trust relationships, which necessarily involves openness to the diverse views and contributions of collaborators. The power of opening up OERs and government data to bring about positive change comes in part from positive outcomes that emerge from unanticipated local uses and adaptations. Complexity isn't a bug, it's a feature.

The chapters in this volume illustrate several implications of working with complexity and open models. Shared understanding of goals and dialogue become central characteristics of many open models, in particular those involving high levels of participation. Working in complex spaces requires emergent responses that are informed by reflexivity and learning. Experimentation and research is needed to find what works and what doesn't in different contexts. When seeking solutions, it is helpful to include a diversity of data, views, and ways of knowing. Open models are also the domain of principles of implementation and local adaptation, not of best practices. Principles travel, the exact models don't—either between contexts or domains. This implies potentially the need for a new type of expert—one who can facilitate open processes rather than one who knows the best way forward.

Embracing uncertainty, however, does run counter to the results-based management paradigm that dominates international development, which lays out a series of preplanned outputs and intermediate outcomes on the path to a project's impact. Diversion from the plan is a risk to be mitigated and managed. In contrast, open models are, ultimately, a process that makes possible a diversity of co-created development paths, rather than a predetermined evolution from less developed to more developed states. It is both a structure and process for development that is ultimately, as de Beer and Oguamanam write in chapter 10, "respectful of different societies' rights to determine their own best paths toward development in a globalized world."

Notes

1. Rebecca Chiao, personal communication, August 17, 2012.

2. Rebecca Chiao, personal communication, August 17, 2012.

3. Palestine: https://streetwatch.crowdmap.com/main; Lebanon: goo.gl/etFze; Yemen: http://thesafestreets.org; Bangladesh: https://bijoya.crowdmap.com; Pakistan: http://www.ryse.pk/bbk; Syria: https://womenundersiegesyria.crowdmap.com.

4. For a more detailed exploration of openness, see chapter 2 of this volume.

5. M. L. Smith, L. Elder, and H. Emdon, "Open Development: A New Theory for ICT4D," *Information Technology and International Development* 7, (Spring 2011): iii— ix.

6. See for example, the collaboratively authored chapter "Exploring Open Development" in *The Open Book* (London, UK: The Finnish Institute in London, 2013), http://issuu.com/finnish-institute/docs/theopenbook_issuu_final.

7. See http://www.worldbank.org/open. The Web page notes: "Phase I of the World Bank's Open Development page aggregates key examples of the Bank's work in promoting openness and transparency in development, from tools and knowledge resources to Bank-wide initiatives. Our second phase will focus on creating a more interactive space to engage." Also see: S. Pradhan and S. Odugbemi, "The Contours and Possibilities of Open Development," Development Outreach, (September 2011), World Bank Institute, http://wbi.worldbank.org/wbi/Data/wbi/wbicms/files/drupal-acquia/wbi/pradhan_odugbemi.pdf. The authors characterize *open development* as follows: (1) open government (transparency, citizen access to official information, and responsiveness); (2) citizens are engaged in development; (3) collective action by citizens to tackle their own development challenges; (4) taking advantage of multiple sources of development knowledge; co-creation of development solutions; and (5) international donors and development institutions have to embrace open data, open knowledge, and open solutions.

8. See http://www.opendta.org/Pages/Home.aspx.

9. See http://www.one.org/us/inside-one/policy.

10. Nagy Hanna, "Open, Smart and Inclusive Development: ICT for Transforming North Africa: Report to the African Development Bank," (2012), http://www.afdb .org/fileadmin/uploads/afdb/Documents/Publications/Brochure   Open   Smart Anglais.pdf.

11. M. L. Smith and L. Elder, "Open ICT Ecosystems Transforming the Developing World," *Information Technology and International Development* 6, no. 1 (2010): 65–71.

12. Y. Benkler, *The Penguin and the Leviathan: How Cooperation Triumphs over Self-interest* (New York, NY: Crown Business, 2011).

Bibliography

Benkler, Y. *The Penguin and the Leviathan: How Cooperation Triumphs over Self-interest.* New York, NY: Crown Business, 2011.

Hanna, N. "Open, Smart and Inclusive Development: ICT for Transforming North Africa: Report to the African Development Bank." (2012). http://www.afdb.org/

fileadmin/uploads/afdb/Documents/Publications/Brochure%20Open%20Smart%20
Anglais.pdf.

Smith, M. L., and L. Elder. "Open ICT Ecosystems Transforming the Developing
World." *Information Technology and International Development* 6, no. 1 (2010): 65–71.

Smith, M. L., L. Elder, and H. Emdon. "Open Development: A New Theory for
ICT4D." *Information Technology and International Development* 7, no. 1 (2011): iii–ix.

2 The Emergence of Open Development in a Network Society

Katherine M. A. Reilly and Matthew L. Smith

In this chapter we explore the nature of open development by examining how open models are reshaping the way we think about and implement international development. Indeed, the emergence of these novel experiments in the international development space has already begun to demonstrate the potential of open models for initiating positive change. We believe that these new open networked models can, and will be, transformative, but they will not necessarily lead to social good. Indeed, in an era of openness that embraces a diversity of perspectives and dialogue, it is difficult to state conclusively what *social good* means. Furthermore, their transformative nature generates points of struggle between the stakeholders of the status quo and proponents of change. The outcome of these struggles will determine much of the distribution of many resources in our future societies.

This chapter lays the foundation for this volume. In the pages that follow we first explain our understanding of the network society and the emergence of new open networked structures and activities we group under the umbrella term *open models*. The concept of open models is explored and defined in the second section of the chapter. We then explore the idea of *open development* both as a set of tools for achieving development and also as a space for transformation and struggle.

The Context of Open Models

In our view, open models are one manifestation of the emerging network society. To understand the nature and relevance of these models for international development, this section briefly explores, theoretically and empirically, the context of their emergence. The story begins with the work of Spanish sociologist Manuel Castells on the movement from the industrial to the information age. Castells's story, however, fails to capture some of the more recent ongoing dynamic changes to society predicated on the massive diffusion of networked technologies. To fill these gaps, the section then draws on Yochai Benkler's notion of the networked information economy and his insight into the increasing significance of information sharing and collaboration. This history takes us from the information and communication technologies for development (ICT4D) moment to the open development moment.

From the Industrial to the Information Age

Scholars debate the timing of the shift from the industrial to the information age,[1] but if we follow Daniel Bell, as Castells does,[2] then it started around 1970. At that time, the United States and the then Union of Soviet Socialist Republics (USSR) came to see the limitations of their Cold War military-industrial complexes, and became conscious of a competitive threat from technologically forward-thinking manufacturers in Japan and Germany. Advances in information and communication technologies (ICTs) were introducing important new efficiencies in manufacturing by revolutionizing the relationship between product design, manufacturing, distribution, marketing, and service. As the Cold War wound down, national protectionism of Fordist assembly lines gave way to globalized capitalism typified by an informational mode of development in which "the action of knowledge upon knowledge itself [is] the main source of productivity."[3] This new model rested, in turn, on neoliberal restructuring of global markets and governance.

The resulting changes ushered in what Castells calls the *information age*, a time period marked by *global informational capitalism* and the *network society*. Thanks to ICTs, economic production could take place on a global scale, in real time, with a high degree of flexibility. The model of organization for this new era was not the hierarchy but the network: "As a historical trend, dominant functions and processes in the information age are increasingly organized around networks. Networks constitute the new *social morphology* of our societies, and the diffusion of networking logic substantially modifies the operations and outcomes in processes of production, experience of power and culture."[4] In the network society economic activity, governance, exploitation, social and cultural activity, and struggles were increasingly organized through transnational digital networks.[5]

This new global economic model implied new challenges for development. In a report written for the United Nations Research Institute for Social Development (UNRISD), Castells argued that the dilemma for development in the information age resulted from the fact that social development was put at the service of globalized informational capitalism, rather than the other way around.[6] Informational capitalism used the new *network morphology* to be footloose and fancy free. This, according to Castells, could lead to a race for the bottom in social and economic policy as localities competed for capital investment. But capital could just as quickly depart again, leaving people behind to suffer their fate. As a result, Castells famously argued, people who were no longer in the network became marginalized or switched off.

The development policy suggested by Castells's work was to ensure that informational capitalism worked in the service of social development so that no one got disconnected or left behind. Ultimately this meant valuing people and putting them first. In the information age, the way to do this, according to Castells, was to ensure access to ICTs and to restructure and improve education so that people would be able to use them. By doing so, we would enable people to take advantage of the benefits of informational capitalism and create the conditions necessary for social development. This, in turn, required not neoliberalism, but social policies that created an environment where people were valued over profit. In other words, we can find support in Castells's work for the idea that globalism needs to be reined in so that it does not run roughshod over communities.

Castells's work gets taken up in the ICT4D literature in two major ways. There are those who argue that we need to close the digital divide in order to ensure that localities can mobilize informational capitalism for social development.[7] A variation on this theme focuses on reforming education and knowledge production.[8] This is the more mainstream interpretation of Castells's work. But there is another, more radical group which argues that informational capitalism, as with any form of capitalism, needs to be fundamentally challenged if we are to tackle the root causes of inequality. Here we find the body of ICT4D literature that advocates appropriation of ICTs for the creation of alternative forms of development.[9] In either case, Castells is a foundational thinker for much of the work in ICT4D that took place during the 1990s and into the new millennium.

But Castells's thesis—that development in the information age depends on access to information and communications technologies, and the education to use them—is challenged in recent times as the network society embeds itself into more and more areas. First of all, Castells's assumption that access to ICTs is the defining feature of development in the information age is becoming less relevant as mobile connectivity penetrates all areas of the planet. Secondly, Castells takes a relatively limited perspective on networks, and as a result misses out on critical new social innovations of the type that we believe are gaining importance for international development. By considering these limitations we can begin to rethink the relationship between ICTs and development in ways that are more appropriate to the current moment. We do just that in the sections that follow.

Moving Beyond Access

For Castells, *access* to ICTs is fundamental to inclusion in the network society, and inclusion in the network society is now a fundamental prerequisite for development. Expanding on this work, many authors suggest that the digital divide excludes regions or groups from participation in the network society.[10] Thus, overcoming the digital divide and unlocking the development potential of these technologies implies overcoming multiple barriers to meaningful access to ICTs, be they a lack of skills, physical access, sufficient financial resources, relevant content, or similar.[11]

The digital divide and the obstacles for meaningful access to ICTs, however, have changed greatly since the millennium. This suggests that we need to move beyond thinking about the digital divide as the principal barrier to development in the information age. There are two relevant trends here: (1) declining prices and expanding reach are allowing more and more people to plug in; and (2) regardless of whether people are plugged in or not, the spread of the network society constitutes an important set of rules that shape the possibilities for development in the world today.

In the 2000s, the relatively rapid diffusion of the Internet, mobile technologies, and social media platforms has expanded the reach and types of information networks in developing and developed countries.[12] By 2010 the world reached a point where 60 percent of the 2 billion Internet users (1.2 million) are in developing countries. This number is skewed by China, where there were an estimated 420 million Internet users. The distribution of these users is, however, still quite uneven, with only 21 percent of developing country population online and Africa being the least connected with only about 11 percent of the population online.[13] While Africa has remained the least connected in terms of Internet access, that situation does look to improve as new cables are being laid that should greatly enhance their connectivity (see figure 2.1).[14]

Globally, mobile phone growth has greatly outpaced the spread of the Internet (see figure 2.2). As of 2011, mobile penetration in the developing world was estimated at ~78 percent (see figure 2.3), with Africa at the lowest level of penetration of ~53 percent.[15] The spread of mobiles has been so great that the rate of mobile growth in the developing world has already begun to decline from above 30 percent growth rates in 2005 and 2006 to (the still fast) 15 percent in 2009 and 2010. This massive increase in

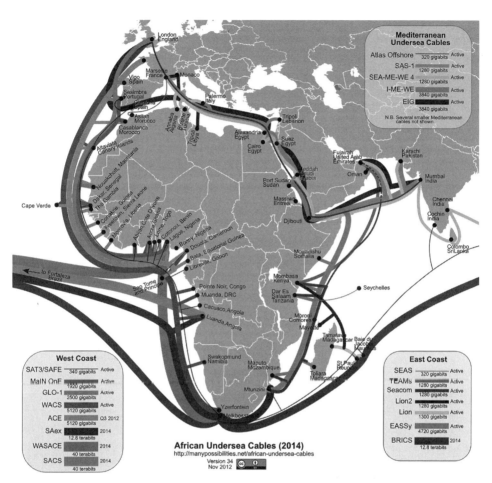

Figure 2.1

Map of projected African undersea cables in 2014. *Source*: http://manypossibilities
.net/african-undersea-cables.

connectivity has arguably already significantly improved the capabilities of
people in developing countries through the strengthening and enabling of
social, economic, and governance networks.[16]

This explosion in mobile phone growth is also expected to facilitate
global Internet connectivity, through third generation (3G), fourth generation (4G) technologies, and beyond. In China, by the end of 2010, there
were 288 million mobile Internet subscribers, up 42 percent from the year
before. China is predicted to surpass 600 million in 2012.[17] In India, the
number has passed 150 million and is growing.[18] In Sub-Saharan Africa,

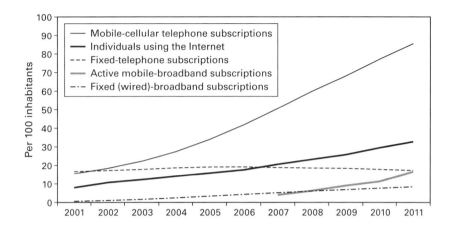

Figure 2.2
Global ICT developments from 2001 to 2011. *Source*: ITU World Telecommunication/ICT Indicators database, http://www.itu.int/ITU-D/ict/statistics.

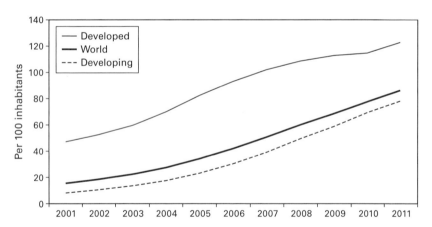

Figure 2.3
Mobile-cellular subscriptions per 100 inhabitants, from 2001 to 2011. *Source*: ITU World Telecommunication/ICT Indicators database, http://www.itu.int/ITU-D/ict/statistics.

Google has seen 50 percent annual growth in search requests coming from the region, with four out of every ten coming from a mobile phone.[19] This should only increase as smartphones become cheaper.[20] As of 2011, of the 500 million mobiles in Africa, there are thirty-two non-smart mobile phones for every one smart mobile phone. The ratio is expected to reduce to 5.6 to 1 by 2015.[21]

This massive diffusion has implications and impacts, regardless of whether people are plugged in or not, as these technologies underpin the expansion of the network society into even more areas. For example, although some groups lack the means to communicate electronically, they will find that their livelihoods are reshaped by the network society. They may recycle electronic waste, or they may have had their labor displaced during processes of market reorganization and optimization stemming from the new efficiencies of ICTs. Others may find themselves working in the factories that produce ICTs, or involved in or are affected by social movements that make use of ICTs to advocate broader changes in governance or social processes. Insofar as globalized informational capitalism constitutes a restructuring of global markets instead of the wholesale transition away from traditional modes of production, such as farming or manufacturing, then it is not access to ICTs that will determine development, but rather the way ICTs have worked to restructure relations of production.

Given this, rather than the digital divide, we find that those who study digital inequality present a more accurate picture.[22] Digital inequality is the inequality among access holders to make meaningful use of that access. Furthermore, in contrast to the more technology-focused notion of digital divide, digital inequality provides a space for a consideration of the longer-term social processes that shape social inequality and social development.[23]

Toward Open Models

A second limitation of Castells's work is that it focuses primarily on a single type of economic transformation—*global informational capitalism*. Global informational capitalism is synonymous with the rise of just-in-time manufacturing and transnational production in multinational corporations. Here the focus is on the shifts in the means of producing manufactured goods, and perhaps the increased production of knowledge-based services in wealthier economies. As a result, Castells's work tends to presume that only capital can use and/or shape networks. In such a world, things can look bleak for marginalized communities; they seem to have very little power in the face of globalized capital. Furthermore, Castells views networks as a rather flat set of nodes and ties. From this, he argues that possibilities for development depend on whether you are inside or outside the network; whether you are connected or not. This position is certainly true to some extent as there is emerging evidence that the costs of exclusion from networks are multiple, "disproportionate and growing."[24]

However, as a consequence of its focus on global informational capitalism, Castells's work is less able to account for the many social innovations that are emerging to take advantage of networked computer technologies. These new social models are better accounted for by the idea of a networked information economy. As Benkler explains: "What characterizes the networked information economy is that decentralized individual action—specifically, new and important cooperative and coordinate action carried out through radically distributed, nonmarket mechanisms that do not depend on proprietary strategies—plays a much greater role than it did, or could have, in the industrial information economy."[25]

Benkler's perspective reveals new and plausible opportunities for bottom-up change and development. The networked information economy offers new possibilities for radically distributed cooperative and coordinated actions that represent important, ongoing changes to the ways in which knowledge is produced and employed. The new systems of knowledge production offered by the networked information economy may provide means to transform or shape global informational capitalism in ways that "offer modest but meaningful opportunities for improving human development everywhere."[26] Overall, knowledge production and use is changing in much more complex and far-reaching ways than were contemplated by Castells.

Benkler explains that "the availability of free information resources makes participating in the economy less dependent on surmounting access barriers to financing and social-transactional networks that made working out of poverty difficult in industrial economies. These resources and tools thus improve equality of opportunity."[27] Inroads into the networked information economy may, therefore, allow local groups to innovate in ways that shift the balance of power in other areas of production, as well as having implications for politics and society. This, more of a Web 2.0 view of the network society, envisions open spaces populated by complex webs of interaction.[28] In other words, the benefits (or challenges) of greater flexibility are available to everyone in the information age, not just corporations, as a result of the ways in which ICTs enable open spaces of interaction. This perspective is captured in recent popular writing, such as the following excerpt from op-ed journalist Thomas Friedman of the *New York Times*:

The second trend we see in the Arab Spring is a manifestation of "Carlson's Law," posited by Curtis Carlson, the C.E.O. of SRI International, in Silicon Valley, which states that: "In a world where so many people now have access to education and cheap tools of innovation, innovation that happens from the bottom up tends to be chaotic but smart. Innovation that happens from the top down tends to be orderly but dumb." As a result, says Carlson, the sweet spot for innovation today is "moving down," closer to the people, not up, because all the people together are smarter than anyone alone and all the people now have the tools to invent and collaborate.[29]

For development practitioners, this implies a shifting of focus. Building on Benkler and others, we argue that the network society involves more than a shift away from hierarchy in the means of production, but also revolves around changes in patterns of information, knowledge, and cultural production and distribution. The ability of a given group to develop in the information age will not entirely depend on their access to ICTs, but rather on their ability to craft and/or take advantage of the new, more open networked social forms made possible by ICTs—the networked social morphologies that we call open models. Thus, there needs to be a shift *beyond* the focus on closing the digital divide by enhancing access to ICTs. We could think of that as the ICT4D moment. In addition, there needs to be increased attention paid to understanding how interactions happening within these open models, these open spaces of the information age, can shift the balance of relations between haves and have-nots (or, as is often the case, between incumbents and newcomers). This could be thought of as the *open development* moment.

What Are Open Models?

In this book, we begin to explore the open development moment by examining various emerging open information network structures and activities (open models) that bring both promise and peril for the processes of international development. To do so, we must first have a deeper understanding of the nature of these open models.

A Brief (Recent) History of Open Models

To better understand these new patterns of social organization, it is helpful to trace their emergence. A good starting point for the origin of ICT-based open models is the open source software production model that took advantage of microcomputers and early networked connectivity. The history of open source began in the late 1970s when Richard Stallman of the Massachusetts Institute of Technology (MIT) launched both the GNU (which stands for "GNU's Not Unix") project and the Free Software Foundation. Free software was understood as a question of liberty, not price (i.e., "free" as in "free speech," not "free" as in "free beer").[30] Software is free if it embodies the following four "essential freedoms:"[31]

- The freedom to run the program, for any purpose.
- The freedom to study how the program works, and change it to make it do what you wish. Access to the source code is a precondition for this.
- The freedom to redistribute copies.
- The freedom to distribute copies of your modified versions to others. By doing this you can give the whole community a chance to benefit from your changes. Access to the source code is a precondition for this.

The term *open source* emerged in the late 1990s as a strategic decision, in particular to position free software as desirable to the business community.[32] Open source emphasizes not only the technical superiority of open code, but the associated business models that emerge from it. By this time there were already several examples of open source software that clearly demonstrated the power of collaborative and freely shared software development.

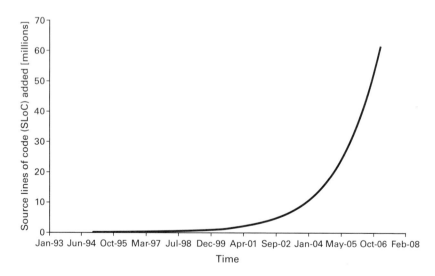

Figure 2.4a

Growth in lines of (open source) source code and in open source projects over time. *Source*: From A. Deshpande and D. Riehle, "The Total Growth of Open Source," http://dirkriehle.com/wp-content/uploads/2008/03/oss-2008-total-growth-final-web.pdf.

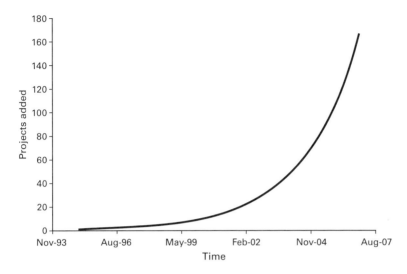

Figure 2.4b
Growth in lines of (open source) source code and in open source projects over time. *Source*: From A. Deshpande and D. Riehle, "The Total Growth of Open Source," http://dirkriehle.com/wp-content/uploads/2008/03/oss-2008-total-growth-final-web.pdf.

For example, the Apache Web server, an open source project, has become the most popular Web server in the world, beating out competing servers created by larger corporations such as Microsoft and Sun.[33] Another example is the development of an enterprise-quality open source medical record system[34] that is being adapted and implemented in developing countries.[35] Figures 2.4a and 2.4b illustrate the dramatic growth of open source production since 1993.

The success of the open source model and the steadily increasing access to digital technologies has meant that the insights, as well as the moral and cultural arguments for openness, were then applied across many domains: "Now we're trying the same trick with the emerging technologies of collaboration, applying these techniques to a growing list of wishes—and occasionally to problems that the free market couldn't solve—to see if they work. . . . At nearly every turn, the powers of socialization—sharing, cooperation, openness, and transparency—have proven more practical than anyone thought possible."[36] This is evidenced in the exponential growth that we are seeing in the application of these ideas such as in open business, open access, open educational resources, and so on (see figure 2.5).

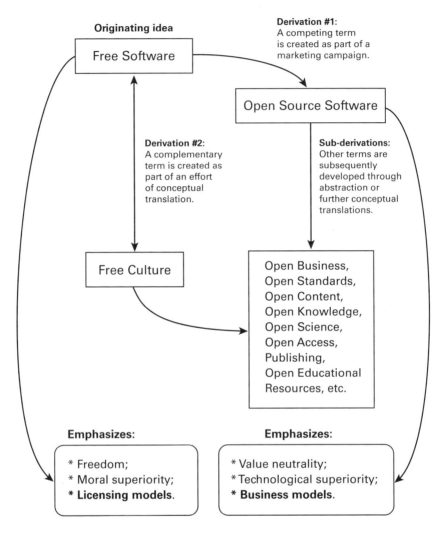

Figure 2.5
A historical-generative map of key terms and ideas. *Source*: P. N. Mizukami and R. Lemos, "From Free Software to Free Culture: The Emergence of Open Business," in *Access to Knowledge in Brazil: New Research on Intellectual Property, Innovation and Development*, ed. Lea Shaver (New Haven, CT: Information Society Project, 2008), 34.

There are many examples available. Ushahidi is a well-publicized application of open thinking that was originally developed to track reports of violence after the Kenyan election in 2008. Ushahidi combines two common components of many open models: open source software and crowdsourcing. Crowdsourcing is the activity of outsourcing a task to a "crowd," which is generally a distributed group of often unknown participants.[37] Rather than attempting to solve a problem through a company or organization, the low transaction costs of ICTs allow one to distribute the task for low costs and take advantage of the knowledge and creativity of interested individuals.[38] The Ushahidi platform takes information that people submit via mobile messages (SMS) or through the Internet, and then plots it according to the geo-location of the message on an online map. The open source nature of the platform and the ease of adaptability were key to its rapid deployment around the world by local actors seeking to tackle a variety of issues. By March of 2011, there have been over eleven thousand deployments of Ushahidi[39] for a wide variety of purposes, such as HarassMap[40] to track incidences of sexual harassment in Cairo, a version that tracked voter fraud in Mexico,[41] and, perhaps most famously, the effort to map issues concerning public health and logistical problems (such as contaminated water, power outages, or security threats) on the ground just after the 2010 earthquake in Haiti.[42]

Another example is the increasing attempts by governments, which have traditionally made public information difficult to access, to make public data freely and openly available to their citizens. Evidence is mounting that opening up data in appropriate modes, such as in structured and easily readable formats, can bring many social and economic benefits. In an early case of open data, one study illustrates the comparative value of open versus restrictive data policies. Europe, with restrictive data policies, invested $9.5 billion in weather data and gained $68 billion in economic value in return. In contrast the United States invested $19 billion and had an estimated economic value return of $750 billion.[43] In 2008, Washington D.C. launched a contest to crowdsource the creation of applications (apps) for mobile phone, Facebook, and the Web that would make use of their open data sets. The contest cost the city $50 thousand and resulted in forty-seven applications with an estimated value to the city of over $2.5 million.[44] In Canada, an open data policy helped the government recover $3.2 billion in taxes, which were recovered from illegal charities perpetrating tax fraud.[45] Developing countries are following suit, with Kenya launching an open data portal.[46] The open data movement has also been embraced by international organizations. For example, the United Nations launched

UN Data,[47] a site that makes many of the UN's statistical databases accessible, and the World Bank has similarly placed many of its data sets openly online.[48] Increased donor transparency can also have a positive impact on reducing recipient corruption levels.[49]

Likewise, openness in scientific knowledge production can bring important benefits. One study showed a significant long-term impact of agreements stipulated by the National Institute of Health (NIH) for funded projects that mandated increased openness of key elements of the research.[50] In particular, the NIH found that openness provided a boost to the amount of follow-on research and expanded the diversity of researchers and projects. In illustrating the potential benefits of openness, the NIH conversely identifies an important restriction of the opposite of openness, which in this case refers to the "the potential restrictions intellectual property rights may place on the diversity of research and researchers who would otherwise take a single powerful idea and experiment across multiple research lines."[51] New open access journals take advantage of the Internet and allow for broader dissemination of research through free access. While these articles are typically downloaded more frequently than those with restricted or subscription access only, this doesn't necessarily translate into more citations or use.[52] Researchers are also taking advantage of new possibilities for researcher collaboration, as indicated by the increase in international scientific collaboration since the advent of the Internet.[53]

The application of openness, including changing approaches to intellectual property, are also being adopted by business—even creating new business models. For example, in Brazil, a music scene called Technobrega has emerged and has produced total sales that now eclipse those of the traditional models existing in the music industry. There are several interesting elements to this story. First, the costs of the production of the digital Technobrega music has dropped so precipitously with the availability and power of PCs that the music is produced out of people's homes. Second, production and sales of Technobrega music happens *in the total absence of IP protection* for that music.[54] Indeed, the very popularity of the musicians and the music depends upon freely distributing the music through a network of street salesmen. The musicians then make money by charging admission to Technobrega parties and from sales of their CDs at those parties.

Growth of openness practices is arguably part of "a more widespread political economic shift towards 'openness.'"[55] Indeed, in many situations, it would seem that openness breeds more openness. When MIT initiated its OpenCourseWare initiative, making many of its courses openly available,[56] it became much harder for other universities to charge for similar content. As governments, NGOs, or other change activists increasingly and more effectively tap into the benefits of collective intelligence to accomplish their goals, we would expect the trend to continue. As these activities increase and spread, sharing and collaboration also spread, further propelling this shift.

Many countervailing trends, however, promote a more closed ecosystem. As we discussed in the introduction, intellectual property rights is one area in dynamic tension with openness, alongside others such as net neutrality and traffic shaping,[57] and open versus closed mobile networks and operating systems.[58] Thus, the shift toward openness is by no means preordained, in particular given how it challenges incumbents.

Indeed, an arguably larger trend plays out, an ebb and flow in the history of communication technologies that cycles between the hype of and movement toward openness and monopoly enclosure.[59] According to Tim Wu, we are entering into a phase of monopolistic consolidation and closing of the Internet and computer-based information and communication technologies. It starts with effusive optimism that the technology will revolutionize the world only to evolve into "privately controlled industrial behemoths, the 'old media' giants of the twenty-first [century], through which the flow and nature of content would be strictly controlled for reasons of commerce."[60] For example, mobile operators are beginning to resist more liberal telecommunication policies as they seek to increase their market share.[61] The final stage is to begin the cycle anew; a system that is closed for long enough becomes vulnerable to being smashed open again by new technological innovations.

Defining Open Models

These open models are made possible by the rapid spread of increasingly low-cost forms of networked computers and communications infrastructure, as discussed above. This communications infrastructure and lower costs of entry enable humans to exploit free distribution of content, plus processes that leverage the power of people, to generate social change.[62] For example, by providing free access to source code, open source software can leverage the efforts of software coders to correct coding errors (bugs). This results in higher quality software. Meanwhile, that software, which is freely available, can be modified to suit local needs. The Ushahidi model relies on people as distributed data collectors as well as an open source software platform. Social media platforms allow for many-to-many communication patterns, which in turn allow people to organize and coordinate in new, locally relevant and productive ways that often challenge existing social structures.

It is helpful to clarify further what we mean by open models. First, while open models rest on technology, they are more properly *social* systems with information-networked structures and activities. These systems can be thought of as *open* along at least three dimensions: (1) content, (2) people, and (3) process.[63]

The dimension of content mirrors the two types of freedoms expressed by the open source community: free access and the freedom to manipulate the content (reuse, revise, remix, and redistribute[64]). For some, there is an important distinction between free content and open content; content can be gratis but unless it is legally licensed to allow for some degree of manipulation, then it isn't truly open.[65]

The second dimension is one of openness to people, referring to who can actively participate and/or collaborate in the model. Note that this implies a broader definition of openness than just open content; open content is only truly open if people can use it, and it is more open if more people can use it. Thus, this dimension highlights that open models are really a form of *social* openness. That is, open models are social, information-network-based, models of sharing, participation, and collaboration. Critically, this implies that the relative openness of an open model extends to factors beyond just the layers of the communication system that underlies it.[66] This includes the capacities of the individuals who are actors in the model, the legal structures, and the implicit/explicit norms, rules, and roles of the structure of the open model, inter alia.

Finally, the third dimension is one of processes. This has at least two potential components: openness as transparency, and openness as contingency. Openness as transparency, such as in the disclosure of politically sensitive documents, was the type of openness talked about when the term "open government" emerged in the 1950s.[67] Openness as transparency is, thus, opening up the internal workings of a process for external scrutiny and accountability purposes. Openness as contingency, on the other hand, is a form of temporal openness with respect to future possibilities. Inherent in a participatory activity, for example, is the notion that the process will emerge from the inputs of the participants. Similarly, placing government data sets online opens up a variety of future and unanticipated possibilities for uses of that data.

It is important to differentiate along these dimensions because each dimension brings a different added value from openness. For example, although free content might expand access, open content allows for the local adaptation of content to a particular context as well as opening up the potential for people to provide feedback to the content creators to improve that content. Openness as transparency might improve accountability and legitimacy of a process, and openness as increased participation can increase buy-in to the process, or provide a diversity of perspectives and ideas that helps to stimulate innovation. These examples are not exhaustive: the literature expounds on the many theories of how openness along these dimensions adds value. These are the mechanism through which openness brings change.

Given the diversity and dimension of openness, clearly openness is not a binary state: categorical statements that something is *open* or *closed* are most likely not helpful to understanding the situation. Rather, the degree or form of openness is a combination of the three dimensions. These combinations give rise to the wide variety of open models that are emerging in many domains of social life. Future researchers might consider if and when a system is "open enough" for the impacts of openness to be felt.

One way to understand openness is by examining its opposite, which we view as the exercise of *control*.[68] More-open social systems allow content to flow and people to participate; they imply decentralized power and distributed controls. More-closed social systems involve centralized controls (like a traditional business firm) that generally treat information as a critical proprietary resource and therefore maintain restricted membership. Thus, openness can be seen as an inverse function of centralization; that is, it defines how exclusive the structure of the platform is (who is allowed to access, participate, and collaborate) and how proprietary the content is (what content can be reused, revised, remixed, and redistributed). Viewing openness as a function of control also illustrates how changes in power are inherent in any movement toward openness; and often it means a loss of power for those who once were in "control."

Whichever way we view open models (more information, more people, or less control), it is important to note that we use the term *models* quite loosely. The term *model* generally implies a finished structure that can be replicated. This is decidedly not the case in this instance. The stability of these models can be quite varied, from fairly stable (Wikipedia) to developmental (governments exploring the process of opening up their data) to highly emergent (political mobilization using various communication means). Furthermore, each example of an open model will be the product of particular groups of people organizing around communications infrastructures to accomplish particular goals within a specific context.

Taken together, these open models of collaboration, production, distribution, and publication are relatively recent manifestations of the network society. By their nature, we believe that these open models could make the benefits of greater flexibility and access to resources available to a much broader audience, offering opportunities to change the relations of power that shape digital inequality. But regardless of how they shift the distribution of opportunities and benefits, we believe that these new models are influencing how development takes place, something that we refer to as *open development.*

What Is Open Development?

Open development implies an end product in itself as well as the means to achieve it. To put it in Amartya Sen's[69] terms, open models are processes that can, in and of themselves, constitute development (the ends) insofar as they establish the conditions for people to escape from the *unfreedom* of poverty, and they can instrumentally bring about development (the means) by allowing more people to more effectively execute those capabilities.

Open Models as and for Development

On the positive side, open models can both expand individual *freedoms* through more participatory processes and by enhancing voice, as well as expand people's *capabilities* through increased access to resources, in particular digital information and connections to people and all they bring.[70] A clear example of this comes from the link between information and development. Transparency in government information about property rights, for example, enables people to leverage their productive resources—such as farm land—more effectively, and also enhances the democratic process by allowing decision making to become more responsive and accountable—for example, to farmers. In another example, greater access to high quality educational resources helps to fulfill the right to education, which enhances freedom, while it can also improve educational outcomes, which expands capabilities.

Openness is also linked to innovation. Indeed, the generally accepted explanation for why the Internet has proved to be an engine for innovation is its open structure. The logic of the Internet is an end-to-end model that places intelligence at the ends rather than the center. The network adheres to a set of open protocols (TCP/IP) that are neutral to the content and applications that run over it.[71] In this way, the more open the network, the greater the conceivable number of users competing in the production of new ideas.[72] As long as users abide by the protocols for communication, anyone can innovate on the network, provided they have the resources to do so. As Vent Cerf, one of the inventors of TCP/IP, the protocol for routing information over the network, wrote in a letter to the United States House of Representatives: "The Internet is based on a layered, end-to-end model that allows people at each level of the network to innovate free of any central control. By placing intelligence at the edges rather than control in the middle of the network, the Internet has created a platform for innovation."[73]

It is particularly important to note that innovation can come from the periphery. Whereas one needed a large capital outlay to start a print media enterprise, now the costs of entry are trivial for an increasing number of people.[74] This means that open models can both enhance the development process as well as make its opportunities and benefits available to a larger group of people.

Being critical is also important when considering open models for development. The history of the use of technologies for development is rife with the uncritical hype that comes when technology drives development spending and interventions. When financial incentives to technology companies are factored in, technology upgrading can displace social change as the end goal of development initiatives. Similarly, openness has normative connotations and can be interpreted as an ideal to strive for, as in the case of the Free Software movement. But it would be a mistake to uncritically accept openness as a social good and to lose focus on what is important: development. Open development does not promote openness at any cost. The desired level of openness (or the method for facilitating openness) should be determined by assessing what works to achieve the best development outcome in a given context.

There is no guarantee that the benefits flowing from open models will be more positive or more evenly distributed than those of less-open models. The possibilities that flow (or not) from openness depend highly on the conditions that shape the possibilities for openness. Furthermore, openness can be employed to both expand and restrict freedoms. Increased government transparency—for example—is good in theory, especially insofar as it enhances accountability. But it can at times foster misinterpretation and mistrust.[75] Information might be easily taken out of context, particularly in highly politicized settings, potentially undermining the credibility of democratic institutions. So while on a technical level the network may be more open, socially the appropriation of the information may result in widely divergent outcomes. Indeed, openness policies that are inappropriately implemented have the potential to reinforce or even erode existing conditions.[76] One example, found in India, illustrates this dynamic.[77] The digitization, centralization, and open access provision of land records was found to contribute to an increase in corruption. Furthermore, "it facilitated very large players in the land markets to capture vast quantities of land at a time when Bangalore experience[d] a boom in the land market."[78] Thus the developmental benefits of openness are not always distributed equally within a society, and can, in fact, be regressive.

The core elements of openness can also go hand-in-hand with the restriction of individuals' freedoms. For example, open models that involve personal information about many people can easily be turned against those who benefit from them. Social media platforms are goldmines for governments looking to gather information on citizens, threatening their right to privacy. While Facebook was arguably important for the Egyptian revolution, it was also a means for the government to uncover information about political activists who used those sites to organize. Indeed, the very pervasiveness of the networked technologies that underlie open models also provides the foundation for the restriction of freedoms. For example, during the 112th session of the U.S. Congress, a piece of anti-child pornography legislation was proposed that aimed to require Internet service providers (ISPs) to track *all Internet activity* and save it for eighteen months.[79] The ubiquity of mobiles phones with global positioning systems (GPS) technologies opens up similar surveillance possibilities for governments, as has been proposed by the city of Beijing, to monitor in real time the movements of its citizens.[80] Were they to be implemented, such invasions of privacy would run counter to core democratic principles, and stifle the potential for social organization and freedom of expression.

Openness may spur innovation, but it can do so in ways that lead to greater concentration of wealth. For example, when industry applies crowdsourcing to creative processes, a small number of people benefit monetarily from the volunteer labor of a large pool of producers. In 2000, Barrick Gold made public its geological data about a fifty-five-thousand-acre property near Red Lake in Ontario, Canada, and launched a competition to see who could come up with the best strategy to identify gold deposits within the territory. Winners shared in $575,000 in prize money, and the success of the experiment saw Barrick's value grow from $100 million to $9 billion.[81] Barrick has since launched similar programs in other regions including in 2007 the Unlock the Value program, which challenged the scientific community to create a cost-effective method for increasing silver recovery from the Veladero mine in Argentina. However, one concern with crowdsourcing in productive sectors is that the losers contribute to knowledge production without being compensated.[82]

Furthermore, the link between openness and innovation is not necessarily straightforward; openness may support some types of innovation, but there can be a dynamic and productive tension between open and enclosed systems. Closed technological innovations can often emerge from open systems, while open initiatives can take advantage of closed technologies or systems. Red Hat developed a user-friendly, Linux-based desktop operating system, and created a for-profit business model around providing user support. Apple's closed and successful operating system Mac OS X was based in part on FreeBSD (also known as Berkeley Unix), an advanced open source operating system. Conversely, closed systems can also be integral to openness. Google's proprietary search engine and translation technologies make navigating and accessing the Web's content much easier for much of the world's population. Similarly, Google Maps provides a key, free component of the Ushahidi platform. Apple's (relatively speaking) closed app marketplace has still generated quite a spate of innovation. There is, in fact, an argument to be made for the power of constraints to drive innovation.[83]

So when the processes of development make use of open models to spur innovation—or are influenced by the trend toward transparency, collaboration, participation, and access—positive impacts are certainly not guaranteed. More work needs to be done to understand how open social processes can be leveraged to enhance freedom, capabilities, and innovation in ways that support development, and how to dampen processes that limit these things. This would be easy to do if these social processes held still so that they could be examined in a leisurely fashion, however in practice the introduction of open models into existing contexts can bring transformative change, up-ending the status quo. As a result, openness can also be understood as a dynamic process that is the site of both transformation and struggle.

Openness as a Space of Transformation and Struggle

The opportunities that open models introduce frequently outstrip the ability of incumbents to adapt. These new models challenge old ways of operating and open up new avenues for social, political, and economic 'entrepreneurs.' This can have great transformative potential, opening up systems of governance, market segments, or cultural production to the influence of a much wider swath of people and increasing the distribution of the benefits of these systems. But this also means that the introduction of openness models are almost always the site of struggle at the border between closed (proprietary, hierarchical) and open (commons-based, networked) ways of doing things. Culturally, openness also challenges theories that see humans as essentially self-interested and incentive driven, since participation in open spaces is often inspired by a broader set of values such as kindness, generosity, cooperation and trust.[84]

This process of transformation is already well underway, and has given rise to several clear sites of struggle. Take for example the widely publicized print media industry's fight for survival: they now seek out new sustainable revenue streams as print readership declines due to the emergence of a wide variety of online news sources. Similarly, creative industries such as music are struggling to hold on to old distribution-based business models in the face of technologies that allow for nearly free distribution with no loss of quality. And, open access to scientific materials and the explosion of open educational resources have the potential to upend highly centralized and controlled knowledge production and distribution systems by redefining who can play the roles of user, creator, publisher, and curator.[85]

The relatively rapid transformation of these information intensive industries has given rise to increasingly tense battles over the legal infrastructure of intellectual property rights (IPRs). Given the centrality of information and knowledge to development processes, intellectual property rights (patents, copyrights) are arguably the central policy debate of the networked age.[86] Originally, IPRs sought to balance the interests of creators with the right to access creative works.[87] This balance is represented by Article 27 in the Universal Declaration of Human Rights: "Everyone has the right freely to participate in the cultural life of the community, to enjoy the arts and to share in scientific advancement and its benefits. Everyone has the right to the protection of the moral and material interests resulting from any scientific, literary or artistic production of which he is the author." However, the emergence of the Internet has upended this balance. In a world where information is digitized and copied at such low costs, making it virtually nonexcludable, how is it possible to protect the interests of creators?[88]

IP law has dramatically expanded over the past decade in an effort to reinforce the rights of creators.[89] For example, the World Intellectual Property Organization manages a slate of international treaties designed around a maximalist position on intellectual property.[90] In the United States, the Copyright Term Extension Act of 1998 (also disparagingly known as the Mickey Mouse Protection Act) extended copyright in the United States to the life of the author plus seventy years. Such protection tilts the balance toward the rights of creators and in favor of industry rents and away from the original intention of IPRs as a means to promote the social good through incentivizing innovation and creativity. The expansion of these copyright and patent protections is now "rapidly tilting the scales towards this stifling of innovation."[91] Furthermore, these policy debates are generally not informed by good empirical data, and the political economy of the situation means that research countering the interests of industry gets ignored.[92]

One effort to restore the balance is the Access to Knowledge movement. This movement seeks to improve access to four elements of the networked information economy: access to human knowledge; access to information; access to knowledge-embedded goods; and access to tools for producing knowledge-embedded goods.[93] This movement views access to knowledge as "a demand for democratic participation, for global inclusion and for economic justice."[94] The seeds of this movement were planted in the 1990s to expand access to the knowledge embedded good of anti-retroviral drugs to developing countries. As Lea Shaver explains, "no situation better illustrated the cruel ironies as an innovation system that would produce life-saving discoveries, but then fail to make them available to most of the world."[95] The relationship between information and development makes access to knowledge of critical importance in marginalized communities.

Another counter to "enclosing the commons of the mind,"[96] is the emergence of copy*left* licenses. A copyleft license employs copyright law to maintain the openness of intellectual property. The first license, the GNU General Public Licenses (GNU GPL), was born out of the free software movement. An open content licensing system by Creative Commons (CC) did for cultural content what GNU GPL did for software; maintain its openness. The goal of these licenses is to maximize the use of information while minimizing transaction costs.[97] CC has been widely successful. In 2010, Creative Commons estimated that there were over four hundred million CC licenses, up from under one hundred million in 2007.[98]

While the battle lines between proponents of strong property rights and supporters of open knowledge are clear, many other struggles over openness are much more complex and nuanced. One tension revolves around the relationship between platforms for communication and the content that flows through them. When a platform is very open, by definition there is very little control over how it is used, which can open the doors to immoral or illicit activities. In order to restrict some uses, the platforms must be made less open (more controlled), which may either alienate some users, or limit the benefits of the platform for innovation or capacity building.

This tension is most evident in the difficulties governments face when trying to regulate undesirable online behavior, such as in the examples of proposed legislation in the United States and in Brazil, to counter the spread of child pornography. A powerful example of this tension can be seen in Zuckerman's "cute cat theory" of digital media.[99] An online platform such as YouTube or Blogger allows people to engage in a wide range of activities, from posting cute images of cats to coordinating protests. The platforms are not activity specific; rather, they have the flexibility to support a wide range of social purposes. If a government cuts off access to the platform as a means to limit one type of activity (organizing protests), it risks incurring the wrath of other users (such as people who post cute images of cats). For example, the government of Pakistan has several times shut down You-Tube, only to restore it later. While they have restored access to YouTube, they would still attempt to block offensive videos (as well as content from other major Web sites like Google, Yahoo, Amazon, and Bing), even though technically it is difficult to keep up with the massive amounts of information (and there are well known methods for working around a ban).[100] Similarly, in an attempt to quell the Egyptian protests in early 2011, the then president of Egypt, Hosni Mubarak, after ordering intermittent blocks on social media tools and independent newspapers, ordered the complete shutdown of access to the Internet in Egypt on January 27.[101] By February 2, he had restored access, as it arguably had further alienated the public by, among other things, damaging the economic interests of the business community.[102] Mubarak stepped down nine days later.

The impact of platforms on innovation is a second source of tension. Controlled platforms provide guidelines for innovation that may facilitate quality products, but uncontrolled platforms allow for more potentially transformative creativity. Consider the very different business strategies of Apple's iPhone platform and Google's Android operating system. The Apple store is centrally controlled, with strict copyright rules and enforcement. If an application challenges the conditions of one of Apple's platforms, such as their iTunes store, it will either be limited in its functionality or rejected outright.[103] However, there are hundreds of thousands of applications available, with whole new businesses forming to make these applications. Obviously, a significant level of innovation is incentivized by this controlled platform, but these innovations are circumscribed by the conditions of inclusion in the platform. There is significantly less control over the Android application marketplace. This lack of control means the scope of innovation can be broader and can potentially threaten existing business models controlled by incumbents, making possible greater distribution of the benefits from innovations. This greater openness has drawbacks, however, as the quality is more variable. For example, there has been an increasing spread of Android applications with embedded malware.[104]

Another source of tension can be seen when comparing centrally controlled mobile telephone networks with the comparatively decentralized

Internet.[105] Unlike the network structure of the Internet that allows for innovations at the ends, the ability to place an application on a mobile phone network requires permission from the mobile phone operator. Thus it is no surprise that a major innovation such as M-PESA, a mobile-phone-based money transfer service, was launched by the Kenyan mobile network operator Safaricom, an affiliate of Vodafone.[106] While this particular innovation has benefitted many Kenyans, the overall scope of innovations that are possible are limited to those backed by the major incumbents, rather than those bubbling up from below. The challenge is to understand how to construct access and communications ecosystems that are open "enough" to facilitate the flow of information and ideas such that they spur innovation.[107]

There's no doubt that additional research is required to understand how open models can impact development. Some cases appear very clear cut. Where incumbents have monopolized power and excluded the masses from opportunities or benefits, openness can offer a much-needed antidote. For example, an open source approach to biotechnology could potentially aid the diffusion of inexpensive drugs to resource poor communities. Similarly, an open approach to the development and maintenance of educational resources can counter the current educational curriculum publication model and greatly expand access by offering high-quality and adaptable curricula for free. But where incumbents fight back against the threat of open processes, such as when they argue for maximalist IPR protection, we may actually see an erosion of the conditions for production, innovation, cultural engagement, or governance. Alternatively, the introduction of open models may simply further entrench those who already have power, or shift the balance of power from one group to another, empowering some people, but disempowering others, such as in the case of opening up the land records in India. Also, openness may come at the cost of quality controls and protections that are traditionally guaranteed by a certain level of control; thus the problems of spam, viruses, identity theft, and other malicious activities on the Internet.

We need to ask what we are losing and gaining from the struggles being waged between incumbents and challengers, or between power holders and power seekers. How do these outcomes structure the potential for development in the information age? Clearly the future of our social change is based on who can innovate, who benefits from those innovations, and how potentially disruptive the changes are. The environment for innovation and change depends upon policy and design decisions we make now. The ability of open models to enhance freedoms, to open up new opportunities, and to build capacity, will all depend on the kinds of open spaces that are put in place, and the ways in which they change production processes and shift relations of power. This in turn will determine the sort of development that takes place, and the distribution of the benefits from those processes.

Notes

1. See, for example: K. K. Robins and F. Webster, "The Long History of the Information Revolution," in *Times of the Technoculture* (London: Routledge, 1999), 89–110.

2. F. Webster, *Theories of the Information Society*, 3rd ed. (New York: Routledge, 2006), 120.

3. M. Castells, *The Rise of the Network Society*, 2nd ed. (Malden, MA: Blackwell, 2010), 17.

4. M. Castells, *The Rise of the Network Society* (Malden, MA: Wiley-Blackwell, 1996), 469.

5. See also: C. Fuchs and E. Horak, "Informational Capitalism and the Digital Divide in Africa," *Masaryk University Journal of Law and Technology* 9, no. 2 (2007): 11–32.

6. M. Castells, *Information Technology, Globalization and Social Development*, UNRISD Discussion Paper No. 114, September, 1999.

7. P. Norris, "The Digital Divide," in *Digital Divide: Civic Engagement, Information Poverty and the Internet Worldwide* (New York: Cambridge University Press, 2000), 3–25.

8. R. Mansell and U. Wehn, "Building Innovative 'Knowledge Societies,'" in *Knowledge Societies: Information Technology for Sustainable Development*, ed. R. Mansell and U. Wehn (Oxford: Oxford University Press, 1998), 5–18.

9. Cees J. Hamelink, "Social Development, Information and Knowledge: Whatever Happened to Communication?," *Development* 45, no. 4 (2002): 5–9; J. Martinez, "The Internet and Socially Relevant Public Policies: Why, How and What to Advocate?," in *Internet and Society in Latin America and the Caribbean*, ed. Marcello Bonilla and Gilles Cliché (Ottawa: IDRC, 2001), 262–385.

10. S. S. Robinson, "Reflexiones sobre la inclusión digital," *Nueva Sociedad*, no. 195, (2005): 126–139; Norris, "The Digital Divide," 2000.

11. See, for example: C. Fuchs and E. Horak, "Informational Capitalism and the Digital Divide in Africa," *Masaryk University Journal of Law and Technology* 9, no. 2 (2007): 11–32; J. Van Dijk and K. Hacker, "The Digital Divide as a Complex, Dynamic Phenomenon," *The Information Society* 19 (2003): 315–326; E. J. Wilson, *The Information Revolution and Developing Countries* (Cambridge, MA: MIT Press, 2006).

12. International Telecommunications Union, "The World in 2010: ICT Facts and Figures," http://www.itu.int/ITU-D/ict/material/FactsFigures2010.pdf .

13. Ibid; See also World Internet Usage Stats, www.internetworldstates.com/stats.htm.

14. "Another Kind of Poverty: www.africa.slow: The Last Continent Without Fast, Easy and Cheap Internet Access," *The Economist*, April 27, 2011, http://www.economist.com/node/21526937?frsc=dg|b. These cables are predicted to increase bandwidth by 2400% and achieve from 50 to 90%/unit connectivity cost reduction in the first few years. See also *East Africa (Kenya) Connectivity Services Category Workbook*. PowerPoint presentation. Washington, DC: Accenture, 2009.

15. Estimated mobile subscriptions per 100 inhabitants in other regions are: Asia and Pacific ~77%; Arab States ~97%; the Americas 105.4%. *Source:* International Telecommunications Union, see http://www.itu.int/ITU-D/ict/statistics/.

16. M. L. Smith, R. Spence, and A. Rashid, "Mobile Phones and Expanding Human Capabilities," *Information Technologies & International Development* 7, no. 3 (2011): 77–88.

17. Unified Communications Industry News, "China's Mobile Internet Users to Surpass Internet Users in 2012, Researcher," February 15, 2011, http://unified-communications.tmcnet.com/news/2011/02/15/5312461.htm.

18. K. Ohri, "The Adoption of Mobile Devices for Surfing Internet Will Happen Faster in India," June 27, 2011, http://www.afaqs.com/news/story/30940_The-adoption-of-mobile-devices-for-surfing-internet-will-happen-faster-in-India:-Mahesh-Narayanan.

19. C. Davies, "Google Search Requests Growing 50 Percent a Year in Africa," *African Business Review*, February 23, 2011, http://www.africanbusinessreview.co.za/tags/twitter/google-search-requests-growing-50-percent-each-year-africa.

20. For example, Jeremy Ford, "$80 Android Phones are Selling Like 'Hotcakes' in Kenya, the World Next?," *Singularity Hub*, August 16, 2011, http://singularityhub.com/2011/08/16/80-android-phone-sells-like-hotcakes-in-kenya-the-world-next.

21. See "Mobile Phones in Africa," Afrographic, http://afrographique.tumblr.com/post/7087562485/infographic-depicting-smart-and-dumb-mobile.

22. See, for example, P. DiMaggio and E. Hargittai, *From the "Digital Divide" to "Digital Inequality": Studying Internet Use as Penetration Increases*, (Working Paper 19). (Princeton, NJ: Center for Arts and Cultural Policy Studies, Woodrow Wilson School, Princeton University, 2001).

23. M. Warschauer, "Dissecting the 'Digital Divide': A Case Study in Egypt," *The Information Society* 19, no. 4 (2003): 297–304.

24. R. Tongia and E. J. Wilson III, "The Flip Side of Metcalfe's Law: Multiple and Growing Costs of Network Exclusion," *International Journal of Communication* 5 (2011): 665–681.

25. Y. Benkler, *The Wealth of Networks: How Social Production Transforms Markets and Freedom* (New Haven, CT: Yale University Press, 2006), 3.

26. Ibid., 10.

27. Ibid., 14.

28. J. Cohen, "Cyberspace as/and Space," *Columbia Law Review* 107, no. 210 (2007): 210–256.

29. T. Friedman, "Advice for China," *New York Times*, June 4, 2011, http://www .nytimes.com/2011/06/05/opinion/05friedman.html.

30. See GNU Operating System, "What is Free Software?," http://www.gnu.org/ philosophy/free-sw.html.

31. Ibid.

32. P. N. Mizukami and R. Lemos, "From Free Software to Free Culture: The Emergence of Open Business," in *Access to Knowledge in Brazil: New Research on Intellectual Property, Innovation and Development*, ed. Lea Shaver (New Haven, CT: Information Society Project, 2008), 25–66.

33. Netcraft, "June 2009 Web Server Survey," http://news.netcraft.com/ archives/2009/06/17/june_2009_web_server_survey.html.

34. See OpenMRS: Open Source Health IT for the Planet, http://openmrs.org.

35. See B. A. Wolfe et al., "The OpenMRS System: Collaborating Toward an Open Source EMR for Developing Countries," *AMIA Annual Symposium Proceedings*: 1146; C. Allen et al., "Experience in Implementing the OpenMRS Medical Record System to Support HIV Treatment in Rwanda," *Studies in Health, Technology, and Informatics* 129, (2007): 382–386.

36. K. Kelly, *What Technology Wants* (New York: Penguin Group, 2010), 317.

37. See Jeff Howe, "The Rise of Crowdsourcing," *Wired*, June, 2006, http://www .wired.com/wired/archive/14.06/crowds.html.

38. C. Shirky, *Here Comes Everybody: The Power of Organizing Without Organizations* (New York: Penguin Press, 2008).

39. See Ushahidi, "Key Deployments and Lessons Learned: Part 1," http://blog .ushahidi.com/index.php/2011/03/21/key-deployments-and-lessons-learned-part-1.

40. See HarassMap, http://harassmap.org.

41. See http://www.cuidemoselvoto.org. The platform has also been applied to 2012 elections in Mexico under a new name, Observación Electoral 2012, http://www.observacionelectoral2012.mx.

42. See http://haiti.ushahidi.com.

43. P. Weiss, *Borders in Cyberspace: Conflicting Public Sector Information Policies and Their Economic Impacts*, (Washington, DC: National Weather Service, US Department of Commerce, 2002); J. Boyle, *The Public Domain: Enclosing the Commons of the Mind* (New Haven, CT: Yale University Press, 2008), 221, http://www.thepublicdomain.org/download.

44. See Apps for Democracy, http://www.appsfordemocracy.org.

45. See http://www.tvo.org/cfmx/tvoorg/theagenda/index.cfm?page_id=3&action=blog&subaction=viewpost&post_id=12404&blog_id=323.

46. See Kenya Open Data, http://opendata.go.ke.

47. See UNdata, http://data.un.org.

48. See The World Bank, "Data," http://data.worldbank.org.

49. Z. Christensen, R. Nielsen, D. Nielson, and M. Tierney, "Transparency Squared: The Effects of Aid Transparency on Recipients' Corruption Levels," Presented at the *International Political Economy Society Conference*, Cambridge, Massachusetts, November 12–13, 2010.

50. F. Murray et al., "Of Mice and Academics: Examining the Effect of Openness on Innovation," Cambridge, MA: NBER Working Paper Series, w14819, 2009, http://www.nber.org/papers/w14819.

51. Ibid., 26.

52. P. Davis, "Open Access, Readership, Citations: A Randomized Controlled Trial of Scientific Journal Publishing," *FASEB Journal* 25, no. 7 (2011): 2129–34, http://www.fasebj.org/content/early/2011/03/29/fj.11-183988.full.pdf+html.

53. The Royal Society, *Knowledge, Networks and Nations: Global Scientific Collaboration in the 21st Century* (London: The Royal Society, 2011), http://royalsociety.org/uploadedFiles/Royal_Society_Content/Influencing_Policy/Reports/2011-03-28-Knowledge-networks-nations.pdf.

54. Mizukami and Lemos, "From Free Software," 2008.

55. C. May, "Opening Other Windows: A Political Economy of 'Openness' in a Global Information Society," *Review of International Studies* 34, (January 2008): 69–92.

56. See MITOpenCourseWare, http://ocw.mit.edu/index.htm.

57. F. Bar et al., "Infrastructure: Network Neutrality and Network Features," in *Networked Publics*, ed. K. Varnelis (Cambridge, MA: MIT Press, 2008), 109–144.

58. Y. Benkler, "Capital, Power, and the Next Step in Decentralization," *Information Technologies & International Development* 618, 11 (SE, 2010): 75–77; E. Zuckerman, "Decentralizing the Mobile Phone—A Second ICT4D revolution?," *Information Technologies & International Development* 6, (SE, 2010): 99–103.

59. T. Wu, *The Master Switch: The Rise and Fall of Information Empires* (New York: Random House, 2010).

60. Ibid.

61. W. Melody, "Openness: The Central Issue in Telecom Policy Reform and ICT Development," *Information Technologies & International Development* 6, (SE, 2010): 89–91.

62. J. Hagel III, J. S. Brown, and L. Davison, *The Power of Pull: How Small Moves, Smartly Made, Can Set Big Things in Motion* (New York: Basic Books, 2010).

63. Prior definitions focused only on two dimensions, openness of content and openness to people. See M. L. Smith, L. Elder, and H. Emdon, "Open Development: A New Theory for ICT4D," *Information Technology and International Development* 7, no. 1 (2011): iv; M. L. Smith and L. Elder, "Open ICT Ecosystems Transforming the Developing World," *Information Technology and International Development* 6, no. 1 (2010): 65–71; M. L. Smith et al., "Open ICT4D," Ottawa: IDRC, 2008, http://web .idrc.ca/uploads user-S/12271304441Open_ICT4D_Draft.pdf.

64. See D. Wiley, "Openness as Catalyst for an Educational Reformation," *EDUCASE Review* 45, no. 4: 14–20.

65. D. Wiley, "Defining 'Open,'" November 16, 2009, http://opencontent.org/blog/ archives/1123.

66. See Yochai Benkler, "From Consumers to Users: Shifting the Deeper Structures of Regulation Towards Sustainable Commons and User Access," *Federal Communication Law Journal* 52, no. 3 (2000): 561–759, http://www.law.indiana.edu/fclj/pubs/ v52/no3/benkler1.pdf; Y. Benkler, The Wealth of Networks, 2006; and J. Hoem, "Openness in Communication," *First Monday* 11, no. 7 (2006), http://firstmonday. org/htbin/cgiwrap/bin/ojs/index.php/fm/ article/view/1367/1286.

67. H. Yu and D. G. Robinson, "The New Ambiguity of "Open Government," UCLA Law Review 59, no. 6 (2012): 178–208.

68. L. Lessig, *The Future of Ideas* (New York: Random House, 2001).

69. A. Sen, *Development as Freedom* (Oxford: Oxford University Press, 1999).

70. For a discussion of the connection between mobile phones and expanding capabilities, see M. L. Smith, R. Spence, and A. Rashid, "Mobile Phones and Expanding

Human Capabilities," *Information Technologies & International Development* 7, no. 3: (2011): 77–88.

71. L. Lessig, *The Future of Ideas*, 2001; T. Wu, "Network Neutrality, Broadband Discrimination," *Journal on Telecommunications & High Technology Law* 2, (2003): 141–179.

72. Wu, "Network Neutrality," 2003.

73. See "Vint Cerf Speaks Out on Net Neutrality," November 8, 2005, http://googleblog.blogspot.com/2005/11/vint-cerf-speaks-out-on-net-neutrality.html.

74. Benkler, *The Wealth of Networks*, 2006.

75. See, for example, L. Lessig, "Against Transparency: The Perils of Openness in Government," *The New Republic*, October 9, 2009, http://www.tnr.com/article/books-and-arts/against-transparency.

76. I. Buskens, "The Importance of Intent: Reflecting on Open Development for Women's Empowerment," *Information Technology and International Development* 7, no. 1 (2011): 61–66.; see Buskens in this volume, chapter 13.

77. See S. Benhamin, R. Bhuvaneswari, and P. R. Manjunatha, "Bhoomi: 'E-governance.' Or, An Anti-politics Machine Necessary to Globalize Bangalore?," A CASUM-m working paper. (Bangalore: CASUM, January, 2007).

78. Ibid., 3.

79. The Protecting Children from Internet Pornographers Act of 2011, H.R. 1981, 112th Cong. (2011–2012).; See C. Friedersdorf, "The Legislation that Could Kill Internet Privacy for Good," *The Atlantic*, August 1, 2011, http://www.theatlantic.com/politics/archive/2011/08/the-legislation-that-could-kill-Internet-privacy-for-good/242853.

80. L. Lewis, "China Mobile Phone Tracking System Attacked as Big Brother Surveillance," *The Australian*, March 4, 2011, http://www.theaustralian.com.au/news/world/china-mobile-phone-tracking-system-attacked-as-big-brother-surveillance/story-e6frg6so-1226015917086.

81. O. Burkeman, "The Wiki Way," September 5, 2007, http://www.guardian.co.uk.

82. F. G. Kleemann and G. Günter Voß Kerstin Rieder, "Un(der)paid Innovators: The Commercial Utilization of Consumer Work through Crowdsourcing," *Science, Technology & Innovation Studies* 4, no. 1 (2008): 5–26.

83. See E. Zuckerman, "Innovating from Constraint," October 17, 2008, http://www.ethanzuckerman.com/blog/2008/10/17/innovating-from-constraint.

84. Y. Benkler, *The Penguin and the Leviathan: How Cooperation Triumphs over Self-interest* (New York: Crown Business, 2011).

85. D. V. Lewis, "The Inevitability of Open Access," *College & Research Libraries Pre-Print*, 2011, http://crl.acrl.org/content/early/2011/09/21/crl-299.full.pdf+html.

86. F. Stadler, *Manuel Castells: The Theory of the Network Society* (Cambridge: Polity Press, 2006); Boyle, *The Public Domain*, 2008; May, "Opening Other Windows," 2008.

87. L. Lessig, *Free Culture: The Nature and Future of Creativity* (New York: Penguin Books, 2006); Boyle, *The Public Domain*, 2008.

88. J. Boyle, "The Second Enclosure Movement and the Construction of the Public Domain," *Law and Contemporary Problems* 66, (Winter-Spring 2003): 33–74, http://ssrn.com/abstract=470983.

89. L. Shaver, "The Right to Science and Culture," *Wisconsin Law Review* 121, (2010): 121–184.

90. Boyle, "The Second Enclosure," 2003.

91. C. Kenny, *Getting Better: Why Global Development is Succeeding—and How We Can Improve the World Even More* (New York: Basic Books, 2011): 185.

92. Boyle, *The Public Domain*, 2008.

93. See Balkinization, "What is Access to Knowledge?," April 21, 2006, http://balkin.blogspot.com/2006/04/what-is-access-to-knowledge.html.

94. L. Shaver, "Chapter One, Intellectual Property, Innovation and Development: The Access to Knowledge Approach," in *Access to Knowledge in Brazil: New Research on Intellectual Property, Innovation and Development*, ed. Lea Shaver, 23. (New Haven, CT: Information Society Project, 2008).

95. Shaver, *Access to Knowledge*, 2008, 10–11.

96. Boyle, *The Public Domain*, 2008.

97. B. Fitzgerald, "Open Content Licensing (OCL) for Open Educational Resources," *OECD Centre for Educational Research and Innovation*, 2007, http://learn.creativecommons.org/wp-content/uploads/2008/07/oecd-open-licensing-review.pdf.

98. See: Creative Commons, "The Power of Open," Creative Commons, 2011, http://thepowerofopen.org; and: http://creativecommons.org/about/history.

99. E. Zuckerman, *My Heart's at Accra*, "The Cute Cat Theory Talk at ETech," http://www.ethanzuckerman.com/blog/2008/03/08/the-cute-cat-theory-talk-at-etech.

100. M. O'Neill, "Pakistan to Restore YouTube But Block Offensive Videos," May 26, 2010, http://socialtimes.com/pakistan-to-restore-youtube-but-block-offensive-videos_b13664; K. Haider, Reuters, May 20, 2010, "After Facebook Pakistan Shuts Down You-Tube"; http://www.reuters.com/article/2010/05/20/us-pakistan-youtube-idUSTRE64J2I920100520; S. Abbot, "Pakistan Blocks YouTube over unIslamic Content,"

Associated Press, May 20, 2010, http://www.nbcnews.com/id/37252270/ns/technology_and_science-tech_and_gadgets/t/pakistan-blocks-youtube-over-un-islamic-content/#.URptPaCk98E; and OpenNet Initiative, "Pakistan," August 6, 2012, http://opennet.net/research/profiles/pakistan.

101. Freedom House, *Freedom on the Net 2011: A Global Assessment of Internet and Digital Media*, ed. S. Kelly and S. Cook (Washington, DC: Freedom House, April 18, 2011), http://www.freedomhouse.org/sites/default/files/FOTN2011.pdf.

102. See N. Scola, *Personal Democracy Media*, "Why'd a Battle Ready Mubarak Turn Egypt's Internet Back On?," February 2, 2011, http://techpresident.com/blog-entry/whyd-battle-ready-mubarak-turn-egypts-internet-back.

103. See C. Cain Miller and M. Helft, "Apple Moves to Tighten Control of App Store," *The New York Times*, February 1, 2011, http://www.nytimes.com/2011/02/01/technology/01apple.html.

104. Google is, however, taking measures to remove these malware apps, see, for example S. Kovach, March 2, 2011, "The 21 Malicious Apps Google Yanked from the Android Market," http://www.businessinsider.com/malicious-android-apps-2011-3.

105. Benkler, "Capital," 2010; Zuckerman, "Decentralizing," 2010.

106. Zuckerman, "Decentralizing," 2010.

107. Thanks to Steve Song for this insight.

Bibliography

Bar, E., W. Baer, S. Ghandeharizadeh, and F. Ordonez. Infrastructure: Network Neutrality and Network Features. In *Networked Publics*, ed. K. Varnelis, 109–144. Cambridge, MA: MIT Press, 2008.

Benhamin, S., R. Bhuvaneswari, and P. R. Manjunatha. "Bhoomi: 'E-governance.' Or, An Anti-politics Machine Necessary to Globalize Bangalore?" A CASUM-m Working Paper. Bangalore: CASUM, January, 2005.

Benkler, Y. *The Wealth of Networks: How Social Production Transforms Markets and Freedom*. New Haven: Yale University Press, 2006.

Benkler, Y. "Capital, Power, and the Next Step in Decentralization." *Information Technologies & International Development* 618, 11 (SE, 2010), 75–77.

Benkler, Y. *The Penguin and the Leviathan: How Cooperation Triumphs over Self-Interest*. New York: Crown Business, 2011.

Boyle, J. "The Second Enclosure Movement and the Construction of the Public Domain." *Law and Contemporary Problems* 66 (Winter-Spring 2003): 33–74. http://ssrn.com/abstract=470983.

Burkeman, O. "The Wiki Way." September 5, 2007, http://www.guardian.co.uk.

Castells, M. *The Rise of the Network Society*. Malden, MA: Wiley-Blackwell, 1996.

Castells, M. (1999) *Information Technology, Globalization and Social Development*. UNRISD Discussion Paper No. 114. Geneva: UNRISD, September 1999.

Castells, M. *The Rise of the Network Society*. 2nd ed. Malden, MA: Blackwell, 2010.

Christensen, Z., R. Nielsen, D. Nielson, and M. Tierney. "Transparency Squared: The Effects of Aid Transparency on Recipients' Corruption Levels," Presented at the International Political Economy Society Conference, Cambridge, MA. November 12–13, 2010.

Cohen, J. "Cyberspace as/and Space." *Columbia Law Review* 107 (210) (2007): 210–256.

Davis, P. "Open Access, Readership, Citations: A Randomized Controlled Trial of Scientific Journal Publishing." *FASEB Journal* 25 (7) (2011): 2129–2134.

Dshpande, A., and D. Riehle. "The Total Growth of Open Source." In Proceedings of the Fourth Conference on Open Source Systems (OSS), 197–209. New York: Springer Verlag, 2008.

Fitzgerald, B. "Open Content Licensing (OCL) for Open Educational Resources," *OECD Centre for Educational Research and Innovation*, 2007, http://learn .creativecommons.org/wp-content/uploads/2008/07/oecd-open-licensing-review.pdf.

Freedom House. *Freedom on the Net 2011: A Global Assessment of Internet and Digital Media.*, edited by S. Kelly and S. Cook, Washington, DC: Freedom House, April 18, 2011, http://www.freedomhouse.org/sites/default/files/FOTN2011.pdf.

Friedman, T. "Advice for China." *New York Times*, June 4, 2011, http://www.nytimes .com/2011/06/05/opinion/05friedman.html.

Hagel, J., III, J. S. Brown, and L. Davison. *The Power of Pull: How Small Moves, Smartly Made, Can Set Big Things in Motion*. New York: Basic Books, 2010.

Hamelink, Cees J. "Social Development, Information and Knowledge: Whatever Happened to Communication?" *Development* 45 (4) (2002): 5–9.

International Telecommunications Union. "The World in 2010: ICT Facts and Figures," http://www.itu.int/ITU-D/ict/material/FactsFigures2010.pdf.

Kelly, K. *What Technology Wants*. New York: Penguin Group, 2010.

Kenny, C. *Getting Better: Why Global Development is Succeeding—and How We Can Improve the World Even More*. New York: Basic Books, 2011.

Kleemann, F. G., and G. Günter Voß Kerstin Rieder. "Un(der)paid Innovators: The Commercial Utilization of Consumer Work through Crowdsourcing." *Science, Technology & Innovation Studies* 4 (1) (2008): 5–26.

Lessig, L. *The Future of Ideas*. New York: Random House, 2001.

Lewis, L. "China Mobile Phone Tracking System Attacked as Big Brother Surveillance." *The Australian*, March 4, 2011, http://www.theaustralian.com.au/news/world/china-mobile-phone-tracking-system-attacked-as-big-brother-surveillance/story-e6frg6so-1226015917086.

Lewis, D. V. "The Inevitability of Open Access." *College & Research Libraries Pre-Print*, 2011, http://crl.acrl.org/content/early/2011/09/21/crl-299.full.pdf+html.

Mansell, R., and U. Wehn. Building Innovative 'Knowledge Societies. In *Knowledge Societies: Information Technology for Sustainable Development*, ed. R. Mansell and U. Wehn, 5–18. Oxford, UK: Oxford University Press, 1998.

Martinez, J. The Internet and Socially Relevant Public Policies: Why, How and What to Advocate? In *Internet and Society in Latin America and the Caribbean*, ed. Marcello Bonilla and Gilles Cliché, 262–385. Ottawa: IDRC, 2001.

May, C. "Opening Other Windows: A Political Economy of 'Openness' in a Global Information Society." *Review of International Studies* 34 (January 2008): 69–92.

Melody, W. "Openness: The Central Issue in Telecom Policy Reform and ICT Development." *Information Technologies & International Development* 6 (Special Edition, Harvard Forum II Essays). Cambridge, MA: MIT Press, 2010.

Mizukami, P. N., and R. Lemos. From Free Software to Free Culture: The Emergence of Open Business. In *Access to Knowledge in Brazil: New Research on Intellectual Property, Innovation and Development*, ed. Lea Shaver, 25–66. New Haven, CT: Information Society Project, 2008.

Murray, F., P. Aghion, M. Dewatripont, J. Kolev, and S. Stern. "Of Mice and Academics: Examining the Effect of Openness on Innovation." Working Paper Series, w14819, Cambridge, MA: NBER, 2009.

Norris, P. "The Digital Divide." In *Digital Divide: Civic Engagement, Information, Poverty and the Internet Worldwide*, 3–25. New York: Cambridge University Press, 2000.

Robins, K. K., and F. Webster. *Times of the Technoculture: From the Information Society to the Virtual Life*. London: Routledge, 1999.

Robinson, S. S. "Reflexiones sobre la inclusión digital." *Nueva Sociedad* no. 195, (2005): 126–139.

Shaver, L. "Chapter One, Intellectual Property, Innovation and Development: The Access to Knowledge Approach." In *Access to Knowledge in Brazil: New Research on Intellectual Property, Innovation and Development*, ed. R. Subramanian and L. Shaver, 23. New Haven, CT: Information Society Project, 2008.

Shirky, C. *Here Comes Everybody: The Power of Organizing Without Organizations*. New York: Penguin Press, 2008.

Smith, M. L., R. Spence, and A. Rashid. "Mobile Phones and Expanding Human Capabilities." *Information Technologies & International Development* 7 (3) (2011): 77–88.

Stadler, F. *Manuel Castells: The Theory of the Network Society.* Cambridge: Polity Press, 2006.

The Royal Society. *Knowledge, Networks and Nations: Global Scientific Collaboration in the 21st Century.* London: The Royal Society, 2011.

Tongia, R., and E. J. Wilson, III. "The Flip Side of Metcalfe's Law: Multiple and Growing Costs of Network Exclusion." *International Journal of Communication* 5 (2011): 665–681.

Warschauer, M. "Dissecting the 'Digital Divide': A Case Study in Egypt." *Information Society* 19 (4) (2003): 297–304.

Webster, F. *Theories of the Information Society.* 3rd ed. New York: Routledge, 2006.

Weiss, P. *Borders in Cyberspace: Conflicting Public Sector Information Policies and Their Economic Impacts.* Washington, DC: National Weather Service, United States Department of Commerce, 2002.

Wu, T. *The Master Switch: The Rise and Fall of Information Empires.* New York: Random House, 2010.

Yu, H., and D. G. Robinson. "The New Ambiguity of "Open Government."." *UCLA Law Review. University of California, Los Angeles. School of Law* 59 (6) (2012): 178–208.

Zuckerman, E. "Decentralizing the Mobile Phone—A Second ICT4D Revolution?" In Information Technologies & International Development 6 (Special Edition, Harvard Forum II Essays). Cambridge, MA: MIT Press, 2010.

Part I   Models of Openness

3 Enacting Openness in ICT4D Research

Melissa Loudon and Ulrike Rivett

This chapter explores the role of information and communication technologies for development (ICT4D) research in producing "actionable knowledge" for development.[1] We consider how a frame of openness, interpreted here as an active process of engagement, knowledge sharing, and co-creation, might guide ICT4D research. We interrogate a research collaboration called Cell-Life, and its project iDART—Intelligent Dispensing of Anti-retroviral Treatment—as examples of an open approach. Both authors have been directly involved in various capacities in iDART and Cell-Life, and as a result, our analysis is grounded in experience, is reflective, and is part of our ongoing learning.

As of early 2010, iDART managed anti-retroviral drug dispensing for approximately 150,000 patients in South Africa, and Cell-Life had been spun off into a separate nonprofit. In iDART and related projects, we have tried to enact a shift toward openness both in the technologies we work with and in the processes used to develop those systems. We have also engaged with the research process itself, trying to establish a developmental understanding of both our work as ICT4D researchers and the work that takes place in university systems. Our analysis is thus directed at both the project and institutional levels, focusing particularly on universities in the Global South. The results demonstrate barriers at both practical and institutional levels, but also encouraging successes. Overall, we find that the success of iDART as a model for knowledge production is well framed by an open approach to ICT4D research.

Background

In the 2003 operational plan for HIV/AIDS, the South African government clarified that anti-retroviral treatment (ART) increased life expectancy of people living with AIDS. This statement, which today is uncontested, has ended a decade of bruising conflict over the state's obligation to provide treatment for people living with HIV/AIDS.

Following a series of successful legal challenges and the development of the operational plan,[2] attention turned to the practical complexity of managing the supply of medication to the most rural areas.[3] With the full ART rollout, the department of health set the ambitious target of treating 80 percent of all people requiring ARVs (anti-retroviral drugs) by 2011.[4] Effective and sustainable treatment with ARVs requires an adherence rate of 95 percent in order to prevent the development of drug resistance in individual patients, as well as possible mutation of the virus. Additionally, the treatment requires a complex time-and-diet regime, and side effects need to be monitored regularly.[5] For under-resourced primary health care centers in disadvantaged areas, HIV/AIDS treatment, and particularly the requirement to monitor patients regularly, seemed a nearly impossible task.

iDART is a pharmacy system designed to increase the capacity of remote and under-resourced clinics providing anti-retroviral treatment; iDART began in 2003 as part of a research collaboration called Cell-Life. From 2001 to 2006, Cell-Life existed within the University of Cape Town and the Cape Peninsula University of Technology (CPUT). Intentionally diverse, the collaboration included students and faculty from engineering, the health sciences, and computer science. In 2006, Cell-Life became a not-for-profit organization and was spun out of the University of Cape Town. This coincided with a shift in focus from being primarily a research organization to a mix of research and implementation support, prompted partly by the growing number of sites using the software and requiring such support. As of mid-2010, over twenty host organizations—nongovernmental organizations (NGOs) or funders—manage sixty-seven iDART sites, covering all nine provinces of South Africa. Approximately 150,000 patients receive their medication through iDART each month. This represents nearly one-sixth of all patients on state- or donor-sponsored ART.

As a research group, Cell-Life originated as a response to a critical development problem—the HIV pandemic—that was unprecedented in both scale and structure. HIV disproportionately affects the rural areas of South Africa, where services are least developed. The public health system, emerging from decades of Apartheid neglect, was already overburdened. An ART rollout of the scale required had never been tried in a developed country, let alone in the developing world. The novelty of the problem mobilized the research community. There was also a very real sense of urgency—people were dying, and the imperative of actionable knowledge was keenly felt.

Theoretical Ingredients for an Open Approach

The idea of open development is attractive because it allows diverse observations about both research and systems implementation to be located within a common framework, while also providing a link to broader questions about the role of universities in national development. A useful starting point for discussing open development is the framework proposed by Matthew L. Smith and Laurent Elder.[6] Here it is defined as a way of organizing social activities in ways that favor:

• Universal over restricted access to communication tools and information.
• Universal over restricted participation in informal and formal groups/institutions.
• Collaborative over centralized production of cultural, economic, or other content.

Translated onto the landscape of university-based academic research, we understand openness as a way of doing research that actively promotes:

• Universal over restricted access to research products.
• Universal over restricted participation in the research process.
• Collaborative over centralized production of knowledge, and recognition of diversity in knowledge systems.

Many theoretical ingredients for a research concept based on openness are already available. Higher education, development studies, and information systems design have all engaged with the issue of participation, whether from a pragmatic standpoint (arguing that involving more stakeholders achieves better outcomes) or an ideological one. The open access movement promotes universal access to research products, as do research initiatives with an ideological commitment to open source software. An established critique of the monolithic and exclusionary nature of traditional academic knowledge production also comes into play, which methodological approaches, such as action research, explicitly confront.

With this in mind, the analytical framework for this chapter organizes observations on openness, both from the literature and the discussion of the iDART case, into three areas:

• System design and implementation.
• ICT4D research.
• The developmental role of universities in the Global South.

This framework reflects our roles in the project, as well as the natural disciplinary division embodied in the literature. It also embodies a sense of combined (sometimes conflicting) roles common among researchers and practitioners who work with ICT4D. We explore each of these points throughout this chapter and offer a map of our combined theoretical framework in table 3.1.

System Design and Implementation

Research in ICT4D has a normative orientation, seeking to influence policy or practice in the ultimate service of development goals. Implemented in the public health sector at local (primary care) level, iDART arose amid an academic discourse of overwhelming optimism about the potential of e-government for development. The fallacy of this soon became clear, and by 2003 it was reported that most government information systems projects in the developing world had ended in either partial or total failure.[7]

There is a vast body of work in the field of information systems (IS) dealing with IS project failure, including many examples from the developing world. (For reviews of this literature see Dada,[8] Pardo and Scholl,[9] and Heeks.[10]) We know that systems have failed because they try to force an unwanted or contentious change in organizational processes. Another reported reason has been that the technology requirements, such as hardware and connectivity, did not exist or were not maintainable due to limited human, technical, and financial resources. In general, the literature on information systems failure suggests that failure occurs because some aspect of the system context—social, technical, or political—is inadequately understood. In developing countries, the potential for "design-reality gaps"[11] is particularly acute.

In addition to factors operating at the project level, the stubborn persistence of information systems failure suggests a broader systemic problem. The structure and realization of the ICT ecosystem—from technologies, implementation, and development processes to ICT research and teaching—does not appear to promote success in ICT4D projects. Crucial gaps exist between technology and context, design and reality, and project planning and development (expensive, high intensity, single-location work amenable to project-based funding approaches) and ongoing support and implementation (low budget, dispersed, and far harder to control and to fund).

If technology is understood broadly, the problem described is a familiar one in studies of failed development projects. Pragmatic prescriptions emphasize tools for project planning, often as a way to highlight potential problem areas. Other tools and methods provide a simplified way to communicate technical and project management concepts to a mixed audience. From the perspective of openness, this last point is crucial. System design methodologies premised on improving communication between technical and nontechnical stakeholder groups, such ETHICS[12] and Soft Systems[13] as well as Edwin Blake and William Tucker's concept of *socially aware software engineering*[14] are potential ingredients for an openness-based approach to system design and development in ICT4D projects. Most mainstream work has emphasized the technical utility of user participation in IS, but there are also authors (including Mumford as well as Hirschheim and Klein,[15] Bryne and Sahay,[16] and Blake and Tucker[17]) who take the more radical view of participation as a condition of worker ownership of the tools of work.

The issue of participation has also been addressed in development studies, from the work of Robert Chambers,[18] through virtual ubiquity in mainstream development discourse, to a backlash against the "tyranny" of participation.[19] In information systems projects Richard Heeks's[20] cautionary article is emphatic on the difficulties of achieving equitable and effective participation. The important point here is that, despite differing views on its purpose and recognizing the practical challenges it poses, the idea of participation enjoys broad support in both IS and development studies. Like broad-based communication, participation seems a natural goal for an approach to system design based on openness.

ICT4D Research

Research approaches privileging participation have also emerged particularly connected to the ideas of socially responsive research and "democratizing knowledge."[21] Action research, which is carried out through continuous engagement with the study community and encourages redefining research objectives based on their self-definition of needs,[22] is clearly aligned with participation. Here, too, there are both pragmatic and ideological justifications for increasing participation. Emma Crewe and John Young,[23] take a pragmatic stance, arguing that wider participation may increase the relevance of research to policy by helping build "legitimacy chains" to informants. For Peter Reason and Hilary Bradbury, on the other hand, action research is "a participatory, democratic process concerned with developing practical knowing in the pursuit of worthwhile human purposes, grounded in a participatory worldview which we believe is emerging at this historical moment . . . in the pursuit of practical solutions to issues of pressing concern to people, and more generally the flourishing of individual persons and their communities."[24] This definition recognizes action research as an expression of a specific worldview. It also makes explicit the normative orientation of action research work, where the primary goal of the research is to effect goal-oriented change. Against positivist claims of an objective reality that exists apart from the research process, action research aims to influence the shifting, subjective *reality* that is uncovered. Participation is a driver of change, but also a democratic means of allowing the people who will be directly affected to determine the kind of change that is desirable. This observation links to openness as a way of favoring universal over restricted participation in the research process—including the defining of research priorities.

The shift away from the positivist paradigm of traditional scientific knowledge production is inherently political. Action research, in its rejection of monolithic knowledge claims, also rejects the objectivity claim of technical expertise. The "legitimating discourse"[25] of interventions based on a supposedly neutral technical goal[26] is similarly denied. In its place, Gordon Wilson[27] imagines a continuous striving toward Jürgen Habermas's "ideal speech situation," with "genuine dialogue between actors, where different knowledges are valued as a source of creative learning and hence new knowledge." The primary goal of the researcher becomes progressive attainment of the ideal speech situation—in itself the ideal of collaborative production of knowledge.

Despite arising from a very different literature, the concept of communities of practice[28] provides a window into understanding collaborative production of knowledge in practical terms. In both production and dissemination, the researcher is understood as embedded within a wide community of information systems stakeholders,[29] with the ultimate aim of the research process to develop "actionable knowledge"[30] for a diverse group. Communities of practice, which develop over time based on shared experience and aligned goals, may describe a mechanism for producing actionable knowledge outside of any formal research agenda, and beyond the timeline of single research projects.

Development in Universities

For Edwin Brett,[31] development is best analyzed—and interventions best operationalized—at an institutional rather than at an individual level. For ICT4D research, this means interrogating the research process not just in individual projects, but also in terms of the role of the university in national development. Brett's '*liberal institutional pluralism* holds that "open, pluralistic and science-based institutions are difficult to create . . . liberal models are crucial to all attempts at social and political emancipation, but institutionalizing them is not just a technical problem but generates practical challenges that demand a credible theory of political agency and practice that has to operate at both macro- and micro-levels."[32] An open approach to ICT4D research, backed by the theoretical ingredients cited in this paper, represents one imagining of a liberal model.

Speaking to knowledge production, Brett acknowledges the research policy–practice gap between development theorists, who "fail to ask who might be willing to implement their recommendations" in a nebulous and ill-defined manner, as a community of "practitioners."[33] An open system of knowledge should be structured such that theorists are encouraged to confront issues of agency and power in the implementer community. Pluralism works only when engaged with local knowledge systems, and the crucial knowledge networks of *organic intellectuals*—a Gramscian concept understood by Brett as "teachers, priests, traditional leaders and local activists."[34]

The starting point of a liberal and pluralistic understanding of the institutional nature of universities has to be that knowledge is developed and used—and should be understood—within a particular context. Speaking to applied fields generally, Michael Gibbons, Camille Limoges, and Helga Nowotny[35] acknowledge context in their concept of "Mode 2" knowledge production—"socially distributed, application-oriented, trans-disciplinary, and subject to multiple accountabilities." Unlike in information systems design or the planning of development interventions, the assumption here is not simply that context should be taken into account as part of the design process. The context of knowledge production, embodied in the structure of institutions and the groups that participate, shapes the knowledge that is produced.

Incentive structures and exclusion are as important as the way knowledge is communicated and disseminated. As Nowotny, Scott, and Gibbons[36] recognize in a follow-up article on the Mode 2 thesis, the reciprocity of "science speaking to society" and "society speaking back to science" is irrevocably marked by exclusion. In familiar dependency terms, Robert Chambers[37] laments the existence of "cores and peripheries of knowledge," with a devastating "centripetal force" that shapes knowledge production according to the priorities of the core. Diversity in knowledge production cannot be achieved without confronting the embeddedness of universities within global networks of wealth and power.

A parallel body of work in science and technology studies is concerned with the social shaping of technology artifacts. The social shaping movement is concerned with the context and process of technology development, and with exposing the power structures it reflects and reinforces. Robin Williams and David Edge[38] describe social shaping of technology (SST) in terms of "choices": "Central to SST is the concept that there are 'choices' (though not necessarily conscious choices) inherent in both the design of individual artifacts and systems, and in the direction or *trajectory* of innovation programs. If technology does not emerge from the unfolding of a predetermined logic or a single determinant, then innovation is a 'garden of forking paths.' Different routes are available, potentially leading to different technological outcomes. Significantly, these choices could have differing implications for society and for particular social groups."

According to social shaping theory, an open system of innovation that enables effective primary control of technology by marginalized groups would result in better outcomes for these groups. This is likely unattainable, however, and even if it were, technology development never takes place in isolation. Jannis Kallinikos[39] observes that human inventions "solidify over time" as they become socially embedded, and malleable along fewer dimensions as they increasingly impose their own logic. The choices we have now are determined by those who walked the path before us and by the long history of technology as a tool in the exercise of political and economic power. A pragmatic response, particularly in the context of widespread information systems failure, is to understand to what extent open innovation is possible in universities, and the role of research in promoting this.

Case Study: iDART, a Pharmacy System for Anti-Retroviral Dispensing

Cell-Life, a group comprising researchers, students, and medical personnel from the University of Cape Town and the Cape Peninsula University of Technology (CPUT), was created in 2001 to investigate IT systems for HIV management in the public health sector. Together with the Desmond Tutu HIV Centre (DTHC), one of the first groups providing ART to people in the townships of Cape Town, a number of tools were developed to support treatment. Once a large-scale ART rollout began to look likely, DTHC increasingly focused on providing treatment at clinical research sites. This necessitated the development of basic infrastructure for tracking drug packages through the supply chain, from initial stock arrival to the creation of monthly supply packets and patient collection at remote clinics.

System Description
With the DTHC, Cell-Life conceptualized the details of a basic dispensing system for anti-retroviral drugs in public primary care centers. The system's core focus was to support pharmacists in dispensing drugs accurately to large numbers of patients, by allowing printing of labels and a simple stock control. Barcode scanning was used to reduce dispensing time, and the system was written in Java using open source components to keep it portable

Table 3.1
Map of Theoretical Framework

	System design and implementation	ICT4D research	Openness and development in Global South universities
Universal over restricted access to research products	Open source software development	Research-policy-practice links, communities of practice, "actionable knowledge"	'Mode 2' knowledge production, alternatives to traditional publication models
Universal over restricted participation in the research process	Socio-technical systems design methodologies	Action research, stakeholder engagement, researcher as facilitator	Recognition of Gramscian "organic intellectuals" in knowledge production and dissemination
Collaborative over centralized production of knowledge, and recognition of diversity in knowledge systems	Emancipatory and neo-humanist approaches ETHICS, soft systems, social shaping	Ideal of knowledge production as a Habermasian "ideal speech situation"	Institutions and development in late-developing countries

across the different operating systems used at primary health facilities, and free of licensing costs.

The iDART project was designed with the following constraints in mind[40]:

1. The software had to support the core functions of dispensing to HIV-positive patients, but was not initially a fully fledged stock management system.

2. The onsite software setup needed to be implemented within one day, and the availability of staff for training was no more than seven hours. Training was nearly always conducted on the job while dispensing to patients.

3. The software needed to be self-explanatory to an extent that new staff could be trained by the existing staff using the software. This was a particularly important point due to the high staff turnover in rural centers. A manual of over one hundred pages was produced but never read; two-page quick guides were routinely found stuck to pharmacy computers.

4. The software needed to run without Internet connectivity, but still back up the dispensing database to an external server. This was accomplished

with a global system for mobile communication (GSM) modem that connected directly to the cell phone network.

5. The software had to be flexible enough to allow for different dispensing models, depending on the setup of each clinic. Models included simple onsite dispensing (one month's supply of drugs), multi-month dispensing for patients with good adherence levels, and down-referral dispensing, in which packages made at a central pharmacy would be collected by patients from a nurse at a local clinic.

Since pharmacy management and dispensing are fundamentally process and number based, it is relatively easy to transfer these particular aspects into an ICT system; on the other hand the realities of public healthcare in resource-constrained settings can make the implementation of systems very difficult.[41] For this reason, iDART evolved to support a small number of basic tasks, including routine dispensing and capturing of basic patient and prescription data. This strong focus on the client and the beneficiary—the public health pharmacist and the HIV-positive person—resulted in a system with very different functionality to commercial alternatives.

Implementation Sites

The initial prototype of iDART was developed in 2004 for a pilot site of DTHC, the Gugulethu Community Clinic in a township near Cape Town. During 2005 iDART was rewritten for use by the DTHC research pharmacy, which was dispensing to small numbers of patients in the greater Cape Town area. During the period from 2003 to 2008, research institutions had started to offer support to government clinics at local level—initially in defiance of national government bureaucracy, which indicated that a plan had to be developed for a national rollout. Capacity was so constrained at the local level that sustainable treatment was not possible without the help, advice, and resources of academics in the health sector. Even so, by 2005, only 14.9 percent of South Africa's registered pharmacists were working in the public sector,[42] and pharmacy services proved to be a major barrier to the rollout.

This atmosphere of social activism, coupled with the notion of having to prove to the government that it was possible to provide treatment even in resource-constrained rural areas, was one of the unforeseen enablers of iDART. Since iDART collaborated with DTHC, other research institutions such as the Medical Research Council of South Africa (MRC), the Reproductive Health Research Unit (RHRU) and the Paediatric Health Research Unit (PHRU) at the University of the Witwatersrand were aware of the system and its early success. Through this network contacts were established in rural areas where the various academic institutions offered support, and Cell-Life began to be asked to implement iDART in other university-supported clinics throughout the country.

The first funding for iDART came from the Elton John Foundation and was focused on equipping four sites in rural South Africa with iDART. After that initial funding, iDART was funded indirectly through grants to the various research institutions involved in providing treatment. International AIDS funds such as PEPFAR (the President's Emergency Plan for AIDS Relief) relied on pharmacy management and reporting capacity to support their treatment plans. Another key enabler of the rollout of iDART was the strong focus on rural clinics. While there was occasionally a sense of competition with other software products in the more urban and peri-urban (township) environments, there was no commercial organization that intended to support rural environments. Highly specialized ARV-dispensing functionality meant that Cell-Life and iDART were not seen to compete with other pharmacy and stock control software suppliers.

When the commitment from government toward a national rollout grew, it became clear that such a rollout had to include research organizations as key stakeholders, many of which had existing treatment programs; iDART became part of the rollout as a consequence of early involvement with research sites. This shift brought increased complexity at some sites when the government began to require formal tender and procurement processes. Meanwhile sites funded by PEPFAR were required to provide specific motivation for using software not developed in the United States.

At the same time, sources of funding diversified. The early model of implementation, in which new sites were assessed individually and managed and supported by Cell-Life, was also changing. Broadreach Healthcare, a private company with responsibility for IT systems at several clinics in KwaZulu-Natal, downloaded iDART from Cell-Life's website and proceeded to implement it themselves (Cell-Life was still involved, but mostly in technical training). This model has since been repeated at several other sites. A front office module for general patient data capture was developed by PHRU, who were using iDART at several sites. The open source license made it possible for Cell-Life to integrate the new module into iDART and make it available to other sites.

Case Study: Cell-Life's iDART Pharmacy Software

In the vast majority of projects undertaken in the South African IT sector, whether in business or government, IT systems are acquired by management, developed by technologists and provided to passive users of systems and services. Whether in a Johannesburg corporation or a rural hospital with intermittent water supply, systems design methodologies and the products and business models of commercial vendors emulate business-oriented models. Progress is explicitly equated with the acquisition of *modern* technology and expertise.[43]

Open Sources and Standards

In Cell-Life projects, we have tried to enact a shift toward openness in the technologies we work with—preferring open source and open standards—and in the system development process through the use of iterative and incremental methods, evolutionary prototyping, and participatory design. This has required a shift in attitude from both the developers of the system and the various user groups. Developers, "specialized [into] academic or professional identities"[44] as technical experts, had to learn to be guided by people whose experiences and modes of expression were often profoundly different from their own. Users, for whom previous engagement with software systems was almost always as passive recipients, needed to work with concepts that were often poorly defined or poorly explained. For most pharmacy users, their involvement was severely time-constrained, balanced with existing work responsibilities that were themselves often overwhelming. The complex setting of post-Apartheid South Africa added particular tension to this relationship, as the developer/user divide often also represented a racial, cultural, and/or language divide.

The urgency of the problem and the severely limited availability and time constraints of pharmacists was key to our decision to use working prototypes, which allow users to form opinions based on actual experience of the system. This in turn fed into iteratively revised design and became a particular strength of iDART. Where software users experienced the system as malleable, they were more likely to provide constructive feedback on changes to the initial design. Similarly, designers and developers who have spent time with system users, soliciting feedback with a mandate to respond to and explore their needs, became an important proxy for users in prioritizing problem areas.

This was, of course, a balancing act. Constantly responding to user requests for changes to iDART became particularly difficult once the exploratory orientation of the initial research project became secondary to considerations of scale. In the transition phase, when iDART was maturing as a research project and growing as an implementation, pressure to make small, individually requested changes to the system needed to be balanced with the need to maintain the technical integrity of the code base, and to align software development priorities with funding. This placed significant strain on the development and implementation teams, and required constant negotiation. Despite this, user and developer relationships had immense value in building and maintaining iDART sites as communities of practice, sustaining knowledge sharing beyond the software itself.

How Openness Affects ICT4D Research

Academic knowledge production suffers from the proliferation of cloistered information silos in which research is conducted and from which it is (often ineffectively) disseminated. Action research, by rejecting positivist claims that the researcher and the researched are independent of each other, and by emphasizing consensus building and co-ownership of the research process, aims to address research production. Communities of practice can serve as gauges for understanding the way research is communicated and made accessible. Action research and communities of practice, informed by observations of participation and the role played by the researcher, form the basis for our understanding of openness in the research process.

The collaborative development of software artifacts (as in Edwin Blake and William Tucker's socially aware software engineering) has been a key factor in developing long-term relationships among developers, implementers, researchers, and stakeholders at project sites in all of Cell-Life's work. In the case of iDART, Ulrike Rivett and Jon Tapson describe multi-stakeholder collaboration in the implementation community: "One of the key partners of the iDART development was the Reproductive Health Research Unit (RHRU) of the University of Witwatersrand. RHRU, being at the forefront of the newest developments in side effects, drug dispensing and other related matters, requested changes to iDART on a regular basis. The changes to the system would subsequently result in Cell-Life offering the updates to all other clinics, which benefited in return from the knowledge of RHRU. A pharmacy assistant in a rural clinic in the North West province described iDART as 'a knowledge transfer system between universities and community clinics.'"[45]

Technical knowledge production, too, can happen beyond isolated innovators at universities. In the case of iDART, open source software components were used throughout, and the software itself is released under an open source license. The motivation for this diverged somewhat from other projects in that attracting contributions from other developers to iDART was not a primary goal. An open source release of the software reflected a philosophical orientation on the part of the developers, which provided induction into a community of open source medical systems developers working on medical records systems (for example, the well-known OpenMRS system, implemented in several South African sites), mobile data collection systems, and related projects. While collaborative software development is the primary activity of these communities, their existence supports much broader knowledge sharing—both formally through mailing lists and project meetings, and informally through relationships between individuals and organizations. The open source model of software development and the community that forms around it are mutually reinforcing. Both the artifact (the software) and the community are also typically in existence for longer than any individual research project, forming a latent network of connections beyond discrete project timelines.

Both situations fit well with the concept of communities of practice, but also highlight their heterogeneous nature. What constitutes actionable knowledge for a health sciences research group, a small IT-sector NGO and a pharmacy assistant at the frontlines of the HIV/AIDS epidemic is likely quite different. The success of iDART lies in the way the process (the implementation of a software system for ARV dispensing) and the artifact (the software itself) have been able to serve and engage diverse stakeholders. Being able to engage over an extended period, long enough for trust to be built and relationships to be developed, has been a key factor in allowing this to happen. The same applies to the open source medical systems communities, which although more technical, are nevertheless heterogeneous in application area and in the kinds of organizations that contribute to projects. Over time, the co-development of the software system provides a concrete basis and a common point of reference for knowledge sharing.

Cell-Life's ability to catalyze knowledge sharing through communities of practice depended on its position as an enduring organization with multiple sources of funding. Unlike most university-based research groups, where highly structured research projects are undertaken with predetermined activities and goals, Cell-Life was able to undertake small pieces of implementation work that bring experience and build the community. Acting as custodians of the iDART system gave the organization a formal intermediary role, facilitating knowledge sharing between heterogeneous groups. Several core groups in similar open source health systems projects are in a similar position, with the added advantage of wider geographical reach.

In terms of methods, iDART offers a promising model to address the common criticism that development research is undesirably disconnected from policy and practice. Traditional academic work, delineated by narrow specializations, offers no incentive to consider the complex political and structural/institutional limits under which policymakers work.[46] Academic work on failed ICT4D projects is often highly critical, particularly where questions of government expenditure and returns are concerned. This may be useful in accountability terms (although the persistence of expensive and contentious failures suggests some limitations), but does little to promote mutually influential relationships between researchers and implementing agencies, and, in turn, fosters negative perceptions of the potential contribution of academic research. Action research, in which the researcher has a stake in delivering a solution that works for all participants, has provided more useful incentives in this regard. iDART, as we've explained, developed as a response to a critical problem. The target user group was pharmacy staff working on the frontlines of the HIV pandemic, and the research was evaluated first by how well it met their needs. At one stage, an integration project was undertaken for the e-Innovation unit of the Western Cape provincial government (PAWC), providing learning on both sides in a clash of institutional cultures that ultimately had to be worked through (and was, with iDART successfully implemented in four PAWC sites). Such a complex, risky, and time-consuming piece of work is unlikely to be undertaken in an academic setting without the incentives provided by action research.

At the same time, the combination of an urgent development problem and an action research response gave rise to the challenge of balancing academic rigor with the awkward compromises arising from a process where everything is understood to be less than ideal. To move from a closed system of expertise, with the researcher as the expert and research participants as subjects, to open collaboration, shared learning, and co-ownership of the research process requires a fundamental shift at both personal and institutional levels.

In traditional academic terms, iDART has produced a tiny fraction of the peer-reviewed academic publications (two journal papers, neither in an ICT4D or information systems journal, and four conference papers) that would be expected of comparable long-running and well-funded projects. The nonresearch focus of the various funders involved, and their focus on instrumental evaluations, provides part of the explanation for this. Another reason may be the inadequacy of our research training—in common with many researchers in ICT4D—in providing tools for reporting action research. Conversely, the position of Cell-Life as an independent NGO with multiple sources of funding has allowed a much more fluid definition of the goals of the iDART project, over which the researchers who write the proposals are not in total control, but the community has some influence.

Openness and Development in Universities

To reconceptualize the role of ICT4D research in national development it is important to grapple with what an enabling institutional environment might look like. For the near future, universities are still best positioned to develop such an enabling environment. However, important structural barriers remain unaddressed. For example, partnerships across disciplines are key to the success of redefining research—social problems are by nature multidisciplinary. Yet discipline-specific journals and conferences are still the dominant means of disseminating academic research. A further barrier is the cost-center approach to research projects, resulting in all projects being hosted within one department or faculty for financial reasons, thereby tacitly discouraging cross- and multidisciplinary research. Cell-Life, which ran projects between the faculties of health science, engineering, and commerce at various stages, constantly encountered barriers to interfaculty collaboration—and it published far less than similar research projects.

Knowledge sharing through intellectual property is another area that requires rethinking. Intellectual property (IP) policies that seem to bedevil the ability to share knowledge require formal mechanisms to exempt certain research and initiatives from the stringent criteria.[47] The concept of collaborative open source development, where ownership of software and code is shared among many groups, is often poorly understood by university IP departments, and poorly addressed in existing guidelines. In the case of iDART, prior work done by Cell-Life in engaging with university management on IP issues was clearly beneficial, as the major concerns of both sides had already been aired and addressed. This experience points to the need to establish a critical mass of initiatives with openness as an organizing principle.

The perspective shift described in the previous sections has also highlighted a need to reconsider the skill set of researchers and practitioners. At the university level, this means reviewing what is currently taught across a wide range of disciplines, as well as critical consideration of areas in which, as with research, disciplinary boundaries of teaching are limited in their ability to promote socially responsive approaches. Unfortunately, curricula reviews of existing programs are often biased toward integrating new developments from industry. Attempts to redefine curricula based on local needs face immense barriers, not least in the attitudes of students themselves. Accreditation processes, which specify fixed requirements for curriculum content, impose additional limitations. This is most obvious for programs seeking international accreditations, as was the case in both computer science and engineering programs at the University of Cape Town during the time that Cell-Life was operating there.

As a result, the area in which Cell-Life has been most successful at influencing teaching and learning is not within the general curriculum but in the supervision of student research projects. iDART was developed in the initial stages as student research. Students benefited by engaging in research within a diverse community of stakeholders, many of whom have very different backgrounds than their own. Our experience has also been that students who are exposed to socially responsive research often continue to incorporate a development orientation in future work. If the role of universities is to serve the public good, sensitizing students to the development potential of their field is extremely valuable.

A final point on institutional arrangements for ICT4D research concerns engagement with institutional stakeholders beyond the university. In the case of iDART, engagement with multiple levels of government was essential to ensure not only the fit of the system in its immediate context, but also its position in relation to other systems and policy directions, all of which evolved rapidly as the government grappled with HIV management. Engagement with the private sector at various points also proved essential in developing a foundation for system support at scale, beyond Cell-Life's own capacity.

In terms of achieving cooperation among institutions, iDART is indebted to the process focus and long timelines of action research. The e-government literature has explored productive engagement with government, but perhaps has failed to emphasize the long timelines necessitated by approval processes, staffing constraints, and budget processes. In relation to the private sector, the advent of iDART as a research collaboration made possible the development of the system that was risky—new, poorly specified, and serving a notoriously difficult sector. The initial research focused on allowing the functional and operational requirements of the new field or anti-retroviral dispensing to emerge.[48] As the focus shifted to broader implementation, the need for flexibility beyond what was available in a university environment resulted in Cell-Life being spun off as a separate nonprofit entity. Because of a shared understanding of the project developed during Cell-Life's multiyear engagement with the university IP office, we were able to negotiate IP policies (in Cell-Life's case, an open source model) that were flexible enough to accommodate the shift. Table 3.2 continues this discussion.

Conclusion

The concept of open development usefully frames reflections on iDART's success as a research-based response to a critical development problem.

Table 3.2
iDART Case Analysis Summary

	System design and implementation	ICT4D research	Openness and development at universities in the Global South
Universal over restricted access to research products	Developing and participating in communities of practice around open source medical systems in the developing world	Research-policy-practice links; action research in context and with a clear organizational outcome; and acceptance of multiple account-abilities: funders, implementers, patients, academic community	Developing and participating in communities of practice around ARV delivery
Universal over restricted participation in the research process	Design by constraints of remote clinics and the public health sector, evolutionary prototyping, time-sensitive training and design sessions with pharmacy staff	Engagement with multiple stake-holders (government, medical/pharmacy professionals, frontline users), action research approach, long timelines	Retraining researchers and students as facilitators/resources, engaging with practitioners as informants for both content and direction of research
Collaborative over centralized production of knowledge, and recognition of diversity in knowledge systems	Longevity of software artifact beyond individual project time-lines, sharing of feature requests and innovation through access by distribution clinics to a common software system, and awareness of alternative IP models	Collaboration (disciplinary, researcher-practitioner) catalyzed by a critical development problem, development and support of enduring communities of practice	Challenges of interdisciplinarity within university structures, interfaculty research teams, teaching outside of internationally recognized syllabi, and nontraditional dissemination channels for research products

Over the past ten years, the project has proven its ability to scale alongside the ART rollout, in the process negotiating a transition from a university research group to an implementation-focused nonprofit.

Both system design and research methods were chosen with the intention of widening participation. In both cases, participatory methods proved both highly valuable but severely constrained by the time-limited nature of participants' work:

• In system design, evolutionary prototyping and the development of working prototypes emerged as valuable method for enabling user participation in system design, while also creating a shared sense of the malleable nature of the systems between users, developers, and researchers.

• Participatory action research and involvement with wider open source developer communities contributed to the development of communities of practice, with diverse stakeholder involvement and the ability to endure beyond individual implementations and systems.

iDART also established the value of a long-running action research approach, where projects are developed over the course of several years, to build a shared, context-sensitive understanding of the system. Openness and co-creation is impossible without relationships at ground level, built in increments as trust is established and, in turn, fundamental to the process of shared development. This in turn supports flexible systems and communities, able to reconfigure themselves over the life cycle of the system.

Action research sees the researcher developing into a resource to the project community rather than an uninvolved observer of a process. By adhering to this principle, iDART succeeded in promoting wider access to research products—both the software and the distributed knowledge developed and shared in the community. However, this came at the expense of traditional academic publication. Action research is challenging to report out of context. The multidisciplinary nature of the project further complicated its relationship with academia in the relatively rigid professionalized disciplines of medicine, engineering, and computer science.

In terms of knowledge production, it is clear that the realization of universities as developmental institutions requires a far wider range of expertise in ICT4D than is usually available in the limited fields of information systems and computer science. On an organizational level, universities often struggle to accommodate projects that span across disciplines and have long timelines, diverse stakeholders, and nontraditional knowledge outcomes. Experience within the university in managing these kinds of projects can lead to productive engagement.

The experience of iDART demonstrates important benefits of open approaches to research, despite practical and structural challenges. Efforts to increase awareness of open alternatives among researchers and practitioners, should be supported, and the results critically evaluated by the ICT4D community.

Notes

An earlier version of this chapter appeared previously in *Information Technologies & International Development*, 9, no. 1 (Spring 2011), Special Issue on Open Development, http://itidjournal.org/itid/issue/view/40.

1. G. Hearn and M. Foth, "Action Research in the Design of New Media and ICT Systems," in *Topical Issues in Communications and Media Research*, ed. K. Kwansah-Aidoo (New York: Nova Science, 2005), 79–94.

2. M. Mbali, "HIV/AIDS Policy Making in Post-Apartheid South Africa," in *Human Science Research Council: State of the Nation 2003–2004,"* ed. J. Daniel, A. Habib, and R. Southall (Cape Town: HSRC, 2003), 312–329.

3. R. Wood, R. Kaplan, L. G. Bekker, S. Brown, and U. Rivett, "The Utility of Pharmacy Dispensing Data for ART Programme Evaluation and Early Identification of Patient Loss to Follow Up," *Southern African Journal of HIV Medicine* 9, no. 2 (2008): 44.

4. DOH, *South African National Strategic Plan for HIV/AIDS and STI 2007–2011* (Cape Town: Department of Health, 2007).

5. L. G. Bekker, C. Orrell, L. Reader, K. Matoti, K. Cohen, K. Martell, F. Abdullah, and R. Wood, "Anti-retroviral Therapy in a Community Clinic: Early Lessons from a Pilot Project," *South African Medical Journal* 93, no. 6 (2003): 458–462.

6. M. L. Smith and L. Elder, "Open ICT Ecosystems Transforming the Developing World," *Information Technology and Development* 6, no. 1 (2010): 65–71.

7. R. Heeks, *eGovernment for Development: Success/Failure Rates Survey Overview*, 2003, http://www.egov4dev.org/success/sfrates.shtml.

8. D. Dada, "The Failure of E-Government in Developing Countries: A Literature Review," *The Electronic Journal of Information Systems in Developing Countries* (2006): 26.

9. T. A. Pardo and H. J. Scholl, "Walking Atop the Cliffs: Avoiding Failure and Reducing Risk in Large Scale E-Government Projects," *Proceedings of the 35th Annual Hawaii International Conference on System Sciences*, 1656–1665.

10. R. Heeks, "Information Systems and Developing Countries: Failure, Success, and Local Improvisations," *The Information Society* 18, no. 2 (2002): 101. doi:10.1080/01972240290075039.

11. Ibid.

12. E. Mumford and M. Weir, *Computer Systems in Work Design:The ETHICS Method*, (London: Associated Business Press, 1979).

13. P. B. Checkland and J. Scholes, *SSM in Action* (Chichester, UK: John Wiley & Sons Ltd., 1989).

14. E. Blake and W. Tucker, "Socially Aware Software Engineering for the Developing World," in *IST-Africa 2006 Conference Proceedings*, ed. P. Cunningham and M. Cunningham (Dublin: IIMC International Information Management Corporation, 2006).

15. R. Hirschheim and H. K. Klein, "Four Paradigms of Information Systems Development" *Communications of the ACM* 32, no. 10 (1989): 1199–1216.

16. E. Byrne and S. Sahay, "Participatory Design for Social Development: A South African Case Study on Community-Based Health Information Systems," *Information Technology for Development* 13, no. 1 (2007): 71–94.

17. Blake and Tucker, "Socially Aware," 2006.

18. R. Chambers, "Poverty and Livelihoods: Whose Reality Counts?," *Environment and Urbanization* 7, no. 1 (1995): 173.

19. B. Cooke and U. Kothari, *Participation: The New Tyranny?* (London: Zed Books, 2001).

20. R. Heeks, "The Tyranny of Participation in Information Systems Learning from Development Projects, http://unpan1.un.org/intradoc/groups/public/documents/NISPAcee/UNPAN015538.pdf.

21. Y. Vaillancourt, "Democratizing Knowledge: Research Experiments Based On University-Community Partnerships," http://www.fimcivilsociety.org/en/library/Democratizing_Knowledge.pdf.

22. J. Rabinovitch, "Transforming Community Practice: [Re] Moving the Margins," Union Institute, http://comm-org.wisc.edu/papers2005/rabinovitch/contents.htm.

23. E. Crewe and J. Young, "Bridging Research and Policy: Context, Evidence and Links," ODI, http://www.odi.org.uk/sites/odi.org.uk/files/odi-assets/publications-opinion-files/184.pdf.

24. P. Reason and H. Bradbury, *The SAGE Handbook of Action Research: Participative Inquiry and Practice* (London: Sage Publications Ltd., 2007).

25. M. Thompson, "Discourse, 'Development' and the 'Digital Divide': ICT and the World Bank, *Review of African Political Economy* 99, (2004): 103–123.

26. F. Wilson, "The Truth is Out There: The Search for Emancipatory Principles in Information Systems Design," *Information Technology and People* 10, no, 3 (1997): 187–204.

27. G. Wilson, "Knowledge, Innovation and Re-inventing Technical Assistance for Development," *Progress in Development Studies* 7, no. 3 (2007):183.

28. L. T. Soeftestad, "Aligning Needs and Means. On Culture, ICT and Knowledge in Development Cooperation," in 24th Information System Research Seminar in Scandinavia (IRIS 24): 47–60, http://rmportal.net/library/content/frame/aligning-needs -and-means.pdf.

29. Blake and Tucker, "Socially Aware,"2006; Byrne and Sahay, "Participatory Design," 2007.

30. Hearn and Foth, "Action Research," 2005.

31. E. Brett, *Reconstructing Development Theory: International Inequality, Institutional Reform and Social Emancipation* (Basingstoke, UK: Palgrave Macmillan, 2009).

32. Ibid., 306.

33. Ibid., 21.

34. Ibid., 306.

35. M. L. Gibbons, C. Limoges, and H. Nowotny, *The New Production of Knowledge: The Dynamics of Science and Research in Contemporary Societies* (London: Sage Publications Ltd., 1994).

36. H. Nowotny, P. Scott, and M. Gibbons, "Mode 2 Revisited: The New Production of Knowledge," *Minerva* 41, no. 3 (2003): 179–194.

37. R. Chambers, *Rural Development: Putting the Last First* (London: Longman, 1999).

38. R. Williams and D. Edge, "The Social Shaping of Technology," *Research Policy* 25, no. 6 (1996): 865–899.

39. J. Kallinikos, "Farewell to Constructivism: Technology and Context-embedded Action," in *The Social Study of Information and Communication Technology: Innovation, Actors, and Contexts*, ed. C. Avgerou, C. Chrisanthi, and F. Land (Oxford: Oxford University Press, 2004), 140–161.

40. U. Rivett and J. Tapson, "The Cell-Life Project: Converging Technologies in the Context of HIV/AIDS," *Gateways International Journal of Community Research and Engagement* 2, (2009): 82–97.

41. S. Brown, D. de Jager, R. Wood, and U. Rivett, "A Pharmacy Stock Control Management System to Effectively Monitor and Manage Patients on ART," The 4th Insti-

tution of Engineering and Technology Seminar on Appropriate Healthcare Technologies for Developing Countries (Savoy Place, London, UK: May 23–24, 2006), 27–36.

42. Health Systems Trust, "Health Statistics 2005: Health Personnel," http://www .hst.org.za/content/health-indicators.

43. S. Moodley, "The Promise of E-Development? A Critical Assessment of the State ICT for Poverty Reduction Discourse in South Africa," *Perspectives on Global Development and Technology* 4, no. 1 (2005): 1–26.

44. P. Ensor, "The National Qualifications Framework and Higher Education in South Africa: Some Epistemological Issues," *Journal of Education and Work* 16, no. 3 (2003): 325. doi:10.1080/1363908032000099476.

45. Rivett and Tapson, "The Cell-Life Project," 2009.

46. Crewe and Young, "Bridging Research," 2002.

47. Rivett and Tapson, "The Cell-Life Project," 2009.

48. Brown and others, "A Pharmacy Stock," 2006.

Bibliography

Bekker, L. G., C. Orrell, L. Reader, K. Matoti, K. Cohen, R. Martell, F. Abdullah, and R. Wood. "Anti-retroviral Therapy in a Community Clinic: Early Lessons from a Pilot Project." *South African Medical Journal* 93 (6) (2003): 458–462.

Blake, E., and W. Tucker. "Socially Aware Software Engineering for the Developing World." In IST-Africa 2006 Conference Proceedings, edited by P. Cunningham and M. Cunningham. Dublin: IIMC International Information Management Corporation, 2006.

Brett, E. *Reconstructing Development Theory: International Inequality, Institutional Reform and Social Emancipation.* Basingstoke, UK: Palgrave Macmillan, 2009.

Brown, S., D. de Jager, R. Wood, and U. Rivett. "A Pharmacy Stock Control Management System to Effectively Monitor and Manage Patients on ART." The 4th Institution of Engineering and Technology Seminar on Appropriate Healthcare Technologies for Developing Countries. Savoy Place, London, UK: 23–24, May 2006, 27–36.

Byrne, E., and S. Sahay. "Participatory Design for Social Development: A South African Case Study on Community-Based Health Information Systems." *Information Technology for Development* 13 (1) (2007): 71–94.

Chambers, R. "Poverty and Livelihoods: Whose Reality Counts?" *Environment and Urbanization* 7 (1) (1995): 173.

Chambers, R. *Rural Development: Putting the Last First* (London: Longman, 1999), http://www.eou.edu/socwomen/support/articles/chambers.pdf.

Checkland, P. B., and J. Scholes. *SSM in Action*. Chichester, UK: John Wiley & Sons Ltd, 1989.

Cooke, B., and U. Kothari. *Participation: The New Tyranny?* London: Zed Books, 2001.

Dada, D. *The Failure of E-Government in Developing Countries: A Literature Review., 26*. The Electronic Journal of Information Systems in Developing Countries, 2006.

DOH. *South African National Strategic Plan for HIV/AIDS and STI 2007–2011*. Cape Town: Department of Health, 2007.

Ensor, P. "The National Qualifications Framework and Higher Education in South Africa: Some Epistemological Issues." *Journal of Education and Work* 16 (3) (2003): 325. doi:10.1080/1363908032000099476.

Gibbons, M. L., C. Limoges, and H. Nowotny. *The New Production of Knowledge: The Dynamics of Science and Research in Contemporary Societies*. London: Sage Publications Ltd, 1994.

Health Systems Trust. "Health Statistics 2005: Health Personnel." http://www.hst .org.za/healthstts/102/data.

Hearn, G., and M. Foth. Action Research in the Design of New Media and ICT Systems. In *Topical Issues in Communications and Media Research*, ed. K. Kwansah-Aidoo, 79–94. New York: Nova Science, 2005.

Heeks, R. "Information Systems and Developing Countries: Failure, Success, and Local Improvisations." *Information Society* 18 (2) (2002): 101.

Heeks, R. *eGovernment for Development—Success/Failure Rates Survey Overview*. 2003, http://www.egov4dev.org/success/sfrates.shtml.

Heeks, R. "The Tyranny of Participation in Information Systems:Learning from Development Projects." http://unpan1.un.org/intradoc/groups/ public/documents/ NISPAcee/UNPAN015538.pdf.

Hirschheim, R., and H. K. Klein. "Four Paradigms of Information Systems Development." *Communications of the ACM* 32 (10) (1989): 1199–1216.

Kallinikos, J. "Farewell to Constructivism: Technology and Context-embedded Action." In The Social Study of Information and Communication Technology: Innovation, Actors, and Contexts, ed. C. Avgerou, C. Ciborra, and F. Land, 140–161. Oxford: Oxford University Press, 2004.

Mbali, M. HIV/AIDS Policy Making in Post-Apartheid South Africa. In *Human Science Research Council: State of the Nation 2003–2004*, ed. J. Daniel, A. Habib, and R. Southall, 312–329. Cape Town: HSRC, 2003.

Moodley, S. "The Promise of E-Development? A Critical Assessment of the State ICT for Poverty Reduction Discourse in South Africa." *Perspectives on Global Development and Technology* 4 (1) (2005): 1–26.

Mumford, E., and M. Weir. *Computer Systems in Work Design: the ETHICS Method.* London: Associated Business Press, 1979.

Nowotny, H., P. Scott, and M. Gibbons. "Mode 2 Revisited: The New Production of Knowledge." *Minerva* 41 (3) (2003): 179–194.

Pardo, T. A., and H. J. Scholl. "Walking Atop the Cliffs: Avoiding Failure and Reducing Risk in Large Scale E-Government Projects." *Proceedings of the 35th Annual Hawaii International Conference on System Sciences*, 1656–1665.

Reason, P., and H. Bradbury. *The SAGE Handbook of Action Research:Participative Inquiry and Practice.* London: Sage Publications Ltd, 2007.

Rivett, U., and J. Tapson. "The Cell-Life Project: Converging Technologies in the Context of HIV/AIDS." *Gateways International Journal of Community Research and Engagement* 2 (2009): 82–97.

Smith, M. L., and L. Elder. "Open ICT Ecosystems Transforming the Developing World." *Information Technology and Development* 6 (1) (2010): 65–71.

Soeftestad, L. T. "Aligning Needs and Means. On Culture, ICT and Knowledge in Development Cooperation," in 24th Information System Research Seminar in Scandinavia (IRIS 24): 47–60, http://rmportal.net/library/content/frame/aligning-needs -and-means.pdf.

Thompson, M. "Discourse, 'Development' and the 'Digital Divide': ICT and the World Bank." *Review of African Political Economy* 99 (2004): 103–123.

Vaillancourt, Y. "Democratizing Knowledge: Research Experiments Based On University-Community Partnerships." http://www.fimcivilsociety.org/en/library/ Democratizing_Knowledge.pdf.

Williams, R., and D. Edge. "The Social Shaping of Technology." *Research Policy* 25 (6) (1996): 865–899.

Wilson, F. "The Truth Is Out There: The Search for Emancipatory Principles in Information Systems Design." *Information Technology and People* 10 (3) (1997): 187–204.

Wilson, G. "Knowledge, Innovation and Re-inventing Technical Assistance for Development." *Progress in Development Studies* 7 (3) (2007): 183.

Wood, R., R. Kaplan, L. G. Bekker, S. Brown, and U. Rivett. "The Utility of Pharmacy Dispensing Data for ART Programme Evaluation and Early Identification of Patient Loss to Follow Up." *Southern African Journal of HIV Medicine* 9 (2) (2008): 44.

4 Transparency and Development: Ethical Consumption through Web 2.0 and the Internet of Things

Mark Graham and Håvard Haarstad

A central problem in contemporary processes of economic globalization is that information about commodities has not been globalized at the same rate as the commodities themselves. Contemporary capitalism conceals the histories and geographies of most commodities from consumers. These consumers rarely have opportunities to gaze backward through the chains of production in order to gain knowledge about the sites of production, transformation, and distribution of products. The complexity of commodity chains leaves us with highly opaque production processes. Transnational companies often strive to maintain this opacity through a separation between the "airbrushed world" communicated through advertising on one hand,[1] and the actual world of production on the other. With this problem in mind, this chapter discusses the potential for emergent practices of collaboration and communication through the Internet to facilitate flows of information about commodity chains. The hope is that, by transcending barriers of time and space, new practices tied to communication and information sharing through the Internet will open up the politics of consumer activism and influence the way goods are produced, particularly those that that originate in the Global South.

Increasingly complex structures of production have been created by transnational corporations (TNCs) in their quest for efficiency, new markets, and new competitive advantages.[2] TNCs generally break production processes into networks and chains that are constituted by complex sets of geographically separated nodes.[3] The lack of association between commodities and information about commodity production has led to an increase in demands from consumers in the Global North for greater transparency in production processes. Many of these demands can be seen in the context of anti-globalization criticisms against transnational corporate practices, and as a battle of information over what goes on in the factories and maquiladoras (that is, export assembly plants) of the Global South. Campaigns around fair trade and corporate social responsibility have convinced large numbers of consumers that their purchasing practices do have global repercussions. In turn, some TNCs have responded by constructing detailed narratives of product histories to ensure consumers of their ethical production practices.

Nongovernmental organizations (NGOs) and social movements have made use of the Internet to spread information about campaigns aimed at the social and environmental effects of corporate practices. Lauren Langman suggests that the Internet provides an infrastructure for "internetworked social movements" and an alternative public sphere, through which information about corporate practices can be exchanged and used for strategy.[4] Yet for the most part, information being transmitted through producers and branders means that narratives constructed about upstream nodes in commodity chains can be difficult to challenge. It has been virtually impossible for actors in the Global South, particularly those subject to oppressive labor practices or destructive environmental practices, to challenge these narratives and communicate counter narratives. At the same time, a number of commentators are now pointing to the potential for a different type of globalization—this one characterized by knowledge and transparency and with the capability to harness the power of the Internet to allow consumers to learn more about the commodities that they buy. This globalization is based on emergent Web 2.0 frameworks and technologies characterized by user-generated information and collaborative development of knowledge.

This chapter discusses whether increased access to commodity chain information can foster progressive social and environmental change by enabling more ethical consumption. More specifically, we discuss the potential for Web 2.0 frameworks to transcend barriers of time and space to facilitate flows of information about the chains of commodities, thereby encouraging consumers to make informed economic decisions by being more aware of the social, political, and environmental impacts of available products. It has already been suggested that information and communication technologies (ICTs) can aid development through access to information, reduced transaction and transportation costs, and new business opportunities.[5] Our perspective on Web 2.0 and commodity chain transparency adds another element to this debate by outlining potential ways for marginalized communities to share information about labor and environmental conditions of production. User-generated content and what has been dubbed the "Internet of Things" have opened up new possibilities for both mapping commodity chains on the Internet and integrating the phenomenon known as *guerrilla cartography* with the politics of production and consumption. This globalization of knowledge and transparency, therefore, offers the potential to alter the politics of consumption and practices of production, as well as to empower marginal individuals and communities. A number of persistent barriers to the creation and transmission of information about commodities (e.g., infrastructure and access, actors' capacities, the continued role of infomediaries, and intelligent capture and use by consumers) can temper these hopes. Unleashing the potential of these technologies, therefore, ultimately depends on technological change being embedded in broader processes of local capacitation, democratization, and social change.

Economic Globalization and Mediated Flows of Information

Transparency and flows of information in commodity chains have traditionally been long-standing links to distance and proximity. Geographers and other social scientists have argued that these relationships are centrally important to understand the distribution and transmission of knowledge,[6] and that transmission costs and boundaries impede the flow of information.[7] Traditionally, consumers have possessed more knowledge about nodes on commodity chains that are close to them in absolute distance than nodes that are further away.[8] For instance, in the eighteenth cen tury most consumers would have been more likely to have had knowledge (related to characteristics such as production practices, ownership, or labor issues) about bakeries in their neighborhood than about wheat farms in southern England, Sweden, or Poland.[9] The transmission of information is thus highly constrained by distance (see figure 4.1).

Early waves of globalization brought new types of goods to consumers in the Global North through increasing trade and by organizing colonies to supply the raw materials for industrialization. By the 1930s, the contours of a consumer economy were emerging with the development of Fordist mass production, the first multinational companies, and an international financial sector. All of this commodity-related activity[10]was aided by new systems of communication, including radio and film.[11] Advertising and films can be considered the trusted infomediaries of that era, communicating what today would be considered gendered and racialized stereotypes without much concern for the production conditions in the colonies or in the domestic factories. Industrialization also went hand in hand with labor organization, and unions systematically used newspapers and pamphlets to communicate and agitate around working conditions.[12] Ethical consumption campaigns grew out of the emergence of NGOs from the 1970s onward,

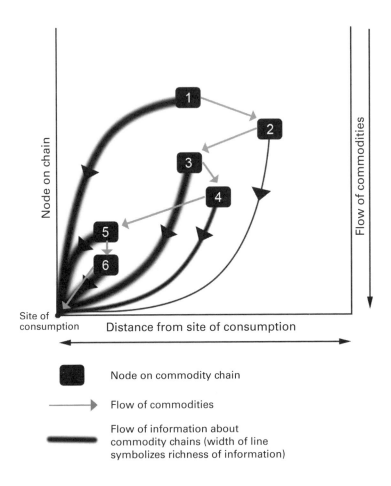

Figure 4.1
Simplified representation of flows of information about nodes on a commodity chain. *Source*: Authors.

and after the advent of the Internet, NGOs have been apt to use it as a tool to network and communicate. Mediators of information about products have therefore changed over time, and new infomediaries have been able to alter the basic relationships between proximity and transparency.

Today a variety of organizations have developed reputations as trusted infomediaries for their critical analysis of the commodity chains of products. Consumer watchdog magazines, such as *Which?* (in the United Kingdom), *Consumer Reports* (in the United States), and *Stiftung Warentest* (in Germany), are targeted primarily at consumers in wealthy countries and reveal information that producers typically conceal. Myriad public interest groups also make it their mission to distribute information about the hidden practices of many TNCs. Reports on Royal Dutch Shell's environmental record in the Niger Delta, Mattel's use of child laborers in Sumatra, and Nike's sweatshops in Vietnam, are just a few of many examples of this sort of investigative interest in the origins of goods and commodities.[13]

Consumer knowledge about distant nodes can have powerful effects on both the consumers and producers of commodities. Without any information transfer about the sites of production, knowledge about products remains highly localized. For example, bananas grown on St. Lucia's plantations, shoes made in Vietnamese factories, and most other items we find in our supermarkets are certainly globalized products, but consumers in distant locations lack information about their production. With media interventions, information about fair trade practices on banana plantations or child labor in shoe factories can become as globalized as the bananas or shoes themselves, potentially reshaping how those commodities are consumed and ultimately produced.

Yet mediated information about nodes on commodity chains is necessarily incomplete and can give rise to the transmission of information about nodes on chains in ways that contradict distance decay models, such as that of figure 4.1. For instance, through documentary reporting and feature stories of coffee growers in Kenya, many consumers in London have a detailed understanding of exploitative production practices on some farms in central Kenya, but they continue to have little or no knowledge about how coffee is roasted in Europe.

Therefore, with the ever increasing importance of infomediaries and their uses of communication technologies, the relationships between distance (either absolute or topological) and the flows of information become less clear (see figure 4.2). In particular, the Internet is frequently thought to alter the link between proximity and transparency in several ways. First, the Internet strengthens what has been called the "spotlight effect,"[14] whereby NGOs, activists, and journalists publicize information about unsavory corporate practices. Such stories are occasionally rebroadcast by mainstream media and have costly and harmful effects on corporate reputations. Second, the Internet can assist with the spreading of campaigns that target general production practices, advocate legal changes, or protest trade agreements. The Internet facilitates both the coordination among activists within a network and the outreach of these networks to potential supporters.[15] Finally, the Internet can function as an alternative public sphere where norms and strategies are communicated and debated.

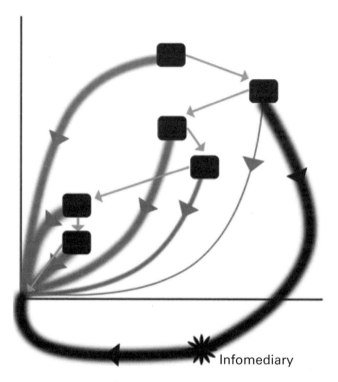

Infomediary

Figure 4.2
Altered flows of information due to media interventions. *Source*: Authors.

The adoption of the Internet to globalize information has inspired a multitude of projects dedicated to mapping, visualizing, and communicating conditions at production sites in the Global South to activists and consumers in the Global North. Richard Welford, for instance, sees the emergence of a "new wave of globalization" where increased transparency aids the struggle for human rights.[16] Similarly, it is frequently argued that communication technologies such as the Internet have unique capacities to create democratic and participatory spaces for information exchange and debates.[17]

Participatory spaces are not solely emerging in the Global North. Ragnhild Overå, for example, illustrates this by a study of how "telecommunication pioneers" in informal trading in Ghana have changed their mode of operation to reduce both transportation and transaction costs.[18] Heeks argues that ICT implementation in the Global South is moving from a first generation, in which designs were imposed and the poor were expected to adapt to them, to a second generation that is increasingly designed around the specific resources, capacities, and demands of the poor.[19] Wikis can be used to keep politicians accountable to the public through projects such as Mzalendo.com in Kenya (subtitled "Eye on Kenyan Parliament"), which allows users to communicate information about the political process.[20] Another example is Ushahidi, an open source tool that allows users to share information on disasters and crises using SMS (short message service, or text messaging), email, and the World Wide Web so that spatially distributed data can be gathered and visualized in timelines or maps. This tool has been used in relation to natural disasters, pandemics, and violence outbreaks in the Democratic Republic of Congo, Haiti, the Gaza Strip, India, and elsewhere.[21] Internet-based social media have played an increasingly important role in American politics, through both Obama campaigns and through the organizing around the so-called Tea Party. A combination of cell phone technology and Internet-based social media also gave the world insight into the repression of the Iranian Green Revolution, which likely restrained the regime's response.

Earlier similar developments lead Steve Weber and Jennifer Bussell to see the contours of a "global shared infrastructure" that is sufficiently disruptive to call into question assumptions about the "natural state" of many economic processes and organizational principles.[22] The most optimistic commentators tend to see the Internet as a new and alternative (or a subcultural) public sphere that subverts the mainstream public sphere controlled by corporate conglomerates.[23] As an extension of Nancy Fraser's work on "subaltern counterpublics,"[24] the Internet is seen as parallel discursive arena wherein members of various social groups invent and circulate counter discourses against power. While conceding the danger that computerization of society might increase inequalities, Douglas Kellner[25] argues that a "democratized and computerized public sphere" is necessary to revitalize capitalist democracies, and that it would provide opportunities to overcome structures of inequality.

The Internet and the public sphere it represents are seen as the backbone of a global civil society or a global social movement that has emerged in opposition to neoliberal globalization. The Internet has enabled new kinds of communities to share common grievances and develop strategies to mobilize in accordance with them. The political activist networks that Langman terms "internetworked social movements"[26] use electronic communication for recruitment, coordination, and leadership, in ways that take them beyond a mere series of isolated "militant particularist" struggles.[27] Social scientists have been interested in movements that attempt to bridge socio-spatial differences and thereby alter the scalar dynamics of opposition to globalization.[28] While transnational solidarities are obviously not new, present alliances are distinct with regard to the means, speed, and intensity of communication among the various groups involved.[29] As these writings make clear, Internet-aided political movements are changing spatial-political practices and the ways in which we conceptualize them.

Traditional advocacy networks composed of NGOs have perhaps become the most effective infomediary in the politics of consumption by collecting information, bringing it to consumer, and pressuring governments and public agencies.[30] Within the activist-based "alter-globalization movement" Anastasia Kavada has found that the use of the Internet is an integral part of an organizational model that is open, flexible, and decentralized.[31] This organizational model has been seen as a new form of collective organization, and it has been argued that these practices should be considered "convergence spaces" rather than formal networks or organizational structures.[32] These convergence spaces represent what is new about Internet-enabled politics—a decentralized and nonhierarchical structure, immediate solidarity, communication and alliance-building across space, and a diffuse networked force that challenges neoliberal globalization. Alternatively, as Laura Illia writes of political campaigns on the Internet, the pressure on companies "is no longer the result of a long aggregation into association, but an immediate and spontaneous network of relationships."[33]

Yet it remains that infomediaries only collect or transfer information about a small proportion of the many long-distance commodity chains that traverse the globe. In cases like the Iranian Green Revolution, transparency is increased by the emergence of a temporary international media event. This creates an outpouring of international sympathy for the duration of the media event, which tends to be quickly forgotten as attention moves on to the next crisis. This is the case for commodity chains as well; infomediaries create temporary media events that work through naming and shaming of prominent companies, rather than through any approach of systematic data collection. Even though much critical research has tracked the chains of coffee, chocolate, sports shoes, and myriad other high-profile objects, spotlight effects rarely touch the mundane objects that surround our every day existences. Chains of cabbage, carburetors, and cat food thus remain largely invisible.

Most importantly, by definition, infomediaries mediate information, adding a dense layer of social, economic, political, and technological arbitration between the nodes and information access points. Therefore, while networked practices and communication technologies have selectively increased transparency in a range of social areas, there remain significant constraints on the transformative potentials of projects designed by infomediaries for commodity chain transparency.

An emerging shift in both virtual production practices and the availability of networked information, however, has left a number of commentators to point to an emerging third model of the relationships between information flows and distance. This alternate model of information flow has not only sparked a new way of imagining the links between place and information, but has also been integral to the implementation of a host of projects that aim to fundamentally transform the politics of consumption.

The Internet of Things

What we're contemplating here is the extension of information-sensing, -processing, and -networking capabilities to entire classes of things we've never before thought of as "technology."
—Adam Greenfield[34]

The distinction between "real" and "virtual" is becoming as quaint as the 19th-century distinction between "mind" and "body." We want to bring about a connectivity between the physical world, its objects and spaces, and the virtual world of Web sites and environments.
—Usman Haque, Pachube.com[35]

The Internet of Things (IOT) refers to the coding and networking of everyday objects and things in order to render them individually machine readable and traceable on the Internet.[36] Much existing content in the IOT has been created through coded radio frequency identification (RFID) tags and Internet Protocol (IP) addresses[37] linked into an electronic product code (EPC) network.

Imagining the Internet of Things being used to track an object like a can of cola or a box of cereal from sites of production to sites of consumption is perhaps not too difficult to stretch the imagination. Indeed, a movement is underway to add almost every imaginable object into the Internet of Things. In New Zealand, for example, all cows were scheduled to have IP addresses embedded onto RFID chips implanted into their skin by 2011.[38] This will then allow producers to track each animal through the entire production and distribution process. Furthermore, objects are increasingly able not just to be characterized by a unique identifier, but also to transmit location and context-sensitive data.

The development of the Internet of Things has been primarily driven by the needs of large corporations that stand to benefit greatly from the foresight and predictability afforded by the ability to follow objects through commodity chains.[39] The ability to code and track objects has allowed companies to become more efficient, speed up processes, reduce error, prevent theft, and incorporate complex and flexible organizational systems.[40] Analysts predict that with the new Internet of Things "users of the Internet will be counted in billions and . . . humans may become the minority as generators and receivers of traffic."[41] Adam Greenfield perhaps best captures this shift by arguing that "ever more pervasive, ever harder to perceive, computing has leapt off the desktop and insinuated itself into everyday life. Such ubiquitous information technology 'everyware'—will appear in many different contexts and take a wide variety of forms, but it will effect every one of us, whether we're aware of it or not.'"[42]

In fact, so many objects were assigned IP addresses that we came to a point at which we would run out of potential new ones.[43] The solution to this problem is the new IP system of addressing. Under the new system there will be 2^{128} potential addresses (this is the equivalent to 39,614,081, 257,132,168,796,771,975,168 addresses for every living person). The sheer number of potential addresses reflects the fact that many powerful voices are within the organizations that oversee the architecture of the Internet (such as the Internet Engineering Task Force) foresee an Internet of Things in which most of the objects that are made and sold are addressable and linked to databases of information.

Blending the physical and the virtual by tagging actual products with networked information produces new spaces for consumption politics. It has also led some commentators to argue that we are approaching a future where codes become part of the "technological unconscious."[44] Martin Dodge and Rob Kitchin argue that this growing pervasiveness of identification codes and informational systems to monitor and regulate population works to create a universal panopticon that will enable its users to "know simultaneously and in real time the what, when, and where of people and things."[45]

In order for the Internet of Things to incorporate the billions of objects that are made, moved, and consumed, every one of those objects requires a unique identifier (through a combination of cheap RFIDs and IP addresses). But a number of commentators are now arguing that it may not be necessary to physically tag and code every single physical thing in order to bring the IOT into being.[46] Such arguments are based on the fact that there has been a change in the ways that information is created and made available on the Internet. Even without barcodes, RFID tags, and IP addresses on every physical object, user-generated content has brought together a critical mass of data about many aspects of the physical world.

The Second and Third Generations of the Internet

The undeclared logic of the machine-readable world is "all data, all the time, on all people, at all places."
—Martin Dodge and Rob Kitchin[47]

This metamorphosis in the production and accessibility of digital information has been most often described as Web 2.0, or the second wave of the Internet. Web 2.0 is generally characterized by user-generated information, user-centered design, sharing of information, and the collaborative development of knowledge.[48] In principle, anyone, anywhere on the planet with the requisite hardware and software and an Internet connection can now contribute to Web 2.0 projects like Wikipedia, YouTube, or Flikr; thus implying that 2.5 billion people (the current number of Internet users), with almost a trillion Internet devices can potentially create, upload, and share information about any aspect of the world (the numbers on the number of connected internet devices is undoubtedly imprecise; however, there is little doubt that we are talking about a LOT of connected machines and sensors).[49] In other words, new tools and forms of collaboration are allowing the cognitive surplus of millions of people to be put to positive use.[50] There has also been talk of another paradigm shift in how people use the World Wide Web: Web Squared. Tim O'Reilly (the inventor of the term "Web 2.0") and John Battelle use the "Web Squared" moniker to refer to the Internet becoming more intelligent as an exponentially increasing amount of content is being created and uploaded. The innovation is that a sufficient body of data exists in order to allow the World Wide Web to learn inferentially, absorbing more knowledge than that is purposely entered into it. To O'Reilly and Battelle, the Internet is "no longer a collection of static pages of HTML that describe something in the world. Increasingly, the Web is the world—everything and everyone in the world casts an 'information shadow,' an aura of data which, when captured and processed intelligently, offers extraordinary opportunity and mind bending implications. Web Squared is our way of exploring this phenomenon and giving it a name."[51]

A variety of authors see what is known as *cloud collaboration* (decentralized and often uncoordinated work or information gathering through the Internet) and Web Squared as the basis of an informational revolution, predicting it to fundamentally change the ways in which decentralized collective intelligence about objects moves through the world.[52] Information about commodities and things is constantly being collected and uploaded (often in real time), and as a result, O'Reilly and Battelle argue that "we'll get to the Internet of Things via a hodgepodge of sensor data contributing, bottom-up, to machine-learning applications that gradually make more and more sense of the data that is handed to them. A bottle of wine on your supermarket shelf (or any other object) needn't have an RFID tag to join the 'Internet of Things,' it simply needs you to take a picture of its label. Your mobile phone, image recognition, search, and the sentient web will do the rest. We don't have to wait until each item in the supermarket has a unique machine-readable ID. Instead, we can make do with bar codes, tags on photos, and other 'hacks' that are simply ways of brute-forcing identity out of reality."[53]

In other words, Web Squared brings about possibilities to tag information directly onto previously non-networked objects. It relies on people to act as networked sensors to fill in gaps not covered by RFID tags, IP addresses, and other forms of tracking and information storage[54] by uploading imagery, video, motion, proximity, and location data. It thus follows that ultimately few objects will be able to exist "outside" of the network.[55]

For the transparency of commodity chains, these developments can significantly decentralize the role of infomediaries in the collection and transmission of information about the sites of production. The technologies theoretically enable bypassing layers of arbitration and provide an immediate online mapping of information on commodity chains. This technological infrastructure can, therefore, become interlinked with an empowering consumer-activist politics that tags commodity chain information onto products in new ways by articulating new relationships between proximity and transparency. Web Squared and the Internet of Things thus potentially provide a model for the future in which a critical mass of data, ubiquitous computing, and systems for data capture using artificial intelligence allow frictions of distance to be effectively negated and the massive amounts of available data categorized and channeled. In other words, the IOT and Web Squared can be used to bring into being a new layer of information that lets consumers see the histories and geographies of any commodity, to see its existence beyond the here and now.

References to ubiquitous information abound within the myriad projects attempting to use the informational model presented in figure 4.3 to inspire a new politics of consumption.[56] It is not just that communication technologies can transport consumer information instantly across space

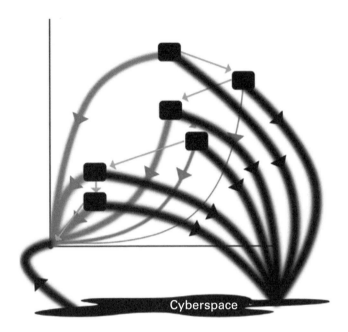

Figure 4.3
Web Squared and ubiquitous information. *Source*: Authors.

(something that has been possible ever since the invention of the tele-
graph). Rather, these new technologies provide a potentially widely accessible infrastructure for virtual mapping of product information, and make
that mapping available in everyday life. They can integrate consumption
practices with on-the-spot product information accessible through mobile
phones, for instance. Consumer activism is thereby shifted from collecting data to a more decentralized model focused on creating the software
that allows consumers to take part in cloud collaboration and make use of
cloud-sourced information. This would, for example, allow a consumer to
pick up a box of Kleenex at the supermarket, scan it with her cell phone,
and get access to user-generated information about the environmental
impacts of the production process, as well as the ways in which those
impacts compare to the competing products. For food products, customers
could, through mobile devices, similarly access information on nutrition
values, gene modification, transportation distance, labor conditions, and
a range of other factors that would allow them to adjust their economic
decisions accordingly.

The leader of one such project, designed at the 2007 London Social Innovation Camp,[57] described his technology by noting, "We set out to try and make something that links products in the real world to information on the Internet using barcodes. So, [that would mean] making any product, anywhere, addressable on the Internet and in real-life." The founder of another project, Rafi Haladjian at Violet.net, similarly claims that: "We are still living in a world where information is trapped in a few of our objects. We stare into our screens, which are like goldfish bowls full of information swimming around, but unable to escape . . . [and] we dream of a world where information would be a butterfly, flitting freely all over the place, and occasionally landing on any of the objects we touch to give them life and enrich them."[58]

These types of visions seem, in many ways, to come dangerously close to technological determinism. Since Marshall McLuhan introduced the concept of the "global village," or the idea that ICTs can bring all of humanity into a shared virtual cyberspace,[59] commentators have speculated that the Internet would be able to eliminate relative distance. Gillespie and Williams, for example, have argued that the convergence of time and space brought about by ICTs would eliminate the geographic frictions that help to shape spatial difference.[60] The idea that the Internet could either render geography meaningless or create a global village accessible from all reaches of the planet is grounded in the notion that the Internet allows an almost instantaneous transfer of information to any connected device, becoming "both an ethereal alternate dimension that is simultaneously infinite and everywhere" and fixed in a distinct, albeit nonphysical, location where all participants "arrive."[61]

Geographers have constantly reminded technological determinists, however, that the Internet is grounded by supporting infrastructures with distinct geographical biases.[62] The "global village," or cyberspace, can therefore only come into being in specific geographic spaces. Furthermore, it has also been shown that interactions and content on the Internet continue to be both socially produced and shaped by geography.[63]

Despite these repeated claims that geography still matters, even a cursory look at most of the projects employing Web Squared and the Internet of Things to alter consumption politics reveals a renewed attachment to the idea that technology can be used to fundamentally transcend the barriers of distance. Given the seemingly unique nature (and powerful combination) of Web Squared and the IOT, however, it is critical to consider more carefully both the potentialities for and constraints on transcending the barriers to flows of information on commodity chains. If Web Squared and the

IOT were to allow ubiquitous access to information about nodes on global commodity chains, the mass of data about all of those nodes would still need to be organized. The following section briefly focuses on the two most widely used methods to index and organize large amounts of data: the wiki model developed by a community of users and the search engine model.

Barriers to the Ubiquity of Information

Wikis allow websites to become containers of user-generated information and knowledge established through consensus. Wikipedia is the prime example of a wiki model, with a stated mission of hosting "the sum of all human knowledge" in every human language.[64] The encyclopedia currently contains 12 million articles in 262 languages. However, other wikis also contain enormous amounts of information created through cloud collaboration (e.g., WikiAnswers, a site containing 9 million questions and 3 billion user-submitted answers; and Baidu Baike, the largest Chinese-language encyclopedia, containing 1.5 million articles). In principle, wikis have the potential to globalize access to information as they allow free access and enable anyone to contribute from anywhere. This is an exercise in both anarchy and democracy that radically opens up the knowledge-creation process.[65] They generally allow anonymous contributions, and so, in theory, do not discriminate based on professional credentials, race, sex, or any other personal characteristics.[66] Mark Thompson argues that wiki technologies enable an "architecture of participation" that poses a challenge for much of the way in which "development" has traditionally been conceptualized and "delivered" to the poor by state apparatuses. Instead it is allowing users to provide input into the content of development projects and policy.[67]

Wikis allow the indexing of structured and codified information (e.g., product codes and ISO numbers), as well as more qualitative, unstructured information (e.g., photographs of factories, videos of production sites, and so forth). The relative lack of hierarchy in the editing process means that content can also, in principle, be moved, changed, and deleted instantly, corresponding to the rapidly changing composition of commodity chains. This allows for a cloud-collaborative development of knowledge about commodity chains without the need for, or interference of, infomediaries. Realistically, infomediaries can be expected to continue to play a significant role in mobilizing data gathering and consumer campaigns, which, in turn, will be conditioned by current structures of commercial media control. But the role of infomediaries is likely to shift away from being central in the actual production of information toward being the facilitators of information usage.

While meaningful participation through wikis in the Global South may be too optimistic in the short term, possibilities such as these should, to a greater extent, be taken into account in debates on how to promote participatory development. And for commodity chains, increased transparency could be achieved even without a wholesale shift in the paradigm of development. With relatively simple technology, marginalized communities can contribute information on labor and environmental conditions of production taking place in their vicinity.

Despite the openness and accessibility of wikis, there remain key barriers for marginalized communities. A core characteristic of wikis is that they necessitate agreement and ultimately only present one representation of any place, process, or thing. Any object or node on a commodity chain can thus only be represented in one way. (See figure 4.4 for an example of how a user-generated page about Starbucks can contain multiple types of content, but must ultimately all be put into the same "space")[68]. So, on any topic or any node of any commodity chain, there is the visible information that gets included and the invisible information that gets excluded.

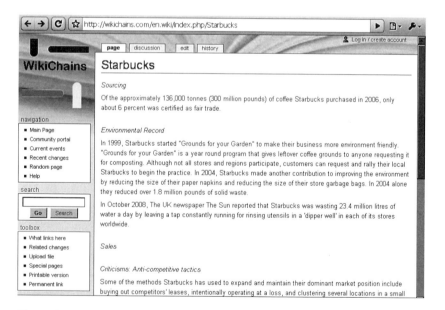

Figure 4.4

An example of a Wiki page. *Source*: http://wikichains.com.en.wiki/index.php/Starbucks (accessed September 14, 2010).

Disagreement and debate about visible content is therefore a necessary feature of wikis, and within those debates there are always winners and los-
ers. Research about Wikipedia, for instance, has shown that not only are
a tiny minority of users the creators of most content,[69] but that methods
employed to resolve disagreements are frequently opaque and usually favor
distinct demographics (young males in Western countries).[70]

Centralized search systems like Google Earth offer a fundamentally different way of organizing information. Multiple representations of the same
nodes on chains can coexist on the Internet by tagging information to
specific points on a chain (or the Earth). In figure 4.5, for example, multiple representations can be tagged to the Cadbury factory in Bourneville,
England, without any need for agreement about which is the most correct
or accurate. Using a centralized search system instead of a wiki to search
through masses of data means that multiple representations of any node
can exist and there is no need for consensus. Thousands of sources could
potentially be tagged to any node on any chain, allowing for multiple
simultaneous representations. But not all information tagged to any node
is equally visible or accessible. Nodes containing rich layers of information necessitate sorting, ordering, and ranking systems that are inherently

Figure 4.5
An example of the search model for Cadbury's Chocolate Factory, Bourneville, England. *Source*: Google Earth.

hierarchical. Research has shown that ranking systems inevitably promote already highly visible parts of the Internet into highly visible positions, and assign less visible parts of the Internet into marginal positions in the rankings. Languages and cultures with large Internet presences (e.g., English and the United States) are also likely to have higher ranks. Ranking algorithms thus essentially become a governance system for the Internet.[71]

These two examples (i.e., the wiki and the search engine) illustrate that even if the IOT and Web Squared could bring together a critical mass of data about global commodity chains, the power-relationships built into any system always serve to make some information visible at the expense of others. A state of ubiquitous information is unlikely to ever come into being due to the distinct geographies of user-created content (e.g., the enormous degrees of unevenness in user-generated content on Wikipedia shown in figure 4.6). Because such a model of information flow relies on the citizen as a sensor to fill in the gaps left uncovered by RFID tags and IP addresses and create a layer of information that is global in scope, the distinct geographical biases to the peer-production of information can serve to contribute to the continuing opacity of information flow about nodes in commodity chains.

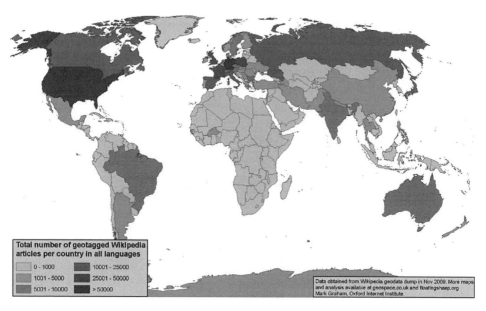

Figure 4.6
Map of content in Wikipedia. *Source*: Mark Graham.

The information shadows of objects will thus always be densest in the most highly digitally networked parts of the world. Studies of ICTs in development have identified a range of barriers to implementation, and challenge the feasibility of "transferring" generic technical know-how into developing countries and their organizations with the expectation that it will result in the same organizational practices and outcomes as in their context of origin.[72] While it is conceivable for a critical mass of people in the Global North to act as sensors for the IOT, it remains perhaps unrealistic to expect Bangladeshi textile workers, coffee growers in Papua New Guinea, or Kenyan flower pickers, and much of the rest of the world, to act as networked sensors, when few workers at those sites of production possess the specific competence or the resources to do so. The degree to which actors in the Global South are participating in articulating the critical narratives on global production is thus unclear. Furthermore, possibilities for effective use of ICTs to encourage ethical consumption also hinge on the intelligent capture and use of commodity chain information in the Global North.

It should be stressed that activist consumers are the ones primarily expected to make use of and act upon information about conditions of production; it is unlikely that a majority of consumers will scan a significant portion of the products they consider buying and act upon the information they find. But given ease of access and reliability of information, it is not unlikely that a group of ethically oriented consumers will make use of such data, or appear to do so, in sufficient degree to create incentives for producers to rethink production practices or to yield to demands of improved working conditions. Infomediaries can potentially create a feedback mechanism in this respect, by placing the spotlight on particularly unsavory production practices of a brand and by influencing more consumers to access cloud-sourced product information and act on it; this creates more incentives for actors to share information, which in turn makes more reliable information available to infomediaries and directly to consumers. At the moment, of course, the complacency of most consumers in the Global North remains one of several barriers to progressive change through commodity chain transparency. These barriers ultimately mean that technological possibilities are, by themselves, a necessary but not sufficient condition for increased transparency in commodity chains.

At the same time, these technological possibilities can potentially make a difference if they are embedded in broader processes of local capacity building, infrastructure development, democratization, and social change. Meaningful participation in wikis and the generation of information does not require an excessive amount of technological competence or social organization on the part of actors in the Global South. Through an incremental process embedded in infrastructure improvement, local capacity building, and linkages to other communities and activists in the Global North, these possibilities could viably empower actors in the South to contribute to a new politics of consumption and production.

In summary, the potential of Web 2.0 technology for increased transparency of commodity chains is conditioned by the following factors:

• Infrastructure and access: the physical technological infrastructure available in the Global South and the access of marginalized communities to the use of these.
• Actors' capacities for meaningful data generation and data entry: the ability of actors in communities in the South to develop the capabilities needed to contribute to peer-to-peer generation of information.
• The continued role of and control over infomediaries: ownership and power relations embedded in organizations and commercial media and the influence of these in communication and information exchange.
• Intelligent capture and use by consumers: the ability of consumers to process information and act upon through practices of consumption.

Conclusions

By globalizing information, the Internet of Things and peer production of information offer an opportunity to empower individuals and communities throughout the world. Transnational corporations would no longer be able to conceal poor production practices and exploitative labor conditions behind the veils of distance that have for so long separated the sites of production and consumption. As Web Squared and the Internet of Things alter the opacity of distance, and as knowledge about sweatshops, child labor, exploitation, and environmental damage becomes widely accessible on a computer or mobile phone, we will see openings for radical shifts in the possibilities for development. Actors in the Global South will have a venue to communicate their knowledge and experience of labor and environmental conditions. Consumers of commodities in the Global North would be better able to distinguish between the glossy (and often exaggerated) claims made by many TNCs that pertain to the benefits they provide to workers in the developing world, and the commodities and chains that truly do result in tangible benefits to producers in the Global South.

However, as many commentators have already noted, the Internet also replicates the structures of class and power of the societies in which it is embedded.[73] A variety of factors will contribute to the continuing opacity of information flow about nodes in commodity chains. In the case of wikis, for instance, methods employed to resolve disagreements are frequently less-than-transparent and often favor distinct demographics, particularly young white males.[74] Control of information continues to characterize much of the technology behind the IOT, and large amounts of data being created through collaboration are often subject to a variety of licensing restrictions, since a majority of Web 2.0 websites are run by for-profit companies.[75] The incorporation of everyday objects into a non-open IOT also raises a plethora of concerns such as privacy,[76] surveillance, black holes of information, bias, and geoslavery.[77]

Further, if people are to act as networked sensors, this necessarily involves only those with the resources, capabilities, and skill sets to do so. At the moment, this excludes large segments of people in the Global South. While Internet coverage in the Global South is increasing rapidly, the Internet and practices of content generation will continue to be characterized by geographical and topological black holes. Access is also a broader issue than just one of infrastructure. Wikis and search engines contain embedded assumptions, laws, and power relations that prevent some information from becoming visible, yet highlight other information. Realization of the potential for transparency depends not only on technological infrastructures but on how these are taken advantage of by social practices seeking to invigorate a politics of consumption. In turn, including the Global South in peer-to-peer generation of information about commodity chains depends on access being embedded in broader processes of development on the ground; local capacity building, building of infrastructure, democratization, and social change.

This chapter has argued that, instead of imagining that ubiquitously available information about any product, anywhere, is addressable on the Internet and in real life, it is important to keep in mind that there will always be nodes on many chains that are kept invisible. Peer production and the networking of everyday objects will in many ways allow for a greater variety of spotlight effects on nodes in chains that would otherwise remain cloaked. It thus remains important to continuously question the invisibility of particular nodes, the geographies of information creation, and the politics of ranking and visibility, rather than uncritically accepting that technologies have brought about a global village of universally accessible information.

Notes

An earlier version of this chapter appeared previously in *Information Technologies & International Development*, 9, no. 1 (Spring 2011), Special Issue on Open Development, http://itidjournal.org/itid/issue/view/40.

1. S. Jhally (writer/director) and K. Garnder (producer), *No Logo: Brands, Globalization & Resistance* (documentary film), USA: Media Educational Foundation, 2003.

2. J. H. Dunning, *Multinational Enterprises and the Global Economy*. (Wokingham, UK: Addison-Wesley, 1993).

3. See G. Gereffi, "The Global Economy: Organization, Governance, and Development," in *The Handbook of Economic Sociology*, ed. N. J. Smelser and R. Swedberg (Princeton: Princeton University Press, 2005), 160–183.

4. L. Langman, "From Virtual Public Spheres to Global Justice: A Critical Theory of Internetworked Social Movements," *Sociological Theory* 23, no. 1 (2005): 42–74.

5. R. Heeks, "ICT4D 2.0: The Next Phase of Applying ICT for International Development," *Computer* 41, no. 6, (2008): 26–33; M. Thompson, "ICT and Development Studies: Towards Development 2.0," *Cambridge Judge Business School Working Paper Series* 27, (2007): 1–17.

6. J. D. Eldridge and J. P. Jones, "Warped Space: A Geography of Distance Decay," *Professional Geographer* 43, no. 4 (1991): 500–511; M. Feldman, *The Geography of Innovation* (Dordrecht, Netherlands: Kluwer, 1994); A. B. Jafe, M. Trajtenberg, and R. Henderson, "Geographic Localization of Knowledge Spillovers as Evidenced by Patent Citations," *Quarterly Journal of Economics* 108, no. 3 (1993): 577–598.

7. D. B. Audretsch and M. P. Feldman, "R&D Spillovers and the Geography of Innovation and Production," *The American Economic Review* 86, no. 3 (1996): 630–640; P. Krugman, *Geography and Trade* (Cambridge, MA: MIT Press, 1991).

8. This is not to imply that there is any necessary correlation between physical proximity to nodes on a commodity chain and topological proximity to positions of nodes on commodity chains.

9. T. K. Hopkins and I. Wallerstein, "Commodity Chains in the Capitalist World Economy Prior to 1800," in *Commodity Chains and Global Capitalism,* ed. G. Gerefa & M. Korzeniewicz (London: Greenwood Press, 1994), 17–50.

10. In this article, we take a commodity to mean any good that results from a production process, meets perceived or actual needs, and has an exchange value, as noted in A. N. Clarke, *Dictionary of Geography* (London: Penguin, 2003). Although Clarke claims different types of commodities react differently to transparency and consumer politics, it is beyond the scope of this article to discuss these topics in detail.

11. D. Shaw, "The Making of the Twentieth-Century World," in *An Introduction to Human Geography*, ed. P. Daniels, M. Bradshaw, D. Shaw, and J. Sidaway (London: Pearson, 2001), 62–84.

12. P. Mason, *Live Working or Die Fighting: How the Working Class Went Global* (London: Harvill Secker, 2007).

13. N. Klein, *No Logo: Taking Aim at the Brand Bullies,* (New York: Picador, 2002).

14. B. Letnes, "Foreign Direct Investment and Human Rights: An Ambiguous Relationship," *Forum for Development Studies* 1, (2002): 33–57.

15. L. Illia, "Passage to Cyberactivism: How Dynamics of Activism Change," *Journal of Public Affairs* 3, no. 4 (2003): 326–337; A. Kavada, "Civil Society Organizations and the Internet: The Case of Amnesty International, Oxfam and the World Development Movement," in *Global Activism, Global Media*, ed. W. de Jong, M. Shaw, and N. Stammers, (London: Pluto Press, 2005), 208–222; M. E. Keck and K. Sikkink, *Activists Beyond Borders: Advocacy Networks in International Politics* (Ithaca, NY: Cornell University Press, 1998).

16. R. Welford, "Editorial: Globalization, Corporate Social Responsibility and Human Rights," *Corporate Social Responsibility and Environmental Management* 9, no. 1, (2002): 1–7.

17. Langman, "From Virtual Public," 2005.

18. R. Overå, "Networks, Distance, and Trust: Telecommunications Development and Changing Trading Practices in Ghana," *World Development* 34, no. 7 (2006): 1301–1315.

19. Heeks, "ICT4D 2.0," 2008.

20. Thompson, "ICT and Development," 1–17.

21. M. Zook and others, "Volunteered Geographic Information and Crowdsourcing Disaster Relief: A Case Study of the Haitian Earthquake," *World Medical and Health Policy* 2, no. 2 (2010): 7–33.

22. S. Weber and J. Bussell, "Will Information Technology Reshape The North-South Asymmetry Of Power In The Global Political Economy?," *Studies in Comparative International Development* 40, no. 2 (2005): 62–84.

23. R. Kahn and D. Kellner, "New Media and Internet Activism: From the Battle of Seattle to Blogging," *New Media & Society* 6, no. 1 (2004): 87–95; D. Kellner, "Globalization from Below? Toward a Radical Democratic Technopolitics," *Angelaki: Journal of the Theoretical Humanities* 4, no. 2 (1999): 101–113; R. D. Lipschutz, "Networks of Knowledge and Practice: Global Civil Society and Global Communications," in *Global Activism, Global Media*, ed. W. de Jong, M. Shaw, and N. Stammers, 17–33 (London: Pluto Press); T. Olesen, "Transnational Publics: New Spaces of Social Move-

ment Activism and the Problem of Global Long-sightedness," *Current Sociology* 53, no. 3 (2005): 419–440.

24. N. Fraser, "Rethinking The Public Sphere: A Contribution to the Critique of Actually Existing Democracy," *Social Text* 25/26 (1990): 56–80.

25. Kellner, "Globalization from Below?," 1999.

26. Langman, "From Virtual Public," 2005.

27. Ibid.

28. N. Castree, D. Featherstone, and A. Herod, "Contrapuntal Geographies: The Politics of Organizing Across Sociospatial Difference," in *The SAGE Handbook of Political Geography*, ed. K. Cox, M. Low, and J. Robinson, 305–321 (London: SAGE Publications, 2008).

29. P. Routledge, "Our Resistance Will be as Transnational as Capital: Convergence Space and Strategy in Globalizing Resistance," *GeoJournal* 52, no. 1 (2000): 25–33.

30. Keck and Sikkink, *Activists Beyond Borders*, 1998.

31. A. Kavada, "The Alter-Globalization Movement and the Internet: A Case Study of Communication Networks and Collective Action," *Cortona Colloquium 2006—Cultural Conflicts, Social Movements and New Rights: A European Challenge*, (Cortona, Italy, October 20–22, 2006), http://www.fondazionefeltrinelli.it/dm_0/FF/FeltrinelliCmsPortale/0072.pdf.

32. Kahn and Kellner, "New Media," 2004; P. Routledge, "Convergence Space: Process Geographies of Grassroots Globalization Networks," *Transactions of the Institute of British Geographers* 28, no. 3 (2003): 333–349.

33. Illia, "Passage to Cyberactivism," 2003, 326.

34. A. Greenfield, *Everyware: The Dawning Age of Ubiquitous Computing* (Berkeley, CA: Peachpit Press, 2006), 19.

35. C. Fong, Internetting Every Thing, Everywhere, All the Time," *CNN*, 2008, http://edition.cnn.com/2008/TECH/11/02/digitalbiz.rfid.

36. E. Biddlecombe, "UN Predicts Internet of Things," *BBC*, November 17, 2005, http://news.bbc.co.uk/2/hi/technology/4440334.stm; D. Butler, "2020 Computing: Everything, Everywhere," *Nature* 440, no. 7083 (2006): 402–405: S. Dodson, The Net Shapes Up to Get Physical," *Guardian*, October 16, 2010, http://www.guardian.co.uk/technology/2008/oct/16/internet-of-things-ipv6; N. Gershenfeld, R. Krikorian, and D. Cohen, "The Internet of Things," *Scientific American* 291, no. 4 (October, 2004): 76–81; R. Lombreglia, "The Internet of Things," *Boston Globe*, July 31, 2005, http://www.boston.com/news/globe/ideas/articles/2005/2007/2031/the_internet_of_Things (accessed October 22, 2010); A. Reinhardt, "A machine-to-machine Internet of Things," http://www.businessweek.com/stories/2004-04-25/a-machine-to

-machine-internet-of-things; V. Shannon, "Wireless: Creating Internet Of 'Things': A Scary, but Exciting," *The New York Times,* November 20, 2005, http://www .nytimes.com/2005/11/20/technology/20iht-wireless21.html.

37. An IP address is a label assigned to any object that uses the Internet Protocol for communication.

38. E. Wasserman, "Riding Herd: RFID Tracks Livestock," *RFID Journal* (October 5, 2005), http://www.rfidjournal.com/article/view/5272.

39. M. Lianos and M. Douglas, "Dangerization and the End of Deviance: The Institutional Environment," *British Journal of Criminology,* 40, (2000), 261–278.

40. M. Dodge and R. Kitchin, "Codes of Life: Identification Codes and the Machine-readable World," *Environment and Planning D: Society and Space* 23, no. 6 (2005): 851–881; T. Ferguson, "Have Your Objects Call My Object," *Harvard Business Review,* 80, no. 6 (2002): 138–144.

41. ITU, *The Internet of Things.* (Geneva: United Nations, 2005).

42. Greenfeld, *Everyware,* 19.

43. Dodson, "The Net Shapes," 2008.

44. N. Thrift, "Remembering the Technological Unconscious by Foregrounding Knowledges of Position," *Environment and Planning D: Society and Space* 22, no. 1 (2004): 175–190.

45. Dodge and Kitchin, "Codes of Life," 2005, 869.

46. For example, T. O'Reilly and J. Battelle, "Web Squared: Web 2.0 Five Years On," paper presented at *Web 2.0 Summit,* San Francisco, CA, October 20–22, 2009.

47. Dodge and Kitchin, "Codes of Life," 2005, 870.

48. M. Graham, "Neogeography and the Palimpsests of Place: Web 2.0 and the Construction of a Virtual eEarth," *Tijdschrift voor Economische en Sociale Geografie [Journal of Economic and Social Geography]* 101, no. 4 (2010): 422–436.

49. D. Beer, "Making Friends with Jarvis Cocker: Music Culture in the Context of Web 2.0," *Cultural Sociology* 2, no. 2 (2008): 222–241; M. F. Goodchild, "Citizens as Sensors: The World of Volunteered Geography," *GeoJournal* 69, no. 4 (2007): 211–221; M. Breen and E. Forde, "The Music Industry, Technology and Utopia: An Exchange between Marcus Breen and Eamonn Forde," *Popular Music* 23, no. 1 (2004): 79–89; M. Graham and M. A. Zook, "Visualizing Global Cyberscapes: Mapping User Generated Pacemarks," *Journal of Urban Technology* 18, no. 1 (2011): 115–132; K. Kelley, "We Are the Web," *Wired* 13, no. 8 (2005). http://www.wired.com/wired/archive/13.08/tech/html (accessed October 22); M. Richtel, "I.B.M. to Invest $100 Million in Cellphone Research," *New York Times,* June 17, 2009, http://bits .blogs.nytimes.com/2009/06/17/ibm-to-invest-100-million-in-cell-phone-research.

50. C. Shirky, *Cognitive Surplus* (New York: Penguin Press, 2010).

51. O'Reilly and Battelle, "Web Squared," 2009, 2.

52. M. Graham, "Cloud Collaboration: Peer-production and the Engineering of the Internet," in *Engineering Earth*, ed. S. Brunn, 67–83. (New York: Springer, 2011); C. Jennings, "The Cloud Computing Revolution," *Computer Weekly*, December 22, 2008. http://www.computerweekly.com/Articles/2008/12/22/234026/The-cloud -computing-revolution.htm; T. O'Reilly, "What is Web 2.0?," http://oreilly.com/ web2/archive/what-is-web-20.html; F. Vogelstein, "The Facebook Revolution," *Los Angeles Times*, October 7, 2007. http://www.latimes.com/news/opinion/la -opvogelstein7oct07,0,6385994.story (accessed September 14, 2010); W. Whitlock, and D. Micek, *Twitter Revolution: How Social Media and Mobile Marketing Is Changing the Way We Do Business & Market Online* (Las Vegas: Xeno Press, 2008).

53. O'Reilly and Battelle, "Web Squared," 2009, 8.

54. See Goodchild, "Citizens as Sensors," 2007.

55. Furthermore, it is increasingly likely that WebCrawlers will be able to harvest enough information from the Internet to automate evaluation and comparison of products, based on their environmental impact, and then link this evaluation to certification standards (Foster, 2001).

56. Examples include alonovo.com, barcodepedia.com, buyitlikeyoumeanit.org, consumergadget.net, en.consumeriamakeitfair.org, and wikichains.org.

57. See: http://web.archive.org/web/20090228093438/http://jonathanmelhuish .com/2009/02/barcode-wikipedia.

58. Rafi Haladjian, Violet.net.

59. M. McLuhan, *The Gutenberg Galaxy: The Making of Typographic Man.* (Toronto: University of Toronto Press, 1962).

60. A. Gillespie and H. Williams, "Telecommunications And The Reconstruction Of Regional Comparative Advantage," *Environment and Planning A* 20 (1988): 1311–1321; See also F. Cairncross, *The Death of Distance: How the Communications Revolution will Change our Lives* (Cambridge, MA: Harvard Business School Press, 1997); H. Coutelis, Editorial, "The Death of Distance," *Environment and Planning B: Planning and Design* 23, no. 4 (1996): 387–389; A. Pascal, "The Vanishing City," *Urban Studies* 24, (1987): 597–603.

61. M. Graham, "Time Machines and Virtual Portals: The Spatialities of the Digital Divide," *Progress in Development Studies* 11, (July, 2011): 216.

62. M. Dodge and R. Kitchin, *Atlas of Cyberspace* (London: Addison-Wesley, 2001); B. Hayes, "The Infrastructure of the Information Infrastructure," *American Scientist* 85, no. 3 (1997): 214–218; M. L. Moss and A. Townsend, "The Internet Backbone

and the American Metropolis," *The Information Society Journal* 16, no. 1 (2000): 35–47; A. M. Townsend, "Network Cities and the Global Structure of the Internet," *American Behavioral Scientist* 44, no. 10 (2001): 1697–1716; M. Zook, M. Dodge, Y. Aoyama, and A. Townsend, "New Digital Geographies: Information, Communication, and Place," in *Geography and Technology*, ed. S. Brunn, S. Cutter, and J. W. Harrington(Norwell, MA: Kluwer, 2004), 155–178.

63. P. C. Adams and R. Ghose, "India.com: The Construction of a Space Between," *Progress in Human Geography* 27, no. 4 (2003): 414–437; Dodge, and Kitchin, *Atlas*, 2001; Graham, "Time Machines," 2011; M. Zook, "Underground Globalization: Mapping the Space of Flows of the Internet Adult Industry," *Environment and Planning A* 35, no. 7 (2003): 1261–1286.

64. S. Dodson, "Worldwide Wikimania," *Guardian Unlimited*, October 3, 2005, http://www.guardian.co.uk/technology/2005/aug/11/onlinesupplement2.

65. A. Ciffolilli, "Phantom Authority, Self-selective Recruitment and Retention of Members in Virtual Communities: The Case of Wikipedia," *First Monday* 8, no. 12 (December, 2003).

66. Graham, "Cloud Collaboration," 2011.

67. Thompson, "ICT and Development Studies," 2007.

68. Wikichains.org is a project being led by Mark Graham and the Oxford Internet Institute.

69. Only about one-tenth of 1% of Wikipedia users are actually regular contributors.

70. M. O'Neil, *Cyber Chiefs: Autonomy and Authority in Online Tribes* (London: Pluto Press, 2009).

71. M. Zook and M. Graham, "The Creative Reconstruction of the Internet: Google and the Privatization of Cyberspace and Digiplace," *Geoforum* 38, no. 6 (2007a): 1322–1343; Zook, M. and M. Graham, "Mapping the Digiplace: Geocoded Internet Data and the Representation of Place," *Environment and Planning B*: Planning and Design 34, no. 3 (2007b): 466–482.

72. C. Avgerou, "Information Systems in Developing Countries: A Critical Research Review," *Journal of Information Technology* 23, no. 3 (2008): 133–146.

73. B. Warf, "Segueways into Cyberspace: Multiple Geographies of the Digital Divide," *Environment and Planning B: Planning and Design* 28, no. 1 (2001): 3–19.

74. O'Neil, *Cyber Chiefs*, 2009.

75. Graham, "Cloud Collaboration," 2011.

76. D. J. Phillips, "Beyond Privacy: Confronting Locational Surveillance in Wireless Communication," *Communication Law and Policy* 8, no. 1 (2003): 1–23.

77. J. E. Dobson and P. F. Fisher, "Geoslavery," *IEEE Technology and Society Magazine* (Spring 2003): 47–52.

Bibliography

Adams, P. C., and R. Ghose. "India.com: The Construction of a Space Between." *Progress in Human Geography* 27 (4) (2003): 414–437.

Audretsch, D. B., and M. P. Feldman. "R&D Spillovers and the Geography of Innovation and Production." *American Economic Review* 86 (3) (1996): 630–640.

Avgerou, C. "Information Systems in Developing Countries: A Critical Research Review." *Journal of Information Technology* 23 (3) (2008): 133–146.

Beer, D. "Making Friends with Jarvis Cocker: Music Culture in the Context of Web 2.0." *Cultural Sociology* 2 (2) (2008): 222–241.

Biddlecombe, E. "UN Predicts Internet of Things." http://news.bbc.co.uk/2/hi/technology/4440334.stm.

Breen, M., and E. Forde. "The Music Industry, Technology and Utopia: An Exchange Between Marcus Breen and Eamonn Forde." *Popular Music* 23 (1) (2004): 79–89.

Butler, D. "2020 Computing: Everything, Everywhere." *Nature* 440 (7083) (2006): 402–405.

Cairncross, F. *The Death of Distance: How the Communications Revolution Will Change our Lives*. Cambridge, MA: Harvard Business School Press, 1997.

Castree, C., D. Featherstone, and A. Herod. Contrapuntal Geographies: The Politics of Organizing Across Sociospatial Difference. In *The SAGE Handbook of Political Geography*, ed. K. Cox, M. Low, and J. Robinson, 305–321. London: SAGE Publications, 2008.

Ciffolilli, A. "Phantom Authority, Self-selective Recruitment and Retention of Members in Virtual Communities: The Case of Wikipedia." *First Monday* 8 (12) (December 2003). http://firstmonday.org/ojs/index.php/fm/article/view/1108/1028.

Clarke, A. N. *Dictionary of Geography*. London: Penguin, 2003.

Couclelis, H. "Editorial, The Death of Distance." *Environment and Planning. B, Planning & Design* 23 (4) (1996): 387–389.

Dobson, J. E., and P. F. Fisher. "Geoslavery." *IEEE Technology and Society Magazine* (Spring 2003): 47–52.

Dodge, M., and R. Kitchin. *Atlas of Cyberspace*. London: Addison-Wesley, 2001.

Dodge, M., and R. Kitchin. "Codes of Life: Identification Codes and the Machine-readable World." *Environment and Planning. D, Society & Space* 23 (6) (2005): 851–881.

Dodson, S. "Worldwide Wikimania," *Guardian Unlimited*, October 3, 2005. http://www.guardian.co.uk/technology/2005/aug/11/onlinesupplement2.

Dodson, S. "The Net Shapes Up to Get Physical," *Guardian*, (October 16, 2010). http://www.guardian.co.uk/technology/2008/oct/16/internet-of-things-ipv6.

Dunning, J. H. *Multinational Enterprises and the Global Economy*. Wokingham, UK: Addison-Wesley, 1993.

Eldridge, J. D., and J. P. Jones. "Warped Space: A Geography of Distance Decay." *Professional Geographer* 43 (4) (1991): 500–511.

Feldman, M. *The Geography of Innovation*. Dordrecht, Netherlands: Kluwer, 1994.

Ferguson, T. "Have Your Objects Call My Object." *Harvard Business Review* 80 (6) (2002): 138–144.

Fong, C. "Internetting Every Thing, Everywhere, All the Time," (2008). http://edition.cnn.com/2008/TECH/11/02/digitalbiz.rfid.

Foster, W. *ISO-14000 Environmental Standards and E-Commerce*. Arizona: Arizona State University, 2001. http://www.fosterandbrahm.com/docs/ISO14000.pdf.

Fraser, N. "Rethinking The Public Sphere: A Contribution To The Critique of Actually Existing Democracy." *Social Text* 25/26 (1990): 56–80.

Gershenfeld, N., R. Krikorian, and D. Cohen. "The Internet of Things." *Scientific American* 291 (4) (October 2004): 76–81.

Gillespie, A., and H. Williams. "Telecommunications And The Reconstruction Of Regional Comparative Advantage." *Environment & Planning A* 20 (1988): 1311–1321.

Goodchild, M. F. "Citizens as Sensors: The World of Volunteered Geography." *GeoJournal* 69 (4) (2007): 211–221.

Graham, M. "Neogeography and the Palimpsests of Place: Web 2.0 and the Construction of a Virtual eEarth." *Tijdschrift voor Economische en Sociale Geografie* 101 (4) (2010): 422–436.

Graham, M. Cloud Collaboration: Peer-production and the Engineering of the Internet. In *Engineering Earth*, ed. S. Brunn, 67–83. New York: Springer, 2011.

Graham, M. "Time Machines and Virtual Portals: The Spatialities of the Digital Divide." *Progress in Development Studies* 11 (July 2011): 211–227.

Graham, M., and M. A. Zook. "Visualizing Global Cyberscapes: Mapping User Generated Pacemarks." *Journal of Urban Technology* 18 (1) (2011): 115–132.

Greenfield, A. 2006. *Everyware: The Dawning Age Of Ubiquitous Computing.*, 19. Berkeley, CA: Peachpit Press.

Hayes, B. "The Infrastructure of the Information Infrastructure." *American Scientist* 85 (3) (1997): 214–218.

Heeks, R. "ICT4D 2.0: The Next Phase of Applying ICT for International Development." *Computer* 41 (6) (2008): 26–33.

Hopkins, T. K., and I. Wallerstein. Commodity Chains in the Capitalist World Economy Prior to 1800. In *Commodity Chains and Global Capitalism*, ed. G. Gerefa and M. Korzeniewicz, 17–50. London: Greenwood Press, 1994.

Illia, L. "Passage to Cyberactivism: How Dynamics of Activism Change." *Journal of Public Affairs* 3, (4) (2003): 326–337.

ITU (International Communication Union). The Internet of Things. Geneva: United Nations, 2005.

Jafe, A. B., M. Trajtenberg, and R. Henderson. "Geographic Localization of Knowledge Spillovers as Evidenced by Patent Citations." *Quarterly Journal of Economics* 108 (3) (1993): 577–598.

Jennings, C. "The Cloud Computing Revolution." *Computer Weekly*, December 22, 2008.   http://www.computerweekly.com/Articles/2008/12/22/234026/The-cloud -computing-revolution.

Jhally, S. (writer/director), and K. Garnder (producer). No Logo: Brands, Globalization & Resistance (documentary film). USA: Media Educational Foundation, 2003.

Kahn, R., and D. Kellner. "New Media and Internet Activism: From the Battle of Seattle to Blogging." *New Media & Society* 6 (1) (2004): 87–95.

Kavada, A. Civil Society Organizations and the Internet: The Case of Amnesty International, Oxfam and the World Development Movement. In *Global Activism, Global Media*, ed. W. de Jong, M. Shaw, and N. Stammers, 208–222. London: Pluto Press, 2005.

Kavada, A. "The Alter-Globalization Movement And The Internet: A Case Study Of Communication Networks And Collective Action." *Cortona Colloquium 2006—Cultural Conflicts, Social Movements and New Rights: A European Challenge*, (Cortona, Italy,   October   20–22,   2006).   http://www.fondazionefeltrinelli.it/dm_0/FF/ FeltrinelliCmsPortale/0072.pdf.

Keck, M. E., and K. Sikkink. *Activists beyond Borders: Advocacy Networks in International Politics*. Ithaca, NY: Cornell University Press, 1998.

Kellner, D. "Globalization from Below? Toward a Radical Democratic Technopolitics." *Angelaki: Journal of the Theoretical Humanities* 4 (2) (1999): 101–113.

Kelley, K. "We Are the Web," *Wired* 13, (8) (2005). http://www.wired.com/wired/archive/13.08/tech/html.

Klein, N. *No Logo: Taking Aim at the Brand Bullies*. New York: Picador, 2002.

Krugman, P. *Geography and Trade*. Cambridge, MA: MIT Press, 1991.

Langman, L. "From Virtual Public Spheres to Global Justice: A Critical Theory of Internetworked Social Movements." *Sociological Theory* 23 (1) (2005): 42–74.

Letnes, B. "Foreign Direct Investment and Human Rights: An Ambiguous Relationship." *Forum for Development Studies* 1 (2002): 33–57.

Lianos, M., and M. Douglas. "Dangerization and the End of Deviance: The Institutional Environment." *British Journal of Criminology* 40 (2000): 261–278.

Lipschutz, R. D. Networks of Knowledge and Practice: Global Civil Society and Global Communications. In *Global Activism, Global Media*, ed. W. de Jong, M. Shaw, and N. Stammers, 17–33. London: Pluto Press.

Lombreglia, R. "The Internet of Things." *Boston Globe*, July 31, 2005, http://www.boston.com/news/globe/ideas/articles/2005/2007/2031/the_internet_of_Things (accessed October 22, 2010).

Mason, P. *Live Working or Die Fighting: How the Working Class Went Global*. London: Harvill Secker, 2007.

McLuhan, M. *The Gutenberg Galaxy: The Making of Typographic Man*. Toronto: University of Toronto Press, 1962.

Moss, M. L., and A. Townsend. "The Internet Backbone and the American Metropolis." *Information Society Journal* 16 (1) (2000): 35–47.

Olesen, T. "Transnational Publics: New Spaces of Social Movement Activism and the Problem of Global Long-sightedness." *Current Sociology* 53 (3) (2005): 419–440.

O'Neil, M. *Cyber Chiefs: Autonomy and Authority in Online Tribes*. London: Pluto Press, 2009.

O'Reilly, T., and J. Battelle. "Web Squared: Web 2.0 Five Years On," paper presented at *Web 2.0 Summit* (San Francisco, CA, October 20–22, 2009).

Pascal, A. "The Vanishing City." *Urban Studies (Edinburgh, Scotland)* 24 (1987): 597–603.

Phillips, D. J. "Beyond Privacy: Confronting Locational Surveillance in Wireless Communication." *Communication Law and Policy* 8 (1) (2003): 1–23.

Reinhardt, A. "A machine-to-machine Internet of Things." http://www.businessweek.com/magazine/content/04_7/b3880607.htm.

Richtel, M. "I.B.M. to Invest $100 Million in Cellphone Research." *New York Times*, June 17, 2009. http://bits.blogs.nytimes.com/2009/06/17/ibm-to-invest-100-million -in-cell-phone-research.

Routledge, P. "Our Resistance Will Be as Transnational as Capital: Convergence Space and Strategy in Globalizing Resistance." *GeoJournal* 52 (1) (2000): 25–33.

Routledge, P. "Convergence Space: Process Geographies of Grassroots Globalization Networks." *Transactions of the Institute of British Geographers* 28 (3) (2003): 333–349.

Shannon, V. "Wireless: Creating Internet of 'Things': A Scary, but Exciting." *New York Times*, November 20, 2005. http://www.nytimes.com/2005/11/20/ technology/20iht-wireless21.html.

Shaw, D. The Making of the Twentieth-Century World. In *An Introduction to Human Geography*, ed. P. Daniels, M. Bradshaw, D. Shaw, and J. Sidaway, 62–84. London: Pearson, 2001.

Shirky, C. *Cognitive Surplus*. New York: Penguin Press, 2010.

Thompson, M. "ICT and Development Studies: Towards Development 2.0." *Cambridge Judge Business School Working Paper Series* 27, (2007): 1–17.

Thrift, N. "Remembering the Technological Unconscious by Foregrounding Knowledges of Position." *Environment and Planning. D, Society & Space* 22 (1) (2004): 175–190.

Townsend, A. M. "Network Cities and the Global Structure of the Internet." *American Behavioral Scientist* 44 (10) (2001): 1697–1716.

Vogelstein, F. "The Facebook Revolution." *Los Angeles Times*, October 7, 2007. http:// www.latimes.com/news/opinion/la-opvogelstein7oct07.0.6385994.story.

Wasserman, E. "Riding Herd: RFID Tracks Livestock." *RFID Journal* (October 5, 2005), http://www.rfidjournal.com/article/view/5272.

Warf, B. "Segueways into Cyberspace: Multiple Geographies of the Digital Divide." *Environment and Planning. B, Planning & Design* 28 (1) (2001): 3–19.

Weber, S., and J. Bussell. "Will Information Technology Reshape The North-South Asymmetry Of Power In The Global Political Economy?" *Studies in Comparative International Development* 40 (2) (2005): 62–84.

Welford, R. "Editorial: Globalization, Corporate Social Responsibility and Human Rights." *Corporate Social Responsibility and Environmental Management* 9 (1) (2002): 1–7.

Whitlock, W., and D. Micek. *Twitter Revolution: How Social Media and Mobile Marketing Is Changing the Way We Do Business & Market Online*. Las Vegas: Xeno Press, 2008.

Zook, M. "Underground Globalization: Mapping the Space of Flows of the Internet Adult Industry." *Environment & Planning A* 35 (7) (2003): 1261–1286.

Zook, M., M. Dodge, Y. Aoyama, and A. Townsend. New Digital Geographies: Information, Communication, and Place. In *Geography and Technology*, ed. S. Brunn, S. Cutter, and J. W. Harrington, 155–178. Norwell, MA: Kluwer, 2004.

Zook, M., and M. Graham. "The Creative Reconstruction of the Internet: Google and the Privitization of Cyberspace and Digiplace." *Geoforum* 38 (6) (2007a): 1322–1343.

Zook, M., and M. Graham. "Mapping the Digiplace: Geocoded Internet Data and the Representation of Place." *Environment and Planning. B, Planning & Design* 34 (3) (2007b): 466–482.

Zook, M., M. Graham, T. Shelton, and S. Gorman, "Volunteered Geographic Information and Crowdsourcing Disaster Relief: A Case Study of the Haitian Earthquake." *World Medical and Health Policy* 2 (2) (2010): 7–33.

5 Open Source Biotechnology Platforms for Global Health and Development: Two Case Studies

Hassan Masum, Karl Schroeder, Myra Khan, and Abdallah S. Daar

Close to ten million children under the age of five die each year. Most of these deaths occur in lower-income countries and are preventable.[1] Chronic noncommunicable diseases, such as heart disease and cancer, are growing in lower-income countries, and they now account for roughly 60 percent of all deaths worldwide.[2] Yet there is hope for moving forward. Millions of lives have already been saved through vaccinations, public health measures, and drugs.[3] Many of these advances can benefit from biotechnology—the use of biological processes for industrial, health, and other purposes.

This chapter examines the potential of collaborative open source biotechnology platforms in global health and development. We start by summarizing the controversial role of patents in innovation, and by considering the open source approach as one response. We then explore two case studies relying on collaborative online platforms: Cambia, a nonprofit based in Australia that specializes in biotech research, and India's Open Source Drug Discovery (OSDD) project. Cambia is addressing neglected diseases by making relevant patent information available through both its Patent Lens project and its Initiative for Open Innovation. OSDD complements this initiative through a collaborative platform and open source practices to accelerate drug development for neglected diseases. While Cambia and OSDD share the goal of addressing basic needs of the developing world, they have implemented the principles of the open source movement in different ways. Finally, we look at related initiatives already underway and suggest issues that merit further exploration.

Overall, we find that open source principles may require adaptation to specific applications. We suggest that, in open source biotechnology for global health and development, at least three linked senses of "open" should be considered: open access, open licensing, and open collaborative platforms. We argue that, supported by collaborative platforms, biotechnology for global health and development holds promise for improving health and food security in developing countries,[4] and that it can move ahead through its own versions of open source practices and collaborative online platforms. We conclude by suggesting what might be needed to build on the modest successes to date.

The Controversial Role of Patents in Innovation

Patents are viewed as being directly linked to innovation,[5] but confounding issues surrounding intellectual property (IP), innovation, and international development have been raised. For patents, these issues include whether patents are being granted for truly novel inventions; when patent protection should be overridden for humanitarian reasons; what barriers to follow-on innovation the patent system might create in itself; and the unique needs of research and development (R&D) for international development.[6] Furthermore, patents themselves can be expensive, time-consuming, and risky to work with.

Innovation rests on a public domain of ideas,[7] yet genes of important organisms like humans, rice, and maize have been patented. Discoveries related to the human genome are vital to future biomedical innovation, but it is estimated that 20 percent of the human genome is claimed by patents. Two-thirds of these patents are owned by private firms, and a similar fraction may be legally questionable on the grounds that they are too broad, not disclosed properly, or overlap other patent claims.[8] Such "patent thickets" have led to what some experts call the "tragedy of the anti-commons"—the proliferation of patents blocking fundamental tools in biotechnology research may have led to the under-use of knowledge due to high costs and lack of cooperation by patent holders,[9] though the extent to which this actually takes place is debated.[10]

Patent pools are consortiums which agree to cross-license patents relating to a particular technology. They are beginning to be used to stimulate research in neglected diseases, allowing both access to select technologies and competitive business practices.[11] Additional enabling tools and collaborative practices, however, are required to harness innovation and the patent landscape for international development.

The Open Source Approach

The open source movement has had an enormous impact on the global software industry,[12] with estimates of an economic value in the tens of billions of dollars. This economic impact nevertheless understates open source's true importance. Richard Stallman emphasizes the value of software that is both open and *free*—in his phrase, "free as in 'free speech,' not free as in 'free beer.'"[13] Free and open software, as Stallman defines it, is software that not only is not proprietary, but that cannot be made proprietary—access to it is an inalienable right, regardless of location or income, and other software can build on it to create new solutions.

A range of incentives motivate participation in open source projects, including building reputation, providing public goods, and undercutting for-profit rivals.[14] Open source methods are now being applied in different sectors, including biotechnology. Yet the metaphor of open source needs adaptation when transferred to biotechnology, since biotechnology research efforts are not structured like the software industry. To take one difference, new biotechnology may require long and expensive laboratory development, followed by even more expensive clinical trials. New software, on the other hand, can be developed in a more incremental and, typically, less expensive fashion.

In the remainder of this chapter, we explore the Cambia and OSDD initiatives, and we discuss how open source approaches are being applied in biotechnology for global health and development, supported by collaborative online platforms. These case studies are based on analyses of transcripts of semistructured interviews conducted by the authors, as well as on secondary data, including journal articles, news reports, books, and websites.

Case 1: Cambia

Cambia is a private, nonprofit institute based in Australia. Founded by Richard Jefferson, Cambia's mission is "to democratize innovation: to create a more equitable and inclusive capability to solve problems using science and technology."[15] Cambia used its first grants from the Rockefeller Foundation to develop training and technology to support rice scientists in Asia, Africa, and Latin America. During the 1990s, Jefferson traveled to many laboratories performing biotechnology in the developing world; this experience influenced his later work.

BiOS: An Open Source Licensing Solution for Biotech

In 2006, Cambia launched the BiOS Initiative (Biological Innovation for Open Society), the aim of which was to create a protected commons to allow users to access, improve, and modify enabling technologies without infringing on proprietary rights. According to Gary Toenniessen, Director of Food Security at the Rockefeller Foundation, "agriculture R&D for the developing world could be lost without a concept like BiOS and open source."[16]

The heart of the BiOS Initiative is the development of BiOS licenses, designed to cultivate collaboration. BiOS licenses derive from Jefferson's belief in the enabling power of legal tools. They aim to allow access to, and improvement of, enabling technologies, which in turn are hoped to ease the development of solutions for local needs. BiOS follows a long line of previous open licenses like the GPL (software) and Creative Commons (cultural goods) that have "some rights reserved."[17]

BiOS licensees must sign a detailed legal contract to preserve the right of others to use the technology—for example by agreeing not to assert intellectual property (IP) rights against others who have also signed the contract. In exchange, they gain access to the technology.[18] Unlike some other open source licenses, BiOS licenses do not prohibit licensed technology from being used to develop downstream proprietary products.

When a developer makes technology available under a BiOS license, the developer retains ownership of the technology, but the company may not assert IP rights over that technology or improvements against other BiOS licensees, nor may it prevent sharing of biosafety data. There is a technology support agreement with each BiOS license in which for-profit companies must pay a fee based on their location and size of operations.

Cambia's first license was developed for plant molecular–enabling technologies, with subsequent licenses including one for health-related technologies, as well as a generic agreement for patented technologies and know-how. Cambia's website sums up the potential benefits of the BiOS licenses as follows[19]:

• Ability to access the intelligence, creativity, goodwill, and testing facilities of a larger and wider community of researchers and innovators.
• Decreased transaction costs relative to out-licensing or obtaining technology via bilateral license agreements.
• Potential for portfolio growth through synergies obtained by combining pieces of technology that may, by themselves, be too small to make a profit or lack sufficient freedom to operate or implement.
• High leverage of costly investments in obtaining proofs of concept, developing improvements, and obtaining regulatory and utility data.
• Ability to commercialize products without an additional royalty burden.

Cambia suggests that BiOS licenses may be of interest to several groups: first, anyone interested in materials and technology from Cambia itself, such as GUSPlus or TransBacter, which are available only under BiOS-compatible agreements; second, research organizations that want access to helpful information; third, smaller enterprises that want protection from the patent thickets described earlier that impede their progress; and fourth, large companies that see how sharing information in particular domains may help them leverage investment by selling services and building on the improvements of others (as has happened with some large companies in the software industry, such as IBM).

Some conclusions can be drawn from Cambia's experience with BiOS. Various firms did express enthusiasm toward the BiOS licensing structure during the first years of the initiative, but the licenses still need to be worked on to have the effect that Cambia desires. Certainly, BiOS has not resulted in a flowering of open projects in the way that the GNU Public License and its offspring produced in software.

The primary reason for this may be that software is intrinsically cheap to produce. One programmer working in her basement may create a new product, requiring none of the sophisticated laboratory equipment on which biotechnology depends. Software does not require large investments to meet regulatory and clinical testing requirements. Once created, software is easy to reproduce.

While large- or midsized organizations will have the resources to pursue Cambia's licensing scheme, small organizations may not. Another problem is that in order to create a pool of components large enough to create new solutions, many distinct methods may need to be licensed.

An analysis of BiOS suggests that IP managers committed to open access might still benefit from the strategic use of patents in certain cases, such as to meet humanitarian goals.[20] For example, by facilitating sales in developed country markets, funding might more easily be found to increase product availability in developing countries. Effective use of licenses like BiOS may depend on a clear understanding of goals, power structures, and the IP landscape.

BioForge: The First Open Biotech Web Portal

Launched by Cambia in 2005, BioForge was a Web portal designed to create an active development community which would collaborate on projects and technologies, develop protocols, discuss experiences, and access tools in a public but secure environment. BioForge was patterned on successful software development portals such as SourceForge.

To kick-start BioForge in 2005, Jefferson seeded it with patented Cambia technologies, including GUSPlus. Within two months of its launch, BioForge had two thousand registered users. The expectation from BioForge was a cooperative development of concepts and solutions, but within the first year of BioForge's launch it became clear that no online collaboration was occurring within the target life sciences community. BioForge did not continue to grow.

Several factors may have contributed. Scientists may not be motivated to collaborate online unless it helps to solve immediate challenges. Similarly, Janet Hope has suggested that collaboration between biotech workers may be harder than in software, because of a lack of standardization.[21] She gives the example of experimental protocols, which may differ from laboratory to laboratory. It is not clear that a portal like BioForge could facilitate the sharing of lab culture. Finally, as Jefferson said in personal communication with the authors in 2009, "Now can we do [BioForge] differently? Absolutely. . . . [When] a sensible accreditation and value is ascribed to a contribution, then it'll have merit. It really will." The BioForge project did not thrive, and it was discontinued. A follow-up platform that learns from BioForge's difficulties may yet prove valuable.

Patent Lens: An Open Patent Research System

Large costs in navigating patent thickets risk hampering follow-on innovation, and some argue that patents have been granted for innovations of dubious novelty.[22] Patent Lens, a free patent informatics resource, is Cambia's response to this complexity. As of 2009, the database contained more than nine million patents, and over sixty-eight million DNA and protein sequences disclosed in patents.

Patent Lens allows diverse players to investigate and analyze key IP issues, facilitating community involvement in guiding the patent system. Cambia plans to integrate business information into the database to make visible IP power chains aimed to reveal who owns what, and dependencies between technologies. As Jefferson told the authors in 2009, "Patents are not about science—they're about the conversion of science into perceived economic value, and that specialized language and capability has emerged as the ecclesiastical elite. What we wish to do is democratize that process."

Patent Lens was first developed with funding from the Rockefeller Foundation, which saw that industrialized countries were seeking patents on the rice genome. These patents could inhibit the improvement of rice in the developing world. Early on, Cambia's team used the Patent Lens technology to map out the patent landscape of *Agrobacterium*—a genus used widely as a tool for making transgenic plants, yet one which Cambia felt was tied up in many patents mainly owned by a few large life sciences companies. Cambia was then able to develop TransBacter, a way to implant genes into a plant using a different family of bacteria than that of *Agrobacterium*. Patent

Lens has been praised by the World Intellectual Property Organization (WIPO) and commentators. The next step Jefferson sees is to develop informatics for analyzing patents, as discussed later in the "Initiative for Open Innovation" section of this chapter.

With an understanding of Cambia's history and projects, we turn now to the second case study in collaborative open source biotechnology platforms.

Case 2: OSDD (Open Source Drug Discovery)

India's OSDD consortium was launched in 2007 by the country's Council of Scientific and Industrial Research (CSIR). OSDD has been strongly supported by CSIR's director, Samir Brahmachari. The OSDD initiative attempts to encompass the drug discovery process: identification of nontoxic drug targets, *in vitro* and *in vivo* validation, *in silico* screening of small molecules, lead optimization, pre-clinical toxicity, and clinical trials. OSDD aims to achieve affordable health care through a platform where talented minds can collectively discover novel therapies, as well as to bring openness and collaboration to the drug discovery process, and keep drug costs low.

Brahmachari has suggested the necessity of retaining patent protection alongside open source development, rather than in opposition to it: "We will not put a wall around drugs that are required by the masses and which we want to sell cheaply (such as Hepatitis or TB drugs), but will put a wall around drugs that have high market affordability, where the diseases that these drugs treat are not yet prevalent among lower income groups. In addition, by patenting, we can also challenge monopolies."[23]

For Brahmachari and OSDD, openness represents an instrument—one that, like patent law itself, is to be used appropriately to achieve specific goals and social results.

How OSDD Works

Developments in bioinformatics have enabled researchers to do some drug discovery *in silico*, while sitting in front of their computers. CSIR has set up a collaborative online platform, SysBorgTb, focused on tuberculosis. The Web portal provides bioinformatics tools, biological information, data on the pathogens, projects for participation in drug discovery, and discussion forums. As of October 2009, there were more than 1,700 registered participants for OSDD.[24]

OSDD aims to break down drug discovery into smaller activities with clear deliverables, which are posted on its Web portal. Participants can contribute ideas, software, articles, IP, or anything else that helps to solve these problems. Users of the portal must comply with OSDD's terms and conditions, which aim to prevent third parties from acquiring proprietary rights based on information available on the portal without contributing improvements made back to OSDD. Like the BiOS license, OSDD allows users to commercially or noncommercially use improvements, additions, or modifications. Users, though, must grant back an unencumbered world-wide nonexclusive right to OSDD for use of any IP rights acquired for their improvements or modifications.

Participants have clear incentives—an element that Jefferson identi-fied as missing from BioForge. All contributions are planned to be peer-reviewed; contributors will receive rights within the system based on credits accrued. A more subtle incentive may come from OSDD's momentum, clear goals, and high-profile backers.

The OSDD project has investigated the genetics of *Mycobacterium tuber-culosis*, with a view to finding new treatments. In October 2009, OSDD announced a collaborative project to re-annotate the entire *Mycobacterium tuberculosis* genome in order to make all information available on each gene easily accessible and searchable. While the success of this project remains to be assessed, it follows the earlier successful completion by OSDD of TBrowse, an analysis tool for the tuberculosis genome.[25] The complexity of developing better tuberculosis treatments highlights the need for the best minds to collaborate and share expertise in an open environment.

Scarecrow or Wall: Using the Right Form of Protection

Samir Brahmachari's approach to open source is to add it to the toolkit next to patent protection. Brahmachari likens the difference between the two approaches to the difference in protecting a factory (by erecting an expensive wall) as opposed to protecting a rice paddy (by erecting a cheap scarecrow): "In growing a paddy, we will use an open source model. While building a factory, we will patent. If my discovery benefits millions, and I want to give it to them cheaply, I do not want to raise the costs by spend-ing a lot of money in protecting. But if the R&D is highly expensive, then we will patent."[26]

Brahmachari sees open source as a methodology that can be used for side-stepping certain issues, rather than meeting them head-on. For instance, by developing free diagnostics based on pharmacogenomic principles, an open source initiative can revive older, inexpensive drugs, thus sidestep-ping the arduous process of developing new drugs.

Looking Ahead

Cambia's Patent Lens project was a significant success, and it is now an open Web resource for patent search and analysis. The BiOS licensing infrastructure was met with enthusiasm by some organizations, but it had problems in becoming truly effective in its goals. BioForge did not complement the culture of scientists, and this first attempt at a collaborative portal for biotech was not successful. With these lessons learned, Cambia and OSDD are looking ahead.

The Initiative for Open Innovation

Cambia is moving ahead with the new Initiative for Open Innovation (IOI). IOI will explore and validate new collaboration and licensing tools with the aim of fostering a commons of capability. This commons is hoped to lower costs of creating new biotechnology solutions by helping non-specialists identify areas of opportunity.

As of 2010, the Bill & Melinda Gates Foundation and the Lemelson Foundation were funding IOI. The initial funding of AU$5 million was focused on creating patent landscapes for malaria, tuberculosis, dengue, and other critical infectious diseases of the developing world. IOI aims to create an evidence base for policy changes for public benefit. Jefferson described to the authors in 2009 how these tools will help to reduce barriers to innovation by reducing the need for expensive IP professionals or "clergy": "What we're trying to do with this, in terms of the low hanging fruit, is to bring in the world's patent information in a form that lends itself to much higher order mark-up and navigation tools. . . . How does it affect your life as a drug developer? Or as a citizen? There's no way to know that right now except through clergy interventions and our job is to break that down." IOI has plans to partner with the Indian government and OSDD. OSDD may benefit both from Cambia's philosophy on system-level barriers, and from its IT tools to navigate patents.

Four Issues for Future Exploration

The case studies in this chapter indicate the potential and modest achievements to date of collaborative platforms and open source methods for development-oriented biotechnology. Many issues remain to be explored.

Viable collaborative platforms. Cambia and OSDD both deployed collaborative platforms. While BioForge was not a success, OSDD and Patent Lens suggest the potential of open platforms. Success factors included low cost of entry for participants and subdivision of complex challenges into simpler sub-challenges.[27] Institutional support, strong leading personalities, and a humanitarian mission encouraged volunteering. As Jefferson and OSDD noted, metrics that reward users' contributions may be helpful. Other factors include interface design and the platform's perceived utility for helping users solve the problems they care about.

Three kinds of "open." The demonstrated value of collaborative platforms in both Cambia and OSDD illustrates a point about the "open source" nomenclature. In the software world, the term "open source" literally refers to the ability to see the source code of programs, but "open source" also embodies a set of cultural practices, licenses, and innovative collaboration methods.

In development-oriented life sciences, therefore, at least three linked senses of "open source" should be considered: open access to underlying information, open licensing practices, and open collaborative methods and platforms. Open access to information by itself, while often the easiest step to take, may be of little value without the freedom and collaborators with which to apply such information to create solutions.

The IP reform debate. Many calls for reform have been raised in IP and international development.[28] Although global health issues have featured prominently in these debates, such as compulsory licenses to permit lower-cost manufacturing of essential medicines, the use of collaborative platforms and open source for global health has, thus far, received little attention. Part of the reason may be the complexity of the issues involved. It is easy to understand a situation where a Brazilian, South African, or Indian company wishes to manufacture a low-cost version of an AIDS drug. It is much harder to grasp the opportunity costs of a complex patent regime, the unrealized potential of drugs that are *not* being developed when barriers to innovation are high, or the potential inhibiting effect on innovation of relaxing IP protection. Tools like Patent Lens help to demystify such issues.

To enable a more informed debate, it may help to look at examples such as Cambia and OSDD. Better metrics and tools might also be created to analyze IP policy options.

Incentives for innovation. A key issue raised by private sector entities in favor of stricter IP regimes is incentives for innovation. If innovators are not rewarded, who will invest in innovation? There is a need to better understand viable business models addressing this issue. For example, Hope has proposed that a biotech company could remain profitable while open-sourcing its core technology.[29] Her model assumes the following to be true: increased access to a product or method will increase its adoption and customer base; wide adoption may lead to improvements in the product or technology; and the company can position itself to profit through analysis and contract research, and to act as the expert in the open-sourced technology. This model is analogous to one that has been successful for companies like Red Hat in the software world: Red Hat's original business model was to give away its core Linux operating system for free, and then to charge for premium support services.

Although such concepts are intriguing, more analysis is needed. Biotechnology innovations may be the result of a complex chain of discoveries, each of which entails risky investments that may fail. At which of these stages are open source approaches most viable? What partial rights regimes might release humanitarian rights that promote use in low-income countries, while keeping core rights that a company needs to maintain profitability (akin to the BiOS and Creative Commons some-rights-reserved approach)? How can investments into enabling collaborative platforms be supported as pre-competitive tools that help all parties achieve more?

Both Cambia and OSDD were largely supported through government and foundation grants. But a variety of innovative funding mechanisms are being explored for global health that span the spectrum from for-profit to grant-based.[30] There is ample room for research into viable open source models that apply at each stage of the biotechnology value chain.

With research into diseases of the poor receiving increasing funding, there may be more receptiveness to the argument that open source approaches can increase the pool of knowledge capital on which downstream innovations will be based, even though they may make private capture of short-term profits more difficult in some cases. Future initiatives may need incentives to attract sufficient early adopters for the innovation or platform to become self-sustaining. Metrics to measure forms of output that add to the global knowledge commons may also be necessary.

Conclusion

In this chapter we explored two case studies of collaborative open source biotechnology platforms and considered the implications for new solutions for international development.

Each area of endeavor that open source principles are applied to may require adaptation. Attempts at mapping collaborative platforms and the software analogy onto such areas (for instance, BioForge as an explicit copy of SourceForge) may fail. They may fail in an educational way, however, indicating which alternative way forward may succeed. For example, the Tropical Disease Initiative is trying open source methods for neglected disease research and drug discovery,[31] attempting to kick-start participation with publication of a small base of seed work,[32] though with limited success to date.

The fact that organizations like India's OSDD are pursuing collaborative platforms for open source drug development is indicative of the potential in the developing world. While OSDD is at a very early stage, it has attracted thousands of contributors and received major funding from the Indian government. Initiatives like OSDD may enable North–South collaborations to tackle international development challenges.

Open source can entail open access to information, open licensing practices, and open collaborative platforms. A project may gain differential benefits from different ways of being open. One universal principle, suggested by Richard Jefferson and others—*a right of access to enabling technologies*—may be more important than the details of a particular license. With this principle and the observations above in mind, the need now is for further research and implementation to harness open source and collaborative approaches for solving challenges in international development.

Notes

An earlier version of this chapter appeared previously in *Information Technologies & International Development*, 9, no. 1 (Spring 2011), Special Issue on Open Development, http://itidjournal.org/itid/issue/view/40.

1. World Health Organization, *Commission on Intellectual Property Rights, Global Health Risks: Mortality and Burden of Disease Attributable to Selected Major Risks* (Geneva: WHO Press, 2006).

2. A. S. Daar, P. A. Singer, and D. L. Persad, "Grand Challenges in Chronic Noncommunicable Diseases," *Nature* 450 (2007): 494–496.

3. R. Levine, *"Case Studies in Global Health: Millions Saved* (Sudbury, MA: Jones and Bartlett Publishers, 2007).

4. H. Masum, J. Chakma, and A. S. Daar, Biotechnology and Global Health. In *Global Health and Global Health Ethics*, ed. G. Brock (Cambridge, UK: Cambridge University Press, 2011), 251–260.

5. N. W. Netanel, *The Development Agenda: Global Intellectual Property and Developing Countries* (Oxford: Oxford University Press, 2009).

6. Commission on Intellectual Property Rights, *Integrating Intellectual Property Rights and Development Policy: Report of the Commission on Intellectual Property Rights* (London: Commission on Intellectual Property Rights, UK Department for Interna-

tional Development, 2002); N. W. Netanel, *The Development Agenda*, 2009; WHO, *Commission*, 2006.

7. J. Boyle, *The Public Domain: Enclosing the Commons of the Mind* (New Haven, CT: Yale University Press. 2008).

8. K. N. Cukier, "Navigating the Future(s) of Biotech Intellectual Property," *Nature Biotechnology* 24, (2006): 249–251.

9. E. R. Gold, W. Kaplan, J. Orbinski, S. Harland-Logan, and S. N.-Marandi, "Are Patents Impeding Medical Care and Innovation?," *PLoS Medicine* 7, no. 1 (2010), e1000208. doi:10.1371/journal.pmed.1000208; S. M. Maurer, "Inside the Anticommons: Academic Scientists' Struggle to Build a Commercially Self-supporting Human Mutations Database, 1999–2001," *Research Policy* 35, no. 6 (2006): 839–853.

10. Y. Joly, "Open Source Approaches in Biotechnology: Utopia Revisited. *Maine Law Review* 59, no. 2 (2007): 386.

11. G. Van Overwalle, ed. *Gene Patents and Collaborative Licensing Models: Patent Pools, Clearinghouses, Open Source Models and Liability Regimes* (Cambridge, UK: Cambridge University Press, 2009).

12. K. St. Amant and B. Still, eds. *Handbook of Research on Open Source Software: Technological, Economic, and Social Perspectives* (Hershey, PA: Information Science Reference, 2007).

13. S. Williams, *Free as in Freedom: Richard Stallman's Crusade for Free Software* (Sebastopol, CA: O'Reilly, 2002).

14. S. Weber, *The Success of Open Source* (Cambridge, MA: Harvard University Press, 2004).

15. Cambia, *Cambia`s Mission and Ethos*, http://www.cambia.org/daisy/cambia/about/590.html.

16. K. L. Miller, "Juggling Two Worlds," *Newsweek International* (November 29, 2004): 56.

17. Boyle, *The Public Domain*, 2008.

18. Biological Innovation for Open Society (BiOS) License, http://www.bios.net/daisy/bios/mta/agreement-patented.html. Archived by WebCite® at http://www.webcitation.org/5m89ua1iz (accessed December 19, 2009).

19. Ibid.

20. S. Boettiger and B. D. Wright, "Open Source in Biotechnology: Open Questions (Innovations Case Discussion: CAMBIA-BiOS)," *Innovations Journal* 1, no. 4 (2006): 45–57.

21. J. Hope, *Biobazaar: The Open Source Revolution and Biotechnology.* (Cambridge, MA: Harvard University Press, 2008).

22. M. Heller, *The Gridlock Economy: How Too Much Ownership Wrecks Markets, Stops Innovation, and Costs Lives* (New York: Basic Books, 2008).

23. M. Kochupillai, "Spicy IP," March 19, 2008, http://spicyipindia.blogspot .ca/2008/03/spicy-ip-interview-with-dr-samir-k.html, archived by WebCite® at http://www.webcitation.org/5kthTApwL.

24. SysBorgTB, http://sysborgtb.osdd.net, archived by WebCite® at http://www .webcitation.org/5ktl4LOQW (accessed October 29, 2009).

25. A. Bhardwaj, D.Bhartiya, N. Kumar, Open Source Drug Discovery Consortium, and V. Scaria, "TBrowse: An Integrative Genomics Map of Mycobacterium tuberculosis," *Tuberculosis* 89, no. 5 (2009): 386–387.

26. M. Kochupillai, "Spicy IP," March 19, 2008.

27. Y. Benkler, *The Wealth of Networks: How Social Production Transforms Markets and Freedom* (New Haven, CT: Yale University Press, 2006).

28. Netanel, N. W., *The Development Agenda*, 2009; WHO, Global Health Risks, 2006.

29. Hope, *Biobazaar*, 2008.

30. R. Hecht, P. Wilson, and A. Palriwala, "Improving Health R&D Financing for Developing Countries: A Menu of Innovative Policy Options," *Health Affairs* 28, no. 4 (2009): 974–985.

31. S. M. Maurer, A. Rai, and A. Sali, "Finding Cures for Tropical Diseases: Is Open Source an Answer?," *PLoS Medicine* 1, no. 3 (2004): e56, doi:10.1371/journal .pmed.0010056.

32. L. Orti, R. J. Carbajo, and U. Pieper, "A Kernel for Open Source Drug Discovery in Tropical Diseases," *PLoS Neglected Tropical Diseases* 3, no. 4, (2009): e418. doi:10.1371/journal.pntd.

Bibliography

Benkler, Y. *The Wealth of Networks: How Social Production Transforms Markets and Freedom.* New Haven, CT: Yale University Press, 2006.

Bhardwaj, A., D. Bhartiya, N. Kumar, Open Source Drug Discovery Consortium, and V. Scaria. "TBrowse: An Integrative Genomics Map of Mycobacterium Tuberculosis." *Tuberculosis (Edinburgh, Scotland)* 89 (5) (2009): 386–387.

Biological Innovation for Open Society (BiOS) License. http://www.bios.net/daisy/bios/mta/agreement-patented.html. Archived by WebCite® at http://www.webcitation.org/5m89ua1iz.

Boettiger, S., and B. D. Wright. "Open Source in biotechnology: Open Questions (Innovations case discussion: CAMBIA-BiOS)." *Innovations Journal* 1 (4) (2006): 45–57.

Boyle, J. *The Public Domain: Enclosing the Commons of the Mind*. New Haven, CT: Yale University Press, 2008.

Cambia. "Cambia`s Mission and Ethos." http://www.cambia.org/daisy/cambia/about/590.html.

Commission on Intellectual Property Rights. *Integrating Intellectual Property Rights and Development Policy: Report of the Commission on Intellectual Property Rights*. London: Commission on Intellectual Property Rights, UK Department for International Development, 2002.

Cukier, K. N. "Navigating the Future(s) of Biotech Intellectual Property." *Nature Biotechnology* 24 (2006): 249–251.

Daar, A. S., P. A. Singer, and D. L. Persad. "Grand Challenges in Chronic Non-communicable Diseases." *Nature* 450 (2007): 494–496.

Gold, E. R., W. Kaplan, J. Orbinski, S. Harland-Logan, and S. N.-Marandi. "Are Patents Impeding Medical Care and Innovation?". *PLoS Medicine* 7 (1) (2010): e1000208. doi:10.1371/journal.pmed.1000208.

Hecht, R., P. Wilson, and A. Palriwala. "Improving Health R&D Financing for Developing Countries: A Menu of Innovative Policy Options." *Health Affairs* 28 (4) (2009): 974–985.

Heller, M. *The Gridlock Economy: How Too Much Ownership Wrecks Markets, Stops Innovation, and Costs Lives*. New York: Basic Books, 2008.

Hope, J. *Biobazaar: The Open Source Revolution and Biotechnology*. Cambridge, MA: Harvard University Press, 2008.

Joly, Y. "Open Source Approaches in Biotechnology: Utopia Revisited." *Maine Law Review* 59 (2) (2007): 386.

Kochupillai, M. "Spicy IP," March 19, 2008, http://spicyipindia.blogspot.com/2008/03/spicy-ip-interview-with-dr-samir-k.html. Archived by WebCite® at http://www.webcitation.org/5kthTApw.

Levine, R. *Case Studies in Global Health: Millions Saved*. Sudbury, MA: Jones and Bartlett Publishers, 2007.

Masum, H., J. Chakma, and A. S. Daar. Biotechnology and Global Health. In *Global-Health and Global Health Ethics*, ed. G. Brock, 251–260. Cambridge, UK: Cambridge University Press, 2011.

Maurer, S. M., A. Rai, and A. Sali. "Finding Cures for Tropical Diseases: Is Open Source an Answer?" *PLoS Medicine* 1 (3) (2004): e56. doi:10.1371/journal. pmed.0010056.

Maurer, S. M. "Inside the Anticommons: Academic Scientists' Struggle to Build a Commercially Self-supporting Human Mutations Database, 1999–2001." *Research Policy* 35 (6) (2006): 839–853.

Miller, K. L. "Juggling Two Worlds." *Newsweek International*, November 29, 2004, 56.

Netanel, N. W. *The Development Agenda: Global Intellectual Property and Developing Countries*. Oxford, New York: Oxford University Press, 2009.

Orti, L., R. J. Carbajo, and U. Pieper. "A Kernel for Open Source Drug Discovery in Tropical Diseases." *PLoS Neglected Tropical Diseases* 3 (4) (2009): e418. doi:10.1371/ journal.pntd.

St. Amant, K., and B. Still, eds. *Handbook of Research on Open Source Software: Technological, Economic, and Social Perspectives*. Hershey, PA: Information Science Reference, 2007.

SysBorgTB. http://sysborgtb.osdd.net. Archived by WebCite® at http://www .webcitation.org/5ktl4LOQW (accessed October 29, 2009).

Van Overwalle, G., ed. *Gene Patents and Collaborative LicensingModels: Patent Pools, Clearinghouses, Open Source Models and Liability. Regimes*. Cambridge, UK: Cambridge University Press, 2009.

Weber, S. *The Success of Open Source*. Cambridge, MA: Harvard University Press, 2004.

Williams, S. *Free as in Freedom: Richard Stallman's Crusade for Free Software*. Sebastopol, CA: O'Reilly, 2002.

Willinsky, J. *The Access Principle: The Case for Open Access to Research and Scholarship*. Cambridge, MA: MIT Press, 2006.

World Health Organization (WHO) Commission on Intellectual Property Rights, Innovation and Public Health. *Public Health, Innovation and Intellectual Property Rights: Report of the Commission on Intellectual Property Rights, Innovation and Public Health*. Geneva: WHO Press, 2006.

World Health Organization (WHO). *Global Health Risks: Mortality and Burden of Disease Attributable to Selected Major Risks*. Geneva: WHO Press, 2009.

6 Open Educational Resources: Opportunities and Challenges for the Developing World

Marshall S. Smith

Over 500,000 students, professors, and life-long learners a month visit OpenCourseWare Consortium (OCW-C) websites, which contain free and reusable course materials published by over 150 institutions of higher education. The content spans fifteen thousand university courses in seven languages from institutions in over forty-five countries including Pakistan, Afghanistan, Indonesia, Kenya, South Africa, China, India, and other developing nations.[1]

The Khan Academy website and its YouTube channel house over three thousand short, five-to-fifteen minute free and reusable videos with problem sets and material for teachers that taken together cover almost all of the mathematics and science found in US kindergarten to grade 12 (K–12) academic curricula. The sites have hosted over 400 million visits from all over the world and many of the materials are being translated into ten languages in addition to English.[2]

Teacher Education in Sub-Saharan Africa (TESSA) is a consortium of eighteen organizations including thirteen institutions of higher education in nine Sub-Saharan African countries. The award winning[3] consortium defines itself as a "research and development initiative creating open educational resources (OERs) and course design guidance for teachers and teacher educators working in Sub-Saharan African countries."[4] TESSA focuses on improving the effectiveness of local schools and teacher training. Their open materials reach over 200,000 educators throughout Africa, and several countries are using TESSA to supplement existing teacher training programs or to serve as the foundation for new programs where none exist.[5]

These are three quite different examples out of hundreds of thousands of open educational resources (OERs).[6] This chapter examines the potential of OERs for improving access and use by students in the developing world to high-quality educational experiences. It first describes OERs and their various forms including how OERs differ from other educational content and software. It then sketches the growth and scope of the OER movement in the developed and developing worlds, including current activities and impediments. The chapter ends by suggesting new directions to improve education in the developing world made possible with open educational resources.[7]

What Are Open Educational Resources?

Open Educational Resources are "teaching, learning, and research resources that reside in the public domain or have been released under an intellectual property license that permits free use and re-purposing by others."[8] Other educational materials that are not covered by such an intellectual property license are not free to download or copy and may not be repurposed.[9] Under international law copyright is automatically conferred to any piece of creative work fixed in a tangible medium (under law a drawing on a napkin is automatically copyrighted).[10] The use of an intellectual property license such as those established by the Creative Commons preserves the copyright of the owner while conferring certain and selected permissions to others to use and even alter the copyrighted works.[11]

How Are OERs Different from Other Content?
The owners of the content in the three examples of OERs in the introduction have granted permissions for users to access, to download and use, and to reuse and/or modify their content, for example by translating the material into another language or by combining it with another OER. The permissions fit into two categories.

One category of permissions granted to users is to allow them to freely access and to download, reproduce, or otherwise use as an intact entity. The owner openly *shares* their materials. OER materials differ from most textbooks, data, educational games and other books and educational materials that are protected behind cyber walls that may only be unlocked by payment, or by passwords available only to selected people. They are also different from the huge amount of digitized content on sites that are available free to all to access but not to download, copy, or otherwise use, except with proper citation and under limited conditions. Such materials are not in the public domain and do not carry an intellectual property license that allows for use that would otherwise violate copyright. Copyright law does not even permit downloading and sharing in most situations without specific permission from the owner. Under the "fair use" provision, in some educational settings, the copyright restrictions on downloading and copying are permitted but within specified limits.[12]

Sharing knowledge to promote the public good is one strong motivating factor for many producers of OERs. Thomas Jefferson wrote in a letter in 1813, "He who receives an idea from me, receives instruction himself without lessening mine; as he who lights his taper at mine, receives light without darkening me. That ideas should freely spread from one to another over the globe, for the moral and mutual instruction of man, and improvement of his condition, seems to have been peculiarly and benevolently designed by nature, when she made them, like fire, expansible over all space, without lessening their density in any point, and like the air in which we breathe, move, and have our physical being, incapable of confinement or exclusive appropriation. Inventions then cannot, in nature, be a subject of property."[13]

Sharing surely was part of the motivation for many of the Massachusetts Institute of Technology (MIT) faculty in 2001 when they voted to freely open the materials for all of their courses on the Web (OpenCourseWare), an action that many believe helped jump start the creation and use of OERs around the world. The act of sharing would have been only part of their decision—there is also pride in imagining and achieving the possibility that hundreds of thousands of people not connected to MIT will appreciate and learn from material they have produced.[14] There is also an economic argument that opening up the flow of ideas greases the paths for others to be creative. Finally, some of MIT's professors may have been responding to a competitive drive and a sense of professional accountability. After all, they were opening their materials to peers who will implicitly or explicitly judge them.

Giving the rights to free access, to copy, and to reshare is one component of the OER equation. Many OERs have licenses that also grant users the right to alter, modify, translate, or otherwise adapt the content to meet their needs. This permission, giving users the right to make *derivative* works, empowers users to modify and thereby add value to the original OER material. This is a game-changing right, particularly for the developing world. For example, copyright law forbids translations of a work without receiving permission from the owner. Being able to take material, translate it into a different language, and then redistribute it multiplies the reach of free access and use, at no cost to the creator/owner. And beyond translations, the possibility of mixing and matching old and new materials from different OERs allows users of all sorts, alone or with others, to create new solutions to their own problems and needs. In the TESSA example, teachers have adapted the social studies modules to incorporate names, regional maps, and references to make the materials more culturally and contextually relevant. With OERs the users become creators and readers become authors.

In a Web 2.0 world the power of this right is amplified by the possibilities for networks of creators and users. For example, networks of teachers across district, state and national boundaries can form to share and improve openly licensed lesson plans, textbooks, research, and other educational materials. Networks for the continuous improvement of materials based on evidence from users, including students in many instances, is becoming an important part of the commercial and noncommercial development processes for many educational materials. Moreover, users who find errors may immediately fix them in their own digitized copy.

How Are the Permissions Organized and Transmitted?

The use of a Creative Commons (CC) license allows OERs to operate under a regime that relies on copyright but changes the default rules from *all rights reserved* to *some rights reserved*. OER owners/producers choose to place their work under a CC or another open copyright license that modifies the copyright requirements and allows the owner to specify which permissible uses or freedoms are allowed with the content.[15] It is important to understand that an owner may permit a specific user a right that is reserved under the open copyright license that applies to a specific work.

All CC licenses allow unrestricted free sharing, regardless of their conditions. A CC license without conditions (CC0) is a Public Domain Declaration that is a waiver of copyright. It puts one's work onto the public domain, which allows unrestricted free sharing and creation of derivative activities. Conditions may then be added to the license by the owner that restrict certain uses or require certain actions by the user. A very common addition to the license is the BY condition that requires that users give recognition and credit to the original creator. Indeed the default of a Creative Commons license is CC BY. Connexions is a popular and easily used platform for OER construction and dissemination that requires that all of the content on it be under a CC BY license.[16]

A second condition that can be exercised using a CC license is to allow no derivatives. This rarely used condition dramatically restricts the rights of the users by not allowing them to edit, translate, mix, remix, or otherwise reuse or alter the original material. A CC BY-ND (Creative Commons, Attribution, No Derivs) license allows sharing with attribution, but without alteration.

The question of whether or not to restrict the user from using the original or altered content for commercial purposes is addressed by a third condition that can be applied to a CC license.[17] The motivation to restrict the user to noncommercial endeavors with the freely open content is straightforward—the creator or owner desires that the content (modified or not), should only be free (zero price)—after all, they embraced the idea of free in the original product. To take this step they would put a CC BY-NC (Creative Commons, Attribution, Non-Commercial) license on the original product. This would constrain users from commercializing the material. Of course, with or without the NC restriction, the original and derivative material would be freely available.

Though the intuitive instinct of an owner/creator may be to place the NC restriction on their material, the drawbacks are potentially substantial. For example, a second party organization might want to modify the original product and add value by simplifying its text and putting scaffolding around it, making it useful to whole new populations. They could do this and then give it away for free, but they may decide to sell the *new* product in order to cover their costs and to have a return on their investments of time. This step is only possible if the original Creative Commons license does not have the NC restriction. To some the use of the NC restriction contradicts the *sharing* motive. If altruism is the motive for the original creator, any new use, commercial or not, should cause pleasure rather than angst. Moreover, the resources from the commercial transaction might be able to support improvement, upgrade, and otherwise sustain the quality of the product over a long period of time. The sustainability and support problems over time loom large for open, free materials that carry a CC BY-NC license.[18]

The last condition is often seen as a compromise solution to the dilemma of sustainability created by the NC condition. The popular condition, (SA—Share Alike) requires the user to place the license of the original work on any derivative work. This license lets others remix, tweak, and build upon the original work even for commercial purposes, as long as they credit the creator and license their derivative under the identical terms as the original material. The derivative work must carry the CC BY-SA license—the work is available for free or to be sold and/or to be altered again.

Wikipedia uses the CC BY-SA license while the Khan Academy, CK-12, and MIT OCW use the more restrictive CC BY-NC-SA license. While a Share Alike license allows a wide range of uses, it does have the drawback that an OER with a CC BY-SA license may only be mixed with OERs that are licensed under a CC BY-SA or CC BY license, or by content in the public domain. Thus, if a content creator wants to share his or her work in the widest way possible, using a CC0 Declaration or CC BY license would be most appropriate.

One conclusion can be drawn from this short discussion: except for public domain materials, OERs could not exist without a Creative Commons or other similar license. A second conclusion is that not all open resources provide the same rights for the user. The choice of license is important.

A third conclusion for some is that the mixture of Creative Commons licenses is complicated and may not be all inclusive. The issues indicated in the discussion of the SA and NC conditions and their implications for sustainability models are one concern. Another issue has been expressed by the Center for the Study of the Public Domain at Duke University. In a recent Center report that considers the rights and wide variation among nations in approach to knowledge and intellectual property, the authors proposed that the "Creative Commons develop a range of indigenous-knowledge-specific licenses."[19]

OERs in the Developed World: Growth and Challenges

In July 2012, UNESCO held a major conference in Paris to celebrate the tenth anniversary of a UNESCO meeting that had coined the term "Open Educational Resources." The celebration included dozens of presentations and demonstrations in one venue. In another meeting, next door, 336 representatives from developed and developing nations all over the world voted unanimously for the 2012 Paris OER Declaration that called for states, within their capacities and authority, to support and facilitate the use, development, and sharing of OERs and to have all appropriate materials paid for with government funds to have an open license.[20]

Although the term Open Educational Resources was not used until 2002, the period prior to the new millennium had produced a variety of open educational resources. Project Gutenberg, for example, was founded in 1971 to publish free books through the ARPA net. Its collection now has forty thousand different books free and available on the Web.[21] Throughout the middle and late 1990s OERs came from governments that routinely published on the Web free public domain materials that were educational and that enterprising employees had digitized to make them available and to protect them for posterity. In 1996, Brewster Kahle started the Internet Archive, a nonprofit digital archive that contains massive collections of books and other cultural materials. The book collection now contains over 1.6 million volumes. Kahle also makes multiple copies of the entire contents of the Web every year and stores the copies in the Archive.[22]

Late in the decade, a public website (www.free.ed.gov) supported by the United States Department of Education published selected open education materials from across the government.[23] At roughly the same time a young graduate student at Brigham Young University, David Wiley, coined the term *open content* and proposed a license granting users rights of use to substitute for the automatically adhering copyright.[24] Of course, there were also thousands of sites of education materials residing on the Web free for all to peruse, but the material was not free to download, copy, or modify, because of their often implicit all-rights-reserved copyright.

The Rise of OERs

In 2001, Lawrence Lessig, Hal Abelson, Eric Eldred, and others built on Wiley's work and founded Creative Commons.[25] By 2011 Creative Commons estimated that over 400 million licenses had been applied to materials on the Web for music, science, and other areas including education. In 2000 MIT's faculty voted to put the materials for all eighteen hundred MIT courses open and available on the Web for use and reuse. Charles Vest, then president of MIT, wrote in his 2000–2001 annual report: "We now have a powerful opportunity to use the Internet to enhance this process of conceiving, shaping and organizing knowledge for use in teaching. In so doing, we can raise the quality of education everywhere. . . . In this spirit, MIT has asked itself, in the words of T. S. Eliot 'Do I dare / Disturb the Universe?' Our answer is Yes. We call this project MIT OpenCourseWare (OCW). We see it as opening a new door to the powerful, democratizing, and transforming power of education."[26] MIT's bold step took place as other universities were considering proprietary models to distribute their educational materials. The combination of Creative Commons being established and MIT's action provided energy and leadership to an alternative conceptualization of the ownership of knowledge. The OER movement that emerged now extends throughout the world.

Although the fundamental concept of an OER and its legal basis are independent of the technology used to make such resources assessable, the magic of the Web and its new tools made it relatively easy to create new open content, capture and modify existing content, reorganize the content and put it on the Web with a license that announces openness. The William and Flora Hewlett Foundation funded much of the early large-scale work in this era and the foundation continues to provide some support for expansion of the use of OER throughout the world. In part to brunt one criticism of open materials (that you get what you pay for) the foundation's early grants were targeted to prestigious institutions. In addition to MIT this included the universities Harvard, Carnegie Mellon, Rice, Stanford, and the Open University of the United Kingdom. Grants also were made for open content including public television video collections, international organizations such as UNESCO and the OECD, and for strengthening the infrastructure of the OER movement by giving general support for Creative Commons, the Internet Archive, and later for Wikipedia, as well as for grants for convening, translating, research, and for creating open platforms for the aggregation and development of OER materials.[27]

Open Access

Simultaneously, Open Access, a special form of OER, was beginning to thrive. (See also chapter 8 in this book.) Wikipedia defines "Open Access" (OA) as "the practice of providing unrestricted access via the Internet to peer-reviewed scholarly journal articles." John Willinsky, in his interesting book *The Access Principle*, wrote: "The year 2003 signaled a breakthrough in scholarly publishing for what might be loosely termed the *open access movement*. The Public Library of Science was beginning to publish an elite open science journal and Nature, Science, The Scientist, and the Wall Street Journal all ranked 'Open Access' among their top science stories for 2003."[28] The Open Society Foundation has been and continues to be a strong supporter of the Open Access movement.

Of course, as with OERs in general, there has not been unanimous consent to change current practice by all academics and academic publishers by making scholarly articles open. The skeptics argue that there are costs to reviewing, editing, printing, and distributing journals and that the current system is fine. Advocates point out that much of the work writing and reviewing the materials is done for free by academics all over the world and that they would continue to do so under an open structure. More importantly, perhaps, advocates worry that the current costs of the journals limit access for unaffiliated academics and higher education institutions that cannot afford them, such as many of the institutions in the developing world. The lack of access can operate to slow scientific progress. The physical and biological sciences have led the way, perhaps because the fields are changing very rapidly and researchers need faster and more universal access to stay abreast of new findings.

One argument supporting Open Access has found substantial recent traction. A great deal of research is paid for by governments supported by the public—to many this is a strong reason to support a policy that leads to government-supported research reports being open and free. In 2008 the National Institutes of Health in the United States adopted Open Access for all of the research that they support. In 2012 the British government and the European Union adopted policies that provide Open Access for taxpayer-supported research.[29]

Finally, in the past few years major international institutions have come to support Open Access. Harvard University and the Wellcome Foundation, the second-largest philanthropy in the world, adopted OA policies in 2011 and the World Bank soon followed adopting their own OA policy on July 1, 2012.[30] In announcing the World Bank policy to use the Creative Commons CC BY license as a default for its research and knowledge publications the president of the bank, Robert B. Zoellick, stated in a press release: "Knowledge is power. Making our knowledge widely and readily available will empower others to come up with solutions to the world's toughest problems. Our new Open Access policy is the natural evolution for a World Bank that is opening up more and more."[31]

OERs in 2013

By the end of the century's first decade, institutions and individuals throughout the developed world were reusing, revising, remixing, and redistributing large quantities of OERs. In addition to those already mentioned, open materials included course modules, full courses, textbooks, simulations, videos for teaching and learning, games, lesson plans and other course materials, book collections, encyclopedias, and many other forms of education content.[32]

While many of the larger and more visible OER projects have been at the postsecondary level, there has also been considerable activity at the K–12 level. For example, hundreds of thousands of teachers now use open portals where they share lesson plans and ideas and draw on videos, simulations, the comments and thoughts of other teachers, and other supporting software and content.[33] Wikiwijs, which provides access to content and learning communities for teachers, is a national OER initiative in the Netherlands. The Learning Resource Exchange from the European Schoolnet provides schools with access to rich amounts of open educational content from its twenty-five partner countries.[34] In the United States Curriki and the OER Commons serve much the same purpose.[35] Tens of millions of K–12 students across the world now use open instructional materials such as the Khan Academy videos of instruction in academic areas and the science simulations (PhET, or Physics Education Technology) designed by Nobel Prize–winning physicist Carl Wieman. Additionally, millions of teachers and students use the open repositories of videos with CC licenses at iTunesU and YouTube EDU.[36] Ironically, many teachers, professors and students may not even know they are using an OER since education institutions can rely on the "fair use" exception under copyright that (under certain conditions) allows limited access and use, and users may not distinguish between OER and non-OER materials.[37]

Also at the beginning of the new decade major foundations, in addition to Hewlett and Mellon, and governments began to invest in OER. The Bill & Melinda Gates Foundation and some others funded a series of projects in 2010 including the expansion of the Khan Academy and work focused on preparing students for credit courses in community colleges.[38] And, in early 2011, the US Department of Labor announced a $2 billion competition for grants for educational and training materials that would be open under a CC license.[39]

The Rise of the MOOCs

Finally, the autumn of 2011 saw another form of possibly open content become known throughout the world. A pair of instructors at Stanford University, Sebastian Thrun and Peter Norvig, designed and constructed their Artificial Intelligence course to go online free to all. Well over 150,000 students from all over the world signed up for the course and over 20,000 completed it; some of them achieved at a level competitive with the Stanford students who were taking the course onsite.

Such courses now labeled massive open online courses (MOOCs)[40] have become the rage in the open education circles, as Stanford has spun off two organizations to create and deliver open courses. One of these, Coursera, is a coalition of sixty-two universities from across the world and now provides hundreds of separate courses. They have served over three million students.[41] A second, Udacity, was started by Thrun and now has over twenty courses. Udacity has announced the decision by Colorado State University's Global Campus to give full transfer credit to students who successfully complete the Udacity Computer Science course.[42] In late spring 2012, MIT and Harvard joined to create edX, an organization that will deliver a wide range of open courses to the world. In mid-summer the two Cambridge institutions were joined by UC Berkeley and have now added another group of institutions including Stanford, Wellesley, Georgetown and the entire Texas University System.[43] EdX has announced that it would provide certificates to all students who successfully complete the courses and pass an independently proctored examination administered in a network of Pearson Corporation assessment centers.[44]

The nature and use of MOOCs will evolve rapidly over time and may begin to be sorted into different categories regarding service delivery, the expectations for students, or other dimensions.[45] One of the shared characteristics of the current mix of MOOCs is the reliance of the instructors on the students to network virtually and support each other's learning using multiple social networking means. Students are expected to provide feedback to the course instructors—whether thoughts, concerns, or corrections—and to post their own work and comment on other student's work. The courses vary in their adherence to any particular pedagogical model.

As with many other open materials, the business models for sustainability or for making a profit for these courses or organizations are not yet clear. The current sources of income include contributions of the universities, private donors, and of foundations in the MIT-Harvard-Berkeley model and venture capital in Coursera. A possible longer-term source of revenue could be to charge fees for students to pass an exam to gain credit in participating institutions or for certification that is acknowledged by a private-sector company. An important point here is that even a small fee from a large number of people can be lucrative.

Finally, it is important to note that both Coursera and Udacity put all of their material under a standard copyright—neither of them are OERs. It is not clear whether any MOOC will have a Creative Commons license. EdX has adopted an open license for its platform. At the time of this writing there was a rumor that edX content also will operate under a Creative Commons license. The nature of the MOOCs, however, may make this question somewhat moot for some of the MOOC vendors. Similar to the design of other materials such as the Carnegie Mellon Open Learning Initiative courses, most MOOCs are built on special platforms that do not allow easy access for users to alter. MOOCs are the latest hot item for the open world but they will not be the last. Individual and multiplayer open learning games, for example, are on the horizon.

Challenges to Overcome

Even with the extraordinary progress over the past decade, as with any innovation the road to general acceptance and extensive use of OERs has potholes. There are at least four significant and inter-related challenges to the expansion of the OER and full use of it in the developed world: (1) concern about quality; (2) publishing companies that fear for the continued viability of their current business model; (3) educational systems that see technology and open content as disruptive threats to conventional practice; and (4) the lack of strong business models for OER.

Quality

Some claims about the low quality of OERs are valid. Like all Web content, there is currently no universally accepted review process or evaluation methodology to determine the quality of an OER before it is published on the Web. Legally, a Creative Commons license may be placed on any product, from the highest quality, state-of-the-art product to a product that is filled with inaccuracies and vile language. Over the years there have been discussions of ways to universally ensure quality, but little has yet to come of them, partly because of the vast quantity of materials, partly because of the concern that regulating openness might bring legitimate cries of censorship, and partly because quality is often impossible to be universally defined, especially when materials are created and used for a number of different purposes and in a wide variety of cultures.

Creators and users have nevertheless instituted some process safeguards. One example is the care taken by the leaders in the open textbook publishing field. The CK12 Foundation is a not-for-profit publisher of eighty-eight "flexbooks." The organization pays close attention to quality relying on expert and user reviews as well as professional copyediting. A number of the secondary school flexbooks have successfully passed review by the California Board of Education. Openstax College, another important player in the open textbook environment, is an initiative of Rice University. Openstax relies on the Connexions software and its publishing infrastructure, uses similar quality-control mechanisms, and a similar CC BY 3.0 license.[46]

The participation of high-quality universities in the OER movement undercuts the low quality claims to some extent, though the charge still exists. The OCW Consortium, with its institutional membership, has relied upon its members' own processes for ensuring high standards. Additionally, the very character of openness or, to use another term, transparency, carries a degree of accountability and an incentive for quality. A number of MIT professors have received emails from colleagues pointing out errors or places to improve their OCW materials. In a discussion with the president of an important Asian university he told me that his institution's few OCW offerings are a powerful incentive for improving instruction in his university. The posted OCW materials at his university are of the highest quality and establish a bar of excellence for all of the other professors.

OER materials for K–12 public schools, such as the online open textbooks, have to meet the same quality criteria that exist for other K–12 educational materials. In the United States, local committees or boards of teachers and educational experts are often responsible for reviewing and approving many of the materials used in classrooms. Partly because of the newness of digitized texts and the arguments by publishers that the free materials lack quality, only a few states, including Florida, California, Washington, Utah and Texas, have agreed to allow K–12 open textbooks that have passed review to substitute for traditional textbooks.[47] Over time the use of online textbooks, both open and commercial, will increase as teachers and students become more accustomed to them. In the case of open textbooks they will also begin to allow their users (teachers, administrators) to modify and adapt the materials for their use—this provides the users with a potentially powerful way to increase their effectiveness.[48]

A recent effort directly addresses the OER quality issue. Achieve, a prominent U.S. nongovernmental organization, has recently developed a useful set of rubrics that provide a way for evaluating the quality of a K–12 OER materials and their alignment with the new U.S. common academic standards.[49] Although these rubrics are only beginning to be used, they represent a positive step to move OER into the mainstream for consideration by educators making decisions about what open materials they will adopt.

Threats to Conventional Business Models

The picture is not entirely rosy. The rise of user-produced digital content, proliferation of free distribution models, and openness in general threaten the traditional business models for academic publishers and for many of the academic societies.[50] OER is a triple threat—it challenges the distribution model by moving to the Web, it challenges the price structure by being free, and it allows users to adapt the materials to better meet their needs.

Not surprisingly publishers and others in the industry have responded rapidly given the opportunity. One approach in the United States has been to lobby Congress and the administration to eliminate government support for OER. If successful this would help the publishers ensure that their existing market models and practices endure, at least for a little while longer.[51]

Other steps have been focused on improving their product. For example, the movement to the Web by publishers has accelerated recently perhaps in partial response to the competition from OER. Some publishers such as Nature, Pearson, and Scholastic are exploring opportunities through which they may capitalize on openness. This overall effort appears now to be at an exploratory stage as publishers try to figure out the best pricing models for their products. The commercial price structure issue is linked to problems of scale and sustainability. This is a two-edged sword for OER, since it makes the OER owners (with a zero price structure) very competitive but may leave them without financial resources to expand participation and sustain their product. The problem of OER sustainability is very significant—and is discussed later in this chapter.

Finally, the threat from the OER-type permission that allows the user to become a creator could be overcome by publishers adopting a Creative

Commons BY-SA license that would allow users to alter their materials to meet their needs and, in exchange, license the derivative works (with all of the changes) back to the publisher and to everyone else. This would allow publishers to keep their current distribution model, use the changes to help modify their product, and to perhaps support their bottom line with an improved product. We should come to expect hybrid business models of this sort.

The Power of the Status Quo

Concerns about quality and publishers are not the only reasons that OERs have faced a somewhat uphill journey. Universities, both public and private, are often conservative organizations that have a difficult time making major changes in their ways of doing business.[52] Moreover, K–12 schools have multiple purposes, among them being safety and socialization. These conditions create an important drive for stability and predictability of structure and function. Technology and some forms of OER are often seen as threatening that stability.

On the nonthreatening list for both postsecondary instructors and K–12 teachers are open online OER lesson plans, high-quality simulations, textbooks, video for teaching and for teacher training, and other open materials that do not disrupt classrooms and that add value to student learning. The materials on this list are now widely adopted. For OER, many professors have embraced open online textbooks because of the cost savings for students.[53]

But teachers and professors may see online courses (commercial or OER) that cover the same material they teach as direct competition. Open online courses can exacerbate this threat because students have full, free access from home or libraries, even while they are taking the course in school. Thus they can learn at home much of what they learn at school. Linear Algebra, taught by Gilbert Strang, is one of the best-known MIT OpenCourseWare courses. The materials include a full set of video lectures taught in a clear, unassuming, and understandable style. Professor Strang has received emails and letters from all over the world from students who thank him for communicating concepts that their own professor did not make clear.[54]

Yet even with the open options, safe and structured environments with adults (such as colleges) and especially K–12 schools will probably be the primary learning environments for academic and technical content for years to come. In these environments there is room for both an instructor and online material, including self-contained courses. Indeed, there is a growing body of data to suggest that the average professor lecturing alone may not be the most effective and efficient facilitator for many students to learn in collegiate settings.

SRI International, an independent nonprofit research institute, recently carried out a meta-analysis of studies of postsecondary teaching methods that examined the effectiveness of using online courses to help teach college courses.[55] Over forty studies were carefully selected for their quality and rigor from a larger population of close to one thousand studies. There were three conditions: a teacher-only condition; a blended technology and teacher condition; and a technology-only condition. The blended condition was statistically the most effective. The difference between the technology-only condition and the teacher-only condition was not statistically significant. The meta-analysis study also looked at K–12 technology courses—the sample was too small for any strong inferences but the general tendency was the same. While the courses in the study were not OER, the results should be indicative of the results that will come about when open full courses are evaluated over the next few years.[56]

Most of the courses included in the SRI meta-analysis were created prior to 2007. Since then the technology and content of online courses has improved rapidly and substantially, in part by becoming more sensitive and adaptive to individual learner differences.

The Carnegie-Mellon Open Learning Initiative (OLI) courses (with CC BY-NC-SA 3.0 licenses), for example, are continuously improved as developers and researchers learn more about how students respond and learn from the course materials. One example of the power of continuous improvement comes from a randomized design study of the effectiveness of the OLI statistics course by Carnegie-Mellon researchers. In the study, one group was in a traditional class and the other, the experimental group, used the technology for learning the material and met with a teacher twice a week for questions and explanations. The traditional lecture group's class completed the course in a full semester—the experimental group was deliberately accelerated and completed the course in only one-half of the semester. Each group took the same exams. The experimental group did better on the final assessments than the traditional group—in effect, the students in the experimental condition learned more in half the time. This statistics course and several others are free and available on the Carnegie-Mellon website.[57]

A second randomized design study was carried out recently by an independent team of researchers using the same OLI statistics course. The sample comprised statistics classes in six universities. One condition was a standard model of three to four hours of face-to-face instruction each week while the other model was a hybrid with machine-guided instruction and one hour of face-to-face instruction each week. The learning outcomes were essentially the same. The authors conclude that the results were the same, but using "speculative models" found that with large class sizes there might be substantial cost savings with the hybrid model.[58]

These findings and opportunities could substantially change education practice. Even a finding of no difference between a professor- or teacher-only course and a technology-only course is a powerful indicator of the potential of technology. One inference from such findings could reasonably be that in some situations students don't need a professor or teacher to facilitate learning the course content. Based on the SRI and OLI studies a professor or teacher might imagine their teaching as replaceable or should be substantially changed. The results of these studies also challenge conventional assumptions about what can be learned in a semester, and that the university or school is the only place a student can learn academic material. MOOCs will reinforce this belief. Indeed an infrastructure is in the works to support such independent learning outside the boundaries of a conventional school or university. OpenStudy is an open social learning network where any learner can join and study in preformed or self-created groups. OpenStudy currently supports some MIT OCW course study groups.[59]

It seems likely that OERs will play an interesting role in these potential changes. On the one hand OERs might be threatening to teachers and their unions or societies. On the other hand they might enable positive new directions. For many OERs the open nature of the materials (digitized or not) provides teachers at all levels with the opportunity to use and modify the materials to adapt to their classrooms and styles of teaching. The data on blended learning approaches to education suggests that a combination of teacher and technology courses (through Internet, TV, CDs, and so forth) is particularly effective. Schools and universities are exploring the possible role of teachers as coaches who will support students learning from technology applications. Open materials also are available for teachers to assign as supplemental out-of-classroom material when students have access to the appropriate technology.

Finding Sustainability

Finally, to be seen as a positive long-term force in education, OERs will need to overcome another hurdle. Until there are viable business models to sustain and improve OERs they will remain problematic for many people. Varieties of possible OER models exist. The Monterey Institute of Technology publishes open secondary school courses on the Web. It also uses a subscription model, with states paying a small fee to be acknowledged as providers of open courses to their schools and students—the courses are curated regularly and placed on websites that identify each participating state.[60]

The field of open source software offers some suggestions that include, for example, charging for activities that support the implementation of the content or add value to the original content (professional development for open courses), or attaching paid advertisements to the open content. The CC BY-SA license might be useful for these models. Other models include obtaining grants from foundations or the government and supporting content with the revenues from other products.

A model that is more attuned to the times arises from Wikipedia and from the original Linux kernel, created by Linus Torvalds and then modified and improved by programmers all over the world who continue to this day to freely devote their time. The possibility that a cluster of educators and content experts could volunteer to either start from scratch or build on past work to create very high-quality OER material is very attractive. Over time the same cluster or others could continue to curate and improve the quality of the OER. The Connexions platform was designed to facilitate this form of collaboration.[61]

OER in the Developing World: Growth and Challenges

Not surprisingly the penetration of OER in the developing world has been slower than in the developed world, following the pattern of access to hardware, connectivity, and support for technology in the schools. Moreover the economies are generally poor, which typically constrains the opportunities for innovation, and some have policies that interfere with the open transmission of knowledge.

Higher Education

As in the developed world context, usage of OERs in higher education has preceded use at K–12 levels, in part because public and private higher education institutions mostly serve the upper economic levels of society in the developing world and many of the institutions have reasonably good connections to the Internet.[62]

But there have been impediments to OER growth in developing world tertiary institutions, just as there have been in the developed world. For example, even while participation in OCW-C has been substantial reports of concern and opposition among faculty exist about the use of content from other institutions. The "not-developed-here" perspective persists in both developed and developing nations. Courses, simulations, modules, and other academic content from the Internet, especially from other nations, may be seen by professors as threatening to traditional patterns of behavior and traditional curricula, as not culturally appropriate, or as not of sufficient quality for their students.[63] In both the developed and developing contexts some professors and educators have argued that spreading content from developed world countries is a form of intellectual neocolonial imperialism.[64] Moreover, as in the developed countries context, there are few, if any, extrinsic incentives (financial or tenure based) that encourage professors to spend their time to develop or adapt OER. Some inkling of these concerns was raised in UNESCO meetings held in the first several years of the 2000s. Representatives of developing world universities strongly represented the importance of their contributions to collections of OER, a position that was soundly endorsed by the participants in the meeting.

Other conditions also constrain growth in OER at the tertiary level. Copyright laws vary among countries, which creates some confusion; the infrastructure for developing and using OER often is not available; the OER from other nations may not be available in the local language; and, as in the developed world, the arrangements affecting publishers' business models are threatened.

Yet even though the conditions may not be conducive, the use of OER at the tertiary level in many developing world nations appears in 2012 to be on the accelerating side of a J curve. The presence and development of thriving virtual and open universities in the developing world nations suggests a source of materials and a commitment to providing education and content to large numbers of people using technology.[65] The opportunity to join OCW-C seems to have been an important factor in the movement to openness. For example, the Virtual University of Pakistan puts many videos of lectures on YouTube.[66] It also posts an open OCW-C site with all of its courses and, as far as I can tell, the lectures for every one of them.[67] Other developing nations and consortia of nations including India, Malaysia, the Philippines, Thailand, a collection of seven Arab countries, and a group of fourteen Sub-Saharan African nations have established virtual universities.[68] The general belief in virtual universities that academic knowledge should be available to all helps create and facilitate openness to OER.

Virtual universities have been important but they are not the whole story. Early in the 2000s, China Open Resources in Education (CORE) began supporting translations of OCW into Chinese, and Universia, a consortium of higher education institutions in Spain, Portugal, and South America followed suit by supporting translations of OCW into Spanish and Portuguese, with both opening channels for international access.[69] The Shuttleworth

Foundation has helped to fund OER in South Africa, and the Open University of the United Kingdom provided assistance to institutions in several African nations to set up TESSA. During that decade as well, Creative Commons developed a local presence in over seventy jurisdictions around the world, many in developing nations. And in 2008, OER Africa, an initiative of the South African Institute for Distance Education (SAIDE), was formed with a mission to "create vibrant networks to . . . develop, share and adapt OER to meet the education needs of African Societies."[70] Two independent international institutions with large country memberships have had particularly broad and important impacts on the growth of OER in the Global South. UNESCO has been an important institution for OER since 2002. Propelled by John Daniel, then the assistant director for education of UNESCO, and an early advocate of OER, UNESCO has served for over a decade as a setting for numerous meetings, affirmed support for, and otherwise introduced representatives of developing world nations to the usefulness and power of OER. Susan D'Antoni, now the executive director of the International OER Initiative at Athabasca University in Alberta, Canada, and on the staff of the UNESCO Institute for International Educational Planning (IIEP) during many of the early years of OER, created and oversaw a virtual community of interest with six hundred participants from ninety countries including sixty in the developing world that lasted for three years as OER was becoming internationally known. The community included grassroots teachers and professors as well as representatives of governments who, over time, have helped to set the groundwork for deepening interest in OER in their nations.[71]

The Commonwealth of Learning (COL) is a voluntary intergovernmental organization of the nations in the British Commonwealth that focuses on the development and sharing of online learning and other educational resources. When John Daniel became president and CEO of COL, just after he left UNESCO, he made OER a priority, a step that took a variety of forms.[72] One of the best known was initial support for the creation of the Virtual University for Small States of the Commonwealth (VUSSC), a network of thirty-two nations. Unlike many other OER creators, the VUSSC supports the collaborative development of OER as well as other ways of building capacity to improve educational opportunities. The focus of the work is on collaboratively building a library of open courses that provide technical and occupational knowledge and skills. The courses are easily altered to adapt to different conditions in the various nations.[73]

UNESCO and COL have also provided joint leadership to the growing OER movement. Most recently they co-sponsored the tenth anniversary of

OER, meeting at UNESCO in the summer of 2012. During 2011 the UNESCO Institute for Information Technologies in Education (IITE) released a set of comprehensive country studies of use of OER in non-English-speaking nations. Among the nations studied are Brazil, China, Lithuania, and Russia.[74] In 2012, COL and UNESCO jointly released a report put together at COL on the use of OERs in higher education in a wide variety of developing world nations.[75] In the same year they also issued the "Survey on Governments' Open Educational Resources (OER) Policies."[76] These valuable reports capture evidence of substantial progress in many developing nations in advancing the policies and practices that support OERs, especially in higher education.

Progress in K–12 Schools

Although the UNESCO IIEP (International Institute for Educational Planning) reports touch on K–12 applications of OERs, they make clear that progress there is much slower than at the tertiary level. At the K–12 level the variation of Internet access among countries and schools is much greater than at the postsecondary level. Many schools in rural areas and city slums lack regular connections to power or the Internet. These conditions call for innovative approaches to using technology and OER.

The social and professional infrastructure for K–12 education is often an impediment as well. Most teachers are not trained in the use of technology, and many have limited teacher training. Education materials and professional development in instructional strategies often are lacking, and the weak management of public education in some places makes it particularly difficult for schools to implement change, such as the use of technology, and therefore the use of OER. Moreover, many well-to-do families in developing world nations send their children to private schools, perhaps making it less likely that they would pay much attention to the quality of the public schools. These conditions may sound familiar to some in the United States, but they are much more extreme in the developing world.

Other obstacles to OER also mirror those in the developed world. In many countries at the K–12 level the curriculum is centralized and the government exerts considerable control over the publication of educational material. In Pakistan, for example, the publishers are in the private sector and follow guidance from the central or provincial governments. In other countries governments have engaged international publishers originating in Singapore, the United Kingdom, other European nations, and the United States. As in the United States many of the private publishers are moving to digitize their materials as access to technology increases. This, of course, does not mean that the content is open. Central control of the textbooks and materials by the government can cut both ways when it comes to whether or not OER is adopted. If the government is happy with the publishers, OER materials may not be adopted. If, however, the publishers' prices are high while the national economy is low, and the appropriate infrastructure exists to make OERs available, the government can make a major move to favor OER.

Activity at the local level also plays an important role in fostering OERs in K–12 education. In small and large communities where there is a healthy and helpful civil society with indigenous and international NGOs, there are pockets of schools (sometimes public and sometimes private, and admittedly scattered), implementing useful technology and even OER projects. Sometimes these NGOs have also worked with governments to provide greater scale to their efforts.

The result is a steadily growing number of efforts in many countries to overcome the problems and to adopt, create, and adapt OERs to be used for K–12 classrooms. The most active areas seem to be the use of OER for pre-service and in-service teacher training, often with open videos that are available on CDs as well as on the Internet. TESSA is a powerful example of countries banding together to support the development of high-quality open materials for teacher training.[77] Teachers Without Borders works in twenty-one different developing nations across five continents providing open high-quality videos for teacher training. Their flagship program is a mentor- and peer-supported teacher professional development program available as a free download (English, Farsi, French, Spanish, and Portuguese), as well as offline through workshops and as a free self-paced online course.[78] In South Africa, under the leadership of SAIDE, nine tertiary institutions recently worked collaboratively to develop online open modules for mathematics teacher education.[79] These are only a few of many examples. One factor in the acceptance of the use of technology and OER in these situations may be the experience that educators all over the world have had with radio and TV delivery of training materials.[80]

Open textbooks and other education materials for K–12 schools are also increasing throughout the developing world. In Bangladesh, all primary and secondary students are provided with free textbooks, in hard copy and online.[81] One Laptop per Child operates in eleven countries serving roughly two million children in South America and another 500,000 in Africa. Many of these laptops use Sugar Labs, an open platform that promotes collaborative learning and places a CC BY license on much of the content that it carries.[82] In Rwanda as part of their roll-out of One Laptop per Child the government is supporting the development of open, locally made content.[83] The Open Learning Exchange is working in Rwanda, Nepal, and several other countries on a variety of projects using OERs, including teacher training and the distribution of education resources.[84]

COL is working with educators in six countries—Botswana, Lesotho, Namibia, Seychelles, Trinidad and Tobago, and Zambia—to develop and share OERs for secondary education, to provide classroom professional development of teachers, and to create learner-support material for teachers.[85] The MIT-initiated BLOSSOMS project works with educators particularly in Jordan and Pakistan to create very high quality open videos and supporting materials for classroom lessons in science and math.[86] The Khan Academy is now translating over one thousand videos, with problem sets and a tracking system for teachers into ten languages. Already the materials are being used extensively in a number of developing world nations, often distributed by third-party organizations.[87] For example, the Learning Place is a very attractive and useful site in the Philippine Islands that has pulled together OERs from around the world, including Khan Academy videos, for distribution across the islands.[88]

It seems clear that though there are often substantial technology and sociopolitical infrastructure problems at the K–12 and postsecondary levels, OERs have substantial momentum in many developing world nations. National and local governments have adopted policies that support one form or another of OERs, and NGOs are giving active support to implementation. For example, in 2011, the national legislature in Brazil debated about whether and how to support OERs, and the Sao Paulo Department of Education adopted a CC BY-SA license for its educational materials, steps not taken in most developed world nations.[89] Brazil is an outlier in South America, but in Asia a number of governments including India, Vietnam, and Indonesia have supported policies that embrace OERs.[90]

Two Emerging Opportunities for OER

Since 2000, two important events have become part of the environments of many developing world nations. Each presents opportunities and challenges for the spread of OER.

The first, the rise of mobile phones, enabled some of the least-developed nations to bypass the stage of laptops and move immediately to using mobile devices (see the introduction to this book) to receive and create or revise educational materials. Use of the cell phone for mLearning (mobile learning) has exploded around the developing world, though most of the activity fits into the small project category.[91]

In the Philippines the Text2Teach project provides teachers with lesson plans and "teacher on demand" videos on their mobile phones. The use of cell phones to deliver language instruction is being tried in a variety of places such as Pakistan's Mobilink/UNESCO project, and SMS for Literacy, which targets girls' literacy and has shown positive findings. In Bangladesh, a multiplatform project uses mobile phones (Janala) to provide language instruction in English. In a nine-month period, Janala had over three million calls.[92]

Some of these projects use OERs though others do not.[93] The World Bank, the United States Agency for International Development (USAID), and other aid agencies and major NGOs are moving rapidly toward using mobile phones to deliver education material of all kinds and to create networks among users with the same interests.[94] The underlying delivery technology for OERs is expanding and creating many powerful opportunities. More OER materials are being designed or redesigned from other platforms for use on mobile phones, and much of that content is locally developed. Here again, local and international NGOs may be more important than governments for support of the users of such innovations.

Secondly, a large component of successful efforts in development areas such as public health and agriculture involve the education of experts and of the populace, as well as sets of local and regional networks for providing, creating, and updating information in a timely way. It turns out that OERs may serve as useful vehicles for this activity. An early example was the development by Johns Hopkins University of OER public health materials.[95] Later on in the 2000s, the University of Michigan launched a public health project in Africa using OERs. Since then other funders, including USAID and the Bill & Melinda Gates Foundation, have supported public health activities in Africa, many of them through OER Africa.[96] Other countries such as Peru are exploring how to use OERs in their public health services.[97] Similar activities are happening in the agricultural field in Africa,[98] and other parts of the developing world.[99]

This chapter provides a very brief sketch of OER in the developing world. If you are a skeptical reader, carry out an experiment to measure the breadth of the OER movement. Enter into a Google search the key words *"open educational resources"* AND *any country name* for a sample of developing world nations. The results are encouraging.

The Future of OER in the Developing World: Two Possible Stories

OER implementation in the developing world is a work in progress, its evolving chapters written and shaped by optimism as well as by pragmatism. One positive storyline arises from several attractive scenarios—an improving technology infrastructure; a growing number of education-oriented local, national and international NGOs; and an abundance of quality OER digitized content of all sorts that is locally developed or rapidly being translated into multiple languages—that are playing out through much of the developing world, particularly at the postsecondary level. OERs give people in the developing world the opportunity and rights to engage in the process of changing, improving, and otherwise managing the content they need to use. The activity is empowering. Some new tools and an increase in the quality of the technical infrastructure are also beginning to give educators and others the capacity to create their own open content from scratch and to establish networks of users. The end of this story seems inevitable— that OER will be widely and effectively used and that access to low-priced technology will accelerate that evolution.

But a second less-positive story line goes something like this: While it is clear that technology is useful for many things at the higher education and K–12 levels, such as research and administrative work, useful technology for teaching and learning is a long way away. Even in the United States the promises of technologists about teaching and learning have been very optimistic for years.[100] Moreover, OERs are not universally appreciated. Adopting OERs raises all sorts of questions about the status quo and threatens many powerful organizations and people's beliefs about how things should be.

The evidence for this second story in the developing world can be seen in a multitude of examples. We have all seen or heard of situations where technology was bought and delivered to schools and then locked up and not used to protect it. Or we have seen classrooms where every student was given a laptop and many end up unused in the classroom closet because the software is not appropriate, or the electricity fails, or the computer crashes, or the operating system is so old it does not support new software. Even more poignantly many schools lack heat or toilets or blackboards or teachers. And, we do not have compelling evidence from the developing world about technology regularly making major changes on student learning and the quality of teaching.[101]

How Might OER Help Equalize Opportunity and Promote Quality in the Developing World

The concept of knowledge being a public good, and of the free distribution of knowledge and of equal opportunity for all to have access to it—like air— is radical in today's hierarchically structured and highly privileged world. The following five sets of activities offer ways to help close the gap between the opportunities of teachers and students in the developed and developing worlds. The first two engage the federal and local governments of nations to create environments that support the development of OERs. The third and fourth activities focus on the use of OERs at the local school level to address important problems in teaching and learning. The fifth suggested activity is applied research that would support the improvement of OERs throughout the world.

Improve the Technical, Political, and Legal Infrastructure

A strong and continuously improving infrastructure in the developing world is one major way to help remedy the inequities and promote high-quality open content and other resources. A significant part of this path is technical. Access to connectivity is proceeding across the world in multiple ways. Massive cabling projects in and around Africa are rapidly increasing access as noted in chapter 2. And, in regions of the world where cell phones are ubiquitous while table computers are rare, the advent of third-generation cell phone technology (3G) providing mobile Internet access has totally changed the access equation. Part of the solution involves ensuring compatible standards for interoperability among different content uses and types.

Another part of the infrastructure is political. Here the leadership from UNESCO, COL, the World Bank, Creative Commons, OECD CERI, and local advocates is critical. Strong support from major country aid agencies such as USAID and DFID would help. Ultimately, national governments will have to step up in the way just as Brazil and others have.[102] Finally, a sound infrastructure for OER requires the implementation of culturally appropriate and interoperable open licensing policies so that open materials from anywhere may be revised and remixed: the Creative Commons global license infrastructure is a good start. All of these issues need continued attention from international NGO and development organizations.

Improve and Expand Content and Academic Capacity of Universities and Schools

One major problem facing schools in low-income developing nations is the lack of educational materials, including textbooks. At the same time, for schools that have access to the Web, there is an abundance of materials that must look entirely chaotic to those not used to searching online. Over time, perhaps, search engines and massive repositories will become more and more adapted to the needs of the users around the world. Teachers then will have less trouble finding the materials that they need—but that will take a while.

There is a way of beginning to addresss this problem that is quicker and more useful. The goal for this activity would be to give every school and university in the developing world the opportunity to have a suite of books and other open and useful educational materials of their very own.

The source of the open materials would be much like an App Store for university, district and school sites. The App Store would be constructed and maintained by UNESCO or some combination of developing world nations and NGOs. Curation would be critical and must be transparent. Governments or individual schools could select materials to meet their needs. The open materials would include but not be limited to open books, virtual laboratories, simulations, online modules and courses, videos, textbooks, tools for constructing and posting OERs, as well as tools for creating and accessing existing professional networks and journals.

Many of these materials should come from the developing world. Language translation would be a challenge, but improved digital translation programs and the use of diaspora might make this less onerous. More important would be to populate the library with content and other materials from the developing and developed worlds that are free and adaptable to local needs.

The idea of a digital library is not new—a very big difference is that this particular activity would be focused on the relatively narrow mission of providing open content specifically for universities and schools. Universities would have immediate access and would be encouraged to add content. As with other ideas of substantial magnitude, it might be useful to start small by creating a prototype for K–12 schools in two to three countries. At the systems level, training the teachers and administrators of the schools and gaining the support of the national education leadership would be crucial. The Open Learning Exchange provides an example of an open library for a small number of schools in Ghana.[103]

Reaching Those Most in Need

Perhaps the most important education problem in the developing world is to reach with quality educational opportunities the four hundred million students who live in poverty (in families that live on one dollar or less a day).[104] Many families in deep poverty are found in places like the slums of Nairobi and Karachi as well as in rural areas. Some of these children are in public schooling where the governments are doing their best to provide effective services. But, others are in families that have shunned the public schools.

One of the recent extraordinary movements in the K–12 education sectors of developing nations is the rapid increase in students attending very low-priced and low-cost neighborhood private schools. Recent reports estimate that over 30 percent of students throughout Pakistan attend low-priced private schools where even the poorest parents pay the tuition.[105] While the numbers in Pakistan may be higher, there are nations in the Middle East, Southeast Asia, and Africa where the same phenomenon is occurring.[106]

These private schools, often started up by parents, have sprung up because of distrust of the public systems fueled by: corruption; lack of accountability; teachers not showing up at the schools; few textbooks; a lack of safety—especially for young girls; and poor facilities. In settings like this the priority is a safe environment and a teacher (preferably a woman) who regularly shows up at the school. These schools typically have large, cramped classes and lack connectivity often due to erratic use of electricity. The teachers in these locations may have less than a secondary school education, very little training to be a teacher, and few opportunities for professional development. Such settings cry out for innovative and inexpensive approaches to using technology and OERs.

The basic idea here is to use Khan Academy or some other coherent body of open materials to teach concepts that are not fully familiar to the teacher, such as those in math and science. Implementation support from a local NGO would be very useful in this situation, though in cities local teachers that form communities of support might play this role. The materials (which would be mapped to local standards) would be loaded onto a USB memory stick or a SD card.[107] If the schools had access to a laptop solution they might be using the raspberry pi, a credit card sized–single board computer plugged in to television.[108] But if a computer were not available they would need another solution.

Since about 2010 small, inexpensive projectors (less than $100) have come on the market.[109] The projectors have rechargeable batteries, read from a SD card and project video on any flat surface.[110] The NGO would buy such a projector and train the teacher(s) to use the content by playing videos that show exemplary teaching of the material. The teachers would project ten-to-fifteen minute videos on the wall and then have a discussion with the class about what they saw. Each video would explain a concept or method of solving a problem. If necessary, a video might be rerun in part or in whole to help clarify the students' understanding. Problem sets on the SD card might be used after the lesson.

This is an extremely low-cost, work-around solution—the cost of the projector may be spread over a few years. The materials are free and reusable and may be adapted for local use. The result is clear, accurate instruction provided in math and science to classrooms where neither topic had been previously well taught. This simple solution also would have the by-product of helping the teacher to better understand the mathematics and science she is responsible for teaching. The biggest challenge in this proposal might be to convince key northern nation development agencies like USAID to take what they might see as a risk and provide local NGOs in the Global South with the funds to give OERs a try.

Changing Teaching and Learning

The opportunities to improve teaching and learning throughout the developing world provided by open materials, the ubiquity of cell phones, very low-cost computers, and the possibility of low-tech solutions using projectors are legion. One idea is that these factors make possible very large-scale (even countrywide) projects of teacher professional development using OER videos. The open structure dramatically reduces costs and allows translation and other modifications to adapt the materials to varying locales. It also creates opportunities for the development of professional networks among teacher and/or administrators. These are critical steps to the implementation of any new curriculum materials and have often been disregarded because of the challenges of implementing to scale.

A second idea would be the introduction of Project Based Learning (PBL) into even high-poverty schools in a country.[111] Projects are typically designed to solve a problem or explore a particular question. These are tasks that often require collaboration among students and the use of evidence, inquiry, time management, and communication skills.

Technology and open content can remove barriers to PBL in the developed and developing worlds. Imagine that teachers had electronic access to a small, curated library of open projects that are fully explained and aligned with their local curriculum and standards. Teachers could select projects from the library that would also include materials explaining the project to the teachers. Teacher networks could share information about their success in using the PBL and modify the materials as they learned how to successfully implement them.

Improvement and Research

A variety of organizations such as the Open University of the UK, COL, Carnegie-Mellon University, and the International Development Research

Centre of Canada (IDRC), Creative Commons, as well as independent scholars including David Wiley at Brigham Young University, are conducting or supporting research about OERs. The studies cover a series of topics but do not together begin to represent a coherent agenda. As OERs begin to be an important factor in education, particularly in the developing world, a crisp and useful research agenda becomes more important. One way of structuring the agenda is to think about the research questions in five categories.

One category addresses knowledge about development and design of technology tools for OERs. The rights of reuse and to create derivative works turns users into creators and sometimes calls for particular design characteristics. For example, open content placed on a platform that makes it impossible or very difficult for a user to modify the content has lost a key ingredient of openness. This also holds for content that is intended to be continuously improved over time.

We need to know more about rapid development strategies that enable improvement through intensive user testing of open products as they are developed. When some of the products such as free online learning programs go into more general use with the right platforms the behavior of the users create massive amounts of data that have considerable promise of improving our understanding of how students learn. When the programs and data are open the usefulness of the data increases exponentially as more researchers become involved.[112]

A second category for OER research addresses the need to understand the effects of the access right. One answer is pretty simple—without MIT OCW, the world outside of Cambridge would not have access to the theory and structure and content of MIT courses. The numbers of users, the answers to questions posed to users, the time users spend on the site and looking at different courses all provide information that indicate the effectiveness and usefulness of the open materials. Another example of the access right comes from an early MOOC. The first MIT course was in electronics. It attracted 155,000 students and 7,157 students passed. One of the 345 perfect scores was by a fifteen-year-old in Mongolia.[113] Access alone is one thing, but making use of access is another. The young person from Mongolia did both. Part of a larger research agenda around access would be analyzing who benefits—are the benefits taken advantage of by rich and poor alike, by Global North and Global South alike, and, if not, is there something that might be done to reduce any differences in opportunity?

A third research area would be the exploration of the use and effects of the derivative right. The translation of open content is an important use of the derivative right—it creates access for many who could not otherwise use the content. But who makes use of the derivative right to translate or to otherwise improve or adapt the content to their needs? Under what circumstances, how often, and to what effect? Are there different ways of making content that is easy to alter? These are important questions for which we have barely scratched the surface. It is entirely possible, for example, that derivative rights are not exercised in situations that call for them because the right is misunderstood or the process is too complex.

A fourth category is research or evaluation on the end/outcome effectiveness of the OER. Seen through one lens, the issue is easy. Most end users in circumstances where technology is aimed to improve teaching and learning do not make a distinction between commercial and OER materials. In almost every setting the effectiveness for end-users of commercial technology in improving teaching and learning could be matched by the use of similar OERs. Thus the effectiveness of a particular OER may be equated with the effectiveness of similar non-OER material. (For example, earlier in this chapter I cited a meta-analysis by SRI International of the effectiveness of online courses and inferred that OER courses could have had such an effect when none of the courses in the meta-analysis had been OER.) This does not mean studies of OER effectiveness should not be carried out. They should, and there should be studies of commercial products. Both sets of studies would provide useful information about the specific products and would provide general information about the quality of the content and instruction that students receive.

If, however, the view of effective OERs is expanded to consider other ways that it adds value beyond what a similar commercial product might give to the user, there is a lot more to explore. In most cases the access right adds value and the open textbook movement has gained a lot of its momentum because it reduces cost to students—reduced cost and increased access clearly added value to users.

The derivative right is also a source of possible "added value" for an OER. It is hard, for example, to argue against the added value gained from translating an effective and needed OER. A strong argument also can be made for assuming added value when teachers or other local people adapt OERs to meet the needs of a local culture. Adapting to local needs has the possible effect of making the materials more effective—it may also create capacity and a sense of accomplishment for the teacher creators at the local level. As a by-product, the capacity to change and improve materials can easily spur the development of networks of practice among the local teachers. These are measurable outcomes, even if they are not test scores. Yet we know little about all of this.

Finally, the last part of a possible OER research agenda would be to support and help strengthen local capacity to carry out research and evaluations in the developing world. The IDRC is currently supporting research focused on better understanding the "value of Open Education Resources in the Global South." This form of research should both improve our knowledge about OERs and create greater local research capacity.

Conclusion

Article 26.1 of the Universal Declaration of Human Rights[114] states that "Everyone has the right to education." Since the 1990s, the Internet has created a tangible way for anyone with access to exercise this right, and more recently OERs have broadened the scope of available educational resources. OERs have also expanded the number of people (students, self-learners, teachers, and professors alike) who benefit from and contribute to the global pool of educational resources, regardless of geographic location or socioeconomic status. That, after all, is the power of "openness for development."

Acknowledgments

The work on this chapter was supported by the William and Flora Hewlett Foundation, the Spencer Foundation, and the Qatar Foundation International. I thank the Carnegie Foundation for the Advancement of Teaching for a quiet work place, and I am grateful to Matthew L. Smith and his colleagues at IDRC, Richard Rowe of the Open Learning Exchange, Kathy Nicholson of the Hewlett Foundation, and Cable Green from Creative Commons for their careful reading, comments, and suggestions on earlier drafts of this chapter.

Notes

1. See www.ocwconsortium.org/en and http://ocw.mit.edu/index.htm.

2. See www.khanacademy.org and http://www.youtube.com/user/khanacademy.

3. See http://tessaafrica.net.

4. See http://www.tessafrica.net/index.php?option=com_content&view=article&id=2&Itemid=353.

5. See http://www.tessaafrica.net.

6. As of April 22, 2013, a Google search of "Open Educational Resources" brought up over 22 million results. In July 2001, that number was effectively zero.

7. This chapter cannot capture the incredible growth and scope of OER: See for example: T. Iiyoshi and M. S. Kumar, eds., *Opening Up Education* (Cambridge, MA: MIT Press, 2008); and J. Glennie, K. Harley, N. Butcher, and T. vanWyk, "Open Educational Resources and Change in Higher Education: Reflections from Practice" (Vancouver: Commonwealth of Learning, 2012).

8. M. S. Smith and C. M. Casserly, "The Promise of Open Educational Resources," *Change: The Magazine of Higher Learning* 38, no. 5 (2006): 8. Wikipedia uses the definition from the William and Flora Hewlett Foundation: "OER are teaching, learning, and research resources that reside in the public domain or have been released under an intellectual property license that permits their free use or re-purposing by others. Open educational resources include full courses, course materials, modules, textbooks, streaming videos, tests, software, and any other tools, materials, or techniques used to support access to knowledge."

9. "In the United States, all books and other works published before 1923 have expired copyrights and are in the public domain.[40] In addition, works published before 1964 that did not have their copyrights renewed 28 years after first publication year also are in the public domain, except that books originally published outside the U.S. by non-Americans are exempt from this requirement, if they are still under copyright in their home country." See Wikipedia article "Copyright," http://en.wikipedia.org/wiki/Copyright.

10. The U.S. Constitution provides the legal framework for the copyright law with the language: "To promote the Progress of Science and useful Arts, by securing for limited Times to Authors and Inventors the exclusive Right to their respective Writings and Discoveries." The Congress with helpful pressure from vested interests interprets and then reinterprets the words "for limited times." For more detail see http://en.wikipedia.org/wiki/Copyright.

11. See the Creative Common website page "About the Licenses," http://creativecommons.org/licenses.

12. See the Wikipedia article "Copyright," http://en.wikipedia.org/wiki/Copyright. For background also see L. Lessig, *Free Culture* (New York: Penguin Press, 2004).

13. T. Jefferson, "Thomas Jefferson to Isaac McPherson," in *The Founders' Constitution*, Volume 3, Article 1, Section 8, Clause 8, Document 12, August 13, 1813, ed. P. B. Kurland and R. Lerner (Chicago: The University of Chicago; The Liberty Fund), http://press-pubs.uchicago.edu/founders/documents/a1_8_8s12.html. See also A. A. Lipscomb and A. E. Bergh, eds., *The Writings of Thomas Jefferson* (Washington: Thomas Jefferson Memorial Association, 1905).

14. MIT faculty also realized that their formal courses were only a part of the overall educational experience of an onsite MIT student.

15. See Wikipedia article on "Copyleft," http://en.wikipedia.org/wiki/Copyleft. Also see http://www.gnu.org/licenses.

16. Connexions is located at http://cnx.org. Connexions' blanket license enables open use of all of the materials on the website.

17. See http://creativecommons.org/licenses/by-nc/3.0.

18. For some materials with a noncommercial (NC) license the creators/owners have specified that a user might ask their permission to waive the NC provision, perhaps even suggesting a revenue sharing deal.

19. See "Indigenous/Traditional Knowledge and Intellectual Property," http://web .law.duke.edu/cspd/itkpaper4.

20. See UNESCO, "2012 Paris OER Declaration," *World Open Educational Resources (OER) Congress* (Paris: UNESCO, June 20–22, 2012), http://www.unesco.org/new/ fileadmin/MULTIMEDIA/HQ/CI/CI/pdf/Events/Paris%20OER%20Declaration_01.pdf.

21. See http://en.wikipedia.org/wiki/Project_Gutenberg and http://www.gutenberg .org.

22. See http://en.wikipedia.org/wiki/Internet_Archive and http://archive.org.

23. Kirk Winters, an innovative staff person in the United States' Deputy Secretary of Education's office in 1997–1998, gathered together a collection of digitized education materials collected from many U.S. government agencies and posted them on the Web at www.free.ed.gov. The site is still healthy and interesting.

24. See http://en.wikipedia.org/wiki/Open_Content_License.

25. See http://www.creativecomons.org and http://en.wikipedia.org/wiki/Creative _Commons.

26. C. M. Vest, "Disturbing the Educational Universe: Universities in the Digital Age—Dinosaurs or Prometheans?," *Report of the President 2000–2001*, MIT, 2001, http://web.mit.edu/president/communications/rpt00-01.html.

27. Marshall S. Smith and Catherine M. Casserly guided the OER work for Hewlett from 2001 to 2009. For general information on the Hewlett approach to stimulating the OER movement see www.hewlett.org; see also D. E. Atkins, J. S. Brown, and A. L. Hammond, "A Review of the Open Educational Resources (OER) Movement: Achievement, Challenges, and New Opportunities," 2007, http://www.hewlett.org/uploads/ files/ReviewoftheOERMovement.pdf; see also Smith and Casserly "The Promise," 2006; and M. S. Smith, "Opening Education," *Science* 323, no. 5910 (2009): 89–93.

28. J. Willinsky, *The Access Principle: The case for open Access to Research and Scholarship* (Cambridge, MA: MIT Press, 2006): 1. "Open Access" has been defined by the Budapest Open Access Initiative (2002) and Bethesda statements on Open Access Publishing (2003); see Willinsky, p. 213; see Public Library of Science, http://www.plos.org; see "The Directory of Open Access Journals," http://www.doaj.org. There are almost 9000 open journals available on this site; see, for a review of the progress of open access since 2006, http://www.plosone.org/article/info:doi/10.1371/journal.pone.0020961.

29. See Reuters, "European Commission Backs Calls for Open Access to Scientific Research," *The Guardian*, July 17, 2012, http://www.guardian.co.uk/science/2012/jul/17/european-commission-open-access-scientific-research; see also E. Sample, "Free Access to British Scientific Research within Two Years," *The Guardian*, July 15, 2012, http://www.guardian.co.uk/science/2012/jul/15/free-access-british-scientific-research.

30. See "Bought to Book," *The Economist*, July 21, 2012, http://www.economist.com/node/21559317; see Wikipedia article "Open Access," http://en.wikipedia.org/wiki/Open_access.

31. See "World Bank Announces Open Access Policy for Research and Knowledge," http://web.worldbank.org/WBSITE/EXTERNAL/NEWS/0,,contentMDK:23164491~pagePK:64257043~piPK:437376~theSitePK:4607,00.html.

32. See open courses, http://www.montereyinstitute.org/nroc; "Open Learning Initiative," http://oli.cmu.edu; open textbooks, http://www.opentextbook.org/; Open Platforms Open University of the United Kingdom, Open-Learn, http://open.edu/openlearn; materials from public television, http://openvault.wgbh.org; academic journals, http://www.doaj.org; book collections, http://www.archive.org/index.php and Google.com; free online science simulations, http://phet.colorado.edu; do a Google search using "open educational resources" or "opencourseware."

33. See for a list of open and partially closed sites for teachers, http://www.leasttern.com/teacher/lessonplans.html

34. See http://lreforschools.eun.org/web/guest;jsessionid=FB89E59535BE844A879420F5BB58EA1B and http://fire.eun.org.

35. See http://www.oercommons.org and http://welcome.curriki.org.

36. See www.Khanacademy.org and http://www.youtube.com/user/khanacademy and http://phet.colorado.edu.

37. See "Fair Use," http://en.wikipedia.org/wiki/Fair_use.

38. See http://www.gatesfoundation.org/press-releases/Pages/fundamental-changes-to-community-college-education-091203.aspx.

39. K. Carey, "The Quiet Revolution in Open Learning," *The Chronicle of Higher Education,* May 15, 2011, http://chronicle.com/article/The-Quiet-Revolution-in-Open/127545.

40. In 2008, Stephen Downes and George Siemens took a course that they were co-teaching at the University of Manitoba and opened it up to the public for free on the Web. Roughly 2,300 people registered. After the course David Cormier of the University of Prince Edward Island called the course a Massive Open Online Course (MOOC), a name that stuck.

41. See https://www.coursera.org.

42. See http://en.wikipedia.org/wiki/Udacity.

43. See "Massive Open Online Course," http://en.wikipedia.org/wiki/massive_open_online_course.

44. See https://www.edx.org/press/edX-announces-proctored-exam-testing.

45. For a discussion of two models of MOOCs, see http://mfeldstein.com/moocs-two-different-approaches-to-scale-access-and-experimentation.

46. See http://www.ck12.org/about/ for information about the CK-12 Foundation. See http://openstaxcollege.org.

47. See, for example, the library of free textbooks that the CK–12 Foundation has created and published under a Creative Commons license. The California State Board of Education recently approved a number of these texts for use in California: http://www.ck12.org/about/freetextbooks. See also Utah Open Textbook Project, http://utahopentextbooks.org/about.

48. See the discussion of how textbooks will morph into teaching programs in the near future in M. S. Smith, "Opening Education," *Science* 323, no. 5910 (2009): 89–93. See also the website for Leadership Public Schools in the United States where teachers have tailored CK-12 math and biology textbooks to teach rigorous content and literacy skills simultaneously, http://www.leadps.org/academic-program/research.

49. See http://www.achieve.org/oer-rubrics.

50. The publishers keep a steady drumbeat against the U.S. government paying for the development of materials that would be open and free and that would compete with their products. An early claim was that OERs were of low quality because they were free—a variation on "you get what you pay for." A troublesome point for the publishers is that they rarely publish data about the effectiveness of their products and independent assessments of education products from commercial entities have not shown particularly positive results. See http://ies.ed.gov/ncee/wwc. The What Works Clearinghouse has data on only a handful of the current most widely used curriculum materials and only a few pass their criteria for high quality.

51. "See http://pandodaily.com/2013/02/18/boundless-challenges-textbook-publishers-to-trial-over-oer and http://chronicle.com/blogs/wiredcampus/publishers-criticize-federal-investment-in-open-educational-resources/31483.

52. The firing and then rehiring of the president of the University of Virginia during early summer 2012 has been attributed to the general tension felt by many higher education institutions between gradual and abrupt change in how to position the university in the area of online learning, including MOOCs.

53. The Student PIRGS is a strong advocate for affordable college textbooks, including openly licensed textbook options. For more information see http://www.studentpirgs.org/campaigns/sp/make-textbooks-affordable.

54. For information about the MIT linear algebra course taught by Professor Gilbert Strang, see http://ocw.mit.edu/courses/mathematics/18-06-linear-algebra-spring-2010.

55. See http://www2.ed.gov/rschstat/eval/tech/evidence-based-practices/finalreport.pdf.

56. Most of the courses included in the SRI meta-analysis were created prior to 2007. Since then, the technology and content of online courses have improved rapidly and substantially, in part by becoming more sensitive and adaptive to individual learner differences. By the end of 2014 there should be a set of evaluations of some of the MITE collection of courses at http://www.hippocampus.org/ and of the Khan Academy materials, www.khanacademy.org and http://www.youtube.com/user/khanacademy.

57. See http://oli.cmu.edu/publications.

58. For the full study and other studies in this series, see http://www.sr.ithaka.org/research-publications/interactive-learning-online-public-universities-evidence-randomized-trials.

59. See http://openstudy.com.

60. The courses are also open to free use by anyone at http://www.hippocampus.org.

61. See "Linux," http://en.wikipedia.org/wiki/Linux; see also "Connexions," http://cnx.org.

62. See R. Winthrop and M. S. Smith, "A New Face of Education: Bringing Technology into the Classroom in the Developing World," in *Brooke Sheaer Working Paper Series 1*, (Washington, DC: Brookings Institution, January 2012) http://www.brookings.edu/research/papers/2012/01/education-technology-winthrop. However, even when the Internet connection is not particularly good, students and professors often have access to the institution's intranet, which can be loaded with much of the educational material necessary for their teaching and learning. Of course, there

are still some higher education institutions where there is no connection and no intranet.

63. See J. Anderson, "III. Current Proposals: Dangers, Problems and Opportunities," in *Indigenous/Traditional Knowledge and Intellectual Property*, Center for the Study of the Public Domain Issues Paper (Durham, NC: Duke University School of Law, 2010), http://web.law.duke.edu/cspd/itkpaper4.

64. In a sweeping talk on technology and learning and OER, Sir John Daniel cites the concerns about neo-colonialism, see J. Daniel "Commonwealth of Learning: Welcome and Introductory Remarks," http://www.col.org/resources/speeches/2010presentation/Pages/2010-09-29a.aspx. In 2009 at a UNESCO meeting in Paris, titled the World Conference on Higher Education, during a debate between Brenda Gourley, then vice chancellor of the Open University of the UK, and Barney Pityana, then vice chancellor of the University of South Africa, Professor Pityana "took issue with the enthusiasm for OER fearing it would lead to a wave of intellectual neo-colonialism whereby the rich north would push these resources at the poor south without thought of reciprocity." See Glennie et al., "Open Educational Resources," 2012.

65. See S. D'Antoni, "The Virtual University," *UNESCO*, 2006 http://www.unesco.org/iiep/virtualuniversity/home.php for some case studies of virtual universities supported by UNESCO in 2006.

66. See http://www.youtube.com/user/vu and http://reganmian.net/blog/2010/05/21/the-virtual-university-of-pakistan-has-6000-hours-of-video-lectures-on-youtube.

67. See http://ocw.vu.edu.pk.

68. S. D'Antoni, "Virtual University," 2012. See also B. Schreurs, (ed.), *Reviewing the Virtual Campus Phenomenon: The Rise of Large-Scale E-Learning Initiatives Worldwide* (Haverlee: EuroPACE, 2007), http://revica.europace.org/Re.ViCa%20Online%20Handbook.pdf.

69. See http://en.wikipedia.org/wiki/China_Open_Resources_for_Education. CORE is now less active having served its original purposes of introducing OCW and other OER to China. For information about Universia and other groups translating MIT OCW see http://ocw.mit.edu/courses/translated-courses/. Also see www.myoops.org and http://www.myoops.org/en. These later URLs are the sites of a Lucifer Chu who uses Diaspora to translate education materials from English to Chinese.

70. See http://www.oerafrica.org/Portals/0/2009.07.30.SAIDE-OERPolicy.pdf.

71. See S. D'Antoni, "Interview on OER: Interview with Susan D'Antoni, IIEP," interview with ICDE, *International Council for Open and Distance Education* (n.d.), https://icde.org/icde.org/filestore/Resources/Taskforce_on_OER/InterviewwithSDAntoni.pdf.

72. See http://www.col.org/Pages/default.aspx.

73. See http://www.col.org/progServ/programmes/Pages/VUSSC.aspx; see also http://www.vussc.info. Daniels wrote his doctoral dissertation at Oxford on online learning.

74. Brazil's report is at http://iite.unesco.org/pics/publications/en/files/3214695.pdf and for a full list of the reports see http://iite.unesco.org/publications/themes/oer (accessed August 30, 2012).

75. Glennie and others, "Open Educational Resources," 2012.

76. See http://www.col.org/PublicationDocuments/Survey_On_Government_OER _Policies.pdf.

77. See http://www.tessafrica.net/.

78. See http://www.teacherswithoutborders.org/programs/core-programs/certificate -teaching-mastery and http://www.teacherswithoutborders.org/resources#.

79. I. Sapire and Y. Reed, "Collaborative Design and Use of Open Educational Resources: A Case Study of Mathematics Teacher Education Project in South Africa," *Distance Education* 32, no. 2 (Special Issue: Distance Education for Empowerment and Development in Africa, 2011): 195–211.

80. R. Winthrop and M. S. Smith, "A New Face of Education," 23–24.

81. Shafiq Islam, "Free Textbooks for Primacy and Secondary Students," *Demotix*, January 2, 2010, http://www.demotix.com/news/215851/free-text-books-primary -and-secondary-students#slide-1; Bangladeshi Information Notifier, "Download Free Bangla and English Textbooks of NCTB for Class 1 SSC Level," *BDTalks.com,* July 3, 2010, http://bdtalks.com/download-free-bangla-english-textbooks-of-nctb-from -class-1-to-ssc-level.

82. See http://www.sugarlabs.org.

83. Replacing Textbooks, http://replacingtextbooks.wordpress.com.

84. See http://www.ole.org/blog.

85. See http://www.col.org/progServ/programmes/education/Pages/openSchooling .aspx.

86. See http://blossoms.mit.edu/partners/current_partners.

87. Khan Academy, http://www.khanacademy.org. See also, http://www.dutiee .com/taking-khan-academy-to-mongolia-in-wireless-routers; http://khanacademy .desk.com/customer/portal/articles/329337-is-khan-academy-available-in-other -languages-.

88. See http://www.thelearningplace.ph (accessed September 10, 2012).

89. See https://creativecommons.org/weblog/entry/27698. Unfortunately the governor of San Palo vetoed the action and the matter is still under consideration at the time of this writing.

90. See S. Hoosen, "Survey on Governments' Open Educational Resources (OER) Policies," *World OER Congress* (COL and UNESCO: June 2012), http://www.col.org/resources/publications/Pages/detail.aspx?PID=408.

91. See the introduction to this volume.

92. See R. Winthrop and M. S. Smith, "A New Face of Education."

93. See GSMA Development Fund, 2010, mLearning: A Platform for Educational Opportunities at the Base of the Pyramid, GSMA Development Fund. http://www.mobileactive.org/files/file_uploads/mLearning_Report_Final_Dec2010.pdf.

94. See, for example, http://www.meducationalliance.org/.

95. See http://ocw.jhsph.edu/?select=www.

96. See Africa Health OER Network, http://www.oerafrica.org/FTPFolder/Website%20Materials/Health/Newsletters/2012/July-2012-edition.htm.

97. See "Workshop on the Regional Network of Open Education Resources Concludes," *Virtual Campus for Public Health,* August, 2012, http://www.campusvirtualsp.org/?q=en/workshop-regional-network-open-educational-resources-concludes.

98. See "AgShare Open Educational Resources (OER) Collaboration," *Saide,* http://www.saide.org.za/resources/newsletters/Vol_16_no.6_2010/Content/Agshare.htm and "eLearning," *World Agroforestry Centre,* http://www.worldagroforestrycentre.org/learning/elearning.

99. See http://openeducation.zunia.org/cat/agricultural-science.

100. See A. Oettinger and S. Marks, *Run Computer Run: The Myth of Educational Innovation* (Cambridge, MA: Harvard University Press, 1969); L. Cuban, *Oversold and Underused: Computers in the Classroom* (Cambridge, MA: Harvard University Press, 2001).

101. See C. P. Bouillon (ed.), *Room for Development: Housing Markets in Latin America and the Caribbean,* (New York: Palgrave MacMillan, 2012), http://www.iadb.org/en/research-and-data/dia-publication-details,3185.html.

102. In the U.S. Department of Education, Under-Secretary Martha Kanter and her senior assistant, Hal Plotkin, have actively supported the use of OER for government-supported content.

103. See http://www.ole.org.

104. The estimate of 400 million is based upon the UNICEF number of 600 million children in poverty. Many of these 600 million would not be of school age. See http://www.unicef.org/mdg/poverty.html.

105. See F. Barrera-Osorio and D. Raju, "Evaluating a Test-Based Public Subsidy Program for Low Cost Private Schools: Regression-Discontinuity Evidence from Pakistan," *The World Bank*, May, 2009 http://www.globalpartnership.org/epdf/uploads/183l; http://siteresources.worldbank.org/EDUCATION/Resources/278200-1126210664195/1636971-1238439091031/RDD-based_Pakistan_FAS_evaluation.pdf and "Low Cost Private School Survey," *Pakistan Education Task Force* (Karachi: September 2010) http://www.affordable-learning.com/research-fieldwork/library/pakistan.html#sthash.VUoknSeu.dpbs; http://enterprisingschools.com/library/documents/low-cost-private-school-survey-highlights.

106. It is very difficult to obtain accurate figures for the percentage of the population of students attending low priced private schools—the national figures appear to mislead as do the figures of the various international aid organizations. Perhaps because most aid from countries and the World Bank and other major banks go to the government they tend to ignore the expansion of the low priced schools. See J. Stanfield, "Self Help and Sustainability Education in Developing Countries," *E.G. West Centre* EFA Working Paper no. 10 (2010): 1–53, http://ebookbrowse.com/gdoc.php?id=383232534&url=dc2f37051ea769f9f494eed9a13d5b75, for an interesting paper that uses Elinor Ostrom's Nobel Prize work on how local people and communities organize to solve their own problems, such as participation in a quality school. See the following papers for studies of the effects of the growth in low cost private schools in India. See S. Pal and G. G. Kindon, "Can Private School Growth Foster Universal Literacy? Panel Evidence from Indian Districts," *IZA*, Discussion paper No. 5274 (October 2010): 1–35, http://ftp.iza.org/dp5274.pdf; J. Tooley and P. Dixon, "Private Schooling for Low-Income Families: A Census and Comparative Survey in East Delhi, India," *International Journal of Educational Development* 27, no. 2 (2007): 205–219; and F. Smith, F. Hardman, and J. Tooley, "Classroom Interaction in Private Schools Serving Low-Income Families in Hyderabad, India," *International Education Journal* 6, no. 5 (2005): 607–618, http://ehlt.flinders.edu.au/education/iej/articles/v6n5/Smith/paper.pdf. For sample case studies of Kenyan schools, see "Private Low Cost Schools in Mathare," *Mathare Sio Kenya*, August 22, 2012, http://matharesiokenya.wordpress.com/2012/08/22/private-low-cost-schools-in-mathare; and C. Epari, A. Ezeh, F. Mugisha, and R. Ogollah, "Oh! So 'We' Have Been Under-reporting Nairobi's Primary School Enrollment Rates?," *African Population and Health Research Center*, APHRC Working Paper No. 35 (2008): 1–16, http://www.aphrc.org/images/Downloads/Working%20Paper%20-%2035.pdf.

107. Many of the Khan Academy materials are being translated into ten languages other than English and, therefore, can probably be delivered in the local language of instruction.

108. See http://www.federicopistono.org/category/stream_consciousness/technology; http://one.laptop.org/; and http://www.raspberrypi.org/. For a discussion of the use of Khan Academy and raspberry pi see http://www.khanacademy.org/about/blog/post/37937773408/introducing-khan-academy-lite.

109. "Portable Pocket Projector," http://www.amazon.com/NEW-PP003-Portable-Pocket-Projector/dp/B004CSZVDM.

110. See http://en.wikipedia.org/wiki/SecureDigital for an explanation of a SD card.

111. See http://www.unescobkk.org/education/ict/online-resources/features/pbl-ict and http://pbl-online.org. See also www.showevidence.com for an example of a platform designed to enable problem-based assessments to be used and made by teachers.

112. See National Science Foundation, "Fostering Learning in the Networked World: The Cyberlearning Opportunity and Challenge," *Report of the NSF Task Force on Cyberlearning*, (2008), http://www.nsf.gov/pubs/2008/nsf08204/nsf08204_1.pdf.

113. See S. Coughlan, "Harvard and MIT Online Courses get 'Real World' Exams," *BBC News,* September 6, 2012, www.bbc.co.uk/news/education-19505776.

114. See http://www.un.org/rights/50/decla.htm.

Bibliography

Carey, K. "The Quiet Revolution in Open Learning." *Chronicle of Higher Education* (May 15) (2011). http://chronicle.com/article/The-Quiet-Revolution-in-Open/127545.

D'Antoni, S. "The Virtual University." *UNESCO,* 2006. http://www.unesco.org/iiep/virtualuniversity/home.php.

Glennie, J., K. Harley, N. Butcher, and T. vanWyk. *Open Educational Resources and Change in Higher Education: Reflections from Practice*. Vancouver: Commonwealth of Learning, 2012. http://www.col.org/resources/publications/Pages/detail.aspx?PID=412.

Jefferson, T. "Thomas Jefferson to Isaac McPherson." In *The Founders Constitution*, Volume 3, Article 1, Section 8, Clause 8, Document 12, August 13, 1813, ed. P. B. Kurland and R. Lerner (Chicago: The University of Chicago; The Liberty Fund).

Sapire, I., and Y. Reed. "Collaborative Design and Use of Open Educational Resources: A Case Study of Mathematics Teacher Education Project in South Africa." *Distance Education* 32 (2) (Special Issue: Distance Education for Empowerment and Development in Africa, 2011): 195–211.

Smith, M. S. "Opening Education," Science 323 (5910) (2009): 89–93.

Smith, M. S., and C. M. Casserly. "The Promise of Open Educational Resources." *Change: The Magazine of Higher Learning* 38 (5) (2006): 8–17.

Vest, C. M. "Disturbing the Educational Universe: Universities in the Digital Age—Dinosaurs or Prometheans?" *Report of the President 2000–2001.* MIT, 2001. http://web.mit.edu/president/communications/rpt00-01.html.

Willinsky, J. *The Access Principle: The Case for Open Access to Research and Scholarship.* Cambridge, MA: The MIT Press, 2006.

Winthrop, R., and M. S. Smith. "A New Face of Education: Bringing Technology into the Classroom in the Developing World." *Brooke Sheaer Working Paper Series 1*, Washington, DC: Brookings Institution, January 2012. http://www.brookings.edu/research/papers/2012/01/education-technology-winthrop.

II Openness in Tension

7 Establishing Public-ness in the Network: New Moorings for Development—A Critique of the Concepts of Openness and Open Development

Parminder Jeet Singh and Anita Gurumurthy

The public sector is at present the decisive actor to develop and shape the network society. Individual innovators, counter-cultural communities, and business firms have done their job at inventing a new society and diffusing it around the world. The shaping and guiding of this society is, as has always been the case in other societies, in the hands of the public sector, regardless of ideological discourses hiding this reality. And yet, the public sector is the sphere of society where new communication technologies are the least diffused and where organizational obstacles to innovation and networking are the most pronounced. Thus, reform of the public sector commands everything else in the process of productive shaping of the network society.

—Manuel Castells[1]

The term *openness* is uniquely associated with the new communication paradigm made possible by the Internet. As the disruptive influence of Internet-based information and communication technologies (ICTs) is felt across social structures and institutions, the dominant techno-utopian vision of openness carries the promise of unbridled freedom. But does the concept of *openness*, or more specifically, related ideas like *open society* and *open development*, provide useful points of departure for thinking about social change and development in the information society? In this chapter we focus on some recent theorizations of openness in relation to development, especially the hypothesis that *open social systems* generate positive development outcomes.[2] This chapter offers a critique of this vision, and briefly addresses alternative theoretical points of departure for development in the information or network society. Specifically, we argue that development in the information society would be better served by the concept of public-ness than the concept of openness.

It is first useful to identify areas where the term *openness* has come to have a relatively clear and well-established meaning, and has proved its conceptual usefulness. These areas are: (1) information and knowledge systems; and (2) information and communication technology (ICT) architectures. In the first case, greater access to information and knowledge, which in essence is a nonrival good, significantly enhances people's overall life opportunities. Given that new ICTs enable near-seamless communication and uninterrupted information flows, a good case can be made for open information and knowledge systems as key enablers of development, in all areas. It is obviously advantageous for people to have as much access to information as possible about the workings of social systems that impact their lives, especially the governance systems that are supposed to be accountable to them. In fact, *open government* is a term that predates the use of the term *openness* in the technology or information society arena. It basically implies "the notion that the people have the right to access the documents and proceedings of government."[3]

The second domain where the term *openness* has been applied usefully is regarding the architecture of ICTs, which increasingly mediate a large part of our social existence. An open ICT architecture, in terms of software, connectivity, hardware, content, and so forth, is important to ensure a level playing field for all, and for egalitarian social outcomes in the information society. Openness in this context means that the basic elements of our socio-technical architecture cannot be captured and controlled by a few powerful entities, and that people not only have easy access to them, but are also enabled to build, change, and rebuild them in a collaborative and bottom-up manner. Many researchers and practitioners, including some contributors to this book, argue persuasively that open technology models may be more favorable to development. Such models can allow freer and easier propagation of technology. Also, contextual modifications can be suited to address marginalized groups who may not be served by proprietary models of technology. Such models also enable faster and richer development of technology, through the collaborative effort of many people.

Whereas open information and knowledge systems, and open ICT architectures, can arguably be expected to promote development, they may not provide enough of a basis to generalize the validity and desirability of the concept of openness across the domain of development. For example, a recent working paper by Matthew L. Smith and colleagues on Open ICT4D argues that: "there are many processes that can be made more open through the use of ICTs and that doing so will generate development outcomes that are accomplished: (a) in a more efficient and/or effective manner, and/or (b) in ways that earlier were not possible."[4] It is not clear on what basis a general connection between openness and positive development outcomes has been made. The feel-good quality of openness seems to simply have been reified uncritically vis-à-vis structures and processes of development.

In the pages that follow, we consider the implications of extending the idea of openness beyond its specific use in the areas of information systems and ICT architectures. We first analyze how terms like *openness, access, participation* and *collaboration* are being subtly co-opted by a neoliberal discourse on the information society. We then consider some specific information society practices that exemplify and reinforce such co-optation, and follow that with a brief examination of how the concept of openness has been employed by those who resist the very ideology of development. We conclude by proposing an alternative approach to theorizing development in the information society founded in the idea of public-ness rather than openness.

The Theory of Openness

We take *openness* to mean, broadly, decreased constraints on social interactions. The principal social impact of new ICTs stems from their ability to reduce the cost, and improve the effectiveness, of mediated social transactions and interactions. Thus, in the emerging information society, a much more complex array of transactions is possible outside the boundaries of existing organizations and institutions. These can take place in relatively unstructured or flexible ways. The resulting social changes are the basis for the claim that networks are emerging as the principal organizational form of the information society.[5]

ICT-mediated social interactions can significantly strain the dominant vertical-hierarchical institutional paradigm, pushing it in the direction of more horizontal and flexible social structures. This shift holds out the promise of a more equitable distribution of power, an idea that informs the typical technocratic worldview. But such a promise cannot simply be taken at face value. As Manuel Castells argues, networks left to their own devices can cause even deeper exclusion than the world has yet known.[6] This insight needs to centrally inform any theorization around new social processes and structures in the emerging information society, especially in relation to development.

New ICTs do provide a new set of possibilities to overcome the typical constraints of vertical-hierarchical organizations and institutions. These possibilities, however, require to be actively harnessed through appropriate institutional design. Such design should follow first, a basic normative vision of the desired society and, second, a nuanced understanding of the full implications of techno-social transformations, going beyond simple techno-optimism.

For example, in their Open ICT4D paper, Smith and his colleagues argue that, "openness is a way of organizing social activities that favours: (a) universal over restricted access, (b) universal over restricted participation, and (c) collaborative over centralized production."[7] At first blush, enabling greater access (to communication tools and information), greater participation (in groups/institutions) as well as greater collaboration (as against centralized production) certainly appears useful. But the Open ICT4D framework seems to overlook the ever-present dimension of power manifest in new forms of networked relationships. The outward appearance of access, participation, and collaboration can mask less desirable social and political outcomes undermining equity and social justice.

For example, enhanced access to information provided by mobiles is often based on privatization and commodification of information and knowledge.[8] It is possible for such enhanced access to have a negative overall impact on development through increasing dependencies and establishing permanent channels of net value outflow from already disadvantaged communities. A similar tendency toward information commoditization characterizes most existing telecenter models (as we will discuss below).

The term *participation* is keenly debated in development studies.[9] Decades of scholarship show how participatory models, through their exclusive focus on specific programmatic processes, can contribute to the de-politicization of development practice.[10] Christian Fuchs describes how labor and consumer participation is subsumed within the narrow profit-seeking parameters of corporate interests.[11] In the information society context, popular media often obtains participation through premium or higher cost short message service (SMS). Apart from serving as a good revenue model, questionable measures of the popular sentiment obtained in this manner can in fact be used to manipulate public opinion.[12] Facebook allows users to vote on its statement of user rights and responsibilities.[13] But user participation in this open governance model does not extend to real hard issues, like whether Facebook needs to clearly distinguish paid-for information/communication from 'regular' interactions on its platform. Some may, therefore, justifiably interpret Facebook's limited user participation model as a preemptive mechanism against public interest regulation. The real issue therefore is not just more participation, but what kind of participation and to what avail, on whose terms does it take place, and how it recasts power.[14]

The term *collaboration* refers to the dynamics of a community, and when used in reference to political economy, implies collective decisions about contributions to, and the appropriation of, the commons. In the context of networked production systems, the use of the term *collaboration* has been critiqued for the selective inclusions and systemic exclusions that networks produce.[15] In the digital order defined by Web 2.0, voluntary community labor is expropriated for private profit. All the high deities of Web 2.0— Google, Facebook, YouTube, Apple—subscribe to a model of collaboration that is mediated, selective, and oriented to private profit. How do such new meanings of collaboration—where the private may encapsulate the public rather than the other way around—correspond to traditional theories of community and the commons?

In sum, what may be touted as greater openness may not translate into positive developmental outcomes given specific institutional contexts, especially with regard to enhancing development capabilities. As we have seen, enhanced access may come at the cost of decreased participation, higher participation may not increase collaborative outcomes, and greater collaboration may lead to private appropriation and decreased overall access to resources for the majority. This puts a question mark on the validity and value of any composite index consisting of these three elements as a measure of openness. There remain critical questions about the actual implications of what gets called access, participation, or collaboration. Any open development framework should address these questions centrally. Use of notions like access, participation, and collaboration will be meaningful only when seen from within larger social realities or constructs. It is therefore necessary to adequately problematize these notions and, for instance, address questions such as:

• Does access to more information and communication resources strengthen the public sphere in developing countries and, if so, under what conditions?
• Given the new opportunities for enhancing participation, how can democracy in the emerging information society bring citizenship to the hitherto marginalized?
• If collaboration through digital means implies new relations of production, what are their distributional implications, and how would they recast the concepts of community and commons?

The Practice of Openness

In this section, we briefly examine how the concept of openness has been employed in some specific areas of contemporary ICTD and information society practice. First we take two examples from the ICTD space, and then two instances of policy development models in information society.

Telecenters and Mobiles as the Centerpieces of ICT4D

The telecenter was arguably the centerpiece of ICT4D thinking and strategy until about 2006, only recently supplanted by a fixation with "mobiles for development."[16] Here we first examine the dominant thinking and practices concerning telecenters for development before turning to the more recent area of mobiles for development. The quest for appropriate business models to ensure telecenter sustainability has been a key imperative in ICT4D. Community level business models involving local entrepreneurs have been invariably prescribed in order to ensure efficiency and innovation in ICT4D practice.[17] It is also common, especially in India, for corporations to own chains of telecenters, whose business models are oriented toward controlling, and later seeking rent from, the new channels of communications and outreach that integrate communities into global market systems.[18]

As can be expected, such new development practices, promoted in the name of opening up access to information and other resources, and open partnerships, do not align well with traditional community-centric development thinking and practice. As a result of this, groups whose interests ought to converge, such as community media (especially community radio) groups and ICT4D practitioners, have had a very difficult relationship, if at all. It is not easy to reconcile exogenous profit-motivated business models with community-centric development models.

One of the main commodities sold at telecenters is information, including information that is fundamental to the process of developing and transforming communities. Commodification of information, through privatization and monetization, is important for the telecenter business model. For example, e-Choupal,[19] one of the world's largest telecenter chains, is owned and run by a multinational commodities company, ITC Limited, which is in the business of agriculture procurement. Its village telecenters were opened with much fanfare as a win-win model of delivering public services more effectively by applying business practices.

But these telecenters have almost exclusively served the needs of better-off farmers.[20] Rather than reducing social disparities within the community, e-Choupal has increased the dependency of local farmers on a monopoly buyer and supplier. The telecentres serve as the primary site for farmers to sell their agricultural produce, as well as for buying agriculture-related services. e-Choupal telecenters have considerable control over both the type of information that farmers access, as well as the services and products that they are able to get. Such significant dependence of local communities on a single corporate entity for their information needs and market linkages erodes local autonomy, with considerable long-term negative impacts. Such key development issues, however, hardly ever find mention in the dominant ICT4D discourse. Rather, value is placed on the financial sustainability of e-Choupal's telecenter model, which ostensibly incorporates the tenets of openness and collaboration across social sectors—profit and nonprofit, public, community, and private.

Interestingly, through its flagship e-governance program, the Indian government is well on its way to building two hundred thousand village telecenters using a model similar to e-Choupal. The primary actors in this scheme are private companies, each of which will run a chain of telecenters within a large geographical area. Like the promoters of e-Choupal, these companies mainly seek to establish ICT-enabled channels for developing new markets for their services and products, which monopoly channels they can then rent out to other service providers, including government departments. Models such as these, which privatize the delivery of public services, may not serve the best interests of the people who most depend on such basic services.[21]

Interestingly, by relying on private companies to run village telecenters, the Indian e-governance scheme uses a model of public service delivery that largely bypasses village self-governance bodies. This goes against the mainstream trend of decentralization and devolution in Indian governance reform efforts. This is a clear instance of how democratic participation can actually be reduced in pursuit of what otherwise appears to be an open, collaborative model of development.

This example demonstrates how development programs that seem to facilitate open collaboration may promote the commoditization of what should be public information, displace the centrality of the notions of community and commons in development, and build new forms of social and economic dependency. Ironically, such so called "open" models can eventually result in more closed channels of information controlled by vested interests and, in the long run, more closed information systems, thus undermining effective access to information as well as information-dependent resources. The new avenues of development information and other services being created through these market-based models also seem to be accompanied by a scaling back of traditional public extension and support services (like marketing support for agriculture produce). The likely impacts of these structural changes have not been examined enough.[22]

While the telecenter model was very popular in the early years of this century, it has more recently come to be seen as something of a failure.[23] But rather than examine the real reasons behind telecenter model failure, the dominant discourse has latched on to mobiles as the new motif for ICT4D.[24] This new approach jettisons the social enterprise (or collaborative/ multi-stakeholder) approach of telecenters, along with its public model of access, even if to priced information. The mobile-for-development model leaves no room even for public private partnership. It is a purely private and commercial affair based on individualized access. Openness, in this new approach, is now seen in terms of the astronomical increase in access that relatively inexpensive mobiles have provided.

Mobiles have no doubt revolutionized peer-to-peer voice and simple text communication, and this underpins important structural shifts that are very meaningful to development. We would argue, however, that to have real transformative potential, mobile phones must be Internet-enabled. However, unfortunately, mobile Internet models typically subvert the traditional openness of the Internet, and its foundational principle of net neutrality.[25] Internet-on-mobile is characterized by tight control and anticompetitive practices by the telecoms and their business partners, with considerable vertical integration across connectivity, hardware, software, application, and content. Interestingly, it seems that the United States Federal Communications Commission was bowing to the pressure of telecommunication companies when it exempted Internet-on-mobile from its most important provisions about net neutrality. Many civil society groups have protested against this exemption.[26] Such problematic aspects of the emerging architecture of mobile Internet means that the mobile for development model can further amplify the commodification of information along with subversion of community-centered development models that began with the commercialization and corporatization of telecenters.

The work of Smith and colleagues on Open ICT4D (previously mentioned) suggests that mobile telephony will be one of two contemporary ICT phenomena that drive open development (the other being Web 2.0, whose dominant characteristics vis-à-vis openness we critique later in this chapter).[27] It is difficult to understand how the concept of openness gets so centrally associated with mobiles, just on the strength of the fact that they have revolutionized the number of people connected to ICT infrastructure in developing countries. What about the considerable danger to openness posed by the currently dominant model of Internet-on-mobile, especially with the mobile platform set to become the main mode of accessing the Internet in the not too distant future? Under closer examination, the theoretical robustness of openness hence comes into question, particularly as a way to inform development practice.

The Open Policy Model of ICT4D

In an increasingly complex society, the limitations of a purely representational democracy are obvious. Efforts aimed at deepening democracy attempt to address these limitations. Democratic ideals face considerable constraints in their practical application, however, not only because of elite resistance but also due to techno-structural constraints of large social systems. It is certainly not easy to organize substantive participation outside elections.

ICTs present exciting possibilities to strengthen and even transform the institutional structures of democracy. But the new political model of multi-stakeholder governance, which seems closely associated with the information society neologism of openness, seems to legitimize the political influence of powerful interests rather than ensuring fundamental rights of participation and collaboration to people. Here we will briefly review two examples of the multi-stakeholder governance model—one at the global level, and another at national level—that, in practice, have caused this kind of a negative impact.

The first case is of the working of the United Nation's Internet Governance Forum (IGF). The Internet is the central paradigm of the emerging information society, but its global governance presents major challenges, particularly as a result of its transnational form and its rapid evolution. The reaction of most developing country governments has been knee jerk, asserting the traditional statist paradigm of international governance. Meanwhile, the fact that the Internet has emerged as a central element in their geoeconomic and geopolitical strategies means that the developed countries also resist exploration of a global Internet governance system that is suitably democratic and participatory.[28]

Distributed global management of the basic technical infrastructure of the Internet, based on technocratic principles, has had an important role in shaping the Internet as it is today.[29] But as the influence of the Internet is increasingly felt in most social, economic, and cultural areas, the imperative for appropriate political governance of the global Internet has grown in urgency.[30]

The IGF[31] is a policy dialogue forum mandated by the World Summit on the Information Society (WSIS) held in Tunis in 2005. Within this space, the business sector and the technical community seem to speak largely in one voice.[32] Together they are motivated by their fear of increased governmental claim over the Internet. Their principal, and perhaps the only, political aim is to resist any such move. This is not an entirely misplaced concern—it is imperative to protect the Internet from the ever growing danger of totalitarian state control. However, a general resistance to any kind of political governance of the Internet has resulted in downplaying many crucial social, economic, political, and cultural issues that the forum should be addressing urgently. Although it was set up as a policy dialogue forum, the IGF has not engaged in any worthwhile discussion toward development of any new policies or institutional frameworks. The incumbent powers that control the IGF, mostly through its Multi-Stakeholder Advisory Group, have effectively repurposed the IGF as a capacity-building forum, circumscribing its political and governance role by simply claiming absence of consensus for any policy or institutional proposal on which consensus may be tough to achieve. It is not difficult to see why big business interests would like to perpetuate the governance vacuum. Any positive movement toward the required political governance of the Internet in global public interest would obviously impede the juggernaut of global capital, which now increasingly controls and shapes the Internet.

At the same time as its political functions are actively circumscribed, the IGF is held out as an exemplary model for enhancing participation of developing countries and marginalized sections in global Internet governance. Meanwhile, real Internet governance is done by industry cartels, the U.S. government through its prime location in the digital ecology, and by plurilateral treaties among the rich nations, a good example of which is the Anti-Counterfeiting Treaty Agreement being currently developed.[33] (In fact, segmentation and fragmentation of governance, and its privatization, is a global phenomenon that has advanced rapidly in the network age.[34]) The OECD has an active Internet policy-making apparatus. Such plurilateral treaties and policy frameworks are bound to form the default Internet governance system globally, given the inherently transnational nature of the Internet. Policies and policy frameworks negotiated in an undemocratic manner (as far as developing countries are concerned) get presented post facto to developing countries for accession. Any such offer may be difficult to refuse unless a country is ready to risk isolation from the Internet economy, a risk few would be willing to take.

Since global governance of the Internet is characterized by obvious democratic deficit, new means for legitimization of the new order are sought. Some prominent actors in the Civil Society Internet Governance Caucus—one of the main global spaces for civil society groups working on Internet governance—openly speak of multi-stakeholderism as a replacement for democratic institutions at the global level.[35] This demonstrates the problem in speaking about the virtues of openness and participation outside specific institutional analyses (in this case, concerning the norms and institutions of democracy). The global Internet governance space is a very pertinent example where the concept of openness has been applied, but with outcomes that cannot be considered conducive to democracy and development.

Another example of how open multi-stakeholder processes can undermine democracy and collaboration comes from India. A few years ago a multi-stakeholder process was used to developing a new "ICT in schools" policy.[36] The whole policy process was initiated and anchored by two civil society groups, one of them a multi-donor initiative of a few countries of the Global North, and another, an Indian civil society organization, a good part of whose funding seems to come from the large number of business-supported ICT4D conferences that it hosts. Not surprisingly, industry interests dominated the process, while educationists, with expertise and legitimacy, were mostly ignored. No further surprise, then, that the draft policy seemed to aim more at institutionalizing avenues for economic exploitation of India's public education system than serving the educational imperatives of the Indian public.[37] The draft policy ignored important progressive possibilities like the use of free and open source software, open and collaborative content, and forming peer-to-peer online communities of teachers.

As a result of pressure by some civil society groups, the minister of education scrapped the multi-stakeholder process, and asked a departmental committee to develop a new policy draft, while taking inputs from all. Although relatively closed and bureaucratic in its processes, the new draft was more progressive on all the counts mentioned above. This example shows how the apparent openness of a policy development process, when not seen critically in light of its actual political context, can lead to negative implications for development.

Certain current practices of the multi-stakeholder governance model, therefore, offers a good example of how the concept of openness can be employed in ways that subvert democratic norms and institutions. Openness may, in such circumstances, become a legitimizing veneer for processes that actually undermine the public interest, especially in terms of equity and social justice.

Openness and the *Problématique* of Development

The concept of open development connects in significant ways to what is emerging as a central problem in development. This problem relates to postmodernist critiques of development, which argue that the development project violates people's subjective notions of what is important to them, and how they should obtain it.[38] This ideology is principally driven by a strong, and considerably successful, neoliberal attack on most nonmarket institutions. It has also gained some mainstream traction in an environment where there is a strong discontent with most public institutions[39] and their perceived nonperformance. There seems to be considerable skepticism in many quarters today about the very idea of development, as it is traditionally understood.[40]

The resulting laissez faire approach advocates leaving people to sort out their strategies and paths, without external assistance or planning. Development defined in this way requires no more than the removal of all constraints to—what are thought to be—autonomous and self-propelled possibilities. The most powerful proponents of such a view are the neoliberals, who basically see public and community institutions as constraining, and market mechanisms as liberating. Such an anarchic view of development, however, also finds sympathy among most techies. In their paper, "The Californian Ideology," Richard Barbrook and Andy Cameron analyze cyberlibertarian thinking in the Silicon valley, describing its neoliberal tendencies and noting its spread across the globe.[41] The coming together of these two, rather different ideologies, results in a powerful challenge to traditional development institutions, especially in the ICT4D space. Whether intended or not, in such a context of ascendant neoliberal ideology, propositions like open development may actually buttress the undermining of traditional development thinking and practice. In their paper on Open ICT4D, Smith and his colleagues approving the "planners versus searchers" typology of William Easterly, an ardent critic of the traditional development project. "Planners attempt to impose from above via top-down plans and structures. In contrast, searchers are the ones close to the ground who search for solutions to local problems. It is only through searchers, Easterly argues, that locally appropriate innovations can emerge. Here we posit that the enhanced spread of information and opportunities for innovation should—theoretically— enable (provided the other contextual supporting aspects are available, for example, bank credit) more opportunities for this type of local searching and innovation."[42] There may be some truth in this assertion. But it is also necessary to recognize that, in reality, good searches benefit greatly from planning and institutionalized support. Participatory development is about locally owned and directed initiatives, situated within such, at least partly exogenous, support structures. Appropriate uses of ICTs can certainly strengthen participatory development. But it is not clear what open development can add that participatory development does not already have, other than, perhaps (1) reducing or abolishing funding and other such public supports for local development; and/or (2) providing ideological support for market-led local community development processes, as has been discussed earlier.

Interestingly, in his paper "The Ideology of Development," William Easterly argues that development is "almost as deadly as the tired ideologies of the last century—communism, fascism, and socialism—that failed so miserably."[43] He goes on to say: "Like other ideologies, this thinking favors collective goals such as national poverty reduction, national economic growth, and the global Millennium Development Goals, over the aspirations of individuals. . . . The only 'answer' to poverty reduction is freedom from being told the answer. Free societies and individuals are not guaranteed to succeed. They will make bad choices. But at least they bear the cost of those mistakes, and learn from them."[44]

The idea of open development may be tilting uncomfortably close to Easterly's radically libertarian vision of development. For example, the Smith Open ICT4D paper argues that:

"If development consists of per-poor innovations [i.e., by the poor for the poor] and peer collaborations—what does this imply for development and development research? Most likely, this is an acceptance of a loss of control, and an increase in trust in the process—that is, the process of openness to lead to relatively unpredictable (hopefully positive) development outcomes."[45]

While this statement may have some validity in itself, the accent on unplanned bottom-up processes of development, with unpredictable outcomes, can easily veer toward antidevelopment views, as articulated by Easterly. Ascribing choices to marginalized communities, subject to deep structural disadvantages, which they simply may not have, and exhorting them to take risks that they may not be able to afford, is not a useful starting point for a new development theory. Creating choices always involve plans, funds, and, of course, capacity building and other enabling conditions. This requires ongoing institutional work close to, and with the participation of, communities. The apparent anti-institutional normativity of the open development model must be treated with great caution.

Establishing Public-ness in the Network: An Alternative to Openness

This chapter visited some practical experiences in the ICT4D and information society arenas in order to examine how certain elements of openness—greater access, participation, and collaboration—get applied in practice.

The analysis has shown these concepts of openness, access, participation and collaboration, as loosely used in ICT4D and information society spaces, to be inadequate, and often quite problematic. A few possible negative outcomes of an uncritical application of the concept of openness to development were touched upon. These include: threat to democratic institutions from multi-stakeholderism; the debilitating dependencies created when weak local markets are suddenly exposed to globalized business systems; displacement of community-centric development approaches by exogenous commercial models; curtailment of the crucial enabling role of public institutions in development; and, the subversion of local public/community informational ecologies and community media through increasing ICT-based commodification of information and communication.

Evidently, access (to information and means of communication) could just mean voice without agency, participation may only ensure presence without politics, and collaboration amounts to labor without appropriation, which provides neither remuneration nor a real commons. It may therefore be preferable to stick to traditional, historically embedded terms of development, such as voice and agency, political participation, and public good—rather than the new sanitized set of terms, such as openness, access, participation, and collaboration.

At the macro-structural level, the reliance on openness as a foundation for a new social paradigm has strong implications for the fine balance between private and public institutions[46] maintained through the social systems of the welfare state. The latter represents the basic political institutional framework that still characterizes all developed countries and most developing ones. The terms (*universal*) *access*, *participation*, and *collaboration* have typically been associated with the public and community institutional space. From such a background, one may well ask, can anything really be open, in its social meaning, without being public?[47] Even an open market is open only because of enabling and regulatory public institutions. Private business houses—singly or put together—cannot by themselves constitute an open market. Open market is a public system. Accordingly, even in digital spaces, private enclosures—however big and benign—cannot meaningfully support the concept of openness.

Openness through private sector provisioning (private openness) is a club good—non-rivalrous. but (potentially) excludable.[48] Because of its early capture by neoliberal forces, most of the digital phenomenon, in areas of its apparent openness, represents private openness (even if this term appears self-contradictory in the light of our earlier analysis). The much-vaunted Web 2.0 phenomenon basically builds on this model of private openness.

Its problems will become more apparent as private monopoly rent-seekers build up power through appropriating collective resources and labor, and use this gained power to achieve even higher levels of appropriation, in unending and perhaps unsustainable cycles.[49] Unfortunately the concept of public has largely been abandoned in the institutional thinking and ecology of the emerging information society. *Public,* as we argued earlier, is the sociopolitical framework and condition for real openness. Public is openness in the explicit context of real social relationships, with the qualities of rights and responsibilities, and with the necessary enabling conditions, all of which derive from a social contract (and not just some private contractual arrangements).

Earlier we mentioned that the considerable hostility against public institutions, and their subsequent creeping withdrawal,[50] is a key contemporary problem for development. It is true that the institution of the State is in considerable crisis, but it would be neither reasonable nor wise to discard or minimize the concept of public. We do not discard the concept of the free market just because it is dominated and manipulated by big business. Instead we work to improve the market while also learning to live with its imperfections. Why then should public institutions not merit similar indulgence? The asymmetrical treatment of public institutions suggests a political economy factor: powerful actors side with market institutions, which help them maintain and enhance their domination, while marginalized actors side with public institutions, which are their hope for equity and social justice. This happens even as the marginalized groups carry on their struggles against the various shortcomings and injustices of public systems. Development is concerned with assisting those who are marginalized from dominant social structures and systems. It is, therefore, quite appropriate for development theory and practice to focus on reestablishing the need, context, and the new meanings of "public" and public institutions in the emerging information-society institutional space. But as we have argued in this chapter, a different, institutionally situated understanding of openness is required if this is to be achieved.

Following the analysis in this chapter, we see an institutional ecology[51] of private openness or commercial openness emerging in the current context. Against this, we posit the need for new forms of public openness. Public openness denotes the commons- and social contract–based network opportunities of the information society, in contrast to those based on markets and private contracts. These new opportunities will need to be supported by an appropriate enabling institutional ecology, which upholds both negative and positive rights. For this purpose, it is important to establish, and strengthen, key elements of public-ness in the network, which is the new dominant social-organizational paradigm of the network age. We, tentatively refer to this institutional ecology as the *network public*. While a full exploration of this alternative concept will not be possible here, a few explanations can be offered as starting points.

First, it is important to understand the difference between the concepts of *openness*, *commons*, and *public*. Openness largely connotes a set of negative rights, whereby freedom from constraints is implied without any further guarantee. The term *commons* is related to specific sharable resources. *Public* represents a much more complex institutional ecology built over ideas of rights, equity, commons, public goods, and distributive justice, arising out of a social contract.

Secondly, in the information or network age, it is difficult as well as illogical, to try and sustain industrial age public institutions in unaltered forms. At present, the relationship between democratic governments and people (or community) is largely determined by elections and mediated by a public sphere dominated by the mass media. The network age calls for innovations, especially at the boundaries between the state and the community, contributing to what we may refer to as the architecture of a new network public. Existing ideas and efforts around deepening democracy represent a good starting point for such innovations. Government adaptation to the networked context[52] is one expression of an emerging network public, but much more will need to be done.

Third, the term *network public* as proposed here is much more than the "networked public sphere" described by Yochai Benkler[53] and others. Network public covers a much wider public institutional ecology, consisting of various public and community institutions in their diverse functions. Basically, the network public represents the public segment or aspect of the network society, formed of its spaces, and its flows. This public segment is not just (all) people-accessible, but also (all) people-owned. Thus the network public is rather different from the dominant conception of the network as a mere collection of connected private realms. In the latter conception, even the connections themselves are seen as private, and as based on private contracts.

While concepts of fluidity and connectedness dominate the network logic, and hence most theorizations of network/information society, the real world public-ness of our emerging social order will be represented by a plurality of considerably bounded, even if interconnected and relatively fluid, institutions. The network logic has to be seen in continuity with the pre-network age, spatially bound, social logic.

A network public at the local level may ensure public funds and other kinds of support for communities, community-based organizations, and local NGOs, among others, to work together in local development networks. Such support may for instance consist of public provisioning of basic connectivity, capacity building, and basic digital tools required to participate meaningfully in the information society. ICT-enabled modes of social interaction may play an increasing part in what Jan Nederveen Pieterse calls "reflexive development," where in response to technological change, "development may become reflexive in a social and political sense, as a participatory, popular reflexivity, which can take the form of broad social debates and fora on development goals and methods."[54] Technology alone cannot ensure such far-reaching social change; it will require a great amount of painstaking work to develop appropriate new institutions and social systems, as public goods, taking into consideration the possibilities presented by the new ICTs.

It is important to note that the new networking possibilities, and thus the network public, extend beyond the purely digital or even the informational realm, to larger social structures. ICTs provide opportunities for different development actors at different levels (micro, meso, and macro) to network together in ways that allow them to share competencies, resources, and outcomes. They can also create an effective space for development dialogue and discourse. This can be a significant improvement over sub-optimal, silo-based approaches to development.

An interesting example of moving from a purely public system to a network public system comes from Brazil's experience with telecenters. Quoting from a posting to the Community Informatics Researcher e-list:

Brazil has had some bad experiences in the past when it tried to implement a national program for Telecentros in which the Federal Government was responsible for maintaining and coordinating the centers. . . . Back then, these Telecentros were called "Casa Brasil." Some of them are still running but very few are providing access to digital technologies. Currently, the federal government, which now has a specific secretary for digital inclusion, is trying to change its role from executors to regulators and fund providers. Brazil's new plan is to provide Telecentro "kits": computers, routers, printers and money to NGOs, City Government and local organizations that are willing to follow the guidelines set up by the federal government. In the case of Vitoria, the Telecentros that I did my field work at, they were maintained by the City, and coordinated by the City and CDI (Committee for the Democratization of Informatics). CDI is an NGO that is specialized in developing Telecentros all over Brazil. The people that work at those Telecentros are called Inclusion Agents, and they are from the community where the centers are implemented. Since they are immersed in the community, they have the freedom to promote whatever workshop they feel the community needs, and it doesn't always need to be related with computers.[55]

Such a public network strategy is a good alternative to either government-run or corporate-run models. We expect such an approach to be more successful in promoting development.

At the meso-social structural level, a network public model will consist of networks of public authorities, development agencies, progressive techies, and the community in general, working together to build and sustain various digital and socio-technical artifacts and platforms that underpin our digital existence (software, social media, search engines, and so forth). Such collaborations can be developed and sustained fruitfully given appropriate networked work cultures and incentive structures. In this way, the voluntary communal labor of techies, other social actors and the wider community can be harnessed for common good, rather than for private appropriation by big businesses, in the Web 2.0 style. Open source software platforms and applications serving the *real* development needs of local communities can be developed and managed collectively, in sync with offline development activities.[56] Similarly, open search engines, open social networking applications, open APIs (Application Programming Interfaces), open content platforms, and the like, need to be developed and iteratively evolved through participatory use by communities. Progressive techie groups have found it very difficult to develop and sustain such basic digital public goods by themselves as a result of insufficient public and community support. On the other hand, regardless of the extent of budget or resource commitments, government alone cannot produce, sustain and distribute these networked digital public goods. Network publics will require institutional innovations by public authorities, NGOs, volunteer groups as well as communities, working together in a flexible but sustained manner.

At the macro-institutional level, the objective will be to understand, anticipate, and nudge the current rapidly moving and powerful techno-social developments toward more equitable forms and outcomes. At this level, the network public will be in the form of structures that can produce appropriate policies and regulations to support developmental efforts at the micro- and meso- structural levels. Appropriate ICT/Internet policies are required to help build a techno-social infrastructure that creates a level playing field for all. In this respect, the tensions that arise between global ICT-enabled networks and the nation-state based policy systems create a significant challenge. New policy/public institutions urgently need to be developed at the global level to meet this challenge. While internationalism may still remain at the core of such institutional developments for the foreseeable future, significant institutional innovations are required that take note of the fact that the Internet creates some uniquely global social realities, such as new transnational publics. In this respect, for instance, the earlier mentioned Internet Governance Forum could become an important new institution contributing to Internet policy making, if it is seriously and sincerely nurtured for such a role. The Forum will have to reclaim its public-ness, meaning, in this case, its embeddedness in the larger political processes around the global Internet and the emerging network or information society.

Notes

1. M. Castells, "The Network Society: From Knowledge to Policy," in *The Network Society: From Knowledge to Policy*, ed. M. Castells and G. Cardoso (Washington, DC: Johns Hopkins Center for Transatlantic Relations, 2005), 17.

2. M. Smith et al., *Open ICT4D*, (IDRC Working Paper: Ottawa, 2008). http://web.idrc.ca/uploads/user-S/12271304441Open_ICT4D_Draft.pdf; M. Smith et al., "Open Development: A New Theory for ICT4D," *Information Technologies & International Development* 7, no. 1 (Spring, 2011): iii—ix. itidjournal.org/itid/article/viewFile/692/290.

3. D. Lathrop and L. Ruma, eds. *Open Government: Collaboration Transparency, and Participation in Practice.* (Sebastopol, CA: O'Reilly, 2010).

4. M. Smith et al., *Open ICT4D*, 2008.

5. M. Castells, *The Rise of the Network Society* (Oxford: Blackwell Publishing, 2000).

6. Ibid.

7. Smith et al., *Open ICT4D*, 2008.

8. E. Noam, "Two Cheers for the Commodification of Information," *Journal of Intellectual Property Law*, Special Issue (June 27, 2001), http://www.citi.columbia.edu/elinoam/articles/Commodification.htm.

9. B. Cooke and U. Kothari, eds. *Participation: The New Tyranny.* (London: Zed Books, 2001).

10. See the discussion on "Varieties of Participation" in C. Sparks *Globalization, Development and the Mass Media* (Los Angeles: Sage, 2007) for an overview of these debates.

11. C. Fuchs, *Internet and Society: Social Theory in the Information Age* (New York: Routledge, 2008).

12. This phenomenon is frequently encountered in television news programs in India.

13. http://www.facebook.com/legal/terms.

14. Cooke and Kothari, *Participation*, 2001.

15. R. Tongia and E. J. Wilson III, "The Flip Side of Metcalfe's Law: Multiple and Growing Costs of Network Exclusion," paper presented at the Beyond Broadband Access Workshop, Washington D.C., March 13, 2010, http://www.cstep.in/node/93.

16. M. Gurstein, "The Mobile Revolution and the Rise of Possessive Individualism," *Gurstein's Community Informatics*, July 21, 2012, http://gurstein.wordpress.com/2012/07/21/the-mobile-revolution-and-the-rise-and-rise-of-possessive-individualism.

17. This was identified as an important issue in the report of the Digital Opportunity Initiative, *Creating a Development Dynamic*, July 2001, by UNDP, Markle Foundation, and Accenture.

18. M. Gurstein, "Towards a Critical Theory of Telecentres: In the Context of Community Informatics," in *Political Economy of the Information Society*, ed. P. Singh, A. Gurumurthy, and M. Swamy (Bengaluru: IT for Change, 2008), 9–23.

19. Insights about e-Choupal and, later in the section, about Indian government's countrywide telecenter project, come from IT for Change's direct field observations and research. For e-Choupal, see IT for Change, *e-Choupal—An Initiative of ITC* (Bengaluru: IT for Change, 2008).

20. N. Dangi and H. Singh, "e-Choupal: Hope or Hype?," *American Journal of Economics and Business Administration* 2, no. 2 (2010): 179–184.

21. UNISON, *Fighting Privatisation in Local Government: A UNISON Guide* www.unison.org.uk/acrobat/19989.pdf.

22. W. M. Rivera and J. W. Cary, "Chapter 22: Privatizing Agricultural Extension," in *Improving Agricultural Extension: A Reference Manual*, ed. B. E. Swanson, R. P. Bentz, and A. J. Sofranko (Rome: Food and Agriculture Organization of the United Nations, 1998), http://www.fao.org/docrep/W5830E/w5830e0o.htm#the%20context%20for%20extension%20privatization.

23. See, for example, J. Jellema and R. Westerveld, "Learning Lessons from Failure: The Ugandan Telecentre Experience in Perspective," *Policy & Development Summit*, 2001, itidjournal.org/itid/article/download/309/14.

24. A. Gurumurthy, "From Social Enterprises to Mobiles—Seeking a Peg to Hang a Premeditated ICTD Theory," *Information Technologies and International Development* 6, (Special Edition, 2010): 57–63.

25. Whereby, all data and content on the Internet has to be treated equally and without discrimination by the carriers.

26. R. Adhikari, "Free Press Sues FCC to Get Real About Net Neutrality," September 29, 2011, http://www.ecommercetimes.com/story/73389.html.

27. Smith and others, *Open ICT4D*, 2008.

28. J. Von Bernstorff, "Democratic Global Internet Regulation? Governance Networks, International Law and the Shadow of Hegemony," *European Law Journal* 9, no. 4 (2003): 511–526.

29. S. O. Siochru, B. Girard, and A. Mahon, *Global Media Governance: A Beginner's Guide* (Lanham, MA: Rowman and Littlefield, 2002): 119–162; 143–162; V. Pickard "Neoliberal Visions and Revisions in Global Communications. Policy from NWICO to WSIS," *Journal of Communication Inquiry* 31, no. 2 (2007): 118–139.

30. This sentiment is strongly expressed in the Tunis Agenda of the World Summit on the Information Society (2005), and annual UN General Assembly resolutions in the subsequent years.

31. Most observations about the IGF are from IT for Change's direct engagement with the IGF. Similarly, later in the section, the insights about ICT in schools policy of government of India come from our direct engagement with the involved processes.

32. J. Malcolm, *Multi Stakeholder Governance and the Internet Governance Forum* (Perth: Terminus Press, 2008).

33. M. Kaminski, "Recent Development: The Origins and Potential Impact of the Anti-Counterfeiting Trade Agreement (ACTA)," *Yale Journal of International Law* 34, (Winter, 2009): 247.

34. http://www.erica.demon.co.uk/EV/EV2122.html.

35. These e-discussions of the Civil Society Internet Governance Caucus are publicly available on its Web site www.igcaucus.org.

36. GeSCI (Centre for Science, Development, and Media Studies), *Toward a National Policy on ICT in School Education in India: A Multi Stakeholder Perspective* (Noidia, IN: Centre for Science, Development and Media Studies, 2008) http://www.gesci.org/assets/files/GESCI%20COMPENDIUM%202008.pdf.

37. A. Raman, "Target Audience," November 24, 2008, http://www.outlookindia.com/article.aspx?239023.

38. F. Schuurman, *Beyond the Impasse*: *New Directions in Development Theory* (London: Zed Books, 1993).

39. M. J. Sandel, *Democracy's Discontent: America in Search of a Public Philosophy* (Cambridge, MA: Harvard University Press, 1996).

40. We mean here a traditional understanding of development, its dominant understanding in discourse around policy and practice. Our view in this regard may be colored to some extent by the Indian context.

41. R. Barbrook, and A. Cameron, "The California Ideology," August 1995, http://www.alamut.com/subj/ideologies/pessimism/califIdeo_I.html.

42. Smith et al., *Open ICT4D*, 14.

43. W. Easterly, "The Ideology of Development," *Foreign Policy*, July/August, 2007, 31.

44. Ibid., 32–33.

45. Smith, *Open ICT4D*, 2008.

46. It is accepted that information society changes are so deep and broad that they affect the relative meaning and nature of the private and public realms as well. This requires serious theorization. However, the contention here is that the blurring of boundaries regarding these concepts hitherto has been mostly opportunistic, as a part of the neoliberal design.

47. The use of the word *public* here includes community institutions.

48. Access to cable television is a typical example of a club good, an entity to which someone can be restricted but a good whose use by one party does not reduce its value to others.

49. The strong parallel with Marxian analysis of the unsustainability of the relations of production in a capitalistic system is obvious. If the collapse of the system as predicted by Marx did not take place, it was because the distributive policies of the welfare state intervened. A similar reestablishing of the balance between public and private institutions will also be required in the emerging information society.

50. D. Grimshaw,and J. Rubery, "The End of the UK's Liberal Collectivist Social Model? The Implications of the Coalition Government's Policy during the Austerity Crisis," *Cambridge Journal of Economics* 36, no. 1 (2012): 105–126.

51. For an analysis of "the battle over the institutional ecology of the digitally networked environment," see Y. Benkler *Wealth of Networks* (New Haven: Yale University Press, 2006).

52. S. Goldsmith, and W. D. Eggers, *Governing by Network: The New Shape of the Public Sector* (Brookings Institution Press: Washington, D.C., 2004).

53. Benkler, *Wealth of Networks*, 2006.

54. J. N. Pieterse, "My Paradigm or Yours? Alternative Development, Post-Development, Reflexive Development," *Development and Change*, 29 (1998): 369.

55. D. Nemer, comment on S. Jalil "South Africa: USAASA Telecentre Fail Revealed," *Community Informatics Researcher*, September 10, 2012, http://vancouvercommunity.net/lists/arc/ciresearchers/2012-09/msg00057.html.

56. IT for Change runs a Public Software Centre with such an objective. A similar initiative is also run in Brazil, where it is led by the government, which partners with other agencies.

Bibliography

Adhikari, R. "Free Press Sues FCC to Get Real About Net Neutrality." September 29, 2011. http://www.ecommercetimes.com/story/73389.html.

Benkler, Y. *Wealth of Networks*. New Haven: Yale University Press, 2006.

Castells, M. *The Rise of the Network Society*. Oxford: Blackwell Publishing, 2000.

Castells, M. The Network Society: From Knowledge to Policy. In *The Network Society: From Knowledge to Policy*, ed. M. Castells and G. Cardoso, 3–22. Washington, DC: Johns Hopkins Center for Transatlantic Relations, 2005.

Cooke, B., and U. Kothari, eds. *Participation: The New Tyranny*. London: Zed Books, 2001.

Dangi, N., and H. Singh. "e-Choupal: Hope or Hype?" *American Journal of Economics and Business Administration* 2 (2) (2010): 179–184.

Fuchs, C. *Internet and Society: Social Theory in the Information Age*. New York: Routledge, 2008.

GeSCI. (Centre for Science, Development, and Media Studies), *Towards a National Policy on ICT in School Education in India: A Multi Stakeholder Perspective* (Noidia, India: Centre for Science, Development and Media Studies, 2008). http://www.gesci.org/assets/files/GESCI%20COMPENDIUM%202008.pdf.

Goldsmith, S., and W. D. Eggers. *Governing by Network: The New Shape of the Public Sector*. Washington, D.C.: Brookings Institution Press, 2004.

Grimshaw, D., and J. Rubery. "The End of the UK's Liberal Collectivist Social Model? The Implications of the Coalition Government's Policy during the Austerity Crisis." *Cambridge Journal of Economics* 36 (1) (2012): 105–126.

Gurstein, M. "Towards a Critical Theory of Telecentres: In the Context of Community Informatics." In Political Economy of the Information Society, ed. P. Singh, A. Gurumurthy, and M. Swamy, 9–23. Bengaluru: IT for Change, 2008.

Gurumurthy, A. "From Social Enterprises to Mobiles—Seeking a Peg to Hang a Premeditated ICTD Theory." *Information Technologies and International Development* 6, (Special Edition, 2010): 57–63.

Kaminski, M. "Recent Development: The Origins and Potential Impact of the Anti-Counterfeiting Trade Agreement (ACTA)." *Yale Journal of International Law* 34 (Winter 2009): 247.

Lathrop, D., and L. Ruma, eds. *Open Government; Collaboration Transparency, and Participation in Practice*. Sebastopol, CA: O'Reilly, 2010.

Malcolm, J. *Multi Stakeholder Governance and the Internet Governance Forum*. Perth: Terminus Press, 2008.

Noam, E. "Two Cheers for the Commodification of Information." *Journal of Intellectual Property Law*, Special Issue (2001, June 27). http://www.citi.columbia.edu/elinoam/articles/Commodification.htm.

Pickard, V. "Neoliberal Visions and Revisions in Global Communications. Policy from NWICO to WSIS." *Journal of Communication Inquiry* 31 (2) (2007): 118–139.

Pieterse, J. N. "My Paradigm or Yours? Alternative Development, Post-Development, Reflexive Development." *Development and Change* 29 (1998): 343–373.

Raman, A. "Target Audience." November 24, 2008. http://outlookindia.com/article.aspx?239023.

Rivera, W. M., and J. W. Cary. "Chapter 22: Privatizing Agricultural Extension." In *Improving Agricultural Extension: A Reference Manual*, ed. B. E. Swanson, R. P. Bentz, and A. J. Sofranko. Rome: Food and Agriculture Organization of the United Nations, 1998. http://www.fao.org/docrep/W5830E/w5830e0o.htm#the%20context%20for%20extension%20privatization.

Sandel, M. J. *Democracy's Discontent: America in Search of a Public Philosophy*. Cambridge, MA: Harvard University Press, 1996.

Schuurman, F. *Beyond the Impasse: New Directions in Development Theory*. London: Zed Books, 1993.

Sen, A. *Development as Freedom*. Oxford: Oxford University Press, 1999.

Siochru, S. O., B. Girard, and A. Mahon. *Global Media Governance: A Beginner's Guide*. Lanham, MA: Rowman and Littlefield, 2002.

Smith, M., N. Engler, G. Christian, K. Diga, A. Rashid, and K. Flynn-Dapaah. *Open ICT4D*. IDRC Working Paper: Ottawa, 2008. http://web.idrc.ca/uploads/user-S/12271304441Open_ICT4D_Draft.pdf.

Smith, M., L. Elder, and H. Emdon. "Open Development: A New Theory for ICT4D." *Information Technologies & International Development* 7 (1) (Spring 2011): iii–ix. itidjournal.org/itid/article/viewFile/692/290.

UNISON. *Fighting Privatisation in Local Government: A UNISON Guide*. www.unison.org.uk/acrobat/19989.pdf.

Von Bernstorff, J. "Democratic Global Internet Regulation? Governance Networks, International Law and the Shadow of Hegemony." *European Law Journal* 9 (4) (2003): 511–526.

8 Centering the Knowledge Peripheries through Open Access: Implications for Future Research and Discourse on Knowledge for Development

Leslie Chan and Eve Gray

Open Access (OA), or free online access, to scholarly and scientific publications has emerged as a significant global movement since the twenty-first century began.[1] OA has also become an area of special interest to the development community, given that access to knowledge is fundamental to all aspects of human development, from health to food security, and from education to social capacity building. The potential of OA to dramatically improve the visibility, usage and, therefore, the impact of publicly funded research is also increasingly recognized by national and international funding bodies, aid agencies, and institutions of higher learning. This has led to the implementation of a growing number of policy mandates that ensure public accessibility to publicly funded research.[2]

Open Access has the potential to facilitate the flow of knowledge in all directions, not only from the Global North to the Global South, but also from the Global South to the Global South, which is far more essential for local and development since Global Southern countries have more in common than with those of the Global North.[3] This at a time in which there are increasing calls by policymakers, particularly in the Global South, for research to demonstrate its impact on the United Nation's Millennium Development Goals. For example, the Namibian prime minister asked of a UNESCO conference in 2010: "How could the application of knowledge end poverty and hunger in Africa? How could higher education empower women and promote gender equity? How can knowledge be considered in an African context to address child mortality and improve maternal health?"[4] This chapter, however, argues that, as OA is currently practiced, its potential to advance development is not being exploited.

Instead of being used to support greater local participation in research that would confront fundamental development issues, OA is all too often focused on improving online access to journal articles, particularly those in expensive Global Northern journals. This is in good part because of the near universal adoption—even in the developing world—of the Thomson Reuter's Science Citation Index and Journal Impact Factor[5] (JIF) as a measure of journal quality and international prestige.

Drawing largely on African examples, this paper seeks to demonstrate how the use of this narrow global yardstick as a one-size-fits-all framework has resulted in the continual invisibility of research publications from the Global South and distortion of research priorities and agendas in many developing countries.[6] The adherence to this approach by developing country governments has led to a situation where research that is of vital importance to national development priorities has been marginalized in the race for improved citation metrics. This applies also to a volume of development-focused publications produced in developing countries that remain invisible as a result of such policies.[7]

Implicit in the acceptance of the JIF as the standard measure for publication impact is an industrial age "innovation system" view that seeks to measure the potential impact of research in terms of commercial exploitation for economic growth.[8] In this discourse there is a particular understanding of what constitutes the center or mainstream research, from which voices and knowledge from the Global South—dismissed as "local knowledge"—are largely excluded and within which different disciplines are valued unequally. This is in contrast to the twenty-first-century network society described by Yochai Benkler,[9] in which a decentered and cooperative environment can lead to different innovation approaches, more likely to contribute to development goals.

This chapter will argue that while OA provides the means to challenge the hegemony of this global publishing system, there is a need to rethink what constitutes scholarly publication, quality, and impact in an open networked knowledge environment. To do so requires the inclusion of a wider range of research objects or outputs and the development of an expanded system of accounting for the social and development impact of research.[10] Such a system would include alternative and enhanced metrics that take into account the multiple outcomes of improved access beyond citation impact, and into less tangible realms including expanded collaboration, inclusive participation, cross disciplinary exchange of ideas, and uptake of research knowledge by development workers and policymakers. Such a system would also provide alternative foundations for allocating research funding that would better recognize the role of publicly funded research institutions in developing countries.

The Geo-Politics of Academic Knowledge Production

Since the mid-1950s, knowledge and knowledge management have come to be seen as key drivers of development. Although this has often been expressed as a matter of economic growth, in recent decades there has been increasing emphasis on the importance of knowledge dissemination and information provision for human and social development. As Benkler argues, "In the global networked information economy, the constituent elements of human welfare and development depend on information and knowledge."[11] These sentiments are echoed in a number of global and regional policy statements from UNESCO and the World Bank,[12] to continental initiatives such as the African Union Plan of Action for Renewing the African University.[13] This is true also for the universities, where the research they disseminate is often seen as lying at the heart of any sustainable effort to build economic growth and foster human development, especially in developing countries.

There seems, however, to be a blockage between these policy ideals and the creation of an effective regime for knowledge dissemination to underpin these development targets. Benkler's analysis of the rise of the information society offers some insights into this situation. He argues that there have been conflicting views on the best way knowledge can be made to contribute to the economy and society. These views are reflected in four sequential but overlapping events: (1) the rise of a neoliberal trading system; (2) the rise of an information economy enshrined in global treaties for intellectual property; (3) the rise of a network society in which the production of culture has been radically decentralized; and (4) the linking of human rights and development as freedom in the face of an inequitable global dispensation.[14]

Ideas about how knowledge can contribute to development will be very different depending on whether they are inspired by the trade related aspects of intellectual property rights (TRIPS), and a TRIPS-governed information economy, or an understanding of the radically decentralized and collaborative network society.[15] The conflation of these two very different development paradigms in global and national research policy creates a similar disjuncture between our understanding of the importance of knowledge for development and the creation of effective policy for the leverage of research for its contribution to the public good.

What has happened, Benkler argues, is that access to knowledge has become essential to developing countries at the same time as the enforcement of control over information flows became of central concern to the major copyright industries, using maximalist models of intellectual property (IP) enforcement and the leverage of trade treaties such as TRIPS.[16] In this contested terrain, developing countries recognize the importance of knowledge for development, but allow commercial publishing values to influence the policies that drive knowledge and educational systems.[17]

Thus UNESCO's report, *Toward Knowledge Societies*, published in 2005, recognized the value of open access initiatives like the Public Library of Science (PLOS) and http://ArXiv.org, but it recommended donor-funded collaborations with commercial providers, such as those evidenced in the reduced-subscription medical and agricultural journal initiatives HINARI and AGORA, as a means to redress global inequality in access to knowledge. The emphasis is thus on greater distribution of commercially produced centralized resources from the Global North over models that favor decentralized production, collaboration, and distribution of knowledge from the Global South. There is little sense in the 2005 report that research might emerge from countries in the Global South; rather, the emphasis falls on enhanced North–South access to (and consumption of) Global Northern knowledge.

The *UNESCO Science Report 2010* continues the endorsement of counts of journal articles and patents as a core measure for judging the effectiveness of national research systems.[18] This is a system that is now deeply entrenched in the academy,[19] which we argue is at odds with the development potential offered by the twenty-first-century networked knowledge society, running counter to policymakers' desire to achieve social and economic impact from research. It is in the *UNESCO Social Science Report 2010*, interestingly in a more marginalized disciplinary research area, that more complex arguments emerge in favor of a changed evaluation system and a wider range of publications.[20]

The Center and the Periphery According to ISI/Thompson Reuters

In *A Geopolitics of Academic Writing*, A. Suresh Canagarajah[21] shows how scholarship from the center has created publication conventions and practices that are simultaneously shaped by technological progress and social institutions. Scholars operating in the peripheries have to adopt these *discursive* practices in order to gain entry into the center, where mainstream knowledge resides. This system of production has been perpetuating itself without reflection. Voices and knowledge from the Global South that do not fit international standards for publishing are excluded from the well-known and largely commercial databases and their citation counts, and so they remain largely invisible.

Even as the Internet has opened new channels for collaboration and dissemination, the journal article has remained the currency of scholarly recognition across the English-speaking world and beyond. In this system, the journals that qualify for inclusion in the indexes are predominantly the publications of large commercial publishing companies based in the Global North. In 2004, four top countries produced 84 percent of the articles in the dominant index, the Institute for Scientific Information (ISI) index, while at the other end of the spectrum, 163 countries contributed 2.5 percent of the indexed articles.[22]

Even after a review of the role of developing country journals in the ISI Web of Science in 2008—which responded to a rising tide of criticism of bias inherent in the indexes and resulted in seven hundred developing country journals being added to the indexes—Africa remained poorly represented. Nineteen journals were added from South Africa, in addition to one from Kenya and one from Nigeria. To put this in perspective, in 2007 there were twenty-eight African journals in the index out of a total listing of around ten thousand according to the Institute for Scientific Information (ISI) report compiled in 2010. More significantly, the criteria for this expanded inclusion of developing country journals remained the extent to which articles in these journals could contribute to *global* understanding of science from the periphery.[23]

Figure 8.1
The map shows the unequal contribution and participation in journal publishing science. *Source*: World Bank's 2005 World Development Indicators.

Thus, it is not a coincidence that the centers of this global publishing system reside primarily in the Global North, dominated by the United States and the United Kingdom in particular, with Japan being the notable exception from Asia. Figure 8.1 depicts the world of knowledge production according to Thomson's Science Citation Index.[24]

This would matter less if the ISI indexes had not been accepted by developing countries as *the* measure of scholarly excellence, as countries, even in the developing world, compete for their position in the global university rankings, such as the Times Higher Education (THE) rankings, as the primary measure of success.

These rankings are, in turn, tied to measures of overall development of a country or an entire region. So, for example, the Global Research Report Africa produced by Thomson Reuters, uses output metrics and citation impact factors as a sole indicator of the state of national research systems. The reports are designed to "inform policymakers and others about the landscape and dynamics of the global research base" and at the global level, they aim to "help provide a further context to that set by the OECD's economic reports, while also furnishing background against which to view the pertinent regional dispatches in the UNESCO Science report 2010."[25]

Implications for Local Research and Development

These metrics "can have perverse and dangerous effects on universities in underdeveloped countries in the global South," Saleem Badat argues.[26] In the place of "uncritical mimicry and 'catching up' with the world class university," which relegates developing country research systems to second-rate status in an idealized global hierarchical system, he argues for the creation of favorable national environments for universities' contribution to society. What is needed, if research is truly to have an impact on social development in the developing world, is a diversity of models and of measures aligned to the realities of a diversity of university systems across the world.[27]

The impact of the wide adoption of this system of evaluation is to render invisible wide swathes of developing country research, and to distort the emergence of knowledge production that serves local development needs. While the journals included in the ISI indexes are only a very small proportion of the publications emerging from developing countries, the publications not included are consigned to oblivion, with very small circulation, little reach beyond the borders of the country of publication, and minimal impact in the global research system.[28] Typically, as the South African Academy of Science discovered, local print journals had a circulation of under four hundred.[29] Moreover, the assumption that locally produced publications in developing countries are of lower quality can become a self-fulfilling prophecy, as researchers from peripheral countries focus their energies on conforming to the requirements of Global Northern journals for the sake of their prospects of recognition and advancement in an idealized global system.[30]

Jean-Claude Guédon argues that as researchers try to achieve their visibility in global journals "the end result is a paradoxical and unexpected form of foreign 'contribution' or aid flowing from poor countries to rich countries."[31] In the political economy of global knowledge production, this tends to go unnoticed by governments and international agencies; they adopt impact factors as the norm for the monitoring of the research systems that they oversee, while at the same time questioning why their research systems are not more responsive to urgent development needs in their regions.[32]

The system, in turn, involves a distortion of research priorities, as researchers seek exposure in international journals, often in contradiction to their own reasons for conducting research[33] and of the research priorities in their region. This has resulted, worldwide, in an emphasis, for example, on research dealing with health issues that are of concern to the United States and Europe and that have economic potential in these markets.

Thus Benkler argues that in the last decade, more attention has been paid to research on curing acne than on malaria.[34] The research system also favors disciplinary production over area studies, while applied disciplines like engineering and agriculture are less well represented.[35]

As a result, social science research of importance to national and regional policy and economic development, health research on neglected diseases that affect the developing world, or agricultural research relevant to food sustainability, are marginalized and under-published.[36]

Limits of Open Access 1.0 as an Alternative Paradigm

In this context Open Access becomes critically important as a way of leveling the playing field and providing a voice for developing country publications. Open Access has emerged as an alternative paradigm to address these concerns. OA refers to online access to scholarly literature that is free from price and most permission barriers. The primary target of OA is the peer-reviewed journal literature, but other research related outputs, including data, software, research reports, and monographs are also being considered. The impetus for OA is that it "gives authors and their works vast and measurable new visibility, readership, and impact."[37]

Two broad approaches have developed in the scholarly community for the use of open access to maximize research exposure and impact. One is to use the potential of open access repositories, institutional or subject-based, in order to provide access to the text of articles published in closed access journals. The posting of preprints (the article before peer review) or postprints (the text revised after peer review but before editing and typesetting) is allowed by a high percentage of journal publishers. This has come to be known as author self-archiving or the "green route" and is promoted by some advocates as the only effective way to get maximum benefit from Open Access while still benefiting from the skills of professional publishers.[38] The use of these institutional repositories has demonstrated considerably increased downloads and increased citations over time.[39]

The other approach, the "gold route," to Open Access is the publication of journals, using a variety of business models. There are now close to nine thousand such journals listed in the major OA journal directory and over one million full text articles.[40] Open Access journals have seen considerable growth in numbers of journals and even higher growth in numbers of articles, in comparison with subscription journals.[41] Early adopters were in the medical and biological sciences: the Public Library of Science (PLOS) as a not-for-profit publisher produces eight broad-based disciplinary journals, and BioMedCentral, now owned by Springer Science+Business Media, is a commercial open access publisher that now publishes hundreds of OA titles based on the authors-pay model of gold OA publishing. These publishers have been quick to point to the impressive citations counts of articles published in their journals, and the rapid rise in JIF of their flagship journals. In essence, they are still using the same yardstick to measure research quality and impact. Numerous studies have now been published on the citation advantage of OA, either through the green or the gold route.[42]

The gold route has a particular appeal in the developing world, which experiences barriers to the effective distribution of research publications. The Academy of Science of South Africa (AASAf), for example, has argued that there is a need to use Open Access as the publication route for journal articles (and books) in order to provide a platform that will grow the volume of research out of the Global South and ensure its wide dissemination.[43] ASSAf, supported by the South African government, has joined the Scientific Library Online (SciELO) platform in Brazil, a large regional platform for the hosting of Latin American publications.[44]

Unfortunately, however, debates over which of these two routes is better often tend to miss out on the bigger question of how best, in a network society, to produce knowledge that addresses the problems of development. As long as the journal article and the scholarly monograph remain the currency of international scholarship, the current hierarchies that limit the potential of developing country research and of research for development will continue. As Nancy L. Maron and K. Kirby Smith argue:

The urge to consider new forms in comparison to the monograph and journal genres that dominate library collections and the consciousness of the Academy is powerful. Yet this frame for interpreting changing practises of scholarly communication carries the risk of falling into a certain circularity of thought—we may acknowledge that scholarly works will change and yet behave as if anything that does not look like a traditional work of scholarship is not a scholarly work; thus the immutability of traditional publishing models becomes axiomatic. Different becomes less by definition.[45]

Cameron Neylon, writing about what scholarly communication would look like if it were invented now in the current digital age, argues that an anachronistic focus on the journal article is limiting the potential impact of research[46]:

It is on re-usability and replication where our current system really falls down. Access and rights are a big issue here, but ones that we are gradually pushing back. The real issues are much more fundamental. It is essentially assumed, in my experience, by most researchers that a paper will not contain sufficient information to replicate an experiment or analysis. Just consider that. Our primary means of communication, in a philosophical system that rests almost entirely on reproducibility, does not enable even simple replication of results. A lot of this is down to the boundaries created by the mindset of a printed multi-page article. Mechanisms to publish methods, detailed laboratory records, or software are limited, often leading to a lack of care in keeping and annotating such records. After all if it isn't going in the paper why bother looking after it?

The resulting impact is described in a study commissioned by the Southern African Regional Universities Association (SARUA). The study's authors argue that the current framework for academic publishing, with its low valuation of local publishing and its exclusion of gray literature from recognition and reward systems, contributes to low publication rates. More damaging, the report found that there was limited access to research publications across the region, limiting the potential for collaborative research and leading to inefficiencies and research duplication.[47]

We must ask, however, whether the problem is what is being *produced*, or what is being *measured*. We would argue that developing countries are producing knowledge, and the problem is increasingly one of what is being measured. While this production is perhaps not in large volumes, it is certain that the hidden research production is far larger and more significant than that published in journal articles. What sort of a publication, metrics and rewards system can ensure that this knowledge is made available to the widest audience possible, in ways that support development efforts?

OA 2.0 and Experiments in Alternative Metrics

In recent years we have seen a proliferation of scholarly metrics, many indeed designed to take advantage of the OA environment and to provide alternative to the JIF.[48] The rationale is that better tools that are easy for scholars to use will form part of the OA toolkit and further drives the uptake of OA. The eigenfactor developed by Carl Bergstrom,[49] which employs Google-like page rank indices to refine citation ranking; the refinement of usage and download metrics from repositories[50]; and the use of recommender and rating systems by PLoS ONE[51] are all welcome developments.

While these new metrics are an improvement over the JIF, such as the longer window of citation and multiple data sources, these measures do not really extend beyond the literature and into the dynamic nature of the research life cycle and the diverse forms of scholarly communications that are taking place. In essence, the journal article in its final form is still being treated by conventional publishers as a static object to be counted, rather than a dynamic artifact at a specific stage in the knowledge production and dissemination cycle. What remains to be developed are tools that capture the multiple benefits at various stages of the research knowledge life cycle and the recognition mechanisms that recognize these multiple benefits, not only at the publication stage, but also during the research process (for example new protocols, data generation, community engagement, and postpublication review).

Happily, we are witnessing an expansion of the ethos of OA to a broadened conception of openness in scientific research and scholarly practices. Beyond citation impact, researchers are beginning to document the multiple benefits of more open practices to research and their dissemination. What we are seeing, in effect, is a merging of open access with open research approaches.

A recent study by the United Kingdom–based Research Information Network[52] found a number of distinct benefits of openness reported by researchers, such as the increased efficiency of research through lower costs of data collection, avoidance of duplication of effort, and sharing of protocols and best practices. Some researchers reported that making methodologies and protocols open for comments and scrutiny led to more rigorous and higher quality of research. Others noted that reuse of data and other material created by other researchers led to new research questions and new ways of engaging existing questions with new data. In particular, the open access to government data in the United Kingdom has allowed epidemiologists to reuse the data in ways that had direct impact on health policy.

Openness has also led to enhanced collaboration and community building. At the same time the enhanced visibility of research leads to new opportunities for much wider engagement, not only across research communities, but also with the broader public in the form of citizen science and public engagement with the process and result of research. Researchers are also using a variety of social media, from initial proposal writing, to data gathering, to publishing and subsequent knowledge mobilization and knowledge translation after formal publication.

A growing number of researchers are experimenting with new forms of publishing. The traditional scientific paper is being deconstructed; an article may be published as a composite of modules, which allows the data, analysis tools, protocols, interpretations, multimedia objects, and supplementary materials to be made available in whole and in parts. These components can also be cited and linked in multiple ways.[53] An author or research group can be cited and given credit for the data made available, or for providing the software tools, or for their interpretation of the data or the subject.

Web 2.0 and semantic mark-up tools now exist that allow for easy implementation of the modular structure of new publications; this may lead to a more fine-grained articulation of the original contributions to knowledge and provide better resolution to authorship and attribution. An example is WikiDashboard,[54] a social dynamic analysis tool for Wikipedia intended to keep track of the contributions by dispersed writers. It is easy to imagine how such a tool could be adapted for credit and reputation attribution in open collaborative research.

Jason Priem and Bradley M. Hemminger compiled and reviewed a growing list of Web 2.0 applications that they grouped into seven categories: "bookmarking, reference managers, recommendation services, comments on articles, microblogging, Wikipedia, and blogging."[55] They pointed out that as researchers increasingly adopt these tools for scholarly purpose, the usage and socially generated data gathered by these tools could be harnessed for building services for "scientometrics 2.0."[56]

But managing the proliferation of data and more metrics is a daunting task, and making sense of these diverse sources would be even more challenging. A key constraint for researchers is time, and services that integrate these diverse tools into the researchers' workflow will be more attractive to busy researchers. Given the early stage of such development, however, the key question of whether these tools will bring the appropriate recognition for researchers remains to be answered. As Neylon has argued, technology solutions are available, as are the licenses, to enable OA. More intractable, however, are issues of research culture.

Open Access 2.0 and the Developing World

Whether Web 2.0 platforms can be harnessed for publishing and dissemination of research from the Global South is an area that is not well researched. This is a significant question, as a large percentage of research conducted in the developing world by local researchers does not make it to the formal publication stage for a variety of reasons. The academic reward and promotion system, which rewards journal articles as the required publication output, fails to recognize the successive transformations of the university's relationship with civil society and industry over the twentieth century and hence the realities of research production. Arguing for increased funding and recognition of use-inspired research in South African universities, David Cooper suggests that this would form part of a necessary realignment with current realities: "[A] national position needs to be articulated .`. . that in the knowledge society of the third industrial revolution, issues of health, housing, transport, etc., are not independent of university research efforts. In fact, university research . . . should directly seek to provide knowledge for the alleviation of such social problems and hence for the condition of poverty of the majority of our population."[57]

This would lead, according to Cooper, to the inclusion, in recognition and reward systems, of the policy and development-oriented publications that were being produced in the research groupings he studied. This concurs with the findings of a study of research communication at the University of Cape Town's Opening Scholarship program,[58] which identified a culture of "translational" scholarship, or what Cooper calls "use-inspired basic research,"[59] in a number of research groupings. These produced, alongside traditional peer-reviewed articles, a range of publications, many of which were posted online on departmental websites, targeting increased impact among policymakers and communities.

In other cases, research of this kind is simply not communicated at all. For example, researchers in Ugandan public universities and research institutions gather data in many areas, such as public health, crop yield, and water quality. But often these data are not analyzed and synthesized due to a lack of funding or appropriate methodologies or analytic tools, and researchers may not have the training or language facility to write up research for formal publication.[60] A good deal of valuable data, therefore, has been languishing in back rooms, often forgotten, resulting in duplication of research. Across Africa, this scenario is being played out repeatedly, contributing to the lack of local knowledge bases needed for solving local problems.

Many policymakers are not aware of the benefits of OA and open science, and most are not familiar with social media and their potential usage for science dissemination. There is a clear need to raise greater awareness, not only in support for capacity building for local research, but also for the use of new tools for dissemination, engagement, assessment, and recognition, while not simply duplicating the power structure of the Global North. At a practical level, one can imagine digital repositories being set up for researchers to upload and store their research materials, including data, draft papers, preprints, research reports, theses, proposals as well as postprints. Support for social networking tools could enhance research collaboration across national boundaries.

Platforms such as AuthorAid,[61] set up by the International Network for the Availability of Scientific Publications (INASP), are laudable experiments in using Web 2.0 to build scientific capacity in the Global South. The site is essentially a social networking platform that allows established researchers to serve as mentors for less-experienced researchers. But additional tools are required, such as repositories, and they should be integrated into the same platform to create collaborative spaces for knowledge development and sharing.

This expanded concept of research communication could also help support more effectively the variety of communicative efforts that African researchers are undertaking in their search for the impact their research can have on development goals. For example, in one of the author's video interviews with a Kenyan crop scientist, Professor Mary Abukutsa-Onyango,[62] the professor discusses the challenges she faced when trying to publish her original research on African Indigenous Vegetables (AIV) in international journals, and notes the importance of OA journals in Africa to ensure that important research relevant to the continent is being published, read, and applied. She also discusses the potential impact that the dissemination of her work (particularly through translated literature in the form of simplified pamphlets to the farmers and policymakers) can have on poverty reduction, improvements in nutrition, agricultural development, and environmental sustainability. She also hints at the wider potential for capability development and the reinforcement of cultural values, which she sees as part and partial of development for countries like Kenya.

It is unlikely that the kinds of impact noted could be easily recorded by existing 2.0 tools, nor is it clear at this stage how metrics can be created to better reflect these uncaptured impacts. But it is important to gather examples such as the research done by Abukutsa-Onyango and to build awareness of the issues and possibilities, to follow the multiple impacts through, and attempt, as far as possible, to measure those impacts and provide a more persuasive policy rationale for research funders and governments.

Such an approach would hopefully enable policymakers to reach better-informed decisions, provide support for the development of access and dissemination policies, and have an effect on assessment initiatives outside the narrow framework of citation metrics.

Policy Alignment

The question then, is how to convince researchers and policymakers alike to take up OA 2.0 as the guiding approach to research metrics. Some proponents of OA see the higher citation impact as a key incentive for authors and assume that this alone would be sufficient to drive the widespread adoption of OA.[63] Economic arguments for better return on research investment have also been made, promoting the idea that funders should therefore favor OA given their interest in seeing the greater impact of the research they fund.[64] But a decade of experimentation with author self-archiving of published papers has shown that left to OA proponents' own initiative, self-archiving rate has hovered around 10 percent to 15 percent for most institutions. This has led some key proponents of OA to advocate for funding and policy mandates in order to propel higher uptake of OA.

It has not been fully acknowledged, however, that these arguments have tended to focus on the leverage of the traditionally accepted publication outputs—formally published journal articles and scholarly books. This narrower vision, this chapter has argued, fails to engage fully with the transformation of research practice in the postwar development of the knowledge economy as well as with the fundamental transformations in communications in the twenty-first-century networked society. Openness generates a host of benefits, and policy needs to reflect the values of these benefits so that researchers are encouraged to embrace them and further amplify them. Institutions and funders need to balance the value placed on the agency (the process and interactions), rather than simply on the output and quantity of research.[65]

In many countries affiliated with the Organisation for Economic Co-operation and Development (OECD), public funders are beginning to place stronger emphasis on the importance of social engagement, public dialogue, knowledge translation, and mobilization as part and parcel of the research life cycle.[66] In countries like Canada, funding is being made available for knowledge translation projects in order to maximize the multiple impacts of research, in public health and in other areas of the social sciences.[67] It may well be the case that if funder policy encouraging social engagement were to be aligned with policy on OA, we may see an increased uptake of both by scientists and a cascade of possible benefits as a result.

At the same time, universities need to revisit the primary mission of knowledge creation and stewardship, and place stronger emphasis on the scholarship of engagement, which "means connecting the rich resources of the university to our most pressing social, civic and ethical problems, to our children, to our schools, to our teachers and to our cities."[68] Indeed the reputation of an institution should be tied to the degree of such engagement, not simply ranking on some international scale based largely on citation impact.

Blade Nzimande, Minister of Higher Education and Training in South Africa, has called for a change in the prevailing ranking system: "Our universities, in particular, should be directing their research focus to address the development and social needs of our communities. The impact of their research should be measured by how much difference it makes to the needs of our communities, rather than by just how many international citations researchers receive in their publications."[69]

Many South African academics are doing what Nzimande advocates, but the policy administered by his department (DHET) and driven by the often conservative senior echelons of the universities still often blocks the full acknowledgment of and reward for much of the research being done. If South African and African research is really to contribute to regional development goals, as the policymakers constantly request, this will need to change. The whole suite of research output will have to be taken into account, beyond the narrow field of journal articles, monographs, and books.

At the same time, new types of data that correspond to the commitment above have to be collected for generating a new metrics, and new kinds of accounting based on social accounting principles that measure multiple values would have to be employed to generate the reputation of such new metrics. A starting point is to expand the vocabulary on impact to include other kinds of success, value, and capital and to recognize that depending on the kind of value we wish to emphasize, we will need to employ the appropriate or correspondent metrics. Metrics, in other words, should serve to support what we value, and not define it. The narrow focus of the journal impact factor as the one-size-fits-all metric for valuing scholarship has had a damaging influence in obscuring the realities of twenty-first-century research, particularly in the developing world, impeding the implementation of the development focus that the policymakers seek.

Conclusion

We live in a time when some of the most pressing problems of humanity are transnational and global in nature. The solution to these problems, such as the growing inequality in health and wealth, and the many negative consequences of climate change, requires a substantial involvement by the public sector and new kinds of thinking centered on nonmarket-based peer production of knowledge. The deep negative effect of the current global recession draws sharp attention to the failures of neoliberal economic theories based on the power of market and growth. It serves as a critical reminder that there is a pressing need to redefine the values that underpin recognition and reward systems for universities, their researchers, and their outputs—and to align them with public good and development goals.

Decision makers, funding agencies, faculty members, and researchers have the responsibility to learn about the value of different emerging metrics, and not to rely solely on commercial providers to dictate the terms of evaluation. Currently we have a highly dysfunctional scholarly communication system, especially in the sciences, where both the means of publishing and the means of evaluation are controlled by private for-profit entities that are not accountable to the public. The OA movement has in part exposed some of this structural imbalance.

The scholarly community has the means and the tools to correct this situation and to bring research back in line for the public interest. Now is the opportune time for stakeholders in the scholarly communication system to work collaboratively toward a new set of tools and policies that reframe scholarship and knowledge in terms of the diversity of processes and research impact.

While we have seen a proliferation of metrics for measuring productivity, so far the rankings of universities have not been particularly good at valuing their roles in social responsibility, environmental sustainability, and community engagement. It is time to produce a new kind of reputation ranking based on the institution's contribution to the public good and their commitment to a global knowledge commons. This will ultimately serve to overcome Benkler's divide between neoliberal informational economy and the cultural ethos of the network society.

Notes

1. M. Laakso et al., "The Development of Open Access Journal Publishing from 1993 to 2009," PLoS ONE 6, no. 6 (2011): e20961, doi:10.1371/journal.pone.0020961; R. Poynder, "Open Access by Numbers. Open and Shut," 2011, http://poynder .blogspot.ca/2011/06/open-access-by-numbers.html; see also "The Global OA Map," http://openaccessmap.org.

2. L. Carr, A. Swan, and S. Harnad, "Creating and Curating the Cognitive Commons: Southampton's Contribution," in *Curating the European University*, ed. M. Simons, M. Decuvpere, J. Vlieghe, and J. Masschelein (Leuven, BE: Universitaire Pers Leuven, 2011), 193–199, http://eprints.soton.ac.uk/271844.

3. L. Chan and S. Costa, "Participation in the Global Knowledge Commons: Challenges and Opportunities for Research Dissemination in Developing Countries," *New Library World* 106, no. 3/4 (2005): 141–163 https://tspace.library.utoronto.ca/bitstream/1807/2388/2/chan_costa.pdf; N. Boshoff, "South–South Research Collaboration of Countries in the Southern African Development Community (SADC)," *Scientometrics* 84, no. 2 (2010): 481–503.

4. The Prime Minister of Namibia, Nahas Angula, speaking at the 2009 World Conference on Higher Education, in the Round Table on African Higher Education. Quoted in E. Reddon "An Academic Revolution," *Inside Higher Ed*, November 22, 2009, http://www.insidehighered.com/news/2009/07/07/unesco.

5. As the result of a number of factors, including the marketization of universities and demands for numeric measures to measure efficiency and outputs, the Thompson Reuters journal impact factor has, over the last fifty years, become the single most dominant measure for research effectiveness, being used to measure national levels of research publication effectiveness in documents such as the UNESCO World Science Report. See B. D. Cameron, "Trends in the Usage of ISI Bibliometric Data: Uses, Abuses, and Implications," *Libraries and the Academy* 5, no. 1 (2005): 105–125; and É. Archambault, and V. Larivière "History of Journal Impact Factor: Contingencies and Consequences, *Scientometrics* 79, no. 3 (2009): 639–653.

6. S. Arunachalam, "The Global Research Village: A View from the Periphery," *Digital Library of Information Science and Technology*, http://arizona.openrepository.com/arizona/handle/10150/105067; L. Velho, "The "Meaning" of Citation in the Context of a Scientifically Peripheral Country," *Scientometrics* 9, no. 1–2 (1986): 71–89.

7. V. Archambault and E. Larivière, "The Limits of Bibliometrics for the Analysis of the Social Science and Humanities literature," in *UNESCO World Social Science Report: Knowledge Divides* (Paris: UNESCO Publishing and International Social Science Council, 2010): 251–254; E. Hazelkorn, "Pros and Cons of Research Assessment," in *UNESCO World Social Science Report: Knowledge Divides* (Paris: UNESCO Publishing and International Social Science Council, 2010): 255–258. http://unesdoc.unesco.org/images/0018/001883/188333e.pdf.

8. M. Castells, *The Rise of the Network Society* (Malden, MA: Blackwell Publishers, 2000).

9. Y. Benkler, *The Wealth of Networks: How Social Production Transforms Markets and Freedom* (New Haven, CT: Yale University Press, 2007).

10. See, for example, C. Neylon and S. Wu, "Article-Level Metrics and the Evolution of Scientific Impact," *PLoS Biology*7, no. 11 (November 2009): e1000242, http://dx.plos.org/ambra-doi-resolver/10.1371/journal.pbio.1000242; see also Neylon's blog, *Science in the Open*, http://cameronneylon.net,where alternative metrics are extensively discussed and J. Priem, "Altmetrics: A Manifesto," 2010, http://www.altmetrics.org.

11. Y. Benkler, "The Idea of Access to Knowledge and the Information Commons: Long-term Trends and Basic Elements," in *Access to Knowledge in the Age of Intellectual Property*, ed. G. Krikorian and A. Kapczynski (New York: Zone Press, 2010): 217.

12. UNESCO, *Toward Knowledge Societies*: *UNESCO World Report* (Paris: UNESCO Publishing, 2005), http://unesdoc.unesco.org/images/0014/001418/141843e.pdf; D. Bloom, D. Canning, and K. Chan, *Higher Education and Economic Development in Africa* (Washington, D.C.: World Bank, 2005), http://ent.arp.harvard.edu/AfricaHigherEducation/Reports/BloomAndCanning.pdf.

13. A ten-year partnership program among the Association of Commonwealth Universities (ACU), the Association of African Universities (AAU), and Higher Education South Africa (HESA).

14. Benkler, "The Idea of Access," 223.

15. C. S. Wagner, *The New Invisible College: Science for Development*, (Washington, D. C.: Brookings Institution Press, 2008).

16. Benkler, "The Idea of Access," 220–221.

17. P. Drahos and J. Briathwaite, *Information Feudalism: Who Owns the Knowledge Economy?* (New York: New Press, 2003).

18. UNESCO, *UNESCO Science Report 2010: The Current Status of Science Around the World*, (Paris: UNESCO Publishing, 2010).

19. B. D. Cameron "Trends in the Usage of ISI Bibliometric Data: Uses, Abuses, and Implications," *Libraries and the Academy* 5, no. 1 (2005): 105–125; A. Paasi, "Globalisation, Academic Capitalism, and the Uneven Geographies of International Journal Publishing Spaces," *Environment and Planning* 37, no. 5 (2005): 769–789; C. Merrett, "The Expropriation of Intellectual Capital and the Political Economy of International Academic Publishing," *Critical Arts: A Journal of South-North Cultural and Media Studies* 20, no. 1 (2006): 96–111.

20. UNESCO, *World Social Science Report*, 248–261.

21. A. S. Canagarajah, *The Geopolitics of Academic Writing* (Pittsburgh, PA: University of Pittsburgh, 2002).

22. D. King, "The Scientific Impact of Nation," *Nature* 430, (2004): 311–316, http://www.nature.com/nature/journal/v430/n6997/full/430311a.html.

23. J. Guédon, "Open Access and the Divide Between 'Mainstream' and 'Peripheral' Scien' ,," in *Como gerir e qualificar revistas científicas* (in English translation), http:// eprints.rclis.org/10778/1/Brazil-final.pdf.

24. See http://www.worldmapper.org/display.php?selected=205. The authors have been granted permission to reproduce this figure under the terms of the Creative Commons Attribution License, which permits unrestricted use, distribution, and reproduction in any medium, provided the original author and source are credited. Source of data used to create map: World Bank's 2005 World Development Indicators.

25. J. Adams, C. King, and D. Hook, *Global Research Report: Africa* (Leeds: Thomson Reuters, 2010), 8, http://thomsonreuters.com/content/corporate/docs/globalresearch report-africa.pdf.

26. S. Badat, "The World-Class University and the Global South," in *UNESCO World Social Science Report: Knowledge Divides* (Paris: UNESCO Publishing and International Social Science Council, 2010): 246.

27. Ibid.

28. L. Chan, B. Kirsop, and S. Arunachalam, "Open Access Archiving: The Fast Track to Building Research Capacity in Developing Countries," (London: SciDev.Net., 2005), http://www.scidev.net/en/features/open-access-archiving-the-fast-track-to -building-r.html; L. Chan, B. Kirsop, and S. Arunachalam, "Towards Open and Equitable Access to Research and Knowledge for Development," PLoS Med 8, no. 3 (2011): e1001016. http://www.plosmedicine.org/article/info:doi/10.1371/journal .pmed.1001016.

29. W. Gevers and X. Mati, eds. *Report on a Strategic Approach to Research Publishing in South Africa* (Pretoria: Academy of Science of South Africa, 2006): 75–77, http://www.assaf.co.za/wp-content/uploads/reports/evidence_based/assaf_strategic _research_publishing.pdf.

30. Badat, "The World-Class," 246–247.

31. Guédon, "Open Access," 9.

32. E. Gray, "Access to Africa's Knowledge: Publishing Development Research and Measuring Value," *African Journal of Information and Communication.* Special issue on Scholarly Communication and Access to Information, edited by Luci Abrahams and Eve Gray, 2010, 4–19, http://link.wits.ac.za/journal/AJIC10-Gray.pdf.

33. J. Mouton et al., "The State of Public Science in the SADC Region," in *Toward a Common Future: Higher Education in the SADC Region: Research Findings from Four SARUA Studies*, Study Series 2008, ed. P. Kotecha (Johannesburg: SARUA, 2008), 199–302, http://www.sarua.org/files/publications/TACF/Chapter4_full.pdf.

34. Benkler, *The Wealth of Networks*, 303.

35. Gevers and Mati, *Report on a Strategic Approach*, 75–77; UNESCO, *World Social Science Report*, 253.

36. Benkler, "The Idea of Access," 329–344.

37. The Budapest Open Access Initiative, http://www.opensocietyfoundations.org/openaccess/read.

38. S. Harnad et al., "The Access/Impact Problem and the Green and Gold Roads to Open Access: An Update," Serials Review 34, no. 1 (2008): 36–40.

39. A. Swan, "The Open Access Citation Advantage: Studies and Results to Date," February, 2010, ECS EPrints.

40. Directory of Open Access Journals, http://www.doaj.org (information from November 1, 2011).

41. B.-C. Björk et al,"Open Access to the Scientific Journal Literature: Situation 2009," PLoS ONE 5, no. 6 (2010): e11273, doi:10.1371/journal.pone.0e011273, http://www.plosone.org/article/citationList.action?articleURI=info%3Adoi%2F10.1371%2Fjournal.pone.0011273.

42. Y. Gargouri et al., "Self-Selected or Mandated, Open Access Increases Citation Impact for Higher Quality Research," PLoS ONE 5, no. 10 (2010): e13636. http://www.plosone.org/article/info%3Adoi%2F10.1371%2Fjournal.pone.0013636.

43. *Gevers* and Mati, *Report on a Strategic Approach*, 75–77.

44. Scientific Electronic Library Online, http://www.scielo.org./php/index.php.

45. N. L. Maron and K. K. Smith, *Current Models of Digital Scholarly Communication: Results of an Investigation Conducted by Ithaka for the Association of Research Libraries*, (Washington, DC: ARL, 2008): 6.

46. C. Neylon, "What Would Scholarly Communications Look Like if We Invented it Today?," Blog posting, *Science in the Open*, 2010, http://cameronneylon.net/blog/what-would-scholarly-communications-look-like-if-we-invented-it-today/.

47. L. Abrahams et al., "Opening Access to Knowledge in Southern African Universities," in *SARUA Study Series* (Johannesburg: Southern African Regional Universities Association, 2008), http://www.sarua.org/?q=publications/opening-access-knowledge-southern-african-universities.

48. M. A. Banks and R. Dellavalle, "Emerging alternatives to the impact factor," *OCLC Systems & Services* 24, no. 3 (2008): 167–173, doi:10.1108/10650750810898200; J. Bollen et al., "A Principal Component Analysis of 39 Scientific Impact Measures," PLoS ONE 4 no. 6 (2009): e6022, doi:10.1371/journal.pone.0006022.

49. C. T. Bergstrom, J. D. West and M. A. Wiseman, "The Eigenfactor™ Metrics," *The Journal of Neuroscience* 28, no. 45 (2008): 11433–11434, doi:10.1523/JNEUROSCI.0003-08.2008.

50. T. Brody et al., "Incentivizing the Open Access Research Web: Publication-Archiving, Data-Archiving and Scientometrics," *CTWatch Quarterly* 3, no. 3 (2007).

51. PLoSOne, is built on the separation of scientific rigor and impact. The former is reviewed before publication, the latter only after publication. PLoSOne is growing exponentially and is being emulated by a number of the big journal publishers. The prediction is that this model of megajournal could account for 50 percent of the literature by 2016. A variety of new impact factors—beyond the citation count—are being explored and the value of the content is being enhanced through the creation of social networking hubs. Mark Patterson described this in a paper, "Re-engineering the Functions of Journals," at the CERN 2011 Workshop on Innovations in Scholarly Communications (A17), 2011, https://indico.cern.ch/contributionDisplay.py ?sessionId=8&contribId=20&confId=103325.

52. "Open Science Case Studies," Research Information Network UK, 2010, http://www.dcc.ac.uk/projects/open-science-case-studies.

53. A. de Waard and J. Kircz, "Modeling Scientific Discourse—Shifting Perspectives and Persistent Issues," in *ELPUB2008. Open Scholarship: Authority, Community, and Sustainability in the Age of Web 2.0*, Proceedings of the 12th International Conference on Electronic Publishing, ed. L. Chan and S. Mornati, Toronto, Canada, June 25–27, 2008, 234–245.

54. http://wikidashboard.appspot.com.

55. J. Priem and B. Hemminger, "Scientometrics 2.0: Toward New Metrics of Scholarly Impact on the Social Web," *First Monday* 15 no. 7 (2010), http://www.uic.edu/htbin/cgiwrap/bin/ojs/index.php/fm/article/view/2874/2570.

56. Ibid.

57. D. Cooper, *The University in Development: Case Studies of Use-Oriented Research* (Pretoria: HSRC Press, 2011): 329, http://www.hsrcpress.ac.za/product.php?productid =2286&freedownload=1.

58. Opening Scholarship, http://www.cet.uct.ac.za/OpeningScholarship.

59. Cooper, *The University in Development*, 2011.

60. P. Nampala, see interview: http://vimeo.com/15370013.

61. AuthorAid, http://www.authoraid.info.

62. M. Abukutsa-Onyango, interview by L. Chan, February 10, 2010, http://vimeo.com/10169351.

63. S. Harnad, "Waking OA's 'Slumbering Giant': The University's Mandate to Mandate Open Access," *New Review of Information Networking* 14, (2008): 51–68.

64. J. Houghton et al., *Economic Implications of Alternative Scholarly Publishing Models: Exploring the Costs and Benefits*, London and Bristol: Joint Information Systems Com-

mittee (JISC), 2009: J. W. Houghton and C. Oppenheim, "The Economic Implications of Alternative Publishing Models," *Prometheus* 28, (2010): 41–54.

65. M. Hall, "Minerva's Owl. A Response to John Houghton and Charles Oppenheim's 'The Economic Implications of Alternative Publishing Models,'" *Prometheus* 28, (2010): 61–71.

66. A. Kitson and S. E. Straus, "The Knowledge-to-action Cycle: Identifying the Gaps," *Canadian Medical Association Journal* 182, no. 2, (2010): E73–E77; Knowledge Translation at the Canadian Institutes of Health Research (n.d.), http://www.ncddr .org/kt/products/focus/focus18.

67. R. Landry et al., "The Knowledge-Value Chain: A Conceptual Framework for Knowledge Translation in Health," *Bull World Health Organ* [online] 84, no. 8 (2006): 597–602, http://www.scielosp.org/scielo.php?script=sci_arttext&pid=S0042-9686200 6000800009&lng=en&nrm=iso.

68. E. L. Boyer, "The Scholarship of Engagement," *Bulletin of the American Academy of Arts and Sciences* 49, no. 7 (1996): 32.

69. Speech delivered at the Women in Science Awards, Johannebsurg, August 21, 2009. Reported on the Department of Higher Education and Training website, http://www.dhet.gov.za.

Bibliography

Abrahams, L., M. Burke, E. Gray, and A. Rens. "Opening Access to Knowledge in Southern African Universities." *SARUA Study Series*. Johannesburg: Southern African Regional Universities Association, 2008. http://www.sarua.org/?q=content/ opening-access-knowledge-southern-african-universities.

Adams, J., C. King, and D. Hook. *Global Research Report: Africa*. Leeds, UK: Thomson Reuters, 2010. http://thomsonreuters.com/content/corporate/docs/globalresearchreport -africa.pdf.

Archambault, V., and E. Larivière. "The Limits of Bibliometrics for the Analysis of the Social Science and Humanities Literature." In *2010 World Social Science Report: Knowledge Divides*. Paris: UNESCO Publishing and International Social Science Council, 2010: 251–254. Arunachalam, S. "The Global Research Village: A View from the Periphery." *Digital Library of Information Science and Technology*, http://arizona .openrepository.com/arizona/bitstream/10150/105377/1/Article_11.pdf.

Badat, S. The World-Class University and the Global South. In *UNESCO World Social Science Report: Knowledge Divides*, 245–246. Paris: UNESCO Publishing and International Social Science Council, 2010.

Banks, M. A., and R. Dellavalle. "Emerging Alternatives to the Impact Factor." *OCLC Systems & Services* 24 (3) (2008): 167–173. doi:10.1108/10650750810898200.

Benkler, Y. *The Wealth of Networks: How Social Production Transforms Markets and Freedom*. New Haven, CT: Yale University Press, 2007.

Benkler, Y. The Idea of Access to Knowledge and the Information Commons: Long-term Trends and Basic Elements. In *Access to Knowledge in the Age of Intellectual Property*, ed. G. Krikorian and A. Kapczynski, 217–236. New York: Zone Press, 2010.

Bergstrom, C. T., J. D. West, and M. A. Wiseman. "The Eigenfactor™ Metrics." *Journal of Neuroscience* 28 (45) (2008): 11433–11434. doi:10.1523/JNEUROSCI.0003-08.2008.

Björk, B.-C., P. Welling, M. Laakso, P. Majlender, T. Hedlund, and G. Gudnason. "Open Access to the Scientific Journal Literature: Situation 2009." *PLoS ONE* 5 (6) (2010): e11273. doi:10.1371/journal.pone.0011273 http://www.plosone.org/article/citationList.action?articleURI=info%3Adoi%2F10.1371%2Fjournal.pone.0011273.

Bloom, D., D. Canning, and K. Chan. *Higher Education and Economic Development in Africa*. Washington, DC: World Bank, 2005.

Bollen, J., H. Van de Sompel, A. Hagberg, and R. Chute. "A Principal Component Analysis of 39 Scientific Impact Measures." *PLoS ONE* 4 (6) (2009): e6022. doi:10.1371/journal.pone.0006022.

Boshoff, N. "South–South Research Collaboration of Countries in the Southern African Development Community (SADC)." *Scientometrics* 84 (2) (2010): 481–503.

Boyer, E. L. "The Scholarship of Engagement." *Bulletin—American Academy of Arts and Sciences. American Academy of Arts and Sciences* 49 (7) (1996): 18–33.

Brody, T., and L. Carr. Y. Gingras, C. Hajjem, S. Harnad, A. Stevan, A. Swan, L. Dirks, and T. Hey,. "Incentivizing the Open Access Research Web: Publication-Archiving, Data-Archiving and Scientometrics." *CTWatch Quarterly* 3 (3) (2007): 42–50.

Cameron, B. D. "Trends in the Usage of ISI Bibliometric Data: Uses, Abuses, and Implications." *Libraries and the Academy* 5 (1) (2005): 105–125.

Carr, L., A. Swan, and S. Harnad. "Creating and Curating the Cognitive Commons: Southampton's Contribution." In *Curating the European University*, edited by M. Simons, M. Decuvpere, J. Vlieghe, and J. Masschelein, 193–199. Leuven, Belgium: Universitaire Pers Leuven, 2011). http://redir.eprints.ecs.soton.ac.uk/redir.php?uri=/21844.

Castells, M. *The Rise of the Network Society*. Malden, MA: Blackwell Publishers, 2000.

Canagarajah, A. S. *The Geopolitics of Academic Writing*. Pittsburgh, PA: University of Pittsburgh, 2002.

Chan, L., B. Kirsop, and S. Arunachalam. "Open access Archiving: The Fast Track to Building Research Capacity in Developing Countries." (London: SciDev.Net., 2005). http://www.scidev.net/en/features/open-access-archiving-the-fast-track-to-building -r.html.

Chan, L., and S. Costa. "Participation in the Global Knowledge Commons: Challenges and Opportunities for Research Dissemination in Developing Countries." *New Library World* 106 (3/4) (2005): 141–163. https://tspace.library.utoronto.ca/ bitstream/1807/2388/2/chan_costa.pdf.

Chan, L., B. Kirsop, and S. Arunachalam. "Towards Open and Equitable Access to Research and Knowledge for Development." *PLoS Medicine* 8 (3) (2011): e1001016. http://www.plosmedicine.org/article/info:doi/10.1371/journal.pmed.1001016.

Cooper, D. *The University in Development: Case Studies of Use-Oriented Research.* Pretoria: HSRC Press, 2011. http://www.hsrcpress.ac.za/product.php?productid=2286 &freedownload=1.

De Waard, A., and J. Kircz. "Modeling Scientific Discourse—Shifting Perspectives and Persistent Issues." In *ELPUB2008. Open Scholarship: Authority, Community, and Sustainability in the Age of Web 2.0*, Proceedings of the 12th International Conference on Electronic Publishing, ed. L. Chan and S. Mornati, Toronto, Canada 25–27 June, 2008, 234–245.

Drahos, P., and J. Briathwaite. *Information Feudalism: Who Owns the Knowledge Economy?* New York: New Press, 2003.

Gargouri, Y., C. Hajjem, V. Lariviere, Y. Gingras, L. Carr, T. Brody, and S. Harnad. "Self-Selected or Mandated, Open Access Increases Citation Impact for Higher Quality Research." *PLoS ONE* 5 (10) (2010): e13636. http://www.plosone.org/article/ info%3Adoi%2F10.1371%2Fjournal.pone.0013636.

Gray, E. "Access to Africa's Knowledge: Publishing Development Research and Measuring Value." *African Journal of Information and Communication.* Special Issue on Scholarly Communication and Access to Information, edited by Luci Abrahams and Eve Gray, 2010, 4–19, http://link.wits.ac.za/journal/AJIC10-Gray.pdf.

Gevers, W., and X. Mati eds. *Report on a Strategic Approach to Research Publishing in South Africa.* Pretoria: Academy of Science of South Africa, 2006: 75–77. http://ideas .repec.org/p/ess/wpaper/id706.html.

Guédon, J. "Open Access and the Divide Between "Mainstream" and "Peripheral" Science." In *Como gerir e qualificar revistas científicas* (in Portuguese). http://eprints .rclis.org/10760/10778/1/Brazil-final.pdf.

Hall, M. "Minerva's Owl. A Response to John Houghton and Charles Oppenheim's 'The Economic Implications of Alternative Publishing Models.'" *Prometheus* 28 (2010): 61–71.

Harnad, S., T. Brody, F. Vallières, L. Carr, S. Hitchcock, Y. Gingras, C. Oppenheim, and H. Stamerjohannes. "The Access/Impact Problem and the Green and Gold Roads to Open Access: An Update." *Serials Review* 34 (1) (2008): 36–40.

Harnad, S. "Waking OA's "Slumbering Giant": The University's Mandate To Mandate Open Access." *New Review of Information Networking* 14 (2008): 51–68.

Hazelkorn, E. "Pros and Cons of Research Assessment." In *UNESCO World Social Science Report: Knowledge Divides*. Paris: UNESCO Publishing and International Social Science Council, 2010: 255–258. http://arrow.dit.ie/cgi/viewcontent.cgi?article=1024&context=cserrep.

Houghton, J., B. Rasmussen, P. Sheehan, C. Oppenheim, A. Morris, C. Creaser, H. Greenwood, M. Summers, and A. Gourlay. Economic Implications of Alternative Scholarly Publishing Models: Exploring the Costs and Benefits. London and Bristol: Joint Information Systems Committee (JISC), 2009.

Houghton, J. W., and C. Oppenheim. "The Economic Implications of Alternative Publishing Models." *Prometheus* 28 (2010): 41–54.

King, D. "The Scientific Impact of Nation." *Nature* 430 (2004): 311–316. http://www.nature.com/nature/journal/v430/n6997/full/430311a.html.

Kitson, A., and S. E. Straus. "The Knowledge-to-Action Cycle: Identifying the Gaps." *Canadian Medical Association Journal* 182 (2) (2010): E73–E77.

Laakso, M., P. Welling, H. Bukvova, L. Nyman, B.-C. Björk, and T. Hedlund. "The Development of Open Access Journal Publishing from 1993 to 2009." *PLoS ONE* 6 (6) (2011): e20961.

Landry, R., N. Amara, A. Pablos-Mendes, R. Shademani, and I. Gold. "The Knowledge-value Chain: A Conceptual Framework for Knowledge Translation in Health." [online] *Bulletin of the World Health Organization* 84 (8) (2006): 597–602. http://www.scielosp.org/scielo.php?script=sci_arttext&pid=S0042-96862006000800009&lng=en&nrm=iso.

Maron, N. L., and K. K. Smith. *Current Models of Digital Scholarly Communication: Results of an Investigation Conducted by Ithaka for the Association of Research Libraries.* Washington, DC: ARL, 2008.

Merrett, C. "The Expropriation of Intellectual Capital and the Political Economyof International Academic Publishing." *Critical Arts: A Journal of South-North Cultural and Media Studies* 20 (1) (2006): 96–111.

Mouton, J., N. Boshoff, L. de Waal, and S. Esau. B, Imbayarwo, M. Ritter, and D. van Niekerk, "The State of Public Science in the SADC Region." In *Towards a Common Future: Higher Education in the SADC Region: Research Findings from Four SARUA Studies*, Study Series 2008, ed. P. Kotecha, 199–302. Johannesburg: SARUA, 2008. http://www.sarua.org/files/publications/TACF/Chapter4_full.pdf.

Paasi, A. "Globalisation, Academic Capitalism, and the Uneven Geographies of International Journal Publishing Spaces." *Environment and Planning* 37 (5) (2005): 769–789.

Priem, J., and B. M. Hemminger. "Scientometrics 2.0: Toward New Metrics of Scholarly Impact on the Social Web." *First Monday* 15 (7) (2010). http://www.uic.edu/htbin/cgiwrap/bin/ojs/index.php/fm/article/view/2874/2570.

Reddon, E. "An Academic Revolution." *Inside Higher Ed*, November 22, 2009. http://www.insidehighered.com/news/2009/07/07/unesco.

UNESCO. *Towards Knowledge Societies: UNESCO World Report*. Paris: UNESCO Publishing, 2005. http://unesdoc.unesco.org/images/0014/001418/141843e.pdf.

UNESCO. *UNESCO Science Report 2010: The Current Status of Science Around the World*. Paris: UNESCO Publishing, 2010. http://unesdoc.unesco.org/mages/0018/001899/189958e.pdf.

Velho, L. "The "Meaning" of Citation in the Context of a Scientifically Peripheral Country." *Scientometrics* 9 (1–2) (1986): 71–89.

Wagner, C. S. *The New Invisible College: Science for Development*. Washington, D.C.: Brookings Institution Press, 2008.

9   Open Government and Citizen Identities: Promise, Peril, and Policy

Aaron K. Martin and Carla M. Bonina

New information and communication technologies (ICTs) promise an era of remarkable and unprecedented change for developing countries around the world, particularly in terms of their capacity to facilitate channels of connectivity, information sharing, and communication between individuals, civil society groups, business organizations, and governments. These new technologies may play an essential role in the near future in enabling new forms of government transparency, citizen participation, collaboration, service provision, and accountability. This is precisely what the advocates of open government suggest.[1]

We repeatedly hear reports on the positive roles that technologies including mobile phones and online social media are already playing in our networked world: organizing the masses in disaffected societies, mobilizing groups to effect positive social and political change, exposing misdeeds, shedding light on abuses of power, and holding wrongdoers to account. For example, the large protests that followed the disputed presidential elections in Iran in 2009 were organized with the help of ICTs, with the events being described as a Twitter revolution in the country. At the time Gordon Brown, the then prime minister of the United Kingdom, commented that the Rwandan genocide would not have happened in a Twitter-enabled world.[2] There is, thus, great excitement around the possibilities for new technology to bring about more open and fairer societies.

As this chapter argues, however, achieving the goals of increased transparency of (and collaboration and political participation in) governance processes (i.e., open government) requires far more than simply adopting new technology. Harnessing the power afforded by ICTs, and particularly mobile telephony and more recent Web applications such as social networking tools, will require additional infrastructure and policy development, particularly in the closely related areas of privacy and identity. These complex infrastructures do not yet exist in many countries. Where legal protections do exist, they are often either overlooked when it comes to practical implementation or there is little enforcement.[3] The fear is that if developing countries create these systems haphazardly they may result in new vulnerabilities, including increased threats to citizens' privacy, greater information security frailties, and more sophisticated means of government surveillance. Such vulnerabilities would challenge the positive and democratic side of open government initiatives.

This chapter explores these issues. Placing the focus solely on government-citizen relationships in open government ventures, our aim is twofold: (1) to address the possible downsides and risks of citizen identity infrastructures in harnessing open government applications; and (2) to advance toward policy principles on how to mitigate these risks. While this chapter draws on empirical examples from diverse countries, mainly in the developed world, the aim is to derive useful policy advice for mitigating the problems that arise no matter the developmental context. The chapter does so in light of the findings of a 2011 report that shows there is a global culture developing in which Internet users worldwide share similar attitudes and values related to online freedom of expression, privacy, trust, and security.[4] More importantly for the chapter's argument, the report reveals that citizens from newer adopting countries such as Brazil, Mexico, China, and India are more liberal in their attitudes and behaviors regarding online privacy, as well as more engaged with Web 2.0 applications and Web usage than users in older adopting countries.[5] This is not to say that developing countries are homogeneous but simply that there are important commonalities that allow us to generalize to a certain degree on these issues. These commonalities include the aforementioned attitudes toward online privacy, freedom of expression, security, and trust as well as a widespread interest across many developing countries in pursuing new e-government platforms based on various technological innovations.

Given the focus on government-citizen relationships, the chapter begins by exploring the emerging debates on open government and its benefits and potential risks in enabling further democratic and participatory channels. The chapter then introduces the main issues linking open government and new forms of digital identity and privacy management. The ensuing analysis revolves around three topic areas that expose just some of the problems with balancing the pursuit of open government applications and maintaining citizens' privacy online. The final section offers a few implementation principles for ameliorating these problems. The hope is that the benefits of open government can be achieved while ensuring individual privacy and minimizing the risks of unnecessary and potentially harmful citizen surveillance.

Openness for Improved Democratic Governance

It is widely accepted that the rapid diffusion of the Internet and related ICTs has provided a new platform with which to improve interactions between citizens and governments.[6] Citizens in the information age can more easily and directly access both government services and public information. Similarly, government agencies are opening new channels of communication and information exchange with citizens, enabling a more efficient, transparent, and responsive government. These developments, broadly understood under the rubric of e-government policy reform,[7] are now being articulated in terms of open government as policy-makers realize the potential of new technologies.[8]

In 2005, the Organisation for Economic Co-operation and Development (OECD) declared that from the public's perspective "an open government is one where business, civil society organizations and citizens can 'know things'—obtain relevant and understandable information; 'get things'—obtain services from and undertake transactions with the government; and 'create things'—take part in decision-making processes."[9] Similarly, the Transparency and Open Government initiative launched by the U.S. government put forward the Obama administration's commitment to achieving an "unprecedented level of openness in Government."[10] The U.S. open government initiative has been designed around three core values:

• Transparency: to enable greater accountability, efficiency, and economic opportunity by making government data and operations more open.
• Participation: to create effective opportunities to drive greater and more diverse expertise into government decision making; to listen to public opinion and to increase opportunities for public engagement.
• Collaboration: to generate new ideas for solving problems by fostering cooperation across government departments, across levels of government, and with the public.

The use of new ICTs to access and disseminate information, in conjunction with the ongoing deployment of e-government programs, is seen as the most promising way to achieve the goals of openness in government.[11]

Pursuing transparency by making government information more publicly available to citizens has been one of the major drivers of many e-government portals worldwide. In Mexico, for example, the freedom of information legislation approved in 2001 mandates a records management system that supports online access to public information.[12] Legislation such as the one in Mexico has the potential to become a cornerstone for more sophisticated e-governance initiatives, as well as for increased online citizen participation.[13] One of a growing number of examples of this participatory trend is Brazil's House of Representatives e-participation website, called "e-Democracia."[14] The initiative provides various mechanisms to encourage citizen participation (i.e., identifying problems that need to be addressed, discussing possible solutions, and even how to draft bills), and it relies on the direct engagement of members of Brazil's parliament via participatory channels such as opinion polls, public forums, and chat rooms.

Collaborative technologies such as Web 2.0 provide attractive cost-effective solutions to facilitate participation, open access, and collaboration, not only in terms of citizen-government interaction but also in terms of how governments do their jobs.[15] In terms of the latter aim, the Internet and related network technologies are conceived as powerful tools to standardize work procedures and smoothen information flows, so that organizational processes become more efficient and accountable, fostering the changes prescribed by the New Public Management wave of reforms.[16]

The assumption behind open government initiatives has been that transparency and participation will enhance public management as well as governance more generally. Indeed, recent analyses and attention among researchers has been especially optimistic, focusing mainly on the potential benefits and usefulness of ICTs in delivering a "better and more open government" (see, for example, the special issue on *Government Information Quarterly 2010* on the topic).

However, more critical voices need to be heard in these debates. Transparency and open access to government information may also have their perils. In a 2009 essay, Lawrence Lessig suggested that the circulation of poorly understood or misleading information may raise confusion, while the misuse of publicly available information may force the political system into crisis[17] (as some argue is the case with the release of confidential U.S. diplomatic cables by WikiLeaks, the transparency organization). Another concern is the increase in government surveillance and potential privacy invasions that accompany governments' access to social networking data.[18] We must also consider the inherent difficulties and complexities in de-identifying large sets of government data that might include personal information on citizens, civil servants, and others before making them publicly available on government-sponsored portals.[19] Public servants are not immune from these risks either, as they also become more accountable and potentially liable if they fail to protect personal or sensitive organizational data.

Selecting the right technologies and appropriate channels to communicate both externally with the public and internally is not straightforward.

The goals of transparency, participation, and collaboration require additional infrastructure and policy development; particularly those related to the handling of personal or identifiable information. Although open government debates are receiving more and more attention,[20] little has been said about the role that digital identity management systems will be required to play as part of these platforms. Given the fact that governments have a unique relationship with citizens, this arguably requires a careful assessment of how information technology impinges upon public values.[21] Moreover, electronic authentication policies and technologies pose several issues, including multifaceted privacy issues,[22] which demand our attention. The next section deals with these issues more deeply.

Citizen Identity Management in a Digital Era

The term identity management covers a wide range of policies and technologies for enabling organizations to identify or authenticate users of a system or service and, conversely, for users to ensure the trustworthiness of the organizations with which they interact.[23] In offline settings, identification technologies include national identity cards, visas, and passports, for example, used most commonly when interacting with a bank or government agency, or crossing international borders. The issue of identity management in the context of open government, however, has taken on newfound importance as it could help to achieve the objectives of transparency and participation by allowing citizens to deal more effectively and assuredly with government online. It also requires systems and processes that potentially alter the interactions and dynamics of trust, information disclosure, and authentication as compared to face-to-face interactions (such as at the border). If leveraged correctly, these identity systems can facilitate many of the platforms that underlie open government in a privacy-sensitive and socially fair manner. If they are poorly conceived and designed, however, such policies and systems will introduce new problems and vulnerabilities. This section provides an overview of the main issues and technologies of digital identity management.

To begin, there are important differences between the concepts of identity, identification, and authentication. David Lyon distinguishes between identity and identification. Acknowledging that we tend to treat the terms as synonyms in practice, he understands the former concept as being deeply personal and relational (i.e., *I am* always *in relation to* other people and objects) and the latter as connoting more technological priorities.[24] Edgar A. Whitley and Ian Hosein further distinguish between identification and authentication.[25] Identification is the process by which a person's identity (or identity attribute) is revealed (e.g., "This is Carlos Gardel"), which is a different process from authentication, although in the common vernacular the two concepts are often conflated. Authentication strictly involves the confirmation of a request or granting of access to something and, importantly, does not necessarily require the revelation of an identity (or identity attribute). For example, some typical authentication requests include:

• "Is this person a citizen of country X?" (e.g., at a border crossing).
• "Is this young person at least eighteen years old?" (e.g., when proving whether someone is of legal age to consume alcohol).
• "Is the person an inhabitant of the local council or county?" (e.g., when accessing a restricted local service).

Importantly, at no point during these requests does a person's identity (or components thereof—his or her name, ID number, or date of birth) need to be revealed. Authentication is, therefore, fundamentally a yes/no type of request (i.e., it relies on the minimal disclosure of personal information in a transaction). Identification and authentication are thus distinct activities— motivated by different policy drivers—and need to be treated differently by systems that collect or process identity information. These concerns are particularly relevant in online settings in which, due to the nature of the medium, it is especially easy to collect information from users that may be irrelevant to the transaction at hand.

The over-identification of users, especially in contexts in which only an authentication-type request is required, may over time lead to the creation of extensive and rich data profiles or "data doubles."[26] Data doubles are the outcome of practices that aggregate information on peoples' past behaviors, transactions, associations, preferences, and so forth. These practices may also trigger concerns about unwarranted profiling and surveillance.[27] There may be a tendency to use these data for purposes that were originally not specified to the citizen (a phenomenon known as "function creep").[28] In societies in which governments have engaged extensively in such profiling activities, critical discourses about the "database state" have emerged.[29] One potential risk resulting from these surveillance practices and attendant discourses is decreased citizen trust in the government institutions pursuing new information strategies.

But appropriate information practices can help to avoid these problems. For example, in many scenarios, what is actually needed to complete a transaction or access a service is an authentication measure rather than the full disclosure of an identity. In these contexts it should be possible for users to use pseudonyms or to remain anonymous in their dealings with organizations, as long as the right information is disclosed for the relevant transaction (e.g., whether the person claiming benefits is entitled to them) and that information may be verified as trustworthy.

Currently, however, as organizations pursue new ways of solving the various problems of online identity, many of these considerations about authentication/identification and fair data collection and retention are being overlooked or neglected. Take, for example, a controversy from the world of online gaming from 2010. Without consulting its users, the gaming company Blizzard® Entertainment (makers of the very popular World of Warcraft®—a multiplayer, online role-playing game) instituted a new identification policy for participants. Its new policy required players to use their real names when participating in discussions in user forums. The original idea was to improve the quality of exchanges on the forums, on which, as one of the website's managers described it, "flame wars, trolling, and other unpleasantness run wild."[30] This Real ID policy did not go over well with gamers, who are accustomed to remaining pseudonymous in gaming environments, for these are perceived as spaces for entertainment and leisure. Under intense pressure from its community, which accused the company of neglecting users' privacy and security, Blizzard quickly retracted the policy. Other online networks, such as Facebook and Google+, are encountering similar problems with their strict user identification policies.

Governments are also trying to leverage new tools for identity management online, although for different purposes, such as simplifying user authentication procedures across different e-government portals, achieving cost savings related to online authentication, and improving government operations. Among these tools of identification and authentication are a range of different technologies and techniques—some well established, others still emerging. The paper documentation of yesteryear is being enhanced with new methods such as the insertion of computer chips and radio frequency identification (RFID) technologies. Supported by encryption techniques (digital certificates and public key infrastructures), these new "smart cards" are said to be more reliable and secure than traditional paper documents. They also require extensive technical infrastructures and organizational routines to make good on their technological promise. Aware of what is to be gained and lost in the online marketplace, the issue of electronic citizen identities is therefore fast becoming a priority for governments.[31]

As governments around the world continue strategizing and making decisions on how best to leverage digital identity systems online, many are opting to use technologies developed in the private sector, including decentralized authentication systems such as OpenID.[32] Others are reappropriating existing Web 2.0 and social networking sites for identity management purposes (see, for example, the United Kingdom's Cabinet Office's proposals to use Facebook as an authentication platform for government services[33]), sometimes with perverse and unintended effects. Many of these platforms are plagued by ongoing privacy concerns, which put agencies that are using these systems as part of their open governance initiatives in a difficult position. For example, strict rules on the use of real names on popular social networking sites may prevent citizens from discussing or campaigning on sensitive moral, social, and political topics, for fear of being personally targeted by opponents. We further discuss these and related consequences in the next section.

Open Government and Online Identity in Practice: Challenges Ahead

This section illustrates the complex dynamics at play in government initiatives to engage citizens in online environments and the implications for identity, privacy, and surveillance. Empirically, these illustrations build on observations from different contexts where the use of new ICTs to achieve more open government has caused considerable controversy. Although these cases originate in so-called developed countries, the lessons learned from them are also potentially applicable to developing countries, if applied intelligently with sufficient attention to the diversity and differences in the context.

The purpose of these illustrations is to look proactively at the benefits and risks associated with the use of these technologies for governance purposes, on which to draw policy principles. The first example relates to the use of social networking websites for political and civil engagement; the second involves the (unintentional) tracking of users on open government websites incorporating new multimedia and Web 2.0 functionality; and the third pertains to the use of mobile phones and open data for new e-government applications (i.e., m-government or mobile government).

Profiling Citizens? Political Engagement in Online Social Networks

Governments are increasingly seeking to connect with citizens online. One way of achieving these connections is by joining existing online social networks on which the public already gather, rather than attempting to create new platforms from scratch. Among these online networks are such popular web sites as Facebook, Google+, Orkut, Myspace, and Twitter. Different authors have observed a range of privacy harms in governments' use of such online social networks to engage citizens:

• Government agencies may trawl information from the profiles on these networks and use it for purposes that users did not previously consent to, including for policing, immigration, welfare administration, or tax administration purposes. A case in Israel from 2010 involved the military searching through Facebook to identify female soldiers who had claimed to be Orthodox Jewish (and thus exempt from military service), using a range of data-mining techniques to root out draft dodgers.[34] These issues are especially salient in the contemporary context in which websites such as Facebook continually update their privacy settings and in doing so expose users to unexpected publicity.

• Government could use the information provided on social networks to make unfair judgments and inferences about individuals, including their political associations[35] and sexual preferences[36]; such uses would also potentially implicate the privacy rights of a user's extended network, as profile information of these friends of friends may also be subject to harvesting and misuse.

• On a more general level, Danielle K. Citron locates harm in governments' use of online social networking information in terms of how it violates privacy norms.[37] Building on Helen Nissenbaum's notion of privacy as "contextual integrity,"[38] she argues that any government use of data gleaned from social networks is problematic as it is likely that users have shared this information based on context-dependent expectations about how it will be used and with whom it will be shared. These expectations are arguably defied when state actors join online social networks for purposes that are incongruent with users' own aims.

Another privacy-related dimension pertains to the circumstances in which government organizations are permitted to block users in these online environments. An incident from late in the year 2010 speaks to the ongoing uncertainty and sensitivity of these issues. It was revealed that the Transportation Security Administration (TSA), the U.S. government agency responsible for overseeing the country's airport security, had blocked a critical member of the public on Twitter who had expressed his opposition to the agency's latest round of security measures (involving "advanced imaging technology" and "enhanced pat-downs"). While he was eventually unblocked by the TSA, the reasons for the original censor remain unclear.[39] More importantly, the event itself raises concerns about the dynamics of exclusion in open government. If, indeed, these technologies are about giving increased voice to citizens, then under what circumstances might voices be silenced and what level of transparency and accountability should be imposed on these actions?

Recent events reveal that cases such as these do not only occur in the sphere of the developed world. After a controversial presidential election in Iran in 2010, journalists reported how the police followed electronic trails left by activists, which ended with the arrest of thousands of protest participants.[40] As well, in June 2011, the Chilean government announced a plan to monitor comments on social networks as a way to measure public perception about the current administration. The government backtracked two months later following considerable public controversy, with many worried about the potential infringement of freedom of expression and citizens' privacy.[41] These examples are indicative of the ongoing tensions surrounding privacy, freedom of expression, and open government initiatives that exist beyond North America and Europe.

Tracking Citizens and Third-Party Access to Personal Information
The technical design of the underlying platforms and technologies that make open government applications possible may also have important and inadvertent privacy consequences. Another example from the United States illustrates these concerns. Every week the U.S. president delivers a video address to the nation, which is now posted on the Internet using Web 2.0 multimedia technology. To transmit these videos the White House originally relied on Google-owned YouTube technology, which by design stores persistent cookies in users' web browsers. The use of such tracking cookies is a common yet controversial practice, especially in the public sector context. Until recently U.S. government agencies were forbidden from using such cookies on their websites due to privacy and civil liberties considerations.[42] Following an outcry from privacy activists who complained about the government tracking users online, the White House switched to another video platform which does not rely on persistent cookies—although they claimed this switch was not motivated by privacy concerns.[43] Regardless of their motivations, this incident and others (e.g., see the case of "supercookies" being used on the challenge.gov site[44]) shows how taken-for-granted design features can complicate the values of open government, while also highlighting the role that third parties play in technology development and how these solutions may implicate privacy laws and norms.

A separate case from the United Kingdom further illuminates the risks of third-party access to personal information on Web 2.0–based government platforms. In November 2010 it was revealed that users of a National

Health Service (NHS) website (known as NHS Choices), which provides general health advice to the public, have had details of their visit unknowingly communicated to Facebook, Google (for analytics purposes), and other advertisers and third parties. The information that was passed on included details of the ailments or conditions that the user was researching. Facebook users who visited the website had information about the date and time of their visit, the Web page browsed, and technical information about their Internet protocol (IP) address, browser, and operating system communicated back to the social network.[45] The only way to opt out of the service was to disable cookies in the Web browser, which is impractical as doing so makes navigating the Web difficult. The NHS has been criticized for these data-sharing practices and a formal investigation is underway.

M-Government, Open Data, and New Frontiers for Surveillance
With the exponential growth of mobile phone usage worldwide, governments have also seen the potential to extend their services and information provision to mobile platforms. M-government allows citizens, businesses, and government employees to access information and services through mobile devices, thereby increasing the range and accessibility of e-government.[46] These mobile technologies also enable the use of location-based services, which utilize mobile networks to access information about the user's current geographical position and deliver tailored information or services based on that location. For example, in Beijing authorities are tracking approximately seventeen million mobile phones to improve traffic flow in the city, which has raised privacy concerns among users.[47]

Despite some initial hype around the promise of m-government, to date there has not been extensive uptake of these services, arguably due to the lack of a unified or consistent strategy by government agencies. Certain mobile phone-based notification or payment services have emerged, but otherwise m-government offerings remain underdeveloped: "The only area of constituent-centric service where mobile technology seems to play a critical role is public safety: mass notification and location-based emergency calling clearly yield a great value to people."[48]

With the development of new smart phones and their accompanying easy-to-use applications, however, this situation is likely to change in the near future, particularly in developing countries (e.g., Android-enabled phones are being widely adopted in countries like Kenya).[49] While it is still very early in the technology development and adoption cycles to try to predict the range of m-government applications that may emerge for these new smart phones, there are emerging trends that shine some light on the issues.

Contemporaneous to the emergence of smart phones is the increased availability of public data sets—another important facet of open government—that has made the creation of mash-ups ever popular. These mash-ups combine data and functionality from different sources to create new services, many of which can be run on mobile phones. Indeed, one of the drivers of the success of smart phones is the wide availability of apps (applications), which often rely on repurposed data sets. One such service that relates to open government (albeit in an atypical sense) is an application for citizens to survey the whereabouts of registered sex offenders.

The best-selling iPhone app known as Offender Locator is a mash-up of sex offender registry data in the United States (which are publicly available online as the result of "right to know" legislation called Megan's Law) and Google Maps. The app allows users to see the last known address of released sex offenders and displays this information on a map (importantly, at the time of writing this is not real-time tracking but rather a static visualization of an offender's most recently registered home).[50]

While this might appear an extreme example of the future of m-government and the use of open data, it illustrates many of the problems that can arise when personal information (such as criminal history and address) are put online by governments without carefully considering the implications of doing so, the range of potential uses to which such information may be put, and how technological innovations might complicate the future use of such data (e.g., its use as part of a mobile phone–based mapping service). These are, of course, matters of policy which need to be democratically deliberated and informed by evidence; however, there is a convincing line of reasoning about the need to provide these and similarly demonized groups an opportunity to restart their lives once they have paid their debt to society.[51] Of course, these points extend beyond the surveillance of sex offenders to other groups and policy areas.[52] The point is that the online publication of government data is not universally desirable and that there might be good reasons to refrain from total transparency, including the protection of civil liberties.

Beyond this example, there are other emergent trends in this space which implicate issues of open government, including crime-mapping applications (see the United Kingdom's Information Commissioner's advice regarding the transparency and privacy aspects of these services[53]), the proposed use of mobile phones for e-voting, and the use of mobile technologies for the transmission of medical information to patients (as public health is often a government function in poorer parts of the world).[54] Such applications introduce a raft of complicated privacy and security issues that must be carefully considered by policymakers before they are adopted and implemented.

Policy Principles for Protecting Identities in Open Government

How can policymakers interested in developing and adopting technologies and platforms for open government purposes build their solutions to engender trust, protect privacy, and limit the potential for harmful citizen surveillance? The answer is neither straightforward nor guaranteed. Moreover, there are several dimensions to explore, ranging from technical and interoperability issues, to ensuring privacy and security, as well as questions of citizen empowerment.[55] While all these dimensions are important, here we focus on two main aspects: privacy and information security. This section builds on three policy principles developed in Scotland for privacy-friendly identity management in the context of public service delivery,[56] tailoring their recommendations to the ongoing discussion on open government.

1: Minimal Disclosure of Identifiable or Personal Information
Citizens should only be asked to prove who they are (i.e., to identify themselves) in order to use government services online when it is absolutely necessary. These systems should instead be designed to authenticate entitlement to information or services using reliable technologies that are appropriate to the medium (e.g., the Internet or mobile network). This involves asking for the minimal amount of information necessary for the transaction. To ensure the reliability and trustworthiness of these transactions, service providers should also offer a provable means for citizens to identify the organizations they are transacting with.

2: Clear, Coherent, and Verifiable Policies for Web 2.0 Platforms
Public sector organizations that aspire to offer their services on Web 2.0 and related platforms must develop clear, coherent, and verifiable privacy and information-security policies specific to these platforms. These policies should encourage Surveillance Impact Assessments or Privacy Impact Assessments (PIAs) prior the project's implementation. The United States' Department of Homeland Security (DHS) recently completed a PIA before incorporating Google Analytics on its website, which led to the decision that "neither DHS nor Google shall collect, retrieve, or retain personally identifiable information (PII) including a visitor's IP address."[57]

These policies should also call for the minimal collection and retention of personal information on open government platforms, and to require user consent for collecting these data whenever necessary. We realize that advanced data analytics and the use of "big data" for open government applications may complicate the data protection principles of notice, consent, and data minimization, but they are nonetheless fundamental to safeguarding privacy. Third parties involved in supporting these services or with access to personal data on these platforms must also abide by these policies. This can be achieved through the creation of contractual obligations specific to these privacy principles. Requiring that technology partners use privacy-enhancing technologies and systems is another way to achieve this policy objective. That way, privacy and accountability can be effectively outsourced to third-party organizations. Making systems transparent so that citizens can see exactly what data about them is being collected and shared will further empower citizens as will providing mechanisms for citizens to restrict third party access.

3: Minimize Personal Information Collected and Stored

Government agencies engaging with citizens online must minimize the personal information they collect and store. Taken to an extreme, this guidance echoes Citron's call for a "one-way-mirror" policy for government's use of data from social media.[58] This policy permits individuals to provide feedback to government on these platforms but prevents governments from using, collecting, or distributing individuals' personal data. It creates a presumption of openness as to policy-related matters and a presumption of privacy as to individuals' personal information. Citron's concept is a legal one, not a technical one. She argues that with strong privacy rules such as these, individuals may be more inclined to participate in open government initiatives.

There are, however, limitations to these sorts of proposals, including the ongoing situation in which government bodies use legal means such as data request letters, subpoenas, and search warrants to obtain these data from social media companies.[59] While outside the scope of debates on open government, these developments cannot be ignored by policymakers who aspire to pursue privacy-friendly e-government using social media and related technologies. This problem becomes worse in countries with less robust data protection laws.

Assuming one-way-mirror-type policies are impractical, government agencies should avoid centralizing the personal information they collect, segregating personal and transactional data separately, and securing access to these databases. Agencies should not track citizens on and across different open government sites and platforms. Government organizations must also consider whether the storage of identifying information is even necessary to provide their services (for often it is not).

Conclusions

Open government initiatives are quickly moving to the fore of many government agendas, and will most likely bring many benefits. Our intent is not to diminish these benefits. Rather, we aim to raise awareness of a set of potential concerns, negative effects, and unintended consequences of open government, in particular in the area of citizen identity and privacy.

We have argued that government programs that encourage and promote openness must simultaneously consider the identity infrastructures that enable such interactions and transactions. If appropriate infrastructures and policies are not put into place, the shift toward these more open spaces, in particular where personal information is concerned, could result in widespread privacy invasions, information security breaches, harmful surveillance, discrimination, or worse. As this chapter is being written, the U.S. government is pursuing new proposals for a National Strategy for Trusted Identities in Cyberspace, which capture many of the policy guidelines offered in the previous section. This is a positive development. It remains to be seen what will happen with these proposals, and importantly for policymakers in developing countries, how these developments will affect the plans for open government and online identity infrastructures in other countries.

As it has been the case with e-government in the past, governments in developing countries are especially well known for adapting models that have been first designed and implemented in developed countries.[60] Although there is no simple way of designing and implementing new digital identity systems that both respect privacy and civil liberties and guarantee all the potential good of openness, in this chapter we have proposed certain pathways worth exploring. Therefore, the policy principles we suggest serve two main purposes: (1) to advance the debate to begin addressing the complexity of dynamics of open government and its potential negative consequences; and (2) to offer some possible ways to keep risks at a minimum. In doing so, we aimed to establish the terms for further debate and discussion on digital identity within the next generation of platforms for online access, participation, and collaboration.

In light of the wide array of technologies, policies, and social and political contexts, we acknowledge that much more research is needed to understand the gamut of privacy consequences of open government ventures in developing countries. For example, what difficulties can we expect when implementing these principles in resource-constrained environments? We urge researchers interested in critical analyses of open development and e-government to consider exploring how new initiatives are impacting citizen privacy in developing country contexts and the strengths and weaknesses of the open government identity and privacy policy principles we offer in this chapter.

Notes

1. P. McDermott, "Building Open Government," *Government Information Quarterly* *27*, no. 4: 401–413.

2. K. Viner, "Internet has Changed Foreign Policy for Ever, Says Gordon Brown," *The Guardian*, June 19, 2009, http://www.guardian.co.uk/politics/2009/jun/19/gordon-brown-Internet-foreign-policy.

3. C. Wolf, "Update on Mexico's New Privacy Law: No Immediate Enforcement, but Companies Expected to Appoint Privacy Officer and Have Written Policies," Hogan Lovells Chronicle of Data Protection. April 6, 2011.

4. S. Dutta, W. Dutton, and G. Law, *The New Internet World: A Global Perspective on Freedom of Expression, Privacy, Trust and Security Online. The Global Information Technology Report 2010–2011* (Geneva: World Economic Forum, 2011).

5. Dutta et al., *New Internet World*, 2011.

6. J. E. Fountain, *Building the Virtual State: Information Technology and Institutional Change* (Washington, D.C.: Brookings Institution Press, 2001); A. Chadwick, "Bringing E-Democracy Back In: Why It Matters for Future Research on E-Governance," *Social Science Computer Review* 21, no. 4 (2003): 443–455.

7. R. Heeks, "Reinventing Government in the Information Age," in *Reinventing Government in the Information Age—International Practice in IT-enabled Public Sector Reform*, ed. by R. Heeks, 9–21 (London: Routledge, 2002); C. Bellamy, and J. A. Taylor, *Governing in the Information Age.* (Buckingham, UK; Bristol, PA: Open University Press USA, 1998); A. Cordella, "E-government: Towards the E-bureaucratic Form?," *Journal of Information Technology* 22, no. 3 (2007): 265–274.

8. H. Yu and D. G. Robinson, "The New Ambiguity of 'Open Government,'" *UCLA Law Review* 59, no. 6 (2012): 178–208.

9. OECD, *Public Sector Modernisation: Open Government* (Paris: Organisation for Economic Co-operation and Development, 2005), 1, http://www.oecd.org/gov/34455306.pdf.

10. B. Obama, *Transparency and Open Government: Memorandum for The Heads of Executive Departments and Agencies* (Washington, DC: United States Executive Office of the President, 2009), http://www.whitehouse.gov/the_press_office/TransparencyandOpenGovernment.

11. OECD, *Public Sector Modernisation*, 2005; S. Dawes, "Stewardship and Usefulness: Policy Principles for Information-based Transparency," *Government Information Quarterly* 27, no. 4 (2010): 377–383.

12. Federal Law of Transparency and Access to Public Government Information, Article 9, Congress of the United Mexican States (2001), http://freedominfo.org/documents/mexico_ley.pdf.

13. UN, *E-Government Survey 2008: From E-Government to Connected Governance* (New York: United Nations, 2008); D. M. West, *Global eGovernment 2005* (Providence, RI: Center for Public Policy, Brown University, 2005); D. M. West, *Global eGovernment 2007* (Providence, RI: Center for Public Policy, Brown University, 2007).

14. F. P. J. A. Marques, "Government and E-participation Programmes: A Study of the Challenges Faced by Institutional Projects," *First Monday* 15, no. 8 (2010), http://firstmonday.org/htbin/cgiwrap/bin/ojs/index.php/fm/article/viewArticle/2858/2583.

15. G. Aichholzer and S. Strauß, "Electronic Identity Management in E-Government 2.0: Exploring a System Innovation Exemplified by Austria," *Information Polity*, 15, no. 1–2 (2010); 139–152.

16. Heeks, "Reinventing Government," 2002; P. Dunleavy and others, *Digital Era Governance* (Oxford: Oxford University Press, 2006); Cordella, "E-Government," 2007.

17. L. Lessig, "Against Transparency," *New Republic* 240, no. 9 (2009): 37–44.

18. D. K. Citron, "Fulfilling Government 2.0's Promise with Robust Privacy Protections," *George Washington Law Review* 78, no. 4 (2010): 101–124.

19. A. Narayanan and V. Shmatikov, "Robust De-anonymization of Large Sparse Datasets," in *Proceedings of the IEEE Symposium on Security and Privacy*, Oakland, California, May 18–21 2008, Chair Y. Guan (Oakland, CA: IEEE Computer Society, 2008), 111–125; P. Ohm, "Broken Promises of Privacy: Responding to the Surprising Failure of Anonymization," *UCLA Law Review* 57 (2010): 1701–1777.

20. Dawes, "Stewardship and Usefulness," 2010.

21. M. L. Smith, M. E. Noorman, and A. K. Martin, "Automating the Public Sector and organizing Accountabilities," *Communications of the Association for Information Systems* 26, Article 1 (2010).

22. S. Holden and L. Millet, "Authentication, Privacy, and the Federal E-Government," *The Information Society* 21, no. 5 (2005): 367–377.

23. E. Whitley and G. Hosein, *Global Challenges for Identity Policies* (Basingstoke, UK: Palgrave Macmillan, 2010).

24. D. Lyon, *Identifying Citizens* (Cambridge: Polity Press, 2009).

25. Whitley and Hosein, *Global Challenges*, 2010.

26. K. D. Haggerty and R. V. Ericson, "The Surveillant Assemblage," *British Journal of Sociology* 51, no. 4 (2000): 605–622; D. Lyon, *Surveillance Studies: An Overview* (Cambridge: Polity Press, 2007).

27. R. Clarke, "The Digital Persona and Its Application to Data Surveillance," *The Information Society* 10, no. 2 (1994): 77–92.

28. B. Schneier, "Security and Function Creep," *IEEE Security & Privacy* 8, no. 1 (2010): 88.

29. See, for example, Anderson and others, *Database State*. A Report Commissioned by the Joseph Rowntree Reform Trust, Ltd. York, UK: Joseph Rowntree Trust Ltd., 2009, http://www.cl.cam.ac.uk/~rja14/Papers/database-state.pdf.

30. BBC News (online), "World of Warcraft Maker to End Anonymous Forum Logins," July 7, 2010, http://www.bbc.co.uk/news/10543100.

31. T. Stevens, J. Elliott, A. Hoikkanen, I. Maghiros, and W. Lusoli, *The State of the Electronic Identity Market: Technologies, Infrastructure, Services and Policies* (Seville: Institute for Prospective Technological Studies, 2011), http://ftp.jrc.es/EURdoc/JRC60959.pdf.

32. D. Recordon, and D. Reed, "OpenID 2.0: A Platform for User-centric Identity Management," in *Proceedings of the Second ACM Workshop on Digital Identity Management*, Alexandria, Virginia, October 30–November 3, Chair Ari Juels (New York: Association for Computing Machinery, 2006), 11–16.

33. K. Fiveash, "Cabinet Office Talks to Facebook & Co about New ID System: Online Access to Public Services Could be Via Social Networks," *The Register*, June 10, 2011, http://www.theregister.co.uk/2011/06/10/caninet_office_id_assurance _facebook/print.html.

34. N. Ungerleider, "Israeli Military Using Facebook to Find Draft Dodgers," *Fast Company*, November 23, 2010, http://www.fastcompany.com/1704908/israeli -military-using-facebook-find-draft-dodgers.

35. D. Wills and S. Reeves, "Facebook as a Political Weapon: Information in Social Networks," *British Politics* 4, no. 2 (2009): 258–265.

36. C. Jernigan and B. F. T. Mistree, "Gaydar: Facebook Friendships Expose Sexual Orientation," *First Monday* 14, no. 10 (October, 2009), http://firstmonday.org/htbin/cgiwrap/bin/ojs/index.php/fm/article/viewArticle/2611/2302.

37. Citron, "Fulfilling Government," 2010.

38. H. Nissenbaum, *Privacy in Context: Technology, Policy, and the Integrity of Social Life* (Stanford: Stanford University Press, 2009).

39. L. Sassaman, "TSA and Social Media: Being Blocked from TSA Twitter Stream," December 10, 2010, http://iwilloptout.org/2010/12/10/tsa-and-social-media-being-blocked-from-tsa-twitter-stream.

40. S. Shane, "Spotlight Again Falls on Web Tools and Change," *New York Times*, January 30, 2011, http://www.nytimes.com/2011/01/30/weekinreview/30shane.html?_r=0.

41. La Tercera, 2011. "Parlamentarios opositores valoran decisión del gobierno de Cancelar monitoreo a redes sociales," August 10, 2011, http://www.latercera.com/noticia/politica/2011/08/674-385449-9-parlamentarios-opositores-valoran-decision-del-gobierno-de-cancelar-monitoreo-a.shtml. (Translation would be "Opposition Parliamentarians assess government decision to cancel monitoring of social networks.")

42. V. Kundra and M. Fitzpatrick, "Federal Websites: Cookie Policy," *Open Government Initiative*. July 24, 2009, http://www.whitehouse.gov/blog/Federal-Websites-Cookie-Policy; P. R. Orszag, "Memorandum for the Executive Heads of Departments and Agencies: Guidance for Online Use of Web Measurement and Customization Technologies. Executive Office of the President Office of Management and Budget," Washington, D.C.: June 25, 2010, http://www.whitehouse.gov/sites/default/files/omb/assets/memoranda_2010/m10-22.pdf.

43. C. Soghoian, "Is the White House Changing Its YouTube Tune?," March 2, 2009, http://news.cnet.com/8301-13739_3-10184578-46.html.

44. A. Soltani, "RESPAWN REDUX (Follow up to Flash Cookies and Privacy II)," July 27, 2011, http://ashkansoltani.org/docs/respawn_redux.html.

45. M. Tuffield, "NHS.uk Allowing Google, Facebook, and Others to TrackYou," http://mmt.me.uk/blog/2010/11/21/nhs-and-tracking.

46. S. Trimi and H. Sheng, "Emerging Trends in M-government," *Communications of the ACM* 51, no. 5 (2008): 53–58.

47. E. Doyle, "Beijing Uses Geolocation To Monitor 'Traffic,'" *TechWeek Europe*, March 3, 2011, http://www.techweekeurope.co.uk/news/beijing-uses-geolocation-to-monitor-traffic-22772.

48. A. Di Maio, "What Happened to Mobile Government?," Gartner Blog Network. January 6, 2009, http://blogs.gartner.com/andrea_dimaio/2009/01/06/what -happened-to-mobile-government.

49. J. Ford, "$80 Android Phone Sells Like Hotcakes in Kenya, the World Next?," *Singularity Hub*, August 16, 2011, http://singularityhub.com/2011/08/16/80-android -phone-sells-like-hotcakes-in-kenya-the-world-next.

50. M. G. Siegler, "The iPhone's Latest Hit App: A Sex Offender Locator," *Tech-Crunch*, July 25, 2009, http://techcrunch.com/2009/07/25/the-iphones-latest-hit -app-a-sex-offender-locator.

51. *Economist*, "Sex Law: Unjust and Ineffective," August 6, 2009, http://www .economist.com/node/14164614?story_id=14164614.

52. V. Mayer-Schönberger, *Delete: The Virtue of Forgetting in the Digital Age* (Princeton, NJ: Princeton University Press, 2009).

53. ICO (Information Commission's Office), *Crime-Mapping and Geo-Spatial Crime Data: Privacy and Transparency Principles*, version 3.4 (Cheshire, UK: Information Commissioner's Office, February 2012), http://www.ico.gov.uk/~/media/ documents/library/Data_Protection/Detailed_specialist_guides/crime_mapping _advice.ashx.

54. G. Hosein and A. Martin, *Electronic Health Privacy and Security in Developing Countries and Humanitarian Operations* (London: Policy Engagement Network, London School of Economics and Political Science, 2010).

55. OECD (Organisation for Economic Co-operation and Development), *The Role of Digital Identity Management in the Internet Economy: A Primer for Policy Makers*. (Paris: Organisation for Economic Co-operation and Development, 2009).

56. Scottish Government. *Identity Management and Privacy Principles: Privacy and Public Confidence in Scottish Public Services (Version 1.0)* (Edinburgh: The Scottish Government, 2010).

57. DHS (Department of Homeland Security), *Privacy Impact Assessment for the Department of Homeland Security Use of Google Analytics*, DHS/ALL/-033, June 2011, 2, http://www.dhs.gov/xlibrary/assets/privacy/privacy_pia_dhs_ga.pdf.

58. Citron, "Fulfilling Government," 2010, 118.

59. J. Lynch, "Social Media and Law Enforcement: Who Gets What Data and When?," *Electronic Frontier Foundation*, January 20, 2011, https://www.eff.org/ deeplinks/2011/01/social-media-and-law-enforcement-who-gets-what.

60. West, *Global eGovernment*, 2007; UN, *E-Government Survey*, 2008.

Bibliography

Aichholzer, G., and S. Strauß. "Electronic Identity Management in E-Government 2.0: Exploring a System Innovation Exemplified by Austria." *Information Polity* 15 (1–2) (2010): 139–152.

Anderson, R. I., T. Brown, P. Dowty, W. P. Inglesant, W. Heath, and A. Sasse. *Database State*. A Report Commissioned by the Joseph Rowntree Reform Trust Ltd. York, UK: Joseph Rowntree Trust Ltd., 2009. http://www.cl.cam.ac.uk/~rja14/Papers/database-state.pdf.

BBC News (online). "World of Warcraft Maker to End Anonymous Forum Logins." July 7, 2010. http://www.bbc.co.uk/news/10543100.

Bellamy, C., and J. A. Taylor. *Governing in the Information Age*. Bristol, PA: Open University Press USA, 1998.

Chadwick, A. "Bringing E-Democracy Back In: Why it Matters for Future Research on E-Governance." *Social Science Computer Review* 21 (4) (2003): 443–455.

Citron, D. K. "Fulfilling Government 2.0's Promise with Robust Privacy Protections." *George Washington Law Review* 78 (4) (2010): 101–124.

Clarke, R. "The Digital Persona and its Application to Data Surveillance." *Information Society* 10 (2) (1994): 77–92.

Cordella, A. "E-government: Towards the E-bureaucratic Form?" *Journal of Information Technology* 22 (3) (2007): 265–274.

Dawes, S. "Stewardship and Usefulness: Policy Principles for Information-based Transparency." *Government Information Quarterly* 27 (4) (2010): 377–383.

DHS (Department of Homeland Security). *Privacy Impact Assessment for the Department of Homeland Security Use of Google Analytics*, DHS/ALL/-033, June 2011. http://www.dhs.gov/xlibrary/assets/privacy/privacy_pia_dhs_ga.pdf.

Doyle, E. "Beijing Uses Geolocation To Monitor 'Traffic'." *TechWeek Europe*, March 3, 2011. http://www.techweekeurope.co.uk/news/beijing-uses-geolocation-to-monitor-traffic-22772.

Dunleavy, P., H. Margetts, and S. Bastow. *S., and J. Tinkler, Digital Era Governance*. Oxford: Oxford University Press, 2006.

Dutta, S., W. Dutton, and G. Law, *The New Internet World: A Global Perspective on Freedom of Expression, Privacy, Trust and Security Online. The Global Information Technology Report 2010–2011* (Geneva: World Economic Forum, 2011).

Federal Law of Transparency and Access to Public Government Information. Article 9. Congress of the United Mexican States (2001), http://freedominfo.org/documents/mexico_ley.pdf.

Fiveash, K. "Cabinet Office Talks to Facebook & Co about New ID System: Online Access to Public Services Could be Via Social Networks." *The Register,* June 10, 2011, http://www.theregister.co.uk/2011/06/10/caninet_office_id_assurance_facebook/print.html.

Ford, J. "$80 Android Phone Sells Like Hotcakes in Kenya, the World Next?" *Singularity Hub,* August 16, 2011. http://singularityhub.com/2011/08/16/80-android-phone-sells-like-hotcakes-in-kenya-the-world-next.

Fountain, J. E. *Building the Virtual State: Information Technology and Institutional Change.* Washington, DC: Brookings Institution Press, 2001.

Haggerty, K. D., and R. V. Ericson. "The Surveillant Assemblage." *British Journal of Sociology* 51 (4) (2000): 605–622.

Heeks, R. Reinventing Government in the Information Age. In *Reinventing Government in the Information Age—International Practice in IT-enabled Public Sector Reform,* ed. R. Heeks, 9–21. London: Routledge, 2002.

Holden, S., and L. Millet. "Authentication, Privacy, and the Federal E-Government." *Information Society* 21 (5) (2005): 367–377.

Hosein, G., and A. Martin. *Electronic Health Privacy and Security in Developing Countries and Humanitarian Operations.* London: Policy Engagement Network, London School of Economics and Political Science, 2010.

ICO (Information Commission's Office). *Crime-Mapping and Geo-Spatial Crime Data: Privacy and Transparency Principles,* version 3.4. Cheshire, UK: Information Commissioner's Office, February 2012. http://www.ico.gov.uk/~/media/documents/library/Data_Protection/Detailed_specialist_guides/crime_mapping_advice.ashx.

Jernigan, C., and B. F. T. Mistree. "Gaydar: Facebook Friendships Expose Sexual Orientation." *First Monday* 14 (10) (October 2009). http://firstmonday.org/htbin/cgiwrap/bin/ojs/iindex.php/fm/article/viewArticle/2611/2302.

Kundra, V., and M. Fitzpatrick. "Federal Websites: Cookie Policy." *Open Government Initiative.* July 24, 2009. http://www.whitehouse.gov/blog/Federal-Websites-Cookie-Policy.

La Tercera. "Parlamentarios opositores valoran decisión del gobierno de Cancelar Monitoreo a Redes Sociales." August 10, 2011. http://www.latercera.com/noticia/politica/2011/08/674-385449-9-parlamentarios-opositores-valoran-decision-del-gobierno-de-cancelar-monitoreo-a.shtml.

Lessig, L. "Against Transparency." *New Republic (New York, N.Y.)* 240 (9) (2009): 37–44.

Lynch, J. "Social Media and Law Enforcement: Who Gets What Data and When?" *Electronic Frontier Foundation*, January 20, 2011. https://www.eff.org/deeplinks/2011/01/socialmedia-and-law-enforcement-who-gets-what.

Lyon, D. *Surveillance Studies: An Overview*. Cambridge: Polity Press, 2007.

Lyon, D. *Identifying Citizens*. Cambridge: Polity Press, 2009.

Marques, F. P. J. A. "Government and E-participation Programmes: A Study of the Challenges Faced by Institutional Projects." *First Monday* 15 (8) (2010). http://firstmonday.org/htbin/cgiwrap/bin/ojs/index.php/fm/article/viewArticle/2858/2583.

Mayer-Schönberger, V. *Delete: The Virtue of Forgetting in the Digital Age*. Princeton: Princeton University Press, 2009.

McDermott, P. "Building Open Government." *Government Information Quarterly* 27 (4) (2010): 401–413.

Narayanan, A., and V. Shmatikov. "Robust De-anonymization of Large Sparse Datasets." In *Proceedings of the IEEE Symposium on Security and Privacy*, Oakland, California, May 18–21 2008, Chair Y. Guan, 111–125. Oakland, CA. IEEE Computer Society, 2008.

Nissenbaum, H. *Privacy in Context: Technology, Policy, and the Integrity of Social Life*. Stanford, CA: Stanford University Press, 2009.

Obama, B. "Transparency and Open Government: Memorandum for The Heads of Executive Departments and Agencies," 2009. http://www.whitehouse.gov/the_press_office/TransparencyandOpenGovernment.

OECD. (Organisation for Economic Co-operation and Development). "Public Sector Modernisation: Open Government." Paris: Organisation for Economic Co-operation and Development, 2005. http://www.oecd.org/gov/34455306.pdf.

OECD. (Organisation for Economic Co-operation and Development). *The Role of Digital Identity Management in the Internet Economy: A Primer for Policy Makers*. Paris: Organisation for Economic Co-operation and Development, 2009.

Ohm, P. "Broken Promises of Privacy: Responding to the Surprising Failure of Anonymization." *UCLA Law Review. University of California, Los Angeles. School of Law* 57 (2010): 1701–1777.

Recordon, D., and D. Reed. "OpenID 2.0: A Platform for User-centric Identity Management." In *Proceedings of the Second ACM Workshop on Digital Identity Management*, Alexandria, Virginia, October 30–November 3, Chair Ari Juels, 11–16. New York: Association for Computing Machinery, 2006.

Schneier, B. "Security and Function Creep." *IEEE Security & Privacy* 8 (1) (2010): 88.

Scottish Government. *Identity Management and Privacy Principles: Privacy andPublic Confidence in Scottish Public Services (Version 1.0)*. Edinburgh: The Scottish Government, 2010.

Shane, S. "Spotlight Again Falls on Web Tools and Change." *New York Times*, January 30, 2011. http://www.nytimes.com/2011/01/30/weekinreview/30shane.html_r=0.

Siegler, M. G. "The iPhone's Latest Hit App: A Sex Offender Locator." *TechCrunch*. July 25, 2009. http://techcrunch.com/2009/07/25/the-iphones-latest-hit-app-a-sex-offenderlocator.

Smith, M. L., M. E. Noorman, and A. K. Martin. "Automating the Public Sector and Organizing Accountabilities." *Communications of the Association for Information Systems* 26, Article 1 (2010).

Soghoian, C. "Is the White House Changing its YouTube Tune?" March 2, 2009. http://news.cnet.com/8301-13739_3-10184578-46.html.

Stevens, T., J. Elliott, A. Hoikkanen, I. Maghiros, and W. Lusoli. "The State of the Electronic Identity Market: Technologies, Infrastructure, Services and Policies." Seville: Institute for Prospective Technological Studies, 2011. http://ftp.jrc.es/EURdoc/JRC60959.pdf.

Trimi, S., and H. Sheng. "Emerging Trends in M-government." *Communications of the ACM* 51 (5) (2008): 53–58.

UN (United Nations). *E-Government Survey 2008: From E-Government to Connected Governance*. New York: United Nations, 2008.

Ungerleider, N. "Israeli Military Using Facebook to Find Draft Dodgers." *Fast Company*, November 23, 2010. http://www.fastcompany.com/1704908/israeli-military-using-facebook-find-draft-dodgers.

Viner, K. "Internet has Changed Foreign Policy for Ever, says Gordon Brown." *The Guardian*, June 19, 2009. http://www.guardian.co.uk/politics/2009/jun/19/gordon-brown-internetforeign-policy.

West, D. M. *Global eGovernment 2007*. Providence, RI: Center for Public Policy, Brown University, 2007.

Whitley, E., and G. Hosein. *Global Challenges for Identity Policies*. Basingstoke, UK: Palgrave Macmillan, 2010.

Wills, D., and S. Reeves. "Facebook as a Political Weapon: Information in Social Networks." *British Politics* 4 (2) (2009): 258–265.

Wolf, C. "Update on Mexico's New Privacy Law: No Immediate Enforcement, But Companies Expected to Appoint Privacy Officer and Have Written Policies." April 6,

2011, Hogan Lovells Chronicle of Data Protection. http://www.hldataprotection.com/2011/04/articles/international-eu-privacy/update-on-mexicos-new-privacy-law-no-immediate-enforcement-but-companies-expected-to-appoint-privacy-officer-and-have-written-policies.

Yu, H., and D. G. Robinson. "The New Ambiguity of 'Open Government'." *UCLA Law Review* 59 (6) (2012): 178–208.

10   Open Minds: Lessons from Nigeria on Intellectual Property, Innovation, and Development

Jeremy de Beer and Chidi Oguamanam

General understanding of the relationship between intellectual property rights (IPRs) and development has changed significantly in recent years. For decades international intellectual property (IP) discourse has been influenced by the belief that development requires strong IP protection and that IP protection invariably causes development. IP is, in the words of a former World Intellectual Property Organization (WIPO) director general, "a power tool for economic growth."[1] The simplistic impression that more IP protection necessarily drives development was one putative reason that international minimum standards were regularly ratcheted up throughout the twentieth century. Developed countries, with the help of key private sector and international organizations, have in various ways pressed upon developing countries the idea that strong systems of IP protection are always good for development, and stronger systems are even better.[2]

With the World Trade Organization's (WTO) Agreement on Trade Related Aspects of Intellectual Property (TRIPs); the WIPO Internet treaties on copyrights, performances, and phonograms; and a host of other bilateral and multilateral agreements international standards of IP protection rose to unprecedented levels. These standards apply homogenously to countries at very different levels of development, regardless of their varying economic, social, and cultural circumstances. A few concessions do exist in terms of the substance and timing of obligations for developing and least-developed countries, but the normative principles animating the last century's international IP laws are presumed to apply globally.

As standards rose, it became apparent that efforts to harmonize IP in domestic legislation could not, alone, yield the results that advocates of stronger protection wanted. Research confirms that, especially in developing countries, there is often a wide gulf between IP laws on the books and day-to-day realities.[3] Effective enforcement requires adequate education about the new laws being enacted.

The TRIPs Agreement in particular, and the legal changes it imposed, created a significant demand for IP education and training in developing countries. In 1996, the WTO and WIPO signed a technical cooperation agreement that gave WIPO a key role in providing technical assistance to developing countries in relation to TRIPS implementation, including IP training and capacity building.[4] That reinforced WIPO's central role in international IP training and education, which actually flowed from its original mandate, established in 1967: "to promote the protection of intellectual property throughout the world."[5] Promoting intellectual property protection meant, in part, educating others about the virtues and details of such protection.

IP education was advocated for more than just technical training. It was necessary to promote and instill in the local culture the value of IP's underlying principles. Government officials, private sector businesses, and the general public in many developing countries needed to be convinced that enacting and enforcing strong IP laws would lead to development and particularly economic growth. The motives of IP trainers and educators were not necessarily nefarious. Programming initiatives were driven by the genuine belief that an IP regime modeled on the leading systems of Europe, North America, and Japan was invariably beneficial for global economic development and should be emulated by developing countries.[6]

Ironically, the successful push for a stronger international IP regime has helped raise awareness of its potentially adverse consequences. Boyle noted that the resulting one-size-fits-all, extra large, global IP paradigm has been widely criticized.[7] A serious backlash has since occurred, even within the developed countries, with some economists suggesting that in some contexts the whole IP system should be completely overhauled.

In this polarized context there is an emerging middle ground. Commissions of respected experts have objectively assessed IP/development linkages.[8] Economic data and analyses of the roles IP does and does not play in development are beginning to appear.[9] There are a growing number of books and other scholarly materials investigating this topic, and especially recently, the promising opportunities for international institutions in reshaping a more development-friendly knowledge governance system.[10] Civil society and academics have begun to work more closely with policy think tanks, intergovernmental agencies, and representatives of developing countries, nurturing the impetus for progressive change. A shared normative critique of IP, rejecting both maximalist and abolitionist extremes in favor of a more moderate and nuanced position, has begun to emerge under the umbrella of "access to knowledge."[11]

The effect of much IP training and capacity building in developing countries is, however, that minds have become more closed rather than more open to a range of different views about the relationship between IP, innovation, and development. Open-mindedness about IP is arguably a prerequisite to, or perhaps a fundamental part of, openness generally and openness in development in particular. Indeed, the contestation and constructive ambiguities inherent in terms such as *openness, accessibility,* and *inclusiveness* (compare Kapczynski and Krikorian 2010 with Chesbrough 2005)[12] require flexibility in operationalizing such concepts. But being open-minded is not the same as being agnostic. It is simply sensitive to the promise of autonomous rather than engineered development and respectful of different societies' rights to determine their own best paths toward development in a globalized world. An important part of openness is, therefore, understanding and respecting the diversity of views and approaches that emerge from being differently situated, and that is what is meant by open-mindedness in this context.

Building capacity for autonomous development requires, among other things, education. As Kempe Roland Hope observes: "Without supportive strategies, policies, laws and procedures, well-functioning organizations, *and educated and skilled people* [emphasis added], developing countries lack the foundation needed to plan, implement and review their national and local development strategies."[13] The IP education system presently in place in many developing countries is rather strongly reinforcing a particular path, while foreclosing alternative perspectives, possibilities, and scenarios for the future. A more open IP system, then, rests on a normative framework that embraces uncertainty, and incorporates or allows space for more diverse views. This is desirable because it allows people the possibility (or perhaps even empowers them) to develop the best system to suit their local circumstances.

A more robust and nuanced understanding of the role IP really plays in society is, in turn, a prerequisite to creating IP systems that drive innovation, economic growth, *and* human freedom. A holistic appreciation of not just laws and policies, but also practices related to IP and innovation will help developing countries design appropriate, context-specific systems of knowledge governance.

To this end, this chapter offers an analysis of WIPO's key role in IP training and education in developing countries, a country-specific case study of the Nigerian experience, and some strategic recommendations for creating a more open-minded IP education system. It argues that, despite some criticism, IP training and education programs offered by WIPO and partners such as the Nigerian Copyright Commission (NCC) are extremely effective in achieving their objectives. If these objectives can be aligned with the principles underpinning WIPO's recently adopted Development Agenda, developing countries could benefit from a richer understanding of the nuanced ways in which IP systems can be creatively designed and exploited to facilitate human development.

Part I: WIPO's Key Role in IP Education

IP training and education occurs in many settings, depending on the target audience and specific objectives for the particular initiative. Because developing-country participants exposed to international IP training and educational activities come from diverse backgrounds and have diverse goals, there are a wide variety of ways in which they may be exposed to the topic. One is through initiatives established by international or regional organizations, including WIPO, African Regional Intellectual Property Office (ARIPO), and similar organizations like the Organisation Africaine de la Propriété Intellectuelle (OAPI). Another is through national IP offices, often in collaboration with foreign government departments or entities. Rights-holders, industry associations and, less frequently, nongovernmental organizations may also organize formal training and education programs for particular stakeholder groups or the public. Finally, substantial training and education takes place in postsecondary institutions including universities and colleges.

Given the diversity of participants and objectives, it should not be surprising that training and education activities can also take many different forms. Events range from intensive training seminars structured over part of one day or several days through to months-long courses or years-long programs of formal study. They may be designed by national or international institutions, independent consultants, or university professors, and delivered by a wide variety of instructors or instructor teams.

In developing countries, some of the aforementioned modes of IP training and education predominate, but all exist. One common thread that runs through IP training and education in developing countries is the involvement of WIPO in one way or another. There are few, if any, developing or least-developed countries where WIPO does not play or has not played some role in developing IP training and education initiatives, and there is almost no aspect of IP training and education that WIPO does not cover in at least some respect.

Indeed, WIPO has played a central role, perhaps *the* central role, in international IP training and education programs developed over the past decades. When the organization became a specialized agency of the United Nations in 1974, it assumed responsibility "for promoting creative intellectual activity and for facilitating the transfer of technology related to industrial property to the developing countries in order to accelerate economic, social and cultural development."[14] Though its UN-related responsibilities are quite different than its former mandate, as the organization has since been required to further the UN's development objectives generally, attitudes and activities have been slow to change. Critics allege that the organization has, in general, adopted the stance that promoting intellectual property protection universally promotes creative intellectual activity, facilitates technology transfer, and accelerates development.

Although WIPO administers a large number and wide variety of training and education activities via its different offices and departments, many are conducted under the auspices of the WIPO Academy. The academy provides teaching, training, and research services related to IP issues through activities grouped into five program areas. Yo Takagi and Mpazi Sinjela have recently described the development of WIPO Academy programming and its strategic direction in detail.[15] The Policy Development Program targets some of the most influential individuals able to help steer the course of national and international IP policies: ambassadors and diplomats; government policymakers; law enforcement authorities; judges; professors; and so on. The Professional Development Program addresses the pragmatic aspects of IP skills development, such as administration and procedural issues. An Education Degree/Diploma Program involves partnerships with various postsecondary institutions in developed and developing countries, in order to create more in-depth training opportunities. There is a Research and Executive Program that is intended to provide a business-oriented perspective on IP issues. Finally, the furthest-reaching activities are run through the academy's Distance Learning Program, which runs a number of IP courses in many different languages. Since its creation, the Academy's tailor-made programs have served tens of thousands of people. WIPO's website puts the number at more than eighty-seven thousand participants[16]; other WIPO sources indicate the number, up to the midway point of 2008, is 105,294.[17]

In light of the academy's mandate, each program aims to meet four strategic goals. These include an international dimension that reflects WIPO's broad membership; an inclusive approach in accommodating the unique cultural, economic and linguistic needs of member countries; in-depth instruction that capitalizes on WIPO's extensive resources and experts; and an interdisciplinary character that is enriched by perspectives from law, economics, environment, business, science, technology and more.[18]

None of the academy's programs were developed by chance; all have been intentionally designed following strategic planning. A major symposium on IP education and research was held at WIPO's offices in Geneva in 2005,[19] just as separate committee meetings on the development agenda were beginning to ramp up. The two-day discussion included some highly respected IP professors from developed and developing countries, representing an appropriately diverse range of views on the topic of IP.[20] Some consensus apparently emerged that a holistic approach toward IP education was appropriate, with increased emphasis on, among other things, interdisciplinary initiatives. The organization was also encouraged to support work specifically addressing the teaching of intellectual property. A book was produced and published several years later[21]; its contents and recommendations for curricular design are discussed in more detail in part IV of this paper. Another international conference was held in Geneva in 2008, which focused on intellectual property management education and research.[22] A broader range of stakeholders—notably private sector industry representatives, IP administrators and business school professors—participated in that conference, the outcomes of which are not yet apparent.

The WIPO Academy has apparently recognized that it cannot fulfill worldwide demand for IP training and education, even working in partnership with various other organizations and institutions at the national level. Given that realization, the obvious response was an attempt to establish a network of academies that can serve as national nodal points for IP education.[23] A symposium held in 2007 led to the creation of the Global Network of IP Academies (GNIPA), of which there are currently seventeen members. Currently, the GNIPA has no African members. That, however, is about to change.

Part II: The Opportunity of WIPO's Development Agenda

In 2007, after several years of discussion, WIPO officially adopted a Development Agenda triggered by a proposal put forward by Argentina and Brazil.[24] In a long series of meetings, many dozens of proposals were advanced, debated, consolidated, and organized.[25] The essence of the Development Agenda is a rejection of a context-neutral, one-dimensional, and oversimplified perspective on IP's impact on development, and its associated implications for IP policies globally and locally. And while that idea may sound laudable in theory, it is difficult to implement in practice.

Thus in 2009, WIPO and its member states agreed to pursue a project-based approach for implementing the Development Agenda recommendations.

For example, an implementation project coded as DA_10_01 is already underway. The project is intended to test a new model for establishing IP training institutions in developing and least-developed countries. New academies were started in four regions—Africa, Arab Middle East, Asia and Pacific, Latin America and the Caribbean—with the goal of building capacity for human resources development in the field of IP.

This idea sounds promising, and if it is done well, it could contribute positively to the agenda's overall implementation. However, it is worth noting that some current members of WIPO's existing global network of IP academies, such as the United States Patent and Trademark Office (USPTO) for example, have been responsible for many of the activities and attitudes that the development agenda seeks to change. The USPTO's own Global Intellectual Property Academy (GIPA), not to be conflated with the network of IP Academies, the GNIPA, described above, has significant influence. This influence is demonstrated by the fact, publicized on its website, that in 2008 alone it trained more than 4,100 officials from 127 countries.[26] The overwhelming emphasis of this training is on IP protection and enforcement of American interests. In fact, the U.S. academy's mandate stems from the American Inventor's Protection Act of 1999,[27] which empowers the USPTO to "offer guidance, conduct programs and studies, and to coordinate with foreign IP offices and international organizations on issues concerning IP protection."

There is a possibility that new or existing activities implemented in collaboration or association with entities like USPTO will merely be labeled or rebranded as implementation projects, without any shift in organizational culture and stakeholder attitudes. If the WIPO Development Agenda implementation project means merely more of the same sorts of activity that have been criticized in the past, the problems that led to the Development Agenda would be exacerbated, not alleviated. Cosmetic changes alone would represent failure for the agenda and its proponents, the organization, and indeed the entire international IP community.

The new, African node in the GNIPA is in Tunisia. WIPO now lists GNIPA members in Kenya, Morocco, and Nigeria. Valuable lessons can be learned from experiences in this region of the world. Pinpointing the discussion by addressing the experience of specific country, such as Nigeria, will help to underscore the risks and opportunities inherent in establishing ostensibly new modes of IP training and education. A case study of IP training and education in Nigeria exemplifies the diverging possibilities that global discourse around IP training and education reform might either fall on deaf ears at the local level or facilitate a more broadly participatory and critically engaging assessment of IP's role in development.

Part III: The Case of Nigeria

With an official population of one hundred and fifty million people, Nigeria is Africa's most populous country. It represents 50 percent of the West African population.[28] After South Africa, Nigeria is the second largest economy in Sub-Saharan Africa. Comprising an estimated 250 nationalities with a corresponding amount of language and cultural groupings, Nigeria represents the cultural hub of Africa. Nigeria's expansive creative activity is perhaps better symbolized in the recent, phenomenal growth of its film/ movie industry, which produces an estimated one thousand low-cost movies annually. The industry, known as "Nollywood,"[29] is rated as "one of the most, if not *the* most productive of the World's movie industries."[30] Nigeria ranks, after India (Bollywood) and the United States (Hollywood), as the third largest movie producing nation.[31] This context makes Nigeria a particularly interesting case study of IP education.

The legal framework for IP governance in Nigeria has remained fairly modest but bureaucratically robust. Most of Nigeria's IP laws, including those governing patents, designs, and trademarks have their roots in Nigeria's British colonial era. They have not undergone any major adjustments. But copyright has, comparatively, followed a different path as a site for active legislative and administrative interventions.[32]

Copyright is administered by the Nigerian Copyright Commission (NCC), which is overseen by the Ministry of Justice. The NCC was established in 1988[33] and is funded primarily by the Nigerian government.[34] Because the NCC has positioned itself as the credible contact point with Nigeria for external stakeholders in IP matters, it has continued to benefit from extensive collaborations, including research, funding, and technical support from international organizations, notably the WIPO, the European Patent Office (EPO), the USPTO, the United States Department of Justice, the International Federation of the Phonographic Industry (IFPI), major multinational software companies, and agencies like the Ford Foundation among others.[35] Such organizations provide various technical supports, including local and international training, workshop, and research collaboration programs, for NCC staff.[36] WIPO tops the list of NCC external partners.

During twenty years of the NCC's existence, it and WIPO have maintained a consistent tradition of mutual courtship. The relationship between the two deepened since the establishment of the WIPO Worldwide Academy in 1998, a timeframe that coincided with the emergence of the Nollywood. A number of Nigerian IP bureaucrats at the NCC and the patent, trademark, and designs registries continue to benefit from the WIPO training programs via the academy and other local collaborative opportunities with WIPO. Perhaps more importantly, WIPO collaborated with the NCC in the establishment of the Nigerian Copyright Institute (NCI), described as "a research training facility for the development of copyright law and administration in the African Sub-region."[37]

Using the NCI as its platform, the NCC embarked on promoting teaching and research in IP law in Nigerian universities. In 2008, the NCC through the NCI developed a document titled *Intellectual Property Law Syllabus for Nigerian Universities,*[38] which it recommends for adoption by Nigerian universities. Despite the paucity of stakeholder consultation in the curriculum project, that initiative encompasses all IP regimes, which is beyond the focus of NCC's statutory mandate on copyright. The NCC's curriculum initiative is commendable; to the extent that it fills the gap in the lethargic state of IP education in Nigerian universities. But the extent to which NCC, as a copyright body, should dominate the overall space for IP policy and education in Nigeria is questionable in light of the country's progress and prospects in other realms of innovation outside the competence and expertise of NCC.

In addition to ongoing NCC-driven IP education and public enlightenment, IP education also happens in other formal or institutional and nonformal sectors. IP entered the curriculum of Nigerian universities, especially the law faculties in the late 1980s, when only a handful of them taught IP on a very modest curriculum, either as a stand-alone course or an integral aspect of commercial law. At the legal professional level, IP remained an integral aspect of the curriculum for commercial law at the Council of Legal Education's Bar program through the Nigerian Law School. There, it has traditionally been limited to a few hours of lecture essentially devoted to the registration of trademarks, designs, the clerical aspects of the filing of convention patents, and the operations of the relevant registries. Since the 2000s, there has been an increase in the number of Nigeria's thirty-two law faculties that teach IP in one form or another. Essentially, most of the curricula used by the universities vary from faculty to faculty. Their emphasis is on the conventional regimes of IP from mainly statutory and case-method frameworks. There is limited policy or developmental content. The same is true of the NCC curriculum initiative, save for its ambiguous reference to "emerging issues."[39]

High-profile professional, executive, and stakeholder workshops on IP are regular occurrences in Nigeria legal and business circles. A coalescing of stakeholders in the legal profession, the movie and music industries, and IP administration nationally and internationally has continued to promote educational and awareness programs on IP in Nigeria. Save for a few exceptional cases,[40] one of the major hallmarks of these initiatives is their focus on the interests of rights owners and the muzzling of public space for the exploration of IP from a critical and developmental context.

IP training and capacity building in Nigeria hardly engages, as Christopher May observed in 2006, with "novel or different solutions to the problems of IPR protection. Rather, countries' specific circumstances are only likely to be accorded weight where this does not conflict with TRIPS agreement's invocation of required legal effect and the 'best practice' acknowledged by WIPO."[41] Top IP bureaucrats are advertently or inadvertently, products of the transformation of that experience into "an important political (and even ideological) program of social orientation."[42] Again, as May rightly notes, "the WIPO's socialization of policy makers can become very important; training and education can produce advocates in domestic policy elites for the new (and/or changed) protection of IPRs, and this may help overcome (if not silence) local objections."[43]

This situation must be understood in light of the fact that Nollywood provides a platform and opportunity for external interests to perpetuate a one-dimensional perspective on IP issues in Nigeria. But while the NCC's characteristically high-profile destruction of movies and books targets the Nigerian domestic market, that effort is only a smokescreen diverting attention from the real threat to Nollywood. Most piracy of Nollywood movies happens through the unauthorized commercial replication outside of Nigeria using sophisticated technologies in remote locations, especially in industrialized countries, where Nigerians and African diasporas constitute the bulk of Nollywood patrons. In other words, developed countries, not exclusively Nigeria, are home to the ones ripping off Nigerian filmmakers. While a compact disc of Nollywood movie sells for an average of US$1.25 in the domestic market, outside of Nigeria's shores, pirated copies sell for an average of US$7.00.

In Nigeria, however, IP is rapidly creeping into the consciousness of the public, courtesy of the NCC's enlightenment campaigns, and educational and curriculum initiatives. In 2005, the NCC launched its flagship program known as Strategic Action against Piracy (STRAP). That program provides the philosophical framework for NCC's approach to copyright and IP in Nigeria, which is essentially reduced to aggressive antipiracy campaigns.

The emerging understanding of IP by the Nigerian public does not extend to the entire interdisciplinary sphere of IP, especially in areas such as biotechnology, food security, human rights, health, and so forth. Rather, the focus is on copyright, and a regime in which the cultural and user communities of creative works are presumed to be pirates until proven otherwise.

Overall, the tone and approach to IP that the NCC champions in Nigeria issues from an unquestioned belief that a strict IP regime, one that stifles access to creative works and that empowers creators only—even at the expense of other stakeholders—is the panacea to economic and social development challenges in the polity. Backed by vocal Nollywood interest groups, NCC's STRAP readily found traction in Nigeria, assuming the status of received wisdom of public education in IP.

This promotion of a strong and unbalanced approach to IP in Nigeria is presented as a historical and context-neutral enterprise. This flies on the face of the leverage, which the later-day champions of IP, such as the United States, Japan, a bulk of EU and lately South Korea and other Asian "Tiger" countries enjoyed. At their early stages in the creative and innovative experiences, these countries were either outliers regarding conventional IP or benefitted from a development friendly and technology transfer approach to IP. Like the United States, the majority of today's industrialized countries were born pirate nations.[44]

In the end, normative regulatory capture for IP policy and administration is a factor in drowning Nigeria's voice in the global policy elaborations on IP, from a development perspective. Thus far, Nigeria has failed to optimize its status as Africa's most populous country and potentially its largest market. Coupled with its creative talents as the heart of African music, movie, literature, and inexhaustible domains of culture, as well as a wealth of biological diversity and biological resources, traditional knowledge, and creative enterprise, Nigeria is also Africa's intellectual powerhouse. Nigeria is, or ought to be, a frontline developing country in a natural position to articulate African regional development agenda in the IP policy-making arena. Nigeria has failed to play in the league of Brazil, India, and China (BRIC) and other frontline countries in the Group of Friends of Development (FOD), whose persistent effort in questioning the United States–led normative approach to IP has resulted in the new development imperative in IP currently symbolized in the WIPO Development Agenda.

In sum, what this suggests is that IP education in Nigeria is lop-sided. This is mainly because the institutional champion of that initiative, the NCC, is constrained by its limited mandate. More importantly, the NCC adopts a normative and uncritical approach to IP. This explains, in part, why the

NCC courts and is courted mainly by right owners locally and internationally. Consequently, the NCC conceives itself and the IP system as essentially beholden to right owners only. So far, Nigeria's evolving IP education demonstrates a bias not only for right holders but also for the copyright regime. While Nigeria has an elaborate bureaucracy and professional and diverse institutional stakeholders in IP, the NCC has dominated the policy space required for a credible curriculum development toward the promotion of a balanced and development-sensitive IP education in Nigeria.

Part IV: The Orthodox IP Pedagogy

There is no doubt that the WIPO Academy has had tremendous success accomplishing its objectives in just over a decade of existence. Any educational institution in the world would be proud to have provided specialized subject-matter training to such a high number and diverse range of people during this relatively short period of time. A review of the academy's programs confirms that the training these participants have received is also high quality and purposive in the context of WIPO's aims; WIPO is not simply trying to churn out graduates but is successfully advancing its broader strategic objectives. One thing the academy does particularly well is emphasize an interdisciplinary approach toward IP training and education, which is a prerequisite to a holistic understanding of how IP actually functions in society. Clearly, much consultation and reflection has gone into curricular development and pedagogical strategies.

WIPO's collaborative work on the design and delivery of IP curricula is, however, far from complete. It was only in 2008 that WIPO produced its first book dedicated to the topic of IP teaching, *Teaching of Intellectual Property: Principles and Methods*.[45] There is further information about teaching method and pedagogy on the Academy's website in a document titled "Intellectual Property Teaching Methods and Pedagogy at the University Level."[46] But WIPO acknowledges that many challenges still exist.[47]

A key issue that has not been independently analyzed or, it seems, adequately explored by WIPO, is the extent to which its IP curricular design, teaching materials, and course delivery are appropriate for training and education in developing countries specifically. Should IP training and education be the same in developed and developing countries? Are there topics or perspectives that might be more heavily, or even just differently, emphasized depending on the target beneficiaries?

There are some indications that the main difference in teaching people in or from developing countries is a belief that developing-country participants need more convincing that the topic is relevant to them, so as to "demystify" IP and overcome their "prejudices" about its impact on things like health and education.[48] To change this perspective, materials include considerable hyperbole about the impact of IP protection on economic development. Yet little time is actually spent critically evaluating the issues that cause developing countries' concerns about IP's intersections with broader public policies and human development.

The academy's literature does not differentiate pedagogical principles better suited for IP education in developing countries. The teaching methods and pedagogical strategies, sample curricula,[49] and resource materials for IP teaching[50] suggested by WIPO acknowledge, in passing, that a one-size-fits-all model of IP education is inappropriate, but contain little substantive content tailored for developing-country participants.

In discussing the question "how should IP be taught?"[51] WIPO differentiates mainly between the face-to-face classroom and tutorial method or the distance education method of course delivery. This is an interesting and important dichotomy, but it doesn't scratch the surface of deeper discussions about student-teacher roles, learning styles, choices of materials, and other pedagogical issues. Other documents touch on the differences between the case method and problem method of teaching, which is also a useful pedagogical discussion. But more detail and richer discussion of these topics is key to delivering the most effective IP training and education possible. It is possible, and even likely, that there are specific strategies better suited to different types of learners in different circumstances, such as those in developing countries, for example.

The WIPO Academy provides particular guidance on setting up an IP curriculum in universities.[52] University programs involving IP may take at least three forms, according to the academy: overview courses for nonlegal disciplines such as business, engineering, or science; introductory or advanced courses on IP law; and specialized, in-depth programs for postgraduates. Topics covered depend on the nature of the program, but might include the scope of rights, procedures for obtaining protection, and enforcement mechanisms. Courses covering these topics might be survey courses, specialized courses, advanced seminars, or practice courses. Full-time faculty members or adjunct lecturers might teach them. Again, course offerings and instructors will vary by program.

Academy documents on pedagogy devote only a few short paragraphs to the topic of teaching IP in developing countries. A lack of topical awareness and scarce resources are identified as obstacles to effective program delivery. University professors and administrators, as well as policymakers who have realized that IP "is an indispensable instrument in achieving desired economic and cultural objectives"[53] can, according to the academy, help overcome these challenges to delivering IP training and education in developing countries. Beyond that point, nothing more substantive is said about this issue.

The rest of WIPO's guidance on IP pedagogy is relatively generic. New teachers are advised to rely on well-established textbooks by recognized experts in the field. A less cautious approach is appropriate only for more experienced professors and practitioners. The academy has compiled links to research and resources that can be used for IP training and education. Most of these are actually WIPO meeting documents and commissioned reports, though there are some independent materials referenced also.

The resource list is, however, several years out of date. Moreover, the topical lists and materials therein fail to adequately cover the range of critical analysis and perspectives that currently exist on important intersections between IP, development, and related public policies. A typical example is a resource on "emerging issues" that purports to present a Nigerian perspective on IP.[54] Like many of the other recommended materials, it contains a rights-focused analysis, with references to development sprinkled throughout but not substantively addressed.

The WIPO academy's most comprehensive output regarding teaching IP is the recently published book on the topic. Contributors to the edited collection include a widely renowned group of IP experts, representing reasonably diverse perspectives on IP issues. Individual chapters cover the staple subjects: patents, copyrights, and trademarks, as well as specialty topics like industrial designs, IP and competition, economics and IP, IP in business schools, IP for nonlawyers, IP practice, distance learning of IP, and current trends. There is no specific discussion of IP and development, IP in developing countries, or anything to that effect. The concluding chapter on current trends and future developments comes closest to representing a critical perspective.

There are statements sprinkled throughout the book that ostensibly reflect different perspectives. In general, however, the book's contents conservatively reflect the standard IP dogma that fueled criticism and led to adoption of recommendations for the WIPO Development Agenda.

The chapter on patents, for example, omits much discussion about contemporary public policy issues, including the intersection between pharmaceutical patents and public health—a topic that is sure to be of interest to many students, especially students from developing countries. That the topic is controversial and generates a wide array of differing perspectives should be a reason to engage it, not to shy away from it.

The chapter on copyrights and related rights expressly advises professors to emphasize to students that the WIPO Internet treaties (including protection for technological protection measures) do not fundamentally change international norms; are "well-balanced, flexible, and duly take into account legitimate interests of all the countries with different levels of development and of all major stakeholders"; are not economically or legislatively burdensome; and do not extend the scope of copyright protection. Such advice is understandable from an expert who played a key role in the formation and promotion of the treaties.[55] It does not, however, objectively reflect the diversity of perspectives on the controversial topics of digital copyright generally nor anti-circumvention legislation specifically. In fact, the advice probably contradicts the views of many experts in and from developing countries, who might counsel IP teachers to deliver a more objective and nuanced instruction.[56]

Part V: Opening Minds about IP and Development

Given the diversity of the purposes for and participants in IP training programs, it would be naïve to believe that this paper can proscribe the key to better pedagogy with respect to IP and development. It is, however, feasible and appropriate to offer some possible suggestions on approaches to better integrate IP training and education with the principles underpinning the development agenda. This can take place via the creation of new programs and activities by the academy, the evaluation and adjustment of existing academy programs, and/or the engagement of external stakeholders.

The simplest, and most modest, tactic for teaching a more development-oriented perspective on IP would be to integrate relevant, critical content into existing activities. Corresponding pedagogical strategies could be adopted to provoke a more open-minded investigation into the complex linkages among IP and development. This requires abandoning unquestioned assumptions that IP protection always facilitates development. At the same time, however, one must not assume that IP protection impedes development, or that greater access to knowledge is preferable to achieve developmental objectives. Open and proprietary systems of knowledge governance are not binary, mutually exclusive options. Further, they are not merely opposite ends of a spectrum. The relationship between IP and open access is even more complex than that.

Often IP can be exploited in innovative ways in order to guarantee openness. Concrete examples include the general public license (GPL) that underpins the open source software community. That mechanism and the communities that embrace it would disintegrate without a strong and enforceable system of IP rights, which are the very things being *licensed* by the GPL. Similarly, one might realize that Creative Commons licenses are essentially a digital rights management (DRM) system. DRM systems include up to three core components: technological protection measures; rights management information practices; and end user license agreements. The Creative Commons licenses rely fundamentally on the latter two components for managing digital rights. Copyright law is the basis for the ability to require users to, for example, attribute authorship, maintain the integrity of a work, or license derivative works on the same terms to other communities of users.

A more ambitious endeavor in IP education (short of a complete curricular overhaul, which seems unnecessary and inadvisable in most cases) would be the creation of new courses specifically concentrating on IP, development, and the global public policy challenges that countries around the world, especially developing countries, struggle with. In framing such a course, one strategy is to consciously place public policy objectives at the fore, and to expose students to the linkages between knowledge governance and key global challenges—such as climate change, food security, population health, public education, gender equity, and poverty reduction—before delving into the specific details of IP statutes or doctrine. Questions for class investigation might include the following:

• How does global patent policy impact the HIV/AIDS crisis in Africa, and why is that relevant to the real threat of other worldwide pandemics?
• What is the link between intellectual property law, environmental biodiversity, and climate change?
• Is copyright constraining access to learning materials and education, and if so, who is affected, where, how and why?
• Are Western-style copyrights, patents, and trademarks appropriate to protect the traditional knowledge and cultures of indigenous peoples throughout the world?
• How is international intellectual property policy affecting the use of the Internet and mobile communication networks as mediums for cultural transformation and more participatory system of democracy?
• Does the increasing concentration of patents over plants' genetic resources threaten the livelihoods of subsistence farmers, or even global food security more generally?

Orienting an entire course around these themes, rather than appending them as a module on current issues to be dealt with at the end of a basic or advanced course, time permitting, could yield extraordinary and perhaps unexpected benefits. In particular, it has the effect of situating students' mindset within an appropriate context, so that IP can be more easily seen for what it is: a means to achieving broader social policy objectives. It can be an effective strategy to open students' minds to a big picture of the role IP plays in society and how IP contributes to, or perhaps impedes, development.

Part VI: Conclusions on IP Education and Open Development

An emerging discourse around the concept of openness applied to international development bears significant promise for shifting the conceptual paradigms that dominated the latter half of the twentieth century. In the area of IP, there is the potential to move from a trade-based framework that emphasized strong, harmonized protection as a means to facilitate technology transfer to spur economic growth in developing countries, to a human-centered system that has freedom and sustainability as its core values. In Nigeria and many other developing countries, however, IP training and education is still driven by narrow-minded beliefs perpetuated over decades of program activities designed to convince people that IP was a solution to their problems.

A failure to acknowledge uncertainty, nuance, and complexity in IP education would undermine efforts to leverage a locally appropriate IP system for economic, social, and cultural growth. Because open-mindedness is crucial to the capacity building that facilitates autonomous development, it must be the cornerstone of both policy and pedagogy of IP training programs in developing countries.

The new WIPO Development Agenda presents an opportunity to reverse previous trends and make this happen. Although some of its recommendations formally treat capacity building as distinct from norm setting, there is undoubtedly and almost inevitably a normative or ideological aspect to all training and educational activities. They reflect values and beliefs in relation to the issue addressed. In this sense, training and education is categorically *not* just technical assistance. More open-minded pedagogical approaches are, therefore, required in order to realize the more nuanced truths about the roles that IP can and cannot play in development. Future research and capacity-building activities conducted by WIPO would benefit from consolidation to facilitate better monitoring and coordination. By assisting rather than administering programs delivered externally, and refocusing support toward students more directly, WIPO and its partner organization should be better placed to respond to the challenges of opening minds to the future possibilities for IP and development.

Notes

This chapter is derived, with substantial revisions, from *Intellectual Property Training and Education: A Development Perspective*, by Jeremy de Beer and Chidi Oguamanam and published through the International Centre for Trade and Sustainable Development (ICTSD) Programme on Intellectual Property Rights and Sustainable Development (Issue Paper No. 31 (2010). The authors acknowledge with gratitude the financial and other support of ICTSD and IDRC, the research assistance of Tavengwa Runyowa, and the editorial and substantive comments of Matthew L. Smith, Katherine M. A. Reilly, and multiple anonymous peer reviewers.

1. K. Idris, *Intellectual Property: A Power Tool for Economic Growth*, 2nd. ed. (Geneva: World Intellectual Property Organization, 2003).

2. P. Drahos and J. Braithwaite, *Information Feudalism: Who Owns the Knowledge Economy?* (London: Earthscan, 2003); C. May, *A Global Political Economy of Intellectual Property Rights: The New Enclosures?* (London; Routledge, 2000); S. Sell, *Private Power, Public Law: The Globalization of Intellectual Property Rights* (Cambridge: Cambridge University Press, 2003); S. Sell and C. May, *Intellectual Property Rights: A Critical History* (Boulder, CO: Lynne Rienner Publishers, 2006).

3. C. Armstrong, J. de Beer, D. Kawooya, A. Prabhala, and T. Schönwetter, *Access to Knowledge in Africa: The Role of Copyright* (Cape Town: University of Cape Town Press, 2010).

4. R. Okediji, "WIPO-WTO Relations and the Future of Global Intellectual Property Norms," *Netherlands Yearbook of International Law* 39, (2008): 69–125.

5. Convention Establishing the World Intellectual Property Organization, Stockholm, July 14, 1967, in *Treaties and International Agreements Registered or Filed or Reported with the Secretariat of the United Nations*, 828, no. 11846 at 11.

6. For example, see H. Arai, *Intellectual Property Policies for the Twenty-First Century: The Japanese Experience in Wealth Creation* (Geneva: WIPO, 1999).

7. J. Boyle, "A Manifesto on WIPO and the Future of Intellectual Property," *Duke Law and Technology Review* 9, (2004): 1–12.

8. Commission on Intellectual Property Rights. 2002. *Integrating Intellectual Property Rights and Development*, http://www.iprcommission.org/graphic/documents/final_report.htm.

9. C. Fink and K. E. Maskus, eds. *Intellectual Property and Development: Lessons from Recent Economic Research* (Oxford: The World Bank and Oxford University Press), pp. 1–15.

10. J. de Beer, ed. *Implementing the WIPO's Development Agenda*. (Waterloo, ON: International Development Research Centre/Centre for International Governance Innovation/Wilfred Laurier University Press, 2009); C. Deere, *The Implementation Game: The TRIPs Agreement and the Global Politics of Intellectual Property Reform in Developing Countries* (Oxford: Oxford University Press, 2008); D. Gervais, ed. *Intellectual Property, Trade and Development: Strategies to Optimize Economic Development in a TRIPS Plus Era* (Oxford: Oxford University Press, 2007); C. May, *The World Intellectual Property Organization: Resurgence and the Development Agenda* (London: Routledge, 2007); N. W. Netanel, ed. *The Development Agenda: Global Intellectual Property and Developing Countries*. (Oxford: Oxford University Press, 2008).

11. A. Kapczynski, "The Access to Knowledge Mobilization and the New Politics of Intellectual Property," *Yale Law Journal* 117, (2008): 804.

12. G. Krikorian and A. Kapcynski, eds. *Access to Knowledge in the Age of Intellectual Property* (New York: Zone Books, 2010); H. Chesbrough, W. Vanhaverbeke, and J. West, eds. *Open Innovation: Researching a New Paradigm* (Oxford: Oxford University Press, 2006).

13. K. R. Hope, "Investing in Capacity Development: Towards an Implementation Framework," *Policy Studies* 32, no. 1 (2011): 59–72.

14. Agreement between the United Nations and the World Intellectual Property Organization, September 27, 1974, in *Treaties and International Agreements Registered or Filed or Reported with the Secretariat of the United Nations*, 956, no. 729, 406–407.

15. Y. Takagi and M. Sinjela, "Harnessing the Power of Intellectual Property Strategy and Programs of the WIPO Worldwide Academy," *World Patent Information* 29 (2007): 161–167.

16. WIPO Worldwide Academy, http://www.wipo.int/academy/en.

17. World Intellectual Property Organization. *WIPO Worldwide Academy 1998–2008, A Decade of Excellence, A Decade of Achievement* (Geneva: WIPO, 2008).

18. Takagi and Sinjela, "Harnessing the Power," 2007.

19. "International Symposium on Intellectual Property (IP) Education and Research," *WIPO* (Geneva, June 30 and July 1, 2005), http://www.wipo.int/academy/en/meetings/iped_sym_05/index.html.

20. The program, including hyperlinks to speakers' presentations, is available at http://www.wipo.int/academy/en/meetings/iped_sym_05/program_detailed.html.

21. Y. Takagi, L. Allman, and M. A. Sinjela, eds. *Teaching of Intellectual Property: Principles and Methods* (Cambridge, Cambridge University Press, 2008).

22. "International Conference on Intellectual Property Management Education and Research Program," *WIPO* (Geneva: July 17–18, 2008), http://www.wipo.int/pressroom/ja/articles/2008/article_0040.html.

23. General information can be found at http://www.wipo.int/academy/en/ipacademies.

24. World Intellectual Property Organization (WIPO), "Proposal by Argentina and Brazil for the Establishment of a Development Agenda for WIPO," Doc. WO/GA/31/11, *WIPO General Assembly*, 31st Session (Geneva, September 27-October 5, 2004), http://www.wipo.int/meetings/en/doc_details.jsp?doc_id=31737.

25. de Beer, *Implementing*, 2009.

26. http://www.uspto.gov/ip/training/index.jsp.

27. *American Inventor's Protection Act of 1999*, Public Law 106–113, 106th Congress (November, 1999).

28. The West African region comprises sixteen countries and has an estimated population of three hundred million people which represents 4.6 percent of the global population and roughly the same population as United States and almost 60 percent of the European Union.

29. *This is Nollywood,* http://www.thisisnollywood.com/film.htm.

30. M. F. Schultz, "The Nigerian movie industry and the lessons regarding cultural diversity from home-market effects of model of international trade in film," http://www.copyrightalliance.org/wp-content/uploads/2012/05/Schultz-Nollywood.pdf.

31. J. Vasagar, "Welcome to Nollywood," http://www.guardian.co.uk/film/2006/mar/23/world.features.

32. This is somehow understandable because copyright is the platform for negotiating and translating aspects of international developments, especially in regard to the protection of folklore and other forms of peripheral regimes considered critical to Nigeria's interests. Also, compared to patents, industrial designs, trademarks, and so forth (i.e., industrial property in general) most of Nigeria's creative industries, such as music, writing, broadcast, performances lie in the cultural domains within the ambit of copyright.

33. Originally, the Copyright Decree of 1988 established the Copyright Council which was later upgraded to a Copyright Commission (as the main outfit for the administration of copyright and neighboring rights) via a 1996 amendment.

34. As in most federal systems, intellectual property is constitutionally within the exclusive legislative list of the federal government of Nigeria.

35. In 2008, the Ford Foundation funded a collaborative initiative with the NCC entitled The *Survey of Copyright Piracy in Nigeria*. The study concluded that the level of piracy of copyrighted works in Nigeria is at 58 percent. Also, Microsoft Corporation provides support for training of NCC and Nigerian IP bureaucrats on copyright infringement detection and enforcement.

36. Presently, WIPO is involved with NCC in a project that would among other things determine the value and contributions of "copyright based industries" to Nigeria's GDP and overall economy. The project is titled *The Survey on the Contributions of Copyright Industries to Nigeria's GDP.*

37. Nigerian Copyright Commission, http://www.copyright.gov.ng.

38. Nigerian Copyright Institute, *Intellectual Property Law Syllabus for Nigerian Universities* (Abuja: NCC, 2008). (Document on file with the authors.)

39. For instance, outside of statutory exploration of copyright the curriculum includes two additional heads of issues under the titles "International Dimensions" and "Emerging Issues." Listed under the latter are: Copyright in the Digital Environment, Copyright and the Internet, Computer Software, and New Development. Similarly after, exploration of textual provision of the Patent Act, it lists some treaties under the head of International Dimensions. It also provides for Emerging Issues under which are listed: traditional knowledge, traditional medicine and biodiversity in Nigeria, biotechnology inventions, and protection of plant variety.

40. Occasionally there are well-resources workshops and learning sessions that provide opportunities for critical and balanced exploration of the promises of intellectual property for Nigeria development. For example, in 2005, the Nigeria National Medicine Development Agency (NNMDA) organized a very successful workshop titled "Traditional Medicinal Practice and Intellectual Property Rights," which provided impetus for a Draft Legislation on the Protection of Traditional Knowledge, Regulation of Access to Biological Resources and Related Matters. In 2009, the IDRC, the NCC and other co-sponsored a successful workshop and learning session titled "Indigenous Knowledge and Intellectual Property: Implications for Nigeria's Development at the University of Ibadan."

41. C. May, "The World Intellectual Property Organization (Global Monitor)," *New Political Economy* 11, no. 3, (2006): 435–445.

42. May, "The World Intellectual," 440.

43. Ibid.

44. L. Lessig, "Piracy," in *Free Culture: How Big Media Uses Technology and the Law to Lock Down Culture and Control Creativity* (New York: Penguin Press, 2004), 63.

45. Takagi et al., *Teaching of Intellectual Property*, 2008.

46. "Teaching Method and Pedagogy," www.wipo.int/academy/en/about/teaching/pedagogy/index.html.

47. Takagi and Sinjela, "Harnessing the Power," 2007; WIPO, *"WIPO Worldwide Academy,"* 2008.

48. WIPO, *WIPO Worldwide Academy*, 2008, 8.

49. "Teaching IP: Sample Curricula," *WIPO*, www.wipo.int/academy/en/about/teaching/sample_curricula/index.html.

50. Idris, *Intellectual Property*, 2003; WIPO, *WIPO Worldwide Academy*, 2008; Takagi and others, *Teaching of Intellectual Property*, 2008.

51. http://www.wipo.int/academy/en/about/teaching/teaching_research/index.html.

52. http://www.wipo.int/academy/en/about/teaching/pedagogy/index.html.

53. World Intellectual Property Organization (WIPO), "The Teaching of Intellectual Property Law," in *Introduction to Intellectual Property: Theory and Practice* (London: UK, 1997), 567.

54. C. T. Owoseni, "Recent Developments and Challenges in the Protection of Intellectual Property Rights. New Developments and Challenges in the Protection of Intellectual Property Rights: A Nigerian Perspective," WIPO/ECTK/SOF/01/2.7, http://www.wipo.int/edocs/mdocs/ip-conf-bg/en/wipo_ectk_sof_01/wipo_ectk_sof_01_2_7.pdf.

55. M. Ficsor, *The Law of Copyright and the Internet: The 1996 WIPO Treaties, Their Interpretation and Implementation* (Oxford: Oxford University Press, 2002).

56. See, for example, R. L. Okediji, "The Regulation of Creativity Under the WIPO Internet Treaties," *Fordham Law Review* 77, no. 5 (2009): 2379–2410; see also Commission on Intellectual Property Rights (CIPR), *Integrating Intellectual Property Rights and Development Policy* (London: CIPR, 2002).

Bibliography

Armstrong, C., J. de Beer, D. Kawooya, A. Prabhala, and T. Schönwetter. *Access to Knowledge in Africa: The Role of Copyright.* Cape Town: University of Cape Town Press, 2010.

Boyle, J. "A Manifesto on WIPO and the Future of Intellectual Property." *Duke Law and Technology Review* 9 (2004): 1–12.

Chesbrough, H., W. Vanhaverbeke, and J. West, eds. *Open Innovation: Researching a New Paradigm.* Oxford: Oxford University Press, 2006.

de Beer, J., ed. *Implementing the WIPO's Development Agenda.* Waterloo, ON: International Development Research Centre; Centre for International Governance Innovation; Wilfred Laurier University Press, 2009.

Deere, C. *The Implementation Game: The TRIPs Agreement and the Global Politics of Intellectual Property Reform in Developing Countries.* Oxford: Oxford University Press, 2008.

Drahos, P., and J. Braithwaite. *Information Feudalism: Who Owns the Knowledge Economy?* London: Earthscan, 2003.

Ficsor, M. *The Law of Copyright and the Internet: The 1996 WIPO Treaties, Their Interpretation and Implementation.* Oxford: Oxford University Press, 2002.

Fink, C., and K. E. Maskus, eds. *Intellectual Property and Development: Lessons from Recent Economic Research.* Oxford: The World Bank and Oxford University Press, 2005, 1–15.

Gervais, D., ed. *Intellectual Property, Trade and Development: Strategies to Optimize Economic Development in a TRIPS Plus Era.* Oxford: Oxford University Press, 2007.

Hope, K. R. "Investing in Capacity Development: Towards an Implementation Framework." *Policy Studies* 32 (1) (2011): 59–72.

Idris, K. *Intellectual Property: A Power Tool for Economic Growth.* 2nd ed. Geneva: World Intellectual Property Organization, 2003.

Kapczynski, A. "The Access to Knowledge Mobilization and the New Politics of Intellectual Property." *Yale Law Journal* 117 (2008): 804–885.

Krikorian, G., and A. Kapcynski, eds. *Access to Knowledge in the Age of Intellectual Property.* New York: Zone Books, 2010.

Lessig, L. "Piracy." In *Free Culture: How Big Media Uses Technology and the Law to Lock Down Culture and Control Creativity,* 62–79. New York: Penguin Press, 2004.

May, C. *A Global Political Economy of Intellectual Property Rights: The New Enclosures?* London: Routledge, 2000.

May, C. "The World Intellectual Property Organization (Global Monitor)." *New Political Economy* 11 (3) (2006): 435–445.

May, C. *The World Intellectual Property Organization: Resurgence and the Development Agenda.* London: Routledge, 2007.

Netanel, N. W., ed. *The Development Agenda: Global Intellectual Property and Developing Countries.* Oxford: Oxford University Press, 2008.

Okediji, R. "WIPO-WTO Relations and the Future of Global Intellectual Property Norms." *Netherlands Yearbook of International Law* 39 (2008): 69–125.

Owoseni, C. T. "Recent Developments and Challenges in the Protection of Intellectual Property Rights. New Developments and Challenges in the Protection of Intellectual Property Rights: A Nigerian Perspective." WIPO/ECTK/SOF/01/2.7. http://edocs/mdocs/ip-conf-bg/en/wipo_ectk_sof_01/wipo_ectk_sof_01_2_7.pdf.

Sell, S. *Private Power, Public Law: The Globalization of Intellectual Property Rights.* Cambridge: Cambridge University Press, 2003.

Sell, S., and C. May. *Intellectual Property Rights: A Critical History*. Boulder, CO: Lynne Rienner Publishers, 2006.

Takagi, Y., and M. Sinjela. "Harnessing the Power of Intellectual Property Strategy and Programs of the WIPO Worldwide Academy." *World Patent Information* 29 (2007): 161–167.

Takagi, Y., L. Allman, and M. A. Sinjela, eds. *Teaching of Intellectual Property: Principles and Methods*. Cambridge: Cambridge University Press, 2008.

World Intellectual Property Organization (WIPO). The Teaching of Intellectual Property Law. In *Introduction to Intellectual Property*, 563–580. London, UK: Theory and Practice, 1997.

World Intellectual Property Organization (WIPO). "Proposal by Argentina and Brazil for the Establishment of a Development Agenda for WIPO." Doc. WO/GA/31/11. *WIPO General Assembly*, 31st Session. Geneva, September 27–October 5, 2004. http://www.wipo.int/meetings/en/doc_details.jsp?doc_id=31737.

World Intellectual Property Organization (WIPO). *WIPO Worldwide Academy 1998–2008, A Decade of Excellence, A Decade of Achievement*. Geneva: WIPO, 2008.

III Constructing Openness

11   Negotiating Openness across Science, ICTs, and Participatory Development: Lessons from the AfricaAdapt Network

Blane Harvey

The advent of new information and communication technologies—particularly of online Web 2.0 technologies that allow for a plurality of information sources and contributors from multiple devices—has stimulated the imagination of practitioners from a wide range of fields, including international development and the sciences. Through these new platforms lies the potential for groups once understood simply as *end users* or *consumers* of information to become active participants and producers, assuming multiple roles as they view, respond to, amend, and share content within and among different communities of interest or practice. This has led to claims that Web 2.0 represents a new "architecture of participation" that will democratize, and thereby challenge conventional paradigms of practice in ICT-mediated environments or relationships.[1] Meanwhile, similar reflections on the evolving roles of end users have been unfolding in parallel in the areas of participatory development[2] and climate science,[3] albeit to varying extents.

These transformations reflect broader challenges made to the notions of official or valid knowledge by critical, feminist, and postmodern theories (among others), as well as an increased awareness of the intimate relationships between power, culture, and the construction of knowledge. They are also indicative of a broader critical reflection on how particular epistemic communities and disciplines construct meaning. With this context in mind, this chapter critically reflects on the prospect of a new architecture of participation emerging from a network using ICTs to collaborate on climate change and international development. Using the case of a Global North–Global South knowledge sharing network on climate change adaptation, it explores how multiple interpretations of concepts such as *openness* and *participation* coalesce around a particular initiative, and explicates the discursive construction of the initiative's ways of working and understanding. The resultant shared meanings and practices, this chapter argues, are a product of existent epistemic and participatory cultures, relations and economies of power, and emergent ways of working that are shaped by engagement with particular technologies and protocols.

The process through which these shared meanings are constructed, however, is rarely transparent or openly reflected on. Rather, these meanings emerge through the normalization of particular practices that "organize" our social relations.[4] This limits our understanding of how a given architecture of participation has been constructed, or of how it has situated those working in it. It has profound implications within and beyond the boundaries of a particular initiative, as "knowledge cultures have real political, economic and social effects"[5]—effects that can lead to the inclusion of some at the expense of others, and that fundamentally shape what can be achieved. Acknowledging this complexity and openly engaging with the invisible processes of negotiation and normalization of meaning can reveal the ways that power and culture construct and constrain our understandings of development practice.

This chapter begins by introducing the notion of epistemic cultures[6] within the contexts of climate science and international development and links it to the production of particular forms of discourse that are supported by mediating technologies, such as ICTs. This is followed by a description of how the intersection of these different communities in a collaborative initiative presents challenges to meaning-making through the case of AfricaAdapt, a North–South network for knowledge sharing on climate change adaptation in Africa. Through discussions with core partners hosting the network, this chapter explores how ways of working were established and interpreted, and examines the influences that have contributed to particular discursive constructions of meaning and purpose within the network. Attention is given to the powerful influence that the development paradigm has had on partners' understandings of participation and openness, and on ways that the ICT-enabled environments within the network privilege certain forms of engagement at the expense of others. Based on these observations, the chapter then considers the influence that these processes of meaning-making have had on the present shape of the network and reflect on what this means for such forms of collaboration more generally.

Theoretical Background

This section introduces the notion of epistemic cultures and links this concept to the power of discourse to validate certain meanings over others. It then considers how ICTs play a mediating role in this negotiation of meaning.

Epistemic Cultures and the Discursive Construction of Meaning

Reflection on the processes and conditions through which knowledge is constructed and validated, and enters into currency has grown steadily since the 1970s. It has shown how power, gender, culture, and professional practice intervene in shaping what we know, and how the power to define what is known both reinforces the authority of certain social groups and disempowers others. The rise of globalization and new technologies in postindustrial societies has also led to a growing emphasis on information and knowledge as a political and economic currency in transnational information or knowledge societies. Given these parallel trends in understanding around the situatedness of knowledge (and its link to power) and the growth of knowledge as currency and commodity, researchers are keen to explore the makeup of what Karin Knorr Cetina calls *knowledge settings* or "the whole sets of arrangements, processes and principles that serve knowledge and unfold with its articulation."[7] These settings, she argues, are shaped by the particular epistemic cultures[8] that determine the policies and practices that sustain or discourage particular outcomes to inquiry. Knowledge settings have historically tended to be bound by time, place, and lifeworld (laboratories within the physical sciences, for example), but the advent of networked social interaction on a global scale—largely facilitated by technological developments in ICTs—has permitted the rise of more distributed settings within which these processes unfold. This evolution involves a merging of different lifeworlds and the negotiation of compatibilities between different administrative and political cultures, Knorr Cetina observes. In the field of climate change and international development, where inquiries overlap multiple epistemic, geographical, and societal divides, there is a need for better understanding of how the products of these knowledge settings circulate, are adopted or subjugated by other communities or cultures with competing knowledge claims, and merge themselves with other truths. It is within this contemporary state of the transnational negotiation of (and trade in) knowledge that the case discussed here finds itself.

As a means to better understanding the link between the production of knowledge claims within particular epistemic communities and their entry into wider circulation, the concept of *discourse* is drawn upon. A focus on the concept and production of discourse is useful for understanding the ways communicative practices both constitute and express our social reality, and also reveal the role that power plays in this process.[9] "Power to control discourse," Norman Fairclough argues, "is seen as the power to sustain particular discursive practices with particular ideological investments in dominance over other alternative (including oppositional) practices."[10] The discursive shaping of words (and the range of concepts to which they refer) ultimately constitutes objects and social relations, as well as the subject positions within these discourses from which individuals or collectives can speak. Thus, the framing of the meanings of terms like *participation* and *openness*[11] in international development effectively shapes the politics of development practice, and, by extension, the potential agency and identity of those who are understood to be (or seek to be) contributing to development. Bill Cooke, in 2003, argues for example, that the term *participation*, as it is put into practice in World Bank/IMF development programming, has more in common with popular governance under late colonial administration than with the types of empowerment with which the term is frequently associated.

A final issue that will be touched on this article is the role of new communication technologies in relation to the production, validation, and circulation of knowledge. Here, ICTs are understood to serve as mediating technologies that play a key role in how people organize and coordinate their (and others') actions. Roger Silverstone describes the process of mediation as "a fundamentally dialectical notion which requires us to address the processes of communication as both institutionally and technologically driven and embedded. Mediation, as a result, requires us to understand how processes of communication change the social and cultural environments that support them as well as the relationship that participants, both individual and institutional, have to that environment and to each other."[12] In this sense, the role of mediating technologies cannot be seen as passive or neutral, but rather, as simultaneous products and producers of the environments and contexts in which they are put to use. By understanding ICTs in this light, it is possible to draw useful comparisons and linkages between the impacts they produce and the impacts of other mediating forces in development, including managerial technologies (such as *the project* and *evaluation*) that "serve to organize and coordinate actions involving people, time, space and money in the interests of efficiency and accountability."[13] Research into the use of information systems and technologies in the context of development have yet to fully explore these issues of "power, politics, donor dependencies, institutional arrangement," yet these are "precisely the type of issues where critical work can open up the 'black box' as an aid to deeper understanding, and a stimulus to appropriate action."[14]

Participation, Openness, and Knowledge in Climate Science

Given that natural sciences have traditionally been more strongly bound to a model of inquiry that privileges distance, objectivity, and authority than the development community, there has been less emphasis on inclusion, community voice, or openness to other knowledge sets within climate science until as recently as the early 2000s. Recent controversies around the transparency of the IPCC's climate modeling and prediction processes highlight the current bias toward closed "expert" dialogue in the establishment of new conclusions and knowledge.[15] However, there is now an increasing acknowledgment of the potential for drawing on traditional practices bound within what are often deemed *nonscientific* knowledge sets (variously termed *local, traditional ecological,* or *indigenous* knowledge) to inform climate prediction, measurement, and adaptation, as well as an increase in support for engaging with communities in the *use* of climate information.[16] This trend has emerged from a growing recognition of the limits of climate science in reliably predicting climate change and variability at the scale of resolution needed for communities to make informed decisions,[17] and of the central role that local knowledge, culture, and practice play in effective responses to climate change.[18]

As such, climate change represents a complex site where natural sciences, social sciences, culture, and politics intersect across multiple levels of action, from global climate models and governance frameworks down to local climatic impacts that stand to dramatically alter people's relationships with their natural environments. This site is further mediated through multiple technologies, including complex information technologies used for data collection, modeling and downscaling, as well as through global and regional institutional regimes in both the areas of climate change and development. These have profoundly shaped the contemporary discourse and body of knowledge around climate change and its link to development, and have also influenced the forms and levels of participation that are available, as this chapter will examine.

AfricaAdapt: Negotiating Meaning through Networked Collaboration

The chapter's discussion will now turn to the case of AfricaAdapt, a network that brings together partners from both the science and development communities, and that, at the time of this study, was hosted by a nongovernmental organization, an intergovernmental organization, a regional center for scientific research, and a development research institute. It provides a clear example of the types of intersections between differently situated epistemic communities, drawing on different forms of technological mediation, within a network whose overarching objective of promoting a culture of knowledge sharing is closely aligned with the notion of promoting openness as it is defined above.

Methodology

This analysis draws primarily on semistructured interviews conducted in October 2009 both face-to-face and virtually with five respondents from the network's implementing partners working at different levels of the network's management hierarchy, and with two respondents closely linked to the network's core partners. These included three of the network's Knowledge Sharing Officers (KSOs), who are charged with implementation of network activities and based in the partner African organizations; the then program manager, based at the Institute of Development Studies; a member of the network management group based in an African partner organization; a UK-based knowledge-sharing advisor who was instrumental in the early development of the network's strategy and later provided mentorship to KSOs; and a representative from a donor institution familiar with the network's activities. Where possible, the respondents' own words are used to describe their impressions of how these processes of meaning-making unfold, often placing their responses alongside one another to illustrate how people's situatedness has influenced their construction of meaning. These interviews were analyzed to draw out commonly recurring themes in the respondents' description of how meanings and ways of working were established within the partnership—themes that are explored below.

Background

AfricaAdapt is a knowledge-sharing network on climate change adaptation in Africa established in 2008 and initially hosted by four partner organizations: Environment and Development Action in the Third World (ENDA-TW), based in Dakar, Senegal; the Forum for Agricultural Research in Africa (FARA) in Accra, Ghana; IGAD Climate Prediction and Applications Centre (ICPAC) in Nairobi, Kenya; and the Institute of Development Studies (IDS) in Brighton, United Kingdom. The network describes its aim as "facilitating the flow of climate change adaptation knowledge for sustainable livelihoods between researchers, policy makers, civil society organisations and communities who are vulnerable to climate variability and change across the continent" (AfricaAdapt, http://www.africa-adapt. net/about). It has since grown to a membership of nearly thirteen hundred, comprising primarily professionals and students from the African climate and development community. AfricaAdapt was funded through the United Kingdom's Department for International Development (DfID) and Canada's International Development Research Centre (IDRC) under a broader program on Climate Change Adaptation in Africa (CCAA), which was designed to promote African participatory action research by African researchers. AfricaAdapt was, therefore, conceived to work within a similar ethos, offering a space for its members to profile the work they are doing, access information and findings from African research in a range of formats and languages, and establish new connections (both virtually and face-to-face) with others who are working on adaptation in Africa. The use of ICTs, therefore, plays an important role in facilitating and mediating relations between the four host partner institutions, as well as between the hosts and the broader AfricaAdapt membership. Among partners, key technologies that are used include Web 2.0 tools such as Skype, wikis, and Delicious, as well as more conventional tools such as email. With its members, however, the network employs a different range of tools including Twitter, YouTube, and its own online platform that allows for the creation of user and project profiles in a style similar to that of Facebook and other networking sites.

Early thinking around the establishment of a knowledge-sharing network (before the selection of other partner institutions) was largely shaped by discussions between IDRC and IDS, including the establishment of what its understanding of what a culture of knowledge sharing actually involved. This was largely guided by one of the network's knowledge-sharing advisors, then based at IDS, who played an instrumental role in first developing its implementation strategy, and then sharing this with the selected partner institutes. It was on the basis of IDS's vision of knowledge sharing and the discussions held at the inception of the network that partners developed a professional profile of the future network drivers, its cohort of Knowledge Sharing Officers, to be based in each partner institution. Each partner institution then took these initial recommendations and tailored them to their particular contexts, and proceeded to hire their KSO. The wide-ranging profiles of the KSOs recruited are indicative of the process of internal interpretation and negotiation between the vision of knowledge sharing conveyed by IDS at the network's inception meeting and the established institutional culture within the partner organizations. Within the agricultural intergovernmental organization, a KSO with a background in library information systems and ICTs for Development was selected. Within the environmental NGO, a KSO with a background in marketing was chosen, while at IDS, it was a KSO with a background in education and development. Meanwhile, within the science-based climate research institute, it was decided that the KSO must be a climate scientist, and as a result, a meteorologist with a background in physics was selected.

The interplay between the promotion of a particular vision of a culture of knowledge sharing at the inception of the network, and the way this vision has been interpreted and ultimately translated into the actual recruitment of

KSOs reveals the multiple institutional and epistemic influences that shaped how knowledge sharing has come to be understood and enacted within the network. This process unfolded in stages that were at times *visible* (through presentation of a concept at a meeting of partners), *partially visible* (through internal negotiations within partner institutes), or *largely invisible* (through the initial development of a vision of knowledge sharing to be presented for review and approval), and that involved similarly varying scales of participation. These processes can unfold with multiple levels and scales of participation and openness being enacted simultaneously, and can greatly influence how particular concepts are collectively understood, embodied, and enacted, particularly within decentralized collaborative networks.

Construction, Validation, and Contestation of Meaning in the Network

To illustrate the process through which meaning has been constructed within the network, it is useful to begin with an examination of some of the core concepts underlying its principles and objectives, and to reflect on how differently situated partners understood these meanings and the process through which they were shaped. Three concepts that were noted by partners to be particularly central *and* challenging were the following: *a culture of knowledge sharing* (as discussed above), *researchers* (as one of the key targeted groups of the initiative), and *quality* (a particularly nebulous concept, but a much debated one for a network aiming to attract, translate, and disseminate climate-related research). As stated at the outset of this article, the shaping of discourse is understood to be constitutive of objects, social relations, as well as the subject positions from which individuals or collectives can speak. Thus, people's reflections on this process can be useful in revealing how power is negotiated among particular actors, institutions, or communities, and how this ultimately impacts who is included, and who is not. The two examples below aim to illustrate how these negotiations unfolded within the network.

Our Researchers Are Not Lab Coat Researchers

As stated earlier, researchers form a core constituency and target audience for participation in the AfricaAdapt network. In the development of the network's strategy, it was generally agreed that researchers should be the first target as part of a phased marketing of the network to its potential stakeholders. However, given the multidisciplinary nature of research into climate change in Africa, the range of possible researchers that might be targeted is wide and varied. Combined with challenges of translating the notion of research across cultural and linguistic divides among network members, this

rather vague identification of a target audience created some initial confusion, according to a number of respondents who serve as network Knowledge Sharing Officers. As one, KSO 1, recounted "One of my colleagues, a
knowledge sharing officer, she's from a francophone background, but she
was always using the word researchers, researchers, and I think she reached
the point where she was confused. So she was like: 'OK people, please clarify.
What do you mean by researchers? For me when I hear researchers I think
of someone in a lab coat, but our researchers are not lab coat researchers.'"

In time, however, the understanding of what is implied by researchers
within the shared discourse of network members narrowed considerably,
and it fell very much in line with the forms of participatory action research
(PAR) that were being funded through IDRC's CCAA program. This evolution was understandable on a number of levels, given that these forms of
research matched well with the overall objectives of the network, and that
there were clear advantages in terms of access to contacts and information for outreach, and, of course, the potential advantage of being seen to
be promoting donor-funded research. However, between members of the
network, the process and justifications for how *researchers* came to mean
this particular set of actors are differently understood, though the influence of the funding partners was noted by all. One KSO, for example, felt
that the network had gradually lost control of its focus due to increasing
attention to donor priorities by group members, while for another KSO,
KSO 2, this arose from a search for focus from *within* the network, alongside
the influence of donors "I think that we said to ourselves, 'let's start with
researchers,' but 'researchers' is so broad. . . . To reassure ourselves we fell
back on CCAA projects because it was easier. We really focused on that and
it helped us a lot. I think it was heavily influenced by the project funders.
Even unconsciously we said to ourselves, *Ah the CCAA projects!*, because
they funded us, but is that the best process?" (translation by Abel Bove). In
discussing this issue with the program manager, however, a very different
perspective is offered; one that sees the network evolving (through some
degree of contestation) *toward* greater inclusiveness, not away from it. As
noted by the program manager: "I think a very important change that happened and something that I fought for, and actually something that the
[donor's] field program manager in Africa was supportive of, and that was
that AfricaAdapt didn't have to serve just the needs of the CCAA program,
that it could actually be seen as covering the whole of the African adaptation domain, it didn't have to just be a client of the program. . . . I think
for us it's allowed us to provide some degree of delinking from CCAA, but
externally viewed people still think of it as some kind of child of IDRC."

The range of perceptions on how the current understanding of targeted researchers evolved is indicative of how significant the hidden transcript of partially or wholly invisible meaning-making can be in shaping differently situated people's understandings of how things work. They also point to the power of particular voices—both heard directly and inferred—in prompting an alignment of understandings (for example, of *researchers*) with the messages they are understood to convey. Thus, while AfricaAdapt is theoretically open to anyone, and indeed those who discover it either online or at an event can be from a range of backgrounds, the extension of invitations to join this *open* space has been conducted in line with particular priorities, whether strategically or unconsciously.

Openness and participation are fluid concepts, and spaces for participation are contingent on a diversity of factors, including, in this case, the types of tools or resources made available for users to participate (climate data sets versus Facebook-style profile pages, for example), the forms of invitation they receive to participate, the incentives for or pressures to accommodate particular actors over others (as alluded to above), and the types of values that a particular space seems to reflect and reinforce (as discussed below).[19] This is recognized by network partners, particularly in discussing the limited engagement of climate scientists as a part of the targeted audience of researchers. The program manager provided some initial reflections on this point, suggesting that both internal and external factors have had an influence on climate scientists' limited participation in the network. He noted: "Science has not played a particularly strong role, but again I think that's partly because there are other networks and other spaces that inhabit the science interactions, and that we've tended to say we're not there to duplicate. . . . And I suppose we haven't really provided the kind of spaces and sharing spaces to really encourage a strong science dimension to the network."

A KSO, however, suggested that the failure to create the necessary incentives to bring climate scientists on board represents a lost opportunity, particularly in light of the fact that one AfricaAdapt partner, ICPAC, is science-focused. As KSO 1 noted: "ICPAC has links to climate scientists and people like that but I don't see any of the scientists on board. So now that I think about it, yes, maybe it would have sort of, not diminished their role, but not made the most out of them. Because we are supposed to target researchers, we are only doing the [PAR] researchers, we are leaving out the climate scientists." These views reinforce the theory that the types of spaces made available for participation, as well as the spaces available elsewhere, have played a determining role on the types of participants that have ultimately joined the network. In effect, the decision to prioritize investing the network's finite human and financial resources into engagement with the action research community may have consequently constrained the ability of other types of researchers to engage, including climate scientists. While such decisions might be seen as a failure to be open and inclusive to all (as suggested by the KSO), on a more pragmatic level, they also reflect an understanding of the challenge (or futility) of being everything to everyone, and instead developing a particular niche alongside other initiatives, as the program manager mentions. This illustrates a key challenge of promoting openness—namely, that the spaces for achieving it do not look the same for everyone, and, therefore, they accommodate some more easily than others. It also highlights the degree to which the prioritization of a particular group of researchers, through processes that are influenced and interpreted differently by differently situated partners, have had a fundamental and lasting impact on the shape of the network. This also leads to a related concept that may have influenced, and been influenced by, the membership to which the network ultimately appealed.

Assessing and Valuing Quality

It isn't surprising that, within a network dedicated to sharing knowledge on a subject as contentious and complex as climate change, questions about the quality and validity of information are considered to be of utmost importance. Knowledge on climate change sits across a range of epistemic, disciplinary and institutional communities drawing on a range of sources of knowledge production that meet with varying levels of acceptance. In many ways, it is at this frontier between the supposed objectivity and verifiability of scientific observation, and the *softer* forms of local observation, traditional or indigenous knowledge that AfricaAdapt finds itself. Given that processes of gathering, appraising, and validating knowledge are central to the structure and practice of epistemic communities,[20] it was clear from the network's inception that decisions would need to be made on the editorial approach to quality control that would be pursued. These decisions would shape the opportunities for contribution among some audiences, while potentially creating a more *or* less familiar space for contribution for others, depending on the conceptions of quality and editorial control that were adopted. The thinking that framed these discussions is recounted by the program manager:

Obviously from the very start we were critically aware of quality issues. But the fact that we wanted to be a reasonably open space, not heavily moderated, and one that appreciated different forms of knowledge, and IDRC pushed this too, they wanted a very strong community dimension to the website and to our action, and that we needed to make sure that we were engaging down to community level, indigenous knowledge and all that kind of thing. So kind of the editorial policy was always being really shaped from the start, to one that was reasonably open and freer than a lot of other editorial policies I've seen. Which obviously sat a little bit in tension with members of the managing group who said: "Well actually we need to be working on the basis of quality climate science, and quality science is the backbone to our work."

Indeed, when asked about how AfricaAdapt should strive to sustain the quality of its knowledge resources, the KSO (KSO 3) with a climate science background appealed for more stringent forms of expert moderation and control: "The knowledge that is generated and the quality of that knowledge has to be maybe supervised or maintained through some mechanism, one could be the sort of review mechanism put in place with experts or our own exchanges or what have you. . . . And also maybe when we put content up we have to be selective, maybe looking for people who are good in a specific specialisation, known scientists or known professors."

These differences of perspective point to wider discussions on the sources of knowledge within climate change and development, as noted at the outset of this chapter. The potential impact of this stance on the contributions that would be sought and accepted within the network were noted by the program manager particularly in terms of how users accustomed to far more prescribed notions of quality, especially climate scientists, might react. The program manager wondered: "If a climate scientist within Africa who's writing, you know, what they think are high-quality papers on climate science, thinks well maybe, you know, 'I won't upload this to Africa-Adapt because there's no kind of validation process, so therefore you know, my work might be compromised.'"

This suggests the possibility that taking an approach of seeking more inclusiveness within a particular space may, in fact, limit the potential for participation from those working within epistemic cultures that privilege adherence to more standardized (or exclusive) measures of quality. It also represents a considerable challenge for initiatives seeking to promote sharing across disciplinary or epistemic boundaries, as archetypes of practice are rarely compared or discussed within this sharing, and yet are often poorly understood from one community to another.

Ultimately, the question of quality control has not yet led to serious conflict within the network's partnership, despite the fact that partners' own perceptions on this issue vary widely. We *do* see, however, a view of quality emerging in line with the particular stance on the broader debate over knowledge taken by both IDS and the donor organization. The implications of this stance are not insignificant, particularly within the political economy of knowledge production in the climate change adaptation community. The stance has also helped to shape the ways in which ICTs have been drawn on to enable users to contribute to knowledge sharing within the network, as this chapter examines in the following section.

ICTs and the Negotiation of Meaning

The decentralized nature of the AfricaAdapt network partners and its targeted audiences has meant that ICTs have played a very central role in both its management and the delivery of its services to members. However, the fact that connectivity and use of online technologies remain limited on the continent where 80 percent of network members are located presents a significant challenge to this role. This issue has been a point of reflection, as partners have sought to balance the selection and use of technologies that allow users to express themselves in a variety of formats (photographs, video, blogs, and so forth) while acknowledging the limiting factors of connectivity, literacy, access to technology, and more. There is also a need to recognize the inscribed logic of the tools that have been selected and their appropriateness of fit with particular knowledge settings. The use of wikis as a space for co-creation, for example, where there is never a "definitive" version of a text, and where one's contributions are always subject to review and revisions by others, has met with unease among some members of the climate research community.[21] Similarly, the absence of climate modeling tools and data sets within the range of tools (which are available on other knowledge platforms) reinforces a particular view of the forms and sources of information and knowledge that the network aims to put into greater circulation, as discussed above.

Beyond the selection and deployment of appropriate ICTs for network members, communication presents broader ongoing challenges to the core partners, who seek to ensure a spirit of openness and collaboration, while at the same time, negotiating different expectations within the bounds of each institution's norms of practice. These issues offer insight into the challenges of openness when collaborating across divides, be they institutional, epistemic, cultural, linguistic, or technological. They also overlap with the challenges of meaning-making raised in the previous section—both reinforcing particular meanings and being shaped by the meanings that have been produced. Core management partners, for example, pointed to an internal struggle of balancing a need for greater openness between partners with the desire to create spaces that allow for safer risk taking, particularly among KSOs, a stance that was strongly advocated by the Institute of Development Studies's knowledge sharing advisor. He explains: "I think at an early stage we felt this was the KSOs and the knowledge sharing advisors coming together, talking about where would be a space that the KSOs could themselves share, and build up their sense of peer support, and the decision to have a wiki space for the KSOs, which was a private space, seemed like a very good idea. . . . And there was actually a desire from the core group to know actively about what the KSOs were talking about in their meetings, and there was a bit of negotiation there about how much would be shared."

These negotiations in promoting openness within the partnership while avoiding the forms of compulsory visibility, or "information panopticism,"[22] point to an important link between openness and the technologies supporting it. A closed online space for KSOs outside of managerial oversight was dissonant with the institutional hierarchies and practices within some partners, as well as with some partners' visions of open sharing, whereas the creation of safe spaces within the model of openness espoused by others was seen as essential.

Beyond ICTs: Mediating Technologies and the Regulation of Practice

Beyond the mediation that ICTs provide, other technologies (using the term in its broader sense) have fundamentally shaped the forms of openness and participation that have emerged from within the network. Of particularly strong influence here is the concept of the project itself, along with its associated techniques and practices. This is particularly pertinent to the field of international development, where action is largely shaped around relationships that are framed by the project structure. As mentioned at the outset of this article, the partially visible process of developing the initial project proposal established the discourse through which understandings of the network's aims and definitions were later formalized. Further, the development of partner work plans and logical frameworks has served to delineate the spaces where partners and particular individuals within partner organizations are expected to take a leading role, essentially delineating and rendering visible spaces and degrees of openness within the activities of the partnership.

One KSO highlighted the potential of these technologies for making visible the activities in which partners are engaged, arguing that "we should work more on putting communication systems into place that are really crosscutting, and project management tools such as worksheets; very simple tools so that any project member can see what's going on." Another KSO, KSO 3, highlighted the importance of these technologies in the governance of partners' actions: "So there is the governance structure of

AfricaAdapt and on top of that we have the project documents which serve as the guidance to execute the project. So those are the things which lead us to decisions. For example, where decisions are made by the core group members for example, based on the project document and then actions are taken by say if a KSO has to do it or if each individual institution has to do it." Thus, the development and use of these forms of project documentation effectively serve to mediate and organize people's actions in line with prescribed norms, both within and among partner institutions,[23] helping to clarify roles and responsibilities—but at the same time, potentially imposing boundaries on actors' agency. The statement by KSO 3 above also points to the hierarchy of engagement perceived by the KSO (flowing from a project document, as developed and ratified by a limited set of actors, to a core management group and on down to KSOs who execute particular decisions), a scale that is differently acknowledged and adhered to within each partner institution.

In AfricaAdapt, as in most other projects, mediating technologies, including ICTs and broader forms of managerial technology, serve to facilitate certain forms of interaction and communication, while precluding others. In developing new insights on openness and participation, unpacking these dynamics can reveal the complexity of attributing the impacts of particular technologies when partners are enmeshed in multiple layers of mediation. For example, the use of new communication tools, such as the KSO wiki mentioned above, may create new spaces for co-construction of meaning, but these benefits may be offset or challenged by forms of institutional hierarchy and limits implied through other managerial technologies, such as the project's logical framework. The concluding section of this chapter draws out some of these observations and considers what they might mean for future research and action.

Discussion and Conclusions

AfricaAdapt has set itself an ambitious challenge of encouraging greater openness and collaboration in knowledge sharing on climate change adaptation across a multitude of divides, and in doing so, it has achieved some remarkable successes, all while revealing important lessons. This article has reflected on these by drawing directly on the viewpoints and experiences of those situated at different positions within the network's core partnership. In particular, it has considered the ways that the negotiation of meaning within partnerships influences the scope for a new architecture of participation, and the ways in which ICTs and other mediating technologies influence (and reflect) this negotiation. An overarching conclusion supported by this study is that, while these new technologies may indeed offer new avenues for contribution and participation in certain contexts, they are subject to a number of other factors that may help to determine whether and in what form this new architecture will emerge. Further, given the varying interpretations of openness and participation, particularly in collaboration across epistemic communities (as we tend to find in climate change and development), consensus views on the suitability of a given architecture may be difficult to establish. Beyond these more general observations, the network's experience highlights the following key points of learning.

First, conceptions of openness and participation are products of particular epistemic and institutional cultures, and they will democratize knowledge production differently. Recalling Knorr Cetina's assertion that "knowledge cultures have real political, economic and social effects,"[24] interpretations of what is implied by "collaborative" rather than "centralised" production of content,[25] for example, are fundamentally shaped by the existing institutional and epistemic traditions onto which these concepts are overlaid. These can, in turn, have a determining influence on when and whether one person's opinion can override another's, as well as on whether opportunities for collaboration must be invited or claimed, and so forth. The influence of these existing knowledge cultures cannot be discounted, and must be better understood within the broader context of a political economy of knowledge generation, validation, and circulation in order to be engaged with effectively. Within networked collaborative environments such as AfricaAdapt, this task becomes even more complex, as these different conceptions of openness intersect, and, therefore, must be negotiated.

Further, in contexts where the promotion and circulation of knowledge from outside of dominant practice is a stated aim, the bias toward aligning spaces and technologies with subjugated knowledge and representations may necessarily entail a limiting of participation and openness to others, as was evidenced in the discussions on quality, for example. Thus, the promotion of openness within networks may involve difficult decisions about whose ways of knowing, working, and so forth, will be modeled at the expense of others—discussions that seldom occur openly. Consequently, it should be acknowledged that the creation of spaces for participation (such as platforms and networks) cannot occur outside of the broader dynamics of power and authority of a given setting or epistemic community. This suggests a more complex relationship between openness and the democratization of knowledge than was assumed by network partners at the outset of the AfricaAdapt program. It also calls on knowledge intermediaries to reflect more closely on the roles they (and others) play in opening or limiting these spaces, and to whom.

A second key point of learning is that formal and informal negotiation of meaning is central to the shared understanding that is ultimately produced in networked collaboration. Building on the previous point, collaboration across divides invariably entails a negotiation of meaning among asymmetrical and differently situated partners. These negotiations can take place in contexts that may be informal or invisible, formal and open, or formal and closed. Meaning often emerges from a combination of these contexts, leading to a lack of clarity on how particular understandings came into use. Actors are not equally placed to influence the outcomes of such negotiations, and understanding how people's positioning (as donors, Northern partners, junior or senior staff, and so forth) affects their access to and influence on these outcomes is central to understanding how meaning has been constructed within the partnership. Beyond this, the study has noted how, frequently, meanings that appear to be shared may be institutionalized or enacted in vastly different ways (as was the case with the hiring of KSOs), and thus may lead to very different outcomes.

Finally, a third point of learning is that ICTs and other mediating technologies play a influential role, both in the negotiation of meaning, and in determining how we move from meaning to action.

It is important to recognize the role that mediating technologies play in facilitating or precluding certain forms of communication and participation. There is a need to recognize the challenge of balancing an intensification of technologies and visibility with the assurance of spaces in which people can struggle to create meaning for themselves before engaging openly. It is also important to bear in mind that particular mediating technologies can either reinforce or clash with the norms of participation established within particular epistemic and cultural norms, and to understand the impacts that this will ultimately have on inclusion. This chapter has also situated ICTs as one group out of a variety of potential mediating technologies (such as the notion of the project itself in the context of development) that can mutually reinforce or contradict one another. Thus, we cannot look to ICTs as guarantors or models of new architectures of development without also looking at the whole range of practices, understandings, and mediations that unfold within this complex arena.[26] Doing so, however, offers us new opportunities to not only strive for better openness through the use of new communication technologies, but to challenge the very ways that development partnerships are enacted.

Moving Forward

At the core of addressing the concerns raised here is acknowledging the inevitability (and normalcy) of these processes of meaning negotiation within collective partnerships from their outset, and considering the forms of visibility and openness that these types of negotiation involve. This might mean spending significantly more time at the earliest stages of collaboration unpacking assumptions that may (from one individual's or institution's perspective) appear obvious and uncontroversial, but which could seem highly contentious to others. It may demand identifying and mapping key influences on discursive production and meaning-making, and reflecting on how differently situated partners are linked to these influences. This point was echoed by the AfricaAdapt program manager in his reflections on how he might have approached the initial phases of network development differently: "I would, we've talked about this a number of times, would have worked harder at the start in engaging the whole institution in a discussion about what knowledge sharing means for them, from the start, rather than thinking that we can build the capacity of a few individuals, and then begin to think that that's going to change the institutional culture." This suggests the need for placing reflexivity and collective learning at the center of efforts to achieve openness, and for appreciating the risks people take in confronting and revising their own practices and understandings, particularly across epistemic divides. This learning could also draw on a review of the evolving appropriateness of the technologies being deployed within an initiative. This form of learning, seen as central to communities of practice,[27] is too often overlooked within networked development practice, or is addressed post hoc, rather than as a starting point. As such, openness is perhaps best understood as a collective process that is continuously under development and review, rather than as a fixed endpoint that can be constructed.

Notes

An earlier version of this chapter appeared previously in *Information Technologies & International Development*, 9, no. 1 (Spring 2011), Special Issue on Open Development, http://itidjournal.org/itid/issue/view/40.

1. M. Thompson, "ICT and Development Studies: Towards Development 2.0," *Journal of International Development*, 20, no. 6 (2008): 821–835.

2. A. Cornwall, "Historical Perspectives on Participation in Development. *Commonwealth & Comparative Politics* 44, no. 1 (2006): 62–83.

3. F. Berkes, J. Colding, and C. Folke "Rediscovery of Traditional Ecological Knowledge as Adaptive Management," *Ecological Applications* 10, no. 5 (2000): 1251–1262.

4. D. Smith, "Texts and the Ontology of Organizations and Institutions" *Studies in Cultures, Organizations and Societies* 7, no. 2 (2001): 159–198.

5. K. Knorr Cetina, "Culture in Global Knowledge Societies: Knowledge Cultures and Epistemic Cultures," *Interdisciplinary Science Reviews* 32, no. 4 (2007): 370.

6. Knorr Cetina, K. *Epistemic Cultures: How the Sciences Make Knowledge* (Cambridge, MA: Harvard University Press, 1999); Knorr Cetina, "Culture in Global," 2007.

7. Knorr Cetina, "Culture in Global," 2007, 362.

8. Knorr Cetina, in her 2007 article cited above, on page 363, defines an epistemic culture as the "interiorised processes of knowledge creation. . . .Those sets of practices, arrangements and mechanisms bound together by necessity, affinity and historical coincidence which, in a given area of professional expertise, make up how we know what we know."

9. M. Foucault, *Power/Knowledge: Selected Interviews and Other Writings, 1972–1977* (New York: Pantheon, 1980).

10. N. Fairclough, *Critical Discourse Analysis: Papers in the Critical Study of Language* (London: Longman, 1995), 12.

11. Use of the term *openness* in this article draws on recent IDRC research that found openness to be characterized by two concepts: egalitarianism and sharing. As noted by M. Smith and others: "Egalitarianism suggests an equal right to participate (access, use and collaborate). Sharing is embedded in the idea of enhanced access to things that were otherwise normally restricted" see *Open ICT4D* (Ottawa: IDRC, 2008): 5.

12. R. Silverstone, "The Sociology of Mediation and Communication," in *The SAGE Handbook of Sociology*, ed. C. Calhoun, C. Rojek, and B. Turner (London: SAGE Publications, 2005): 189.

13. R. Kerr, "International Development and the New Public Management: Projects and Logframes as Discursive Technologies of Governance," in *The New Development Management: Critiquing the Dual Modernization*, ed. S. Dar and B. Cooke (London: Zed Books, 2008), 99.

14. G. Walsham and S. Sahay, "Research on Information Systems in Developing Countries: Current Landscape and Future Prospects," *Information Technology for Development* 12, no. 1 (2006): 13.

15. R. Tol, R. Pielke, and H. Von Storch, "Save the Panel on Climate Change!," *Spiegel Online International*, January 25, 2010, http://www.spiegel.de/international/world/ 0,1518,673944,00.html.

16. C. Roncoli, K. Ingram, and P. Kirshen, "Reading the Rains: Local Knowledge and Rainfall Forecasting in Burkina Faso," *Society and Natural* 15 (2002): 409–427.

17. S. Dessai, M. Hulme, R. Lempert, and R. Pielke Jr., "Climate Prediction: A Limit to Adaptation?," in *Adapting to Climate Change: Thresholds, Values, Governance*, ed. W. N. Adger, I. Lorenzoni, and K. O'Brien (Cambridge: Cambridge University Press, 2009), 64–78.

18. J. Ensor, and R. Berger, "Community-based Adaptation and Culture in Theory and Practice," in *Adapting to Climate Change: Thresholds, Values, Governance*, ed. W. N. Adger, I. Lorenzoni, and K. O'Brien (Cambridge: Cambridge University Press, 2009), 226–239.

19. A. Cornwall, *Making Spaces, Changing Places: Situating Participation in Development*. (Brighton: Institute of Development Studies, 2002).

20. Knorr Cetina, *Epistemic Cultures*, 1999.

21. IDS. (2009). "IDS submission to the Nairobi Work Programme synthesis report." Unpublished report, Institute of Development Studies, Brighton.

22. S. Zuboff, *In the Age of the Smart Machine: The Future of Work and Power* (New York: Basic Books, 1988).

23. Kerr, "International Development," 2008; Smith, "Texts," 2001.

24. Knorr Cetina, "Culture in Global," 370.

25. M. Smith et al., *Open ICT4D*, 2008.

26. C. Avgerou, C. Ciborra, and F. Land, *The Social Study of Information and Communication Technology: Innovation, Actors, and Contexts* (Oxford: Oxford University Press, 2004).

27. E. Wenger, *Communities of Practice: Learning, Meaning, and Identity*. (Cambridge: Cambridge University Press, 1998).

Bibliography

Avgerou, C., C. Ciborra, and F. Land. *The Social Study of Information and Communication Technology: Innovation, Actors, and Contexts*. Oxford: Oxford University Press, 2004.

Berkes, F., J. Colding, and C. Folke. "Rediscovery of Traditional Ecological Knowledge as Adaptive Management." *Ecological Applications* 10 (5) (2000): 1251–1262.

Cornwall, A. *Making Spaces, Changing Places: Situating Participation in Development.* Brighton: Institute of Development Studies, 2002.

Cornwall, A. "Historical Perspectives on Participation in Development." *Commonwealth and Comparative Politics* 44 (1) (2006): 62–83.

Dessai, S., M. Hulme, R. Lempert, and R. Pielke, Jr. Climate Prediction: A Limit to Adaptation? In *Adapting to Climate Change: Thresholds, Values, Governance*, ed. W. N. Adger, I. Lorenzoni, and K. O'Brien, 64–78. Cambridge: Cambridge University Press, 2009.

Ensor, J., and R. Berger. Community-based Adaptation and Culture in Theory and Practice. In *Adapting to Climate Change: Thresholds, Values, Governance*, ed. W. N. Adger, I. Lorenzoni, and K. O'Brien, 226–239. Cambridge: Cambridge University Press, 2009.

Fairclough, N. *Critical Discourse Analysis: Papers in the Critical Study of Language.* London: Longman, 1995.

Foucault, M. *Power/Knowledge: Selected Interviews and Other Writings, 1972–1977.* New York: Pantheon, 1980.

Kerr, R. International Development and the New Public Management: Projects and Logframes as Discursive Technologies of Governance. In *The New Development Management Critiquing the Dual Modernization*, ed. S. Dar and B. Cooke, 91–110. London: Zed Books, 2008.

Knorr Cetina, K. *Epistemic Cultures: How the Sciences Make Knowledge.* Cambridge, MA: Harvard University Press, 1999.

Knorr Cetina, K. "Culture in Global Knowledge Societies: Knowledge Cultures and Epistemic Cultures." *Interdisciplinary Science Reviews* 32 (4) (2007): 361–375.

Roncoli, C., K. Ingram, and P. Kirshen. "Reading the Rains: Local Knowledge and Rainfall Forecasting in Burkina Faso." *Society & Natural Resources* 15 (2002): 409–427.

Silverstone, R. The Sociology of Mediation and Communication. In *The SAGE Handbook of Sociology*, ed. C. Calhoun, C. Rojek, and B. Turner, 188–207. London: Sage Publications, 2005.

Smith, D. "Texts and the Ontology of Organizations and Institutions." *Studies in Cultures, Organizations and Societies* 7 (2) (2001): 159–198.

Smith, M., N. J. Engler, G. Christian, K. Diga, A. Rashid, and K. Flynn-Dapaah. *Open ICT4D*. Ottawa: IDRC, 2008.

Thompson, M. "ICT and Development Studies: Towards Development 2.0." *Journal of International Development* 20 (6) (2008): 821–835.

Tol, R., R. Pielke, and H. Von Storch. "Save the Panel on Climate Change!" *Spiegel Online International*, January 25, 2010. http://www.spiegel.de/international/world/0,1518,673944,00.html.

Walsham, G., and S. Sahay. "Research on Information Systems in Developing Countries: Current Landscape and Future Prospects." *Information Technology for Development* 12 (1) (2006): 7–24.

Wenger, E. *Communities of Practice: Learning, Meaning, and Identity*. Cambridge: Cambridge University Press, 1998.

Zuboff, S. *In the Age of the Smart Machine: The Future of Work and Power*. New York: Basic Books, 1988.

12 Open Data, Knowledge Management, and Development: New Challenges to Cognitive Justice

Katherine M. A. Reilly

If people put data onto the Web—government data, scientific data, community data, whatever it is—it will be used by other people to do wonderful things in ways that they never imagined.

—Tim Berners-Lee, TED, February 2010

Our experience shows that what gets measured can be changed. That is why it's so important to make this information available to everyone.

—Robert Zoellick, World Bank president, April 2010

According to Tim Berners-Lee, the year 2010 saw the emergence of a "worldwide open data movement."[1] The buzz around open data has been building for some time now, driven by larger debates over proprietary versus open systems of production. It has also been moved forward by specific events, such as the Organisation for Economic Co-operation and Development (OECD) Committee for Scientific and Technological Policy's Declaration on Access to Research Data from Public Funding signed by thirty-four countries on January 30, 2004, and, U.S. president Barack Obama's Open Government Initiative which was put into motion on his first day in office in January 2009. It was during the year 2010, however, that open data began to be applied in meaningful ways that grabbed the public's imagination. For example, in the wake of Haiti's January 2010 earthquake, volunteers around the world used open data to generate real-time street maps showing the locations of hazards, refugees, aid stations, and the like, which greatly facilitated relief efforts.

This new movement is being widely praised as a force of empowerment. Its supporters argue that open data will democratize dialogue and make decision making more transparent. We should not jump to conclusions. There is much more to open data than cracking open the books and inviting public involvement. Open data is not just about the possibility of making formerly closed data publicly available, thanks to the Internet. Open data is also about the massive amount of data that is being generated and made publicly available *because* of the Internet. The result is a flood of material that must somehow be managed, processed, and represented. In this new context, increasing amounts of data are being managed in new ways.

Visual analytics and data visualization, for example, are being used to make sense of the meanings held within complex data sets. These techniques allow alternative approaches to knowledge production, such as abduction and interpretation, to join the stage alongside traditional scientific approaches. This is an interesting development, but it isn't clear what sort of play these actors will put on when take the stage together. The techniques that are emerging to grapple with open data are changing dominant structures of information circulation and knowledge production with important implications for how social structures are produced and reproduced within social systems. These new forms of digitized knowledge management will affect how production takes place, how governance is realized, and how subjectification happens, and, therefore, will affect relations of production, power, and equality in ways that reshape processes of development and change.

In short, we are facing the question of how the open data movement will reshape people's ability to "participate in the governance of their own lives."[2] This is ultimately a question of cognitive justice (CJ), which can be defined as the search for equality within processes of decision making that shape development and change. In the past the main threat to CJ came in the form of hegemonic science because, as a legitimating framework, science served to prioritize some ways of knowing and marginalize others.[3] The argument developed in this chapter, however, is that the worldwide open data movement has gone a long way toward resolving exclusionary practices within processes of decision making. In particular, thanks to the new techniques that are emerging to contend with open data, different ways of knowing are being put into dialogue with each other as a matter of course. This is good news, but we need to now recognize that the systems of knowledge management that bring together different ways of knowing introduce new threats to CJ given how they obligate and structure dialogues between the forms of knowledge that they contain. Threats to equality of opportunity in spaces of policymaking will, in the future, be less likely the result of the delegitimation or exclusion of unscientific logics. Instead it is more likely they will originate from competition among the parameters used to incorporate and weigh a range of ways of knowing within knowledge management systems.

Open Data and Data Visualization

The currently exploding field[4] of data visualization offers an excellent starting point for thinking about how knowledge management is changing to grapple with the flood of open data. This is because data visualization is a method for making sense of large volumes of information so as to manage the complexity of global networked flows. A widely accepted definition of data visualization is the use of visualization to amplify cognition[5] or more colloquially, using vision to think. It does so by bringing together the quantitative work of visual analytics (computer-assisted statistical analysis) with the qualitative work of graphical representation (infographics). But recent discussions in the data visualization community suggest that this definition ought to be expanded to include communication as well[6] given the growing roles of collaboration, mediation, and dissemination in sense-making work. In total, data visualization encompasses an important epistemological shift arising directly from the problem of having too much data. It represents both a challenge to old paradigmatic divides (such as between the sciences and humanities), as well as the playing field on which new paradigms are being constructed.

Given its current celebrity, it may come as a surprise to learn that data visualization is not new. Several recent projects have documented its lengthy history, such as Eugene F. Provenzo's Web curation of the data visualizations created by W. E. B. Du Bois for the *Exhibit of American Negroes* displayed at the 1900 Paris Exposition.[7] The work of the Milestones Project at York University goes back much further in time noting that contemporary data visualization has deep roots in early statistics, cartography, the expansion of planning and commerce with colonialism and the rise of the nation-state, advances in mathematics, advances in data management, and the development of new technologies for drawing and reproduction.[8] Here we see the suggestion that data visualization can be historically linked to processes of Western colonization in that it would serve to establish dominant ways of knowing (for example, cartographic understanding of geographical space) and to marginalize other ways of knowing (for example, ecological understanding of human space).

We can nevertheless point to a series of factors that have conspired to give rise to a new moment in data visualization. The first of these is the declining cost of information processing and storage that is a hallmark of the information age (e.g., Moore's Law or Butler's Law). The second is the rise of ubiquitous computing[9] and digital surveillance that allow for the generation of massive data sets about everything from financial markets and climate patterns to human dynamics (the study of human motion and behavior), the human genome, and cultural artifacts. Together these two factors mean that a range of different types of knowledge can be codified, stored, and processed within knowledge management systems, thus reducing the exclusion of certain ways of knowing from systems of decision making.

There is still the issue, however, of how that data is processed. This, too, is changing given the application of data mining techniques to computer-supported statistical analysis. As Shneiderman explains, early computer-assisted analytics were applied in controlled scientific experiments that followed the hypothetico-deductive model and used an objective, reductionist approach designed to avoid human subjectivity in analysis.[10] This produced, for example, the familiar two-dimensional line graphs that correlated a variable on the x-axes with a variable on the y-axes suggestive of a linear, causal relationship. The application of deductive logic, however, meant the exclusion of any data that did not fit a proposed model, a problem which, it is often pointed out, works to marginalize ways of knowing that do not fit dominant models of knowing.[11]

As limitations to this approach have become clear, and the size and complexity of data sets have gown, advocates of exploratory data analysis have come to the fore. In this approach, analysts use computer-assisted visualization, which often relies on sophisticated data mining algorithms, to extract patterns, clusters, gaps or outliers within massive and complex data sets. As Ben Shneiderman explains:

> Those who believe in data or information visualization are having a great time as the computer enables rapid display of large data sets with rich user control panels to support exploration. Users can manipulate up to a million data items with 100-ms update of displays that present color-coded, size-coded markers for each item. With the right coding, human pre-attentive perceptual skills enable users to recognize patterns, spot outliers, identify gaps, and find clusters in a few hundred milliseconds. When data sets grow past a million items and cannot be easily seen on a computer display, users can extract relevant subsets, aggregate data into meaningful units, or randomly sample to create a manageable data set.[12]

While mathematics plays a role in identifying patterns, as data sets get larger and more complicated, human beings play a larger role in shaping the inquiries driving data mining and in interpreting the results. Deductive techniques are joined by abduction and induction allowing for diverse approaches to creating knowledge. And narrative, metaphor, and imagery play a larger role in shaping both exploration and presentation of results making the exercise of knowledge production much more creative.

The turn toward visual analytics has sparked a sort of gold rush, as a range of actors try to make sense of, or manage, the knowledge contained in the massive, complex, and emergent data flows of the information age. It has been of particular interest to scientists working in fields where such data sets are the norm, such as climatology.[13] But the field received its biggest boost from the response to the 9/11 terrorist attacks in the United States. Facing the results of increased surveillance, plus pressure to produce actionable intelligence, the United States Department of Homeland Security established the National Visualization and Analytics Centre (NVAC) to coordinate industry and academic advances in the field of visual analytics.[14] Data analytics has since drawn the attention of law enforcement experts, managers of critical infrastructure (such as the electrical grid), fraud detection and insurance experts, and actors who work with real-time situation assessment such as the military, disaster response teams, and large businesses.[15]

As these examples suggest, visual analytics is aligned with important changes in the way knowledge feeds into processes of decision making. As Dave Snowden's[16] Cynefin framework suggests, linear, reductive science remains useful in controlled situations that can justifiably exclude extraneous information. In more complex, nonlinear, uncontrolled situations, however, there are fewer constraints as the system is open, and actors continuously modify the situation through their actions. In these conditions, Snowden argues, it becomes necessary to work emergently. He recommends finding ways, through trial and error, to amplify desirable feedback and dampen undesirable feedback.[17] It then becomes necessary to consider all available data, all different ways of knowing. Visual analytics offers a useful tool for monitoring changing circumstances in ways that allow managers to drive these processes. What, however, counts as desirable feedback? When the whole of our thinking was circumscribed by reductive science, what counted as a desirable feedback was constrained to a large extent by our epistemological parameters. But now that our thinking has been opened up, what counts as desirable feedback is itself in motion, as is our vision of how any given end might be achieved.

Open data can support the democratization of these open-ended processes. Not only are many large publicly financed data sets becoming publicly available (such as the World Bank's Open Data initiative: http://data .worldbank.org), but it is also well within the reach of the general public to generate their own data using simple software to troll the Internet (as was done for http://www.wefeelfine.org). There is also work being done to link up the data contained on the web such that related data can be easily pooled.[18] Freely available and/or open source software supports a variety of tools and resources to leverage this data, resulting in a democratization of analytics.[19] And finally a range of applications is available to visualize the results of those analytics (http://www.data-visualization-tools.com). This, in turn, has generated a renaissance in the application of graphic design to data visualization as is exemplified by the popular website We Love Data-vis (http://www.datavis.tumblr.com) and projects like Radical Cartography (http://www.radicalcartography.net). Some data sets are mounted on websites where users can interact in real time with the data to generate and share their own visualizations and interpretations (for example, http://www.theyrule.net).

In this sense, data visualization can be seen as collaborative and iterative—inductive in the purest sense of the idea—creating the potential for democratized and cumulative analytics. In an ideal world this suggests the potential for data to be simultaneously produced and consumed, for collaboration and implementation to happen simultaneously. Both the visual analytics and graphical representation of data visualization can serve to uncover and/or challenge the assumptions hidden within dominant narratives. It can also serve to locate and/or monitor patterns or gaps within reference populations. Data visualization can be applied to manage complex situations. And, crucially for those who are interested in cognitive justice, all of this can be done from the local point of view. This ought to serve not only to empower and nurture alternative forms of knowledge, but it should also allow them to enter into dialogue with each other in creative new ways. In this sense, open data and data visualization seem to resolve the problem of hegemonic science posed by supporters of cognitive justice.

So then why should we be worried about data visualization as a way to manage large data sets? Some obvious complaints have been leveled against data visualization. Visual analytics in the field of law enforcement has raised widespread fears about surveillance and the invasion of privacy, for example. But more fundamental concerns arise from the question of how decisions will be made in such a system, and according to whose logic. How do open data, alternative approaches to analysis, and emergent thinking contribute to changes in social structures, and what is the impact of these changes on relations of power or equality? More broadly, how will these processes change the way we coordinate social relationships, what will this mean for the kinds of social structures that emerge within social systems, and how will this impact relations of power and inequality, particularly where decision making is concerned?

Knowledge Management as Social Process

Answers to these questions require new approaches to theorizing knowledge management. The term *knowledge management* has been around in business studies since the early 1990s. As a business practice, it consists of a wide range of strategies aimed at enhancing collaboration and decision making within groups in ways that maximize returns on intellectual capital. The commonly used term *knowledge hierarchy*, originating from systems theory, informs a great deal of this work.[20] Here data is defined as a raw material that has no inherent significance; it only gains meaning when it is organized into information. Knowledge is then defined as the application or use of information.[21] Following this idea, knowledge management consists of a range of strategies used to facilitate and/or drive the transformation from one level of the hierarchy to the next in ways that will best inform decision making.[22]

As techniques have emerged to make sense of the range of different forms of knowledge that are brought together within open data, some authors have suggested that these are forms of corporate knowledge management that aim to organize and absorb *all* forms of knowledge so that its potential can be controlled and exploited by powerful actors. The problem with the knowledge management hierarchy, however, is that it treats knowledge like a material good from which value can be extracted. In fact, the framework arose in the context of labor flexibilization within large corporations during the 1980s. Corporations needed a way to separate knowledge from bodies, and to stockpile and manage that knowledge, so that its value could be retained even when workers were not. In treating knowledge like a good, this model of knowledge management removes human agency and power relations from the communicative processes that underlay knowledge production. Thinking about knowledge in this way leads to reductionist social analysis.

For example Sunil Sahasrabudhey and Avinash Jha[23] warn us not to mistake the apparent democratization of knowledge for a victory of local pluralism over centralizing hegemonies. In the current moment, according to Sahasrabudhey "all that is organizable by the new technologies, all that can be processed by a computer, all that can be networked through the new means of communication, deserves to be called knowledge. And the science and art of doing this is called knowledge management."[24] This "shift of command in the knowledge domain from scientificity to the virtual realm tends to break the hierarchies of the old house of knowledge. Arts, management, design and software activity fetch greater value and have high esteem in the public realm than scientific and industrial activity."[25] As a result, Sahasrabudhey argues, "We have now moved to an era, where knowledge is every one's concern. Each one of us worr[ies] about having access to and possession of valuable knowledge which would increase our chances of survival and success in the emerging knowledge society."[26] Additionally, Sahasrabudhey observes "this entire show is being played out within a minority which thinks that the rest of the world, those on the other side of the digital divide, peasants, workers, artisans, women and tribal do not know and even if they do what they do, they are suppliers of sorts and not players."[27] To summarize, in a globalized, networked economy the value of knowledge is ascendant, and, therefore, powerful actors seek out new legitimating frameworks (i.e., openness) for the organization and exploitation of knowledge (such as visual analytics). This extraction of knowledge from the human realm is perceived to be a threat to communal processes of knowledge production, particularly since "ex-situ storage and preservation of natural processes endangers its in-situ existence."[28]

Here lies the suggestion that preservation of local knowledge requires local autonomy from global corporate systems of knowledge management. But in attempting to protect local knowledge processes, this set of arguments treats knowledge like precisely the sort of fixed good that can be exploited by corporate systems of knowledge management. Knowledge is treated like a mineral resource that once extracted causes the closure of the mine and the creation of a ghost town. This sort of thinking leads to the museumization of culture, meaning that knowledge is treated like something unchanging and static, as well as a romanticizing of processes of knowledge production such that the power struggles involved in processes of cultural change are ignored, along with the implications of these processes for social justice. In treating knowledge like a fixed good, this approach ignores ongoing knowledge production, provides few options outside of autonomy, and leaves communities unable to engage with foreign cultures or technical systems. In other words, linkages between different systems of knowledge management are ignored, and we are left with no tools to understand how those interactions are (or could be) negotiated to the advantage and/or disadvantage of specific communities.

Christian Fuchs[29] offers an alternative, dialectic approach to thinking about knowledge management that better captures the way knowledge interacts with social processes. Instead of treating knowledge as either subjective (i.e., a state of mind), or objective (an object that can be manipulated by management systems), Fuchs sees knowledge as both informing and arising out of the processes of cognition, communication, and co-operation that drive complex processes of social emergence. In this view, "Cognition refers to the individual dimension, that is, to the elements of social systems, communication refers to the interactional dimension, co-operation to the integrational dimension, that is, to the social system itself that is constituted by the interaction of its elements."[30] Within the context of a particular social system, individual actors use their cognition to process data into subjective knowledge. Communication requires the objectification of that knowledge so that it can be transmitted to others. When two actors plan to cooperate then, their knowledge must be codified into social norms, institutions, or traditions since it is necessary to solidify the assumptions that form the basis on which projects and programs will be constructed. These norms, institutions, commitments, and investments serve to constrain our cognitive processes.

This constant interplay between knowledge production and social structures is what "enables the system to change, maintain, adapt and reproduce itself."[31] For Fuchs, therefore, knowledge management is defined as "a fundamental human process in the sense that human beings permanently have to co-ordinate their cognition, communication, and co-operation in social relationships."[32] When we understand knowledge management to be a dialectical process of social emergence, information becomes a driving force in social change. With this in mind, Fuchs argues that knowledge is a social manifestation of information. To this we can add the further observation that information is a technical manifestation of knowledge.

According to Fuchs, knowledge management has always been taking place. All societies are knowledge societies because all societies seek to manage knowledge resources (in different ways) and all societies emerge through cognition, communication, and cooperation. What makes the current period different is that, thanks to computers and the Internet, knowledge forms a foundation for production, and, therefore, security and equality in an increasingly interconnected world. This is due to the informational intensity of production activities including labor, manufacturing, distribution, content, servicing, and promotion. Fuchs describes this as the difference between knowledge societies in general, and the knowledge-*based* society in particular.[33] In short, what makes the current moment different is the informational intensity of processes, and the fact that knowledge management frequently occurs through digital channels.

Fuchs' dialectical approach to understanding knowledge management is a preferable framework to the knowledge hierarchy. In his model knowledge management is seen as a living, breathing process both at the local level, as well as in its negotiation with supralocal processes. We can study how subjective thinking is shaped by uneven or hegemonic patterns of information flows, as well as how local patterns of knowledge production emerge to shape alternative responses. Using this model, communities may well suffer unequal patterns of information circulation, but they are also in a position to examine evolving interactions between technical and social processes, and to make decisions about what knowledge they want to protect, what knowledge they need to import, and what knowledge they wish to exploit, and how they might do this. They can also examine how these decisions are getting made, and think about how to alter those processes. In other words, the model allows us to consider how knowledge production shapes information flows in ways that either condition the outcomes of larger debates, or limit the parameters of more local debates.

The question then becomes how the new socio-technical ensembles resulting from open data and visual analytics reflect and shape social structures with implications for patterns of development and change. That is to say, how do the distributed structures of the Internet plus the social processes of analysis that they enable, come together both to reflect and to shape certain sets of social relations? As described in the previous section, in the current moment, those socio-technical ensembles are made up of a combination of open data, ubiquitous computing, new techniques for processing, and democratized access. Here it becomes important to separate the combined context of open data flows from the uneven realities of specific processes of knowledge production. What this means is that different groups will be involved in separate efforts of objectification and systematization that respond to competing logics.

This is very important; when we eliminate science as a single arbiter of legitimate knowledge and open up processes of decision making to all kinds of knowledge, then the game is completely changed. Decision making is no longer controlled through exclusion of knowledge that falls outside of the dominant framework, but rather it is controlled through the successful designation of legitimate spaces and criterion for a particular desirable outcome. Often these battles will revolve around questions of autonomy— whether it is more beneficial to make these parameters local or whether benefits can be derived from integration into larger spaces. As a result the issue is not whether and how knowledge management serves the interests of the all-powerful, but rather how power enters into processes of knowledge management. In the end, these patterns may organize themselves into the very channels of exploitation that are of concern to Sahasrabudhey and Jha. It is key to recognize, however, that this need not necessarily be the case. By recognizing knowledge management to be a social process, we also shine light on local power dynamics, and open the door to local agency.

Open Data, Data Visualization, and Development

When we look at open data and data visualization in the context of international development, we can examine the extent to which open data corresponds with an opening up of the legitimate criterion for decision making about the means and the ends of development. A quick overview shows that there is no dominant measure of what counts as legitimate knowledge, but there are different patterns of control over the way open data is indexed and analyzed. At times open data initiatives function as addendums to a particular paradigm of development assistance in ways that ensure a measure of control over the parameters of the conversation. But in other cases open data and data visualization do seem to be cracking open processes of knowledge production and knowledge management with interesting implications for decision making.

Much of the open data and data visualization work happening in large international development organizations subscribes to a "continuity variant" of modernization theory.[34] Here we find open data programs that are designed to make the existing system function more effectively, rather than to rethink the functioning of the existing system. In these cases the availability of open data does little to change existing patterns of knowledge management. Quite the opposite—open data is being presented in ways that reinforce old approaches to doing development. Open data does little to open up debates or to allow for competing logics of decision making, but rather invites wider participation in highly structured processes such that those processes are more efficient or have greater legitimacy.

These include efforts within the international development community to make statistics publicly available on the Internet. For example in October 2010, the United Nation's Commission on Trade and Development harmonized and integrated their statistical databases, commodity and price indices, foreign direct investment (FDI) statistics and world trade information and made them available on the United Nations Conference on Trade and Development (UNCTAD) statistics website (http://unctadstat.unctad .org). Additionally, in April 2010, the World Bank launched its Open Data Initiative (http://data.worldbank.org), which provides access to a catalog of over seven thousand World Bank indicators. Then, in July 2011, the World Bank made available data about its investments, financial statements, and the assets it manages for global funds (https://finances.worldbank.org). The announcement for this latest initiative points out that the new website makes publicly accessible data "available in a social, interactive, visually compelling, and machine-readable format."[35] National donor organizations have followed suit by making data about their aid activities available online. For example, the former Canadian International Development Agency (CIDA) made data about its activities available on the Government of Canada's transparency website (http://www.data.gc.ca).[36]

This new form of transparency allows watchdog organizations to hold international organizations accountable, as well as to ensure that aid achieves its intended ends. For example www.aiddata.org is a website dedicated to tracking global flows of development finance and foreign aid, while www.aidinfo.org works to ensure that local people are aware of programs and resources that have been promised to their communities so that they can keep local officials accountable. These initiatives are, of course, wonderful insofar as they improve the impact of aid dollars and ensure that they reach the intended populations. But as knowledge systems they are limited to traditional accounting methods that are used to make existing approaches to development more efficient. They do not represent new approaches to knowledge management, nor do they represent a fundamental challenge to dominant thinking about development.

In this sense it is important to study how dominant players are shaping the criteria for decision making in the spaces where open data flows. For example, when the World Bank introduced its Open Data Initiative, a blogger in the Bank's Development Marketplace noted the Bank would "lead amongst multilateral institutions and demonstrate by example that *liberating data* can pave the way for others to create valuable products, tools, and mash-ups to understand trends, correlations, and development outcomes in new ways."[37] But what sorts of initiatives would these be? In one celebrated case, the Global Adaptation Institute launched the Global Adaptation Index, called GAIN for short. The Index uses data from the World Bank's open data program to rank countries according to their vulnerability to climate-induced environmental change, ability to adapt to these changes, and ability to utilize investment capital to respond to vulnerabilities. "The beauty of this tool," said the Institute's Bob Edwards, "is it allows us as investors to look forward . . . to see where a country's trajectory is and its ability to create an attractive area to invest."[38] This is troubling because it means that the index maps future investment potential resulting from past investment externalities, and as a result promotes the sort of capitalist activity that contributed to climate change in the first place. The initiative is a clear example of how criteria for indexing open data can be used to maintain a system of knowledge management that upholds existing approaches to development.

Initiatives like these are legitimated by a certain data fetishism that blinds us to the bigger picture of how new approaches to making sense of open data might open up debates about how development happens, and to what end. Hans Rosling,[39] a veritable apostle of open data, actually offers an excellent example of this issue. According to Rosling, we do not face any lack of data about the problems of underdevelopment—it's just that progress is undermined by preconceived ideas about the nature of underdevelopment. This is the problem of being data rich but insight poor. For example, there is a widespread belief that HIV in Africa is linked to poverty, but Rosling uses conventional statistical correlations to show that some of the poorest nations in Africa also have some of the lowest rates of HIV. This suggests that research on HIV prevention needs to focus on cultural practices rather than resource distribution, and that interventions will achieve greater success if they focus on education rather than poverty reduction. Observations such as these lead Rosling to argue that "if people better understand what's happening in the world, they can make better decisions."[40] What Rosling overlooks is the very real possibility that there will be a variety of different interpretations of the rich data resources at our disposal. There is no epistemological shift here—just an insistence that if more people do more analysis of the conventional variety, and make their results available to a wider audience, then the problems of underdevelopment will be solved.

The development community has not been immune to the influences of open data, however. For example, in February 2008, in the wake of the global financial meltdown, then French president Nicolas Sarkozy convened a Commission on the Measurement of Economic Performance and Social Progress headed by Joseph Stiglitz, Amartya Sen, and Jean-Paul Fitoussi. The goal of the commission was to identify the limits of GDP as an indicator of both economic performance and social progress, and to propose alternative indicators, measurement tools, and ways to present information that would enable better understanding of social and economic progress. The limitations of GDP as an economic, social, and ecological measure have long been understood, but the spectacular failure of the GDP to capture the disastrous effects of the housing bubble on the U.S. economy created a window of opportunity to discuss new national and international measures of progress.

The results of the commission were made public in September 2009. The report finds that the role of statistics "has increased significantly over the past two decades" in part because "In the 'information society,' access to data, including statistical data is much easier. More and more people look at statistics to be better informed or to make decisions."[41] The authors go on to point out that people's decisions "depend on what we measure, how good our measurements are and how well our measures are understood."[42] To that end, the authors recommend traditional objective measures of progress be complemented by new, subjective indicators of well-being and sustainability including "measures of people's health, education, personal activities and environmental conditions."[43] As one commentator explains, "The idea is to build indicators that would be closer to the experience of the citizen, rather than an abstract, expert top-view of a system."[44] The report provides suggestions about what these measures might be, but the authors conclude that these issues require "global debate" about "what we, as a society, care about, and whether we are really striving for what is important," as well as national-level dialogues to "identify and prioritise those indicators that carry to potential for a shared view of how social progress is happening and how it can be sustained over time."[45]

Although it is true that official indices of progress will continue to rely on "robust, reliable measures . . . that can be shown to predict life satisfaction,"[46] the commission's work opens up room for debate about the different types of indicators that are chosen, how data is collected and represented, how it is analyzed, and how findings are visualized. More than this, however, it has been recognized that the production and distribution of a variety of types of data will allow different groups to monitor well-being in ways that make sense to them. For example, the OECD has released an interactive tool called the Create Your Better Life Index (http://www.oecdbetterlifeindex.org), which allows users to study national performance according to the criteria that matter to them. While still rudimentary, this experiment is a nod in the direction of greater openness and diversity in measures of progress. A diversity of measures and indexes are more likely to catch problems (such as the housing bubble) before they become crises. But this raises the question of how to balance opposing viewpoints. One might well ask, when different groups champion different measures, which set of measures will have the greatest legitimacy in which political arenas?

Open data creates the possibility for political competition between different interpretations, a situation that has not been lost on organizations working at the forefront of the open data movement. Political change organizations realize that politics is increasingly shaped by data prowess, and they are working with communities to help them manage knowledge in ways that will advance their agendas. For example, the international nongovernmental organization (NGO) Tactical Tech is accompanying a sex workers' collective in Cambodia in the design of research for evidence-based advocacy. Project Coordinator Maya Indira Ganesh explains that the conditions for sex workers in Cambodia are very difficult right now thanks to a draconian antitrafficking law that criminalizes sex workers.[47] Advocates for sex workers in that country understand that in order to change the law, they need to change public perception about sex workers. In order to do so, they not only need to show how the law fails to achieve its ends, and the harm that it does in society, but they also need to change the local public image of sex workers.

They have set out to produce a survey that will provide the kinds of data required to change people's opinions. They recognize that this work requires careful selection of indicators, ones that will be easy and inexpensive to gather, measure, understand, and visualize, all in ways that will have an impact within their community. The project is particularly interested in being able to visual the resulting data, as they feel visual material will have the greatest political impact. This work requires an intimate engagement with how people *know* within a very specific cultural space. By gathering data about how long sex workers spend in lock-up when they are arrested, they can show the impact of the law on the children of sex workers, and also the ability of sex workers to manage HIV by taking medications at the proper times. By gathering data about the sorts of abuses suffered by sex workers, they can demonstrate that landlords and police are a more significant source of social ills than the clients of sex workers, or sex workers themselves. The collective is very clear on the story they need to tell, the indicators that will help them paint a particular picture, but also the methods of analysis they need to use to create change within their particular context. Here we see an example both of the power of open data to change knowledge management within communities, but also its potential to become wrapped up in deep questions of how a community knows itself.

Experiments such as these point to a shift from a paradigm of knowledge about development, in which external experts measure development or progress against scientific criterion, to a paradigm of knowledge-intensive development, in which different ways of knowing enter into dialogue in decision making about development or progress. New approaches to knowledge management seek to advance the second of these two visions. For example, Laszlo Pinter from the International Institute for Sustainable Development (IISD) has worked on two community level projects to develop sustainability indicators, one for the Lake Balaton region in Hungary (http://www.balatonregion.hu/bam) and the other for the city of Winnipeg in Canada (http://www.mypeg.ca). In each case, indicators of sustainability and well-being are produced through a grassroots process and data is made available on a Web-based platform as a means to facilitate dialogue between community members. Pinter argues that these sorts of community-driven data consortiums are fundamental to sustainable development because they are the building blocks of community resilience: "Policies should not only be simple aiming for finding solutions to current pressing problems and negative trends identified through indicator analysis, but they should be centred on promoting resilience, setting-up institutional arrangements, networks and capabilities to facilitate interaction between stakeholders and thus foster learning and adjustments as society evolves."[48]

If the goal of development is to produce greater well-being in our societies, then what Pinter is suggesting is that we should move beyond externally produced measures as a foundation for top-down decision making to internally produced measures as a foundation for sense-making that takes place through the knowledge systems of our communities. This is about moving beyond treating data as an instrument of decision making. Instead, the way in which the data is produced, analyzed, and presented needs to be integrated into the development processes of the community. And this means that the data will necessarily reflect a variety of ways of knowing that will be coordinated through communal processes of decision making. But it also means that communities will become the sites of struggle over legitimate criteria for decision making, and that those struggles will take place on the plain of knowledge management expressed through new patterns of data visualization.

Rethinking Cognitive Justice

All of this suggests that we need to rethink the foundations for cognitive injustice. Cognitive justice can be broadly defined as the search for equality in processes of decision making that shape development and change. But the argument for CJ emerged in a very particular context, and this means that it is usually defined in a much narrower way that highlights the struggle between hegemonic, scientific legitimating frameworks for processes of decision making, and diverse local processes of knowledge production.

Indian scholar Shiv Visvanathan coined the term *cognitive justice* with reference to a community in India that suffered from sickle cell anemia. This group approached Visvanathan and his colleagues to discuss the possibility of organizing a dialogue between the various stakeholders in the treatment of their condition. As Visvanathan explains, the group wanted more than to *participate* in the treatment of their condition—they wanted *cognitive representation* in a dialogue about their care. This example highlights a problem encountered by many early proponents of cognitive justice. They found that what limited social justice within decision-making processes was not the opportunity to participate, but rather the dominant legitimating framework within spaces where decision making took place, where "modern science"[49] overrode tacit knowledge, knowledge of local ecosystems and cultures, and ethical or cosmological constructs as the arbiter of legitimate choices for the future of a community.[50] This led to the conclusion that "the social injustice that is rampant in the world today is in part the result of the cognitive injustice that a narrow and imperial conception of modern science has produced and legitimized."[51] Thus CJ is most often defined as the possibility for different systems of knowledge to exist in dialogue with each other or as "the constitutional right of different systems of knowledge to exist as part of dialogue and debate."[52] This challenge to science was seen as necessary for true equality of opportunity in debates and true equality of outcomes in policy making.

As a result, CJ has tended to mark a shift away from participatory models of technology transfer and scientific democratization. Participatory development models emerged as a response to the failures of top-down modernization projects. These projects were often implemented by outside experts who lacked sufficient knowledge about target communities.[53] Channels for community participation were not meant to challenge the parameters of the project, but rather were seen as a way to secure project success through consultations, information sessions, and promotional materials. Sparks calls such efforts the "continuity variant" of modernization theory.[54] In these cases, he argues, even when planning exercises attempt to be fully pluralistic, it is the expert who will determine what scientific knowledge is relevant to a given debate, and it is often also the expert who will determine what indigenous knowledge should be referenced. Thus, "the practical outcome of this apparently participatory and pragmatic approach to the problem is to leave all of the decision making power in the hands of elites who possess scientific knowledge of the recognized western kind."[55] In Visvanathan's words, in participatory development projects the "dream of democracy was still diffusionist. It was a dream of taking science to the villages. What was invented was the idea of the scientific temper, a pedagogic vision that a scientific world-view could be induced in a people."[56]

This produced a problem where CJ was concerned. As a dominant framework for decision making, the modern scientific criterion served to delegitimize and exclude alternative ways of knowing. As Boaventura de Sousa

Santos explains in his classic work *A Discourse on the Sciences* (2007), the modern scientific paradigm focuses on the creation of law-like generalizations through the conduct of ordered experiments with the objective of generating ever-greater certainty about the machinations of the natural and social world. Universal causal laws of nature rely on the establishment of fixed starting points, however their results must, by definition, be independent of time and place. In order to generate laws of social order, the modern paradigm depends on identifying social facts and representing them in terms of measurable dimensions. These measures need to be made consistent so as to facilitate verifiability, falsifiability, and transparency, but they serve to eliminate "the virtuoso technique, the random flash, the generalist's epiphany, and other private sources of confidence,"[57] as well as the ethical or moral voice. However, as Randall Arnst points out, "The largely unquestioned assumption that scientific knowledge is more valid or valuable than other knowledge is erroneous. The traditional or indigenous knowledge is simply different knowledge formulated in response to differing environments, conditions, and cultures."[58] Thus the dominant scientific framework represented a systematic stereotyping and oppression of alternative ways of knowing, and thus a fundamental *cognitive* injustice.

Efforts to overcome these problems often focus on helping marginalized groups recover their voice and achieve greater inclusion within decision making processes. Those who accompany marginalized groups play an explicitly political role in helping to articulate agendas, mobilize support, influence public opinion and the like.[59] But the spaces that these groups participate in are still arbitrated by science. Thus participation is not sufficient because, "However democratized social practices may become, they are never democratized enough if the knowledge guiding them is not democratized itself. Antidemocratic repression always includes the disqualification of the knowledge and ways of knowing of the repressed ones."[60]

CJ takes the additional step of tackling the knowledge systems that set the parameters of legitimate dialogue. As Visvanathan explains, "The idea of participation fundamentally accepts the experts' definition of knowledge. It seeks only to modify or soften it. It seeks a blend of expert knowledge and ethnoscience. But it is a world where expert knowledge is presented as high theory and the layperson's ideas as a pot-pourri of practices, local ideas and raw material. There is no principle of equivalence." Note how expert knowledge exists in a vertical relationship with indigenous knowledge systems in this discourse. Visvanathan continues by noting that "cognitive justice, however, recognizes the plurality of knowledge systems. It also recognizes the relation between knowledge and livelihood and lifestyle. It is in this context that it holds the policy must not be articulated within one monochromatic frame of knowledge but within an existential plurality of them."[61] Thus, the group that approached Visvanathan asking for help with their healthcare dilemma was seeking a dialogue with healthcare professionals at the level of knowledge systems. When decisions were being made about the delivery of healthcare to their community, they wanted the parameters of the dialogue to be established by both Western health experts *and* tribal doctors. In this sense cognitive justice demands not just participation or voice or resistance vis-à-vis science, but rather it demands, as well, a dialogue between alternative ways of knowing.

But as it turns out, open data brings a plurality of different ways of knowing together as a matter of course. Not only can a variety of different types of data be digitized and incorporated into online knowledge management systems, but open data, ubiquitous computing, new techniques for processing, plus democratized access have made it possible for different groups to bring different ways of knowing to bear in the interpretation of open data, rendering hegemonic science a thing of the past. With the rise of data visualization, for example, it becomes possible (even fashionable) to introduce visual representations of ideas into evidence with implications for how decisions get made. This suggests that open data has gone a long way toward resolving the exclusionary practices that gave rise to concerns about cognitive justice in the first place.

This does not mean, however, that cognitive justice has been resolved; it does mean that we need to reconsider the threats to equality in processes of decision making the might arise in the context of open processes. Now greater attention needs to be paid to the ways in which these new dialogues, and the compromises they represent, inhere within specific spaces of decision making. Thus CJ needs to be rethought in terms of the structuration of dialogue between competing/contrasting/complementary logics. Threats to equality of opportunity in spaces of policy making will be increasingly less likely the result from exclusion of views, and more likely to originate from the ways in which the inclusion of a wide variety of views is crunched by decision-making processes. As Julie E. Cohen argues "For law and technology alike, relevant questions will include the allocation of rights and abilities to access, control, and alter these flows. . . . Another way of putting this point, perhaps, is that the nature of networked/embodied space, and of the networked/embodied self, will depend critically on the construction of differentially bounded space, which I will define provisionally as space within which information flows are defined by a semantic and technical structure of permissions and authentications. Networked / embodied space can be a space of domination or a space of critical practice, depending on who keeps the boundaries and controls the permissions."[62] With this in mind, we can turn our attention to issues such as how the commodification of information or the spatialization of flows influences the ways in which different forms of knowledge get taken up in decision processes. But we can also look at *how* differing logics are harmonized, or reconciled or integrated, for instance, and with what implications for policy outcomes.

So, following Cohen's assessment, rather than defining CJ as the right of different knowledge forms to enter a debate, we need to think about CJ in ways that will frame innovative agendas for research. One possibility is to think in terms of the dignity of knowledge and propose that different forms of knowledge and their sources be accorded due respect within processes of knowledge production. What this would mean in practice requires consideration within the emerging context of open data, and the new forms of knowledge production to which it gives rise. For example, in chapter 11 in this volume, Blane Harvey considers how different logics contributed to the construction of a space for online discussion. Recognizing that different types of knowledge come together in the formation of open spaces, cognitive justice might seek protections against exploitation, marginalization, ridicule, or disrespect within such interactive spaces.

Another possibility is to focus on how spaces for decision making are constructed by processes of cognition, communication, and collaboration. In doing so it becomes possible to think about CJ in terms of equal opportunity (to think subjectively, to communicate, to collaborate) and equal outcomes (in which benefits of information flows are distributed fairly). Returning to Fuchs's model of knowledge management, we can imagine various asymmetries in the construction of spaces for decision making that would have implications for CJ. For example, deeply entrenched socio-technical systems and patterns of information flow can undermine cognition and communication in ways that limit the freedom of people to pursue independent thought and to express themselves. In chapter 4, Mark Graham and Håvard Haarstad look at how a particular pattern of information flow concerning the production and marketing of consumer goods limits the ability of people to make informed choices in the marketplace. In this case, cognitive justice would seek the possibility for consumers to access information about products that would allow them to apply different ways of knowing (such as environmental sustainability or labor responsibility) when making purchase decisions.

Similarly, too little information flow and too few frameworks for cognition and communication can undermine independent thought and leave people without the grounds for productive conversation. This situation can create a void in which people fail to exploit the potential gains from collaboration, or in which spaces for collaboration become occupied by opportunistic frameworks. In this case it becomes necessary to consider what types of institutional frameworks are necessary or desirable within particular contexts. This stance accords well with the arguments made by Parminder Jeet Singh and Anita Gurumurthy in chapter 7 of this volume. They argue that neoliberal frameworks have filled the void left by government retrenchment, and that open processes require institutional frameworks to ensure adequate financial and administrative support, as well as to establish fundamental principles of fairness—beyond what is suggested by neoliberal policy. The difficulty here lies in determining how much support is required and what types of principles ought to shape open processes. Ideally these supports would be sufficiently flexible so they could be adapted to particular circumstances.

Finally, there is also the possibility that contending circuits of information flow can lead to entrenched competition between groups in ways that undermine dialogue or collaboration. This is the concern expressed by the idea of a "filter bubble" recently introduced by Eli Pariser.[63] Pariser found that certain search engines (such as Google) and websites (such as Facebook) had begun to use algorithms that biased search results toward patterns of previous searches. The result according to Pariser is both an "invisible algorithmic editing of the web" and the creation of "personal information ecosystems" that close us off to ideas different from our own. This can create the impression that the world agrees with our own narrow view of issues, and at an extreme, could make people less open to contrasting points of view. There has been some debate about the seriousness of the "filter bubble" problem on the Internet,[64] but the concept remains useful for capturing the possibility of entrenched patterns of cognition, communication, and collaboration that limit the democratizing impacts of open data flows.

In sum, in a world of open data it is more useful to think of cognitive justice not as the right of different ways of knowing to enter the spaces of decision making, but rather in terms of the quality of the space into which different ways of knowing enter. Since knowledge production and the decisions it informs arise out of specific circumstances and specific communities, it is difficult to suggest universal principles for cognitive justice. It becomes necessary, however, to study how the parameters used to index information and the spaces designated for decision making shape the patterns of knowledge management that give rise to particular development practices. Indeed, the very tools provided to us by open data and data visualization can be used to reveal patterns of information flow and knowledge production. Having access to analysis can foster open dialogues about the types of spaces that are appropriate for knowledge management in particular contexts.

Acknowledgments

Thank you to Matthew Smith, Ineke Buskins, Deepak Sahasrabudhe, Tom Longley, Avinash Jha, Richard Arias Hernandez, and Tyler Morgenstern for their helpful comments and suggestions.

Notes

1. T. Berners-Lee, "Tim Berners-Lee: The Year Open Data Went Worldwide," *TED-Talk* (Long Beach, CA: TED University, February 2010), http://www.ted.com/talks/tim_berners_lee_the_year_open_data_went_worldwide.html.

2. A. Kaplan, *The Development of Capacity*. NGLS Development Dossier. (Geneva: UN Non-Governmental Liaison Service, 1999): 19.

3. Santos, B. S. "A Discourse on the Sciences," In *Cognitive Justice in a Global World: Prudent Knowledges for a Decent Life*, ed. by B. S. Santos (Toronto: Lexington Books, 1987/2007): 13; V. Shiva, "Western Science and its Destruction of Local Knowledge," in *The Post-Development Reader*, ed. M. Rahnema and V. Bawtree, 161–167 (London: Zed Books, 1997); A. Nandy, *The Intimate Enemy* (Bombay: Oxford University Press, 1987).

4. C. Chen, "Information Visualization is Growing," *Information Visualization* 1, (2002): 159–164.

5. Fekete, J.-D. et al., "The Value of Information Visualization," in *Information Visualization*, ed. A. Kerren et al. (Berlin; Heidelberg: Springer-Verlag, 2008), 1–18.

6. A. Kerren, J. T. Stasko, J.-D. Fekete, and C. North, "Workshop Report: Information Visualization–Human-Centered Issues in Visual Representation, Interaction, and Evaluation," *Information Visualization* 6, no. 3 (2007): 189.

7. The exhibit can be viewed at http://www.education.miami.edu/ep/paris/home.htm.

8. M. Friendly, "A Brief History of Information Visualization," in *Handbook of Data Visualization*, ed. C. Chen, W. K. Hardle, and A. Unwin (Berlin; Heidelberg: Springer-Verlag, 2008), 15–56.

9. L. Kleinrock, "History of the Internet and its Flexible Future," *Wireless Communications, IEEE* 15, no. 1 (February, 2008): 8–18.

10. B. Shneiderman, "Inventing Discovery Tools: Combining Information Visualization with Data Mining," *Information Visualization* 1, no. 1 (2002): 6.

11. See, for example, L. T. Smith, "Research through Imperial Eyes," in *Decolonizing Methodologies* (London: Zed Books, 1999): 42–57.

12. Shneiderman, "Inventing Discovery Tools," 8.

13. P. Ball, "Picture This," *Nature* 417, no. 4 (July, 2002): 11.

14. J. J. Thomas, Visual Analytics: Why Now? *Information Visualization* 6, (2007): 104–106; N. C. Roberts, "Tracking and Disrupting Dark Networks: Challenges of Data Collection and Analysis," *Information Systems Frontiers* 13, no. 1 (2011): 5–19.

15. J. Kielman, "Foundations and Frontiers in Visual Analytics," *Information Visualization* 8, no. 4 (2009): 239–246.

16. D. Snowden, "Cynefin: A Sense of Time and Space, the Social Ecology of Knowledge Management," in *Knowledge Horizons: The Present and the Promise of Knowledge Management*, ed. C. Despres and D. Chauvel (Woburn, MA: Butterworth Heinemann, 2000), 237–266.

17. D. Snowden, *The Cynefin Framework*, YouTube.com, posted July 11, 2010, http://www.youtube.com/watch?v=N7oz366X0-8.

18. T. Berners-Lee, Linked Data, last posting June 18, 2009, http://www.w3.org/DesignIssues/LinkedData.html.

19. P. K. Janert, *Data Analysis with Open Source Tools: A Hands-on Guide for Programmers and Data Scientists* (Sebastopol, CA: O'Reilly, 2010).

20. According to Wallace the notion of a knowledge hierarchy has informed information science for decades. The origins of the concept are unclear, and so the default citation has become a 1989 paper by R. L. Ackoff, see "From Data to Wisdom," *Journal of Applied Systems Analysis* 16, (1989): 3–9; P. Wallace, "Introduction," in *Knowledge Management: Historical and Cross-Disciplinary Themes*, ed. P. Wallace (Westport, CT: Libraries Unlimited, 2007), 1–10.

21. This basic framework is sometimes extended with further concepts, such as understanding (analytical processes in which existing knowledge is incorporated into new knowledge) or wisdom (responsible or novel applications of knowledge).

22. A. Liew, "Understanding Data, Information, Knowledge and Their Inter-Relationships," *Journal of Knowledge Management Practice* 8, no. 2 (June, 2007), http://www.tlainc.com/articl134.htm.

23. S. Sahasrabudhey, "Knowledge Flux and the Demand on Thought: Dialogue at Indian Association for Cultivation of Sciences," unpublished paper presented at *The Indian Association for Cultivation of Sciences* (Calcutta, India: April 15, 2008), http://vidyaashram.org/publications.html, 1–17; A. Jha, "Internet and the Shifting Grounds of Knowledge," presented at *The Conference on The Emerging Organisation of Knowledge and the Future of Universities*, December 19–20, 2008 (New Delhi: Jamia Milia Islamia University, 32nd Indian Social Science Congress, 2008), http://www.vidyaashram.org/papers/ISSC_Avinash_Jha_Internet.pdf.

24. Sahasrabudhey, "Knowledge Flux," 7.

25. Ibid, "Knowledge Flux," 11.

26. Jha, "Internet and the Shifting," 1.

27. Sahasrabudhey, "Knowledge Flux," 12.

28. Ibid., 17.

29. C. Fuchs, "Knowledge and Society from the Perspective of the Unified Theory of Information (UTI) Approach," in *Proceedings of FIS 2005: Third Conference on the Foundations of Information Science*, ed. M. Petitjean (Paris: July 4–7, 2005): 1–29, http://www.mdpi.org/fis2005/F.24.paper.pdf; C. Fuchs, "Knowledge Management in Self-Organizing Social Systems," *Journal of Knowledge Management Practice*, May 2004, http://www.tlainc.com/articl61.htm?newwindow=true.

30. Wallace, "Knowledge Management," 1.

31. Fuchs, "Knowledge and Society," 9.

32. Wallace, "Knowledge Management," 10.

33. Ibid., "Knowledge Management," 6.

34. C. Sparks, *Globalization, Development and the Mass Media* (Los Angeles: Sage, 2007).

35. "World Bank Opens Financial Data with Launch of Web Pilot," July 13, 2011, http://data.worldbank.org/news/wb-opens-financial-data-with-launch-of-web.

36. In March 2013, the Canadian Conservative government announced that CIDA would be folded into the Department of Foreign Affairs, the latter to be renamed the Department of Foreign Affairs, Trade and Development.

37. A. Walji, "Open Data for an Open World," *Development Marketplace*, April 20, 2010, http://blogs.worldbank.org/dmblog/node/741.

38. A. Howard, "Global Adaptation Index Enables Better Data-driven Decisions," *O'Reilly Strata*, September 15, 2011, http://radar.oreilly.com/2011/09/global-adaptation-index-open-data-speed.html.

39. Rosling is the chairman of the Gapminder Foundation, an organization dedicated to using statistics about social, economic, and environmental development to better understand and achieve sustainable development. In an effort to root out preconceptions and misunderstandings, the Gapminder Foundation dedicates itself to gathering data on development and making it freely available. It also advocates for open access to government statistics related to development. Rosling also recognizes the importance of making statistics accessible to non-experts. Gapminder makes much of this information available through a Web-based platform called Gapminder World (available at http://www.gapminder.org/world) which allows users to explore global development trends visually on graphical interfaces. Rosling is famous for the lectures (such as his much-lauded TED talk) and public relations stunts (he is a sword swallower) that he uses to reveal and deliver the stories contained within his data.

40. P. Fjällström, *Rosling's World* (Sweden: SVT, 2010), http://www.youtube.com/watch?v=y_7howQzatw.

41. J. E. Stiglitz, A. Sen, and J.-P. Fitoussi (2009), *Report by the Commission on the Measurement of Economic Performance and Social Progress*, Paris: Commission on the Measurement of Economic Performance and Social Progress, 2009, http://www.stiglitz-sen-fitoussi.fr/en/index.htm, 7.

42. Ibid., *Commission on the Measurement*, 9.

43. Ibid., *Commission on the Measurement*, 15.

44. J. Cukier, "The Stiglitz-Sen-Fitoussi Commission," *Communicating with Data*, September 15, 2009, http://www.jeromecukier.net/blog/2009/09/15/the-stiglitz-sen-fitoussi-commission/.

45. See Stiglitz et al., *Commission on the Measurement*, 2009; R. Tamburri, "Canadian Researchers Launch National Index of Well-Being," *University Affairs*, October 19, 2011, http://www.universityaffairs.ca/canadian-researchers-to-launch-national-index-of-wellbeing.aspx.

46. Stiglitz et al., *Commission on the Measurement*, 15.

47. Interview conducted Monday, August 1, 2011.

48. L. Pinter et al., "Developing a System of Sustainability Indicators for the Lake Balaton Region," *Tajokologiai Lapok* 6, no. 3 (2008): 291.

49. See Santos, "A Discourse," 1987/2007.

50. See Shiva, "Western Science," 1997.

51. B. Santos, "Introduction," in *Cognitive Justice in a Global World: Prudent Knowledges for a Decent Life,* ed. S. Santos (Toronto: Lexington Books, 2007): 1.

52. S. Visvanathan, "Knowledge, Justice and Democracy," in *Science and Citizens: Globalization and the Challenge of Engagement*, ed. M. Leach, I. Scoones and B. Wynne (New York: Zed Books, 2005), 83.

53. See Sparks, *Globalization*, 2007.

54. Ibid., 50.

55. See Sparks, *Globalization*, 2007.

56. Visvanathan, "Knowledge," 88.

57. A. Appadurai, "Grassroots Globalization and the Research Imagination," *Public Culture* 12, no. 1 (2000): 11.

58. R. Arnst, "Participation approaches to the research process," in J. Servaes, T. Jacobson, and S. White (eds.), *Participatory Communication for Social Change* (New Delhi: Sage), 109–22.

59. See Sparks, *Globilization*, 2007.

60. B. S. Santos, *The Rise of the Global Left: the World Social Forum and Beyond*. (New York: Zed Books, 2006), 45.

61. Visvanathan, *Knowledge*, 92.

62. J. E. Cohen, "Cyberspace as/and Space," *Columbia Law Review* 107, no. 1 (January 2007): 248.

63. E. Pariser, *The Filter Bubble: What the Internet is Hiding From You* (New York: Penguin Press, 2011).

64. P. Boutin, "Your Results May Vary: Will the Information Superhighway Turn into a Cul-de-sac because of Automated Filters?," *The Wall Street Journal*, May 20, 2011, http://online.wsj.com/article/SB10001424052748703421204576327414266287254.html.

Bibliography

Appadurai, A. "Grassroots Globalization and the Research Imagination." *Public Culture* 12 (1) (2000): 1–19.

Arnst, R. Participation approaches to the research process. In *Participatory Communication for Social Change*, ed. J. Servaes, T. Jacobson, and S. White, 109–122. New Delhi: Sage.

Ball, P. "Picture This." *Nature* 417 (4) (July 2002): 11–13.

Berners-Lee, T. "Tim Berners-Lee: The Year Open Data Went Worldwide." *TEDTalk*. Long Beach, CA: TED University, February 2010. http://www.ted.com/talks/tim_berners_lee_the_year_open_data_went_worldwide.html.

Boutin, P. "Your Results May Vary: Will the Information Superhighway Turn into a Cul-de-sac because of Automated Filters?" *The Wall Street Journal*, May 20, 2011. http://online.wsj.com/article/SB10001424052748703421204576327414266287254 .html.

Chen, C. "Information Visualization is Growing." *Information Visualization* 1 (2002): 159–164.

Cohen, J. E. "Cyberspace as/and Space." *Columbia Law Review* 107 (1) (January 2007): 210–256.

Fekete, J.-D., J. Van Wijk, and J. Stasko. The Value of Information Visualization. In *Information Visualization*, ed. A. Kerren, J. Stasko, J.-D. Fekete, and C. North, 1–18. Berlin, Heidelberg: Springer-Verlag, 2008.

Friendly, M. A Brief History of Information Visualization. In *Handbook of Data Visualization*, ed. C.-h. Chen, W. K. Hardle, and A. Unwin, 15–56. Berlin, Heidelberg: Springer-Verlag, 2008.

Fuchs, C. "Knowledge Management in Self-Organizing Social Systems." *Journal of Knowledge Management Practice*, May 2004. http://www.tlainc.com/articl61 .htm?newwindow=true.

Fuchs, C. "Knowledge and Society from the Perspective of the Unified Theory of Information (UTI) Approach." In *Proceedings of FIS 2005: Third Conference on the Foundations of Information Science*, ed. M. Petitjean, 1–29. Paris: July 4–7, 2005. http:// www.mdpi.org/fis2005/F.24.paper.pdf.

Howard, A. "Global Adaptation Index Enables Better Data-driven Decisions." *O'Reilly Strata*, September 15, 2011. http://radar.oreilly.com/2011/09/global-adaptation -index-open-data-speed.html.

Janert, P. K. *Data Analysis with Open Source Tools: A Hands-on Guide for Programmers and Data Scientists*. Sebastopol, CA: O'Reilly, 2010.

Jha, A. "Internet and the Shifting Grounds of Knowledge." Presented at *The Conference on The Emerging Organisation of Knowledge and the Future of Universities*, December 19–20, 2008. New Delhi: Jamia Milia Islamia University, 32nd Indian Social Science Congress, 2008, 1–9. http://www.vidyaashram.org/papers/ISSC_Avinash _Jha_Internet.pdf.

Kaplan, A. *The Development of Capacity. NGLS Development Dossier*. Geneva: UN Non-Governmental Liaison Service, 1999.

Kerren, A., J. T. Stasko, J.-D. Fekete, and C. North. "Workshop Report: Information Visualization–Human-Centered Issues in Visual Representation, Interaction, and Evaluation." *Information Visualization* 6, no. 3 (2007): 189–196.

Kielman, J. "Foundations and Frontiers in Visual Analytics." *Information Visualization* 8 (4) (2009): 239–246.

Kleinrock, L. "History of the Internet and its Flexible Future." *Wireless Communications, IEEE* 15 (1) (February 2008): 8–18.

Liew, A. "Understanding Data, Information, Knowledge and Their Inter-Relationships." *Journal of Knowledge Management Practice* 8 (2) (June 2007). http://www.tlainc.com/articl134.htm.

Nandy, A. *The Intimate Enemy*. Bombay: Oxford University Press, 1987.

Pariser, E. *The Filter Bubble: What the Internet Is Hiding from You*. New York: Penguin Press, 2011.

Pinter, L., L. Bizikova, K. Kutics, and A. Vari. "Developing a System of Sustainability Indicators for the Lake Balaton Region." *Tajokologiai Lapok* 6 (3) (2008): 271–292.

Roberts, N. C. "Tracking and Disrupting Dark Networks: Challenges of Data Collection and Analysis." *Information Systems Frontiers* 13 (1) (2011): 5–19.

Sahasrabudhey, S. "Knowledge Flux and the Demand on Thought: Dialogue at Indian Association for Cultivation of Sciences." Unpublished paper presented at *The Indian Association for Cultivation of Sciences*. Calcutta, India: April 15, 2008, 1–17, http://vidyaashram.org/publications.html.

Santos, B. S. A Discourse on the Sciences. In *Cognitive Justice in a Global World: Prudent Knowledges for a Decent Life*, ed. B. S. Santos, 13–48. Toronto: Lexington Books, 1987/2007.

Santos, B. S. *The Rise of the Global Left: the World Social Forum and Beyond*. New York: Zed Books, 2006.

Santos, B. S. Introduction. In *Cognitive Justice in a Global World: Prudent Knowledges for a Decent Life*, ed. B. S. Santos, 1–12. Toronto: Lexington Books, 2007.

Shneiderman, B. "Inventing Discovery Tools: Combining Information Visualization with Data Mining." *Information Visualization* 1 (1) (2002): 5–12.

Shiva, V. Western Science and its Destruction of Local Knowledge. In *The Post-Development Reader*, ed. M. Rahnema and V. Bawtree, 161–167. London: Zed Books, 1997.

Snowden, D. Cynefin: A Sense of Time and Space, the Social Ecology of Knowledge Management. In *Knowledge Horizons: The Present and the Promise of Knowledge Management*, ed. C. Despres and D. Chauvel, 237–266. Woburn, MA: Butterworth Heinemann, 2000.

Sparks, C. *Globalization, Development and the Mass Media*. Los Angeles: Sage, 2007.

Stiglitz, J. E., A. Sen, and J.-P. Fitoussi. *Report by the Commission on the Measurement ofEconomic Performance and Social Progress*, Paris: Commission on the Measurement of Economic Performance and Social Progress, 2009, 1–292, http://www.stiglitz-sen-fitoussi.fr/en/index.htm.

Tamburri, R. "Canadian Researchers Launch National Index of Well-Being." *University Affairs* 19 (October) (2011). http://www.universityaffairs.ca/canadian -researchers-to-launch-national-index-of-wellbeing.aspx.

Thomas, J. J. "Visual Analytics: Why Now?" *Information Visualization* 6 (2007): 104–106.

Visvanathan, S. Knowledge, Justice and Democracy. In *Science and Citizens: Globalization and the Challenge of Engagement*, ed. M. Leach, I. Scoones, and B. Wynne, 83–94. New York: Zed Books, 2005.

Wallace, P. Introduction. In *Knowledge Management: Historical and Cross-Disciplinary Themes*, ed. P. Wallace, 1–10. Westport, CT: Libraries Unlimited, 2007.

13 Open Development Is a Freedom Song: Revealing Intent and Freeing Power

Ineke Buskens

Events since the year 2008 give cause for reflection about the nature of the global economy and its impact on our world. As we look back on the global financial crisis of 2008 from the perspective of the U.S. credit rating crisis of 2011, it has become apparent that the global systems of finance, production, and governance face real limits. But until this series of crises was upon us, the majority of people, among them even economic experts, were apparently unaware of the impending collapse. For the billions of people who contributed their labor, time, energy and genius, and who had invested their dreams and savings, the financial system was never intended to function as it did, and the current outcry is a sign of deep sentiments of loss and betrayal.

Lessons about this historical moment need to be applied to open development. The information age (a term coined by Daniel Bell) and the network society (a concept introduced by Manuel Castells) that form the backdrop for this volume have given rise to a new networked social morphology that has transformed the mechanisms of governance, production, and subjectification.[1] These transformations are important. We need to understand them as potential models of open development, and as sites of struggle, because they may offer solutions to problems of underdevelopment and marginalization. But we cannot artificially isolate the idea of a networked social morphology from the overarching myth of the global economy. In the wake of the global financial crisis, it has become clear that we need to theorize and practice open development in ways that will keep our minds alive to the intentionality of open processes, especially given the larger political-economic discourses that shape our thinking and our actions.

Peter Moddel frames the term *intent* as "the impetus to form meaning or to perform a specific act" and he asserts that intent is "ignored in classical science and without a place in cybernetic emitter/receptor descriptions of communication, the ubiquity of intent has been left unacknowledged and yet without it no unit of meaning would enter our minds and we would be zombies in a world totally out of reach."[2] Open development, as a conceptual constellation comprising both concepts and practices, holds a dream for change[3] that is grounded in human intentions. We need to acknowledge human intentions as comprising and constituting open development initiatives because this asserts the agency of open development designers, thinkers, practitioners, and participants, and therefore enhances the transformative potential of these efforts.[4] This approach is consistent with Amartya Sen's vision of development as freedom.[5]

It is, furthermore, important to examine the conceptual environment in which open development operates. Concepts have great power in directing and structuring human thought and behavior. Conceptual constellations exist in and interact with other conceptual constellations within dynamic force fields of power relations. Mutual influence between conceptual constellations is happening all the time. Outcomes of such encounters depend on how the intensity of human intent interacts with mechanisms of power in concrete and specific situations. Furthermore, concepts have "bewitching power": even when conceptual constellations do not deliver on their promise, in the sense that there is no logical link between the apparent intentionality of a concept and its actual real impact, human beings will persist in believing in the concept. This is particularly true when the intentionality of the concept has emotive and persuasive power.

It is, therefore, important to not only examine the conceptual environment in which open development operates, but also how the mechanisms of conceptual bewitching work. In becoming aware of these conceptual dynamics, human beings committing themselves to open development can keep course as they intended.

With this in mind, part I of this chapter examines the broader conceptual environment shaping international development in the world today. In part II of this chapter, mechanisms of conceptual bewitching will be examined with reference to a series of examples: gross domestic product, separate development, structural adjustment, connectivity through mobile phones, and the ideal of first come, first served.[6] This sets the scene for part III of this chapter where I sketch open development as an expression of a new worldview that could be framed as both a critique of and an alternative to the current mainstream econocentric worldview. International development deals with humans—with human aspirations and human suffering—and it is inspired by the human drive to reach out to those among us who are less advantaged in terms of circumstances, opportunities, and capabilities. This chapter will offer a way of thinking about open development that makes agency central to openness in ways that can keep us alive to our intentions and less prone to conceptual bewitching.

Part I: What Is This Age We Live In?

Every society is characterized first and foremost by its implicit assumptions about who we think we are as human beings, what the world is about or should be about, what the right way of living is, and what our purpose in this world is or should be. These basic assumptions form a grid that sustains and creates our thinking, doing, relating, being, and knowing. From this grid we will gather the data, glean the information, construct the knowledge, distill the understanding, and design the wisdom that we think we need and that makes sense to us, from the perspective of that grid. This same grid will also provide for us the justifications for the way we go about our thinking, doing, relating, being, and knowing: every paradigm or worldview comprises its own parameters for rationality and hence the reason for its existence.

The most powerful institution in our society will invariably determine the parameters of this grid and thereby shape our understandings in this regard. In the current age, this institution is the global economy. As the previous president of the Institute of Noetic Sciences, the futurist Willis Harman,[7] said in an interview with Sarah van Gelder: "Every society has some kind of an organizing myth; traditional societies had one, medieval society had one, we have one. Very central to our modern myth is the idea that it's perfectly reasonable that the economy should be the paramount institution around which everything else revolves, and that economic logic and economic values should guide our decisions." Harman argues that our particular econocentric worldview is deeply elitist, as it "works to the benefit of the few and penalizes masses of people today and in the future."[8]

Because the underlying value system of our global civilization is grounded in an economic ideology that has made monetary value its keystone, human beings and the natural environment do not hold intrinsic value. Furthermore, because economic value has become equated with monetary value, unpaid caring work that serves to maintain and repair our world has been made invisible. This affects women in particular ways as it makes their responsibilities—for bearing and raising children, taking care of the elderly and the sick, and contributing to important causes in their communities—unrewarded and hence invisible. Failing to acknowledge such important contributions to human life and the human species is not only unjust toward women as individual humans, but it also makes the global economic focus on money quite unsustainable. Our global economic dispensation's propensity to exacerbate inequality and hence instability is succinctly characterized by Harman: "At one time, it was a dominant belief in Western society that if you behaved pretty well here on this earthly plane you'd go to heaven; that belief system held the society together in certain ways. Then we changed that belief and essentially said if you can trample on others and succeed then you'll get the most toys in the end and you'll win the game, and people behaved accordingly."[9]

According to one Nobel laureate economist, Joseph Stiglitz: "We have created a society in which materialism overwhelms moral commitment, in which the rapid growth that we have achieved is not sustainable environmentally or socially, in which we do not act together to address our common needs. Market fundamentalism has eroded any sense of community and has led to rampant exploitation of unwary and unprotected individuals."[10]

Given that the global economy has become a threat to sustainable human progress we need to question its influence on processes dedicated to development.[11] The United Nations Research Institute for Social Development (UNRSID) 2005 Gender Report asserts that it will not be possible to secure gender equality in a world in which the "dominant policy model tends to deepen social and economic inequality and reinforce marginalization; in which redistribution has no place; and in which governments compromise the interests of their citizens to accommodate global forces."[12] Furthermore, as the countries that reported the greatest economic growth, India and China, also accounted for the greatest number of missing women, it is clear that there is no guarantee that economic growth will enhance human progress and development.[13] Even if the global economy were functional (recent events clearly demonstrate that it is not) the dominant economic model would fail to create a suitable set of normative guidelines for human development.[14,15]

How Does This World View Effect International and Open Development?

The current mainstream worldview not only steers and regulates economic thinking and economic behavior, it also influences concepts and practices in more general ways, and in other areas of human life, because it is the main institution of our world; it is our global organizing myth. Open development and international development will inevitably be influenced by this conceptual force field in many ways. In the following section I discuss three areas of conceptual influencing that are pertinent to the question of whether open development could realize its dream of transformation.

In the first place, the mere use of the terms *information age* or *networked society* is obscuring the lived reality of many people on this planet, even before the financial crises took place. We would have good reason to call our era "the Era of Predators Gone out of Control" instead. Just as there were good reasons to call the European Middle Ages the "Dark Ages" and not the "Age of Messengers." In the Middle Ages, important news spread by people traveling on foot, on horseback, or on boats, and learning and teaching took place face to face. But there was much more going on in the European Middle Ages than that: there were witch hunts, the Holy Inquisition, the Crusades—and scientists like Galileo were imprisoned because they valued scientific integrity above authoritarian, religious dogma. These were the traits seen to have the most important effect on human civilization and progress in this era and hence it entered history as the Dark Ages.

Along the same vein, the world we are transitioning into cannot be characterized primarily in terms of the communication technology we use. In our human experience, we cannot separate the informational network character of our world from its aspect as "the era of predators gone out of control." Doing so would lead us to fall in the same trap as the people who described the Egyptian uprising as the Facebook revolution—as if the revolution happened because Facebook exists—rather than recognizing the material and political basis of the uprising. In fact, the uprising was a response to systemic injustice perpetrated by an authoritarian regime. Similarly, using the concepts of information age or networked society in an unqualified way obscures the destructive power of our mainstream worldview. But worst of all, the mystifying of so many aspects of this world's lived reality disqualifies and disempowers the human perspective—and with that, the possibility for developing a humanist perspective on the information age.

As the global financial crisis has unfolded, commentators and protestors have taken to blaming individual bankers or Wall Street for the economic collapse.[16] But despite what many people, including President Obama, had to say about their depravity, the bankers still took their multimillion dollar bonuses. It is thus obvious that the immorality in the financial sector is exactly the mentality that the economic system creates and rewards.[17] Instead of placing blame, we need to reflect on what we have created: a predatory global system where trampling on others is indeed rewarded. Its power to suffuse our intentions and permeate our concepts and practices should not be underestimated. By using concepts that correspond with and hence maintain this predatory global culture, we may unwittingly contribute to the failure of open development efforts—thwarting the intentions for transformation that we had chosen consciously.

In the second place, the concept of a human being that emerges in this mainstream worldview is that of a greedy person, driven mainly by ruthless competition and self-interest without much room for moral conflict. It is this idea of a human being as a greedy competitor that is used to justify the current economic world order,[18] and it emerges in debates around alternatives for a global economic order, such as the Venus Project suggested by Jacques Fresco.[19] But we must question whether this conceptualization of the nature of a human being is valid and correct. By giving prominence to conceptualizations of human nature that are propagated by proponents and beneficiaries of this predatory economic world order, the dominance of the system and its rewards is reinforced. This is one of the points Jacques Fresco makes in discussions that propose his idea for a different global economic dispensation.[20] It is obvious that human beings appreciate the values of caring and sharing. A lot of caring and sharing work does take place, monetarily rewarded or not. Furthermore, the values of collaboration are acknowledged in the ways the new information and communication technologies are used, which only seem surprising if we still hold on to the erroneous conception of human beings as isolated units driven by self-interest and competition.[21] The systemic and systematic denial of the important values of caring and sharing in our lives distorts who we as humans are and what we do, *also in our economic expressions*. The reflection we receive from the mainstream global dispensation as selfish, greedy beings is thus distorted. More importantly, the systematic denial of the actual existence and importance of human caring and sharing reveals the mainstream econocentric ideology as an irrational projection. Harman seems to be closer to reality in the following passage:

If you were to look at the goals that not only this society but any human society seems to aim toward, you would come up with: We want a wholesome environment in which to raise our children. We want a good relationship with nature. We want to feel safe. We hold dear certain values like democracy, liberty, the rule of law, equity and justice and so on.[22]

In the third place, an econocentric worldview by its own nature would favor knowledge construction processes that frame human beings as passive consumers. It is no coincidence that the mainstream research paradigm is still geared toward creating knowledge for prediction and control, framing human beings as passive objects of study, and deemphasizing their interpretive capacities and their potential to change their world as emancipatory actors.[23]

But this epistemic bias is actually detrimental to international development and open development. It will negatively influence research, design, monitoring, and evaluation in two major ways. First, framing researchers as technocrats devoid of intent and research respondents as mere objects of study makes the human capacity for individual intent and interpretation invisible. Failing to acknowledge these human capacities will make it more difficult to understand human agency. As human agency is key to the success of development efforts, development research that fails to acknowledge human intent and interpretation will make international development and open development less effective.[24]

Second, the underutilization of hermeneutic-interpretive and critical-emancipatory approaches will lead to many missed research opportunities for open development. Much of the collaborative design work that is so essential to many open development efforts can only be done justice to, in and through research that makes the design process—the actual developmental action process—visible. This is done best through action research approaches, which acknowledge researchers and research participants as *emancipatory actors*. Furthermore, as Matthew L. Smith, Laurent Elder, and Heloise Emdon state, ICT and open development initiatives open up possibilities for participatory methodologies.[25] Both action research and participatory research need to appeal to methodological criteria that do justice to their particular research practice and hence need justification through a different paradigmatic logic.[26]

It is inevitable that the econocentric mainstream worldview and the way in which it frames human beings influences international development and open development in many more ways than I have been able to suggest here. Such influence should not be underestimated; it is powerful because it is implicit, unexamined, and hence insidious.

Part II: Power, Concepts, and Intentions

In this section I examine mechanisms of conceptual influencing which could be transferred to the area of open development. Certain conceptual constellations deliver the opposite of what they promise regardless of the intentions behind them.

The Case of the GDP

A specific conceptual constellation that is pertinent to the fields of open development and international development is the gross domestic product (GDP).[27] The GDP represents the value of all the goods and services in an economy based on prices being charged.[28] It is conceivable that a country's GDP rises, but that the actual income of its people deteriorates while the loss in livability gets hidden. The GDP as an economic measure has set up false choices, such as the choice between promoting growth and protecting the environment.[29] Furthermore, reliance on the GDP metric masked the bad state of the U.S. economy before the credit crisis hit. Stiglitz admitted that "there has long been discussion of the metric's alleged deficiencies; namely, that it does not take into account factors such as disparity in the distribution of wealth, depletion of natural resources, underground economies, and the quality of goods and services."[30] Alternative development indicators have been available for some time that do not have these drawbacks, such as the Genuine Progress Indicator[31] and the Human Development Index, which further evolved into the Inequality-Adjusted Human Development index; the Gender Inequality Index and the Multidimensional Poverty Index,[32] And yet, the GDP as a concept is still used as a measure for growth in development discourses (in the World Bank blog, African Development Bank blog, and so forth).

Separate Development and Structural Adjustment

Similar unveilings of conceptual constellations have taken place before, involving terms and concepts that were key to development such as *separate development* and *structural adjustment*. The concept of separate development was used to denote and justify the practice of treating different peoples in different ways during Apartheid South Africa. The apparent intentionality of the concept was to respect peoples' different cultural background so that real and sustainable development could take place. From looking at the practices and outcomes of how the concept of separate development was put into actual operation, it was clear that separate development had nothing to do with real development. Its practices created a core-periphery opposition in South Africa in a way that had not existed before, where the homelands provided an ongoing flow of cheap labor to the actual white-only state. But it took a long time before this situation was seen for what it was.

The concept of structural adjustment is another example of mismatch between a conceptual promise and resulting effects. Structural adjustment was intended to whip untidy economic houses into productive order, which, in the abstract, seems a logical enough goal. But in practice, these reforms were requirements of debt repayment programs. Many African institutions were insufficiently developed to successfully implement the proposed reforms, and the debt repayment programs left them unable to generate sufficient resources to make the institutions function properly. The devastating effects of putting structural adjustment into operation can still be felt all over Africa. And yet it has guided economic development theory and practice for a very long time.

How is it that reality departs so radically from intentions in practice? And how is it that this kind of disjuncture between discourse and reality is sustained for such a long time? Two cases of information and communication technologies for development (ICT4D) reveal some of the dynamics at work in inverted promises.[33]

Conceptualizing Gender Discrimination as Fair and Empowering

At the University of Zimbabwe in Harare, access to the free library computers was governed on the basis of the rule of *first come, first served*. But the librarians noticed that the overwhelming majority of the students using the computers were male. When asked about their perspectives and experiences around access, the female students spoke about their duties as wives and mothers at home, which they had to fulfill exactly during the time at which the computers were free, and about the fact that when they lined up, they ran the risk of being pushed out of the line by the male students. While they acknowledged the *first come, first served* rule as democratic, fair, and even empowering, at the same time they lamented that they had to put in extra efforts to get access to computers in other ways. These female students did not have a concept—a way of thinking about this access rule that really matched their experience of this rule—just the lived reality that was a consequence of this rule. When the researchers subsequently deepened their research efforts and created opportunities for these women to face their experiences, emotions, reflections, and dreams, these female students were able to bring more coherence to their thinking and to acknowledge their lack of access as inconvenient and disempowering. Without the researchers' interventions, the female students would not have been able to do the conceptual work that gave them a position from which to question the fairness of this rule.[34]

The *first come, first served* rule, which was undoubtedly established by the university management with the intent to guarantee as much as possible universal access to both genders, became a tool of gender discrimination in a patriarchal environment. Even more problematic was the fact that the rule itself had become a corruptive force: it provided a logical frame for the students' experiences and thus functioned as a conceptual smokescreen, making it more difficult for them to realize what was really going on. As such, the rule was very effective in removing female competition from the computer access arena. It also kept in place the stereotypes about women and their nonuse of ICTs.

Division because of Connection: The Irony of Mobile Phone Use

The use of mobile phones enhances the possibility for connection, mobilization, and social advocacy, especially in environments where, due to lack of landlines, human messengers and face-to-face contact have to do much of this work. In such a context the innovative use of mobiles, such as paging through missed calls, seems to make more participation possible for people who cannot afford to use a mobile because of the prohibitive costs. However, K. B. Abraham found in his research regarding mobile phone networks and advocating women's rights in Zambia[35] how it was exactly this innovative use of exercising the missed-calls option that created a divisive effect within a group of women using their phones for the explicit purposes of connection, mobilization, and social advocacy; as some women could afford calling costs and others could not, the women users started speaking of "callers" and "beepers" and hence a "virtual class system" emerged that had not existed before. Because the use of ICTs takes place within a monetary system that is divisive, ICTs can become the handmaidens of this system and ICT users will perpetuate these divisive dynamics.[36] While the women organizations' intentions to enhance the effectiveness of their connection through the use of mobile phones got thwarted to a degree through the monetary aspects of the financial economic environment, they did not question this divisive aspect of the economy but took the critique to themselves and each other.

The Mechanisms of Conceptual Bewitching

Unequal access to the library computers in Zimbabwe was caused by the democratic intentionality of the first come, first served rule. The students' acceptance of these connotations in the process of giving meaning to their experiences created a smokescreen that prevented them from making a clear analysis of the actual effects of the open-access rule. The discourse of connectivity surrounding mobile phone use caused divisive results from mobile phone use among activists in Zambia. In both cases, it can be argued that the actors' conceptualizations collaborated with and contributed to the mismatch between their intentions and the effect of their actions.

Why does it take us so long to understand that certain constellations of concepts and practices are not delivering on their promises? There is, of course, the habit factor: a conceptual constellation has its mechanisms of action and chains of activities that cannot be easily interrupted and changed because human beings are creatures of habit.

But there is more to it than simply habits. As the Zimbabwe case shows, there was power involved on various levels: there was the power of the unquestioned schedule of the library opening times, which was an expression of cultural male-centeredness, and there was the actual physical power abuse of the male students. Both forms of power influenced the behavior of the female students, and of this they were aware. The case can be made however that both these powers in tandem would also have influenced the female students' conceptualization processes. Living in a patriarchal environment not only means that the threat of male abuse of physical power is always present and real, it also means that the male-dominated culture has infused all general rules, norms as well as the representations and images of such norms and rules. It was the female students' conceptualization work that created the smokescreen preventing a clear understanding of what was actually happening. It can be argued as well that the first function of this smokescreen for the female students was thus to prevent them from realizing what was going on—"adapting their preference" to what they had come to accept as possible, rather than questioning and rebelling against the status quo.[37] To keep this pretense up, it would have been imperative not to become conscious of their part in this conceptualization process. But in making their conceptual work of supporting the male-dominated culture invisible, the female students would also have made the male interest in the status quo invisible. Power and invisibility were playing out an intricate dance where the women did the work and the men got the benefits.

This adaptive preference in which disempowered people adjust their choice or priority to what seems acceptable in the mainstream culture helps explain other cases of failed promise. The concepts of GDP, structural adjustment, and separate development come from the most powerful echelons of our econocentric world: the financial-monetary sector. It would be logical to assume that most people would have adjusted their preference to this all-pervasive conceptual constellation. It can also be argued that the more disempowered people are, the more absolute this adaptation would be. It is a fact well known to feminist researchers "that the viewpoint of the dominant groups, which permeates the common knowledge of how society should function, has obscured the true interests of other groups."[38]

This analysis resonates with how the Zambian women organizations took the divisive aspect of the monetary system toward themselves and each other, instead of realizing the significance of mobile telephony causing divisions that were not there before. The Zimbabwe case study shows how the social and individual gender power dimensions create and maintain each other: the dynamic of disempowered people accepting the concepts of the powerful to give meaning to their own personal experiences. Women and other disempowered people may thus not even be aware of the ways in which they are agents to their own disempowerment—not only because of the way they give meaning to their experiences influenced by the power in their environments, but because they may give up their alignment to their own intent in the face of outside pressure without being totally aware of this. In this example as well, power and invisibility may be playing out an intricate dance where the disempowered do the work and the empowered get the benefits.

If we turn our focus to the way human beings process theoretical concepts internally, the reason for the need to have reality match concepts (instead of the other way around) becomes even more understandable: concepts are powerful tools that, once accepted as an intricate part of a collective consciousness, create the parameters for people's thoughts, emotions, experiences, and realities. Concepts become the places and spaces we humans dream in and reach out from. In that process they form us and inform us about what we perceive inside as well as outside of us. There is no real separation between a thinker and a thought: the moment one inhabits a concept, thinker and thought have become one, unless one takes special effort to observe oneself in thought.

Because of the generally unreflective nature of the thought process, concepts have the power to reveal reality while at the same time masking other aspects of that same reality. Hence, concepts that evoke the understanding of a genuine intent of what *development* means will lead people with the noblest of intentions astray, even though the practices that accompany that concept affect the opposite of what seems to be promised. As our perception is so guided by the conceptualizations we have embraced, and because conceptualizations are often tautological (in the sense that they harbor the reason for their existence within their specific explanatory field), concepts are thus the ideal smoke screens.

Lifting the Veil

It has become clear from examining the scenarios above that it can take a long time before the internal inconsistency in a conceptual constellation is detected and hence can be identified as a problem. The lack of coherence reveals that somewhere a link is missing in the logical sequence between: The "promise" that the conceptual constellation holds; the apparent intentionality of actual manifestation of the promise; the "official" meanings that were given to the measures and activities which the intent gave rise to in terms of conceptualizations; the outcomes in terms of human experiences and lived realities; the impact in terms of manifested state.

The fact that this lack of coherence remains invisible for so long contributes to the situation of the concept not delivering on its promise. As we have seen, power plays a crucial role here: whether this power was vested in patriarchal or financial control, the invisibility of the incoherence served the interest and intentionality of the more powerful entity in the wider environment. Conceptual constellations such as the GDP, separate development, structural adjustment, the *first come first served* rule, and mobile connection reflect the interests and intentions of the systems that created these conceptual constellations. The more powerful entity may not always have been the creator of the original, bewitching, conceptual constellation. But because of its relative power, it was in a position to sway whatever was initially intended to fit its own interests. The disempowered meanwhile undertake the conceptualization work that keeps the status quo of incoherence intact, and this serves to make the interest of the more powerful entity invisible. This total complex amounts to a typical tautological feedback loop, where the disempowered become agents in and of their own disempowerment by not only accepting the perspective of the greater power in their environment, but also by giving up (in degrees) on their own intent.

In both the Zambian and the Zimbabwean case, a caring outsider was needed to lift the smokescreen and make the discrepancy visible, conscious, and debatable. It is possible that similar process dynamics made the unveilings of separate development, structural adjustment, and the GDP possible. But how can we lift the veil on open development in ways that will ensure that the intentions behind this concept are transmitted accurately in reality? How can we ensure that open development becomes a mechanism that injects humanity and sustainability into the dominant econocentric model, rather than becoming a handmaiden of that model? In many ways this book was an important step down the road toward answering these questions. We need to understand open processes both as models and as sites of struggle. But given what has happened with the global financial crisis, it also becomes apparent that we need to study them as potential sites in which the disempowered give their power away to the powerful merely by the way they think.

We thus need to understand open development as a conceptual constellation that operates in a force field of human interest, intentionality, and power. Conceptual constellations invite users (insiders) to perceive their processes, outcomes, and even impact on the environment through the lens of their conceptualizations. But as a result, they may create a smokescreen, making any lack of coherence between intent and impact in the environment invisible.

It is of crucial importance to understand whether a conceptual constellation one engages with is in conflict with more powerful conceptual constellations in the wider environment, in terms of intentionality and interest. When the intent behind the conceptual constellation one engages with conflicts with a more powerful constellation in the environment, the concepts and practices of the greater power may thwart the intent and interest of the original constellation until it fits its own intentionality and interest. Because of the smokescreen created by the conceptualizations of the less powerful, the lack of coherence between intent and desired impact may remain invisible for a long time. This invisibility serves the more powerful conceptual constellation in the environment. Power and invisibility go hand in hand in this situation.

But when there is dialogue between insiders and outsiders (those who are subject to a conceptual mirage and those who are not), the lack of coherence between intent and impact and between conceptual constellations in terms of intentionalities and interests can be made visible and named. In this process of making visible and naming, the pervasive conceptual constellation in the environment that influences the original conceptual constellation to get off track can be managed and neutralized.

Most importantly, however, the most powerful defense against the co-option and colonization of a conceptual constellation by a more powerful conceptual constellation with conflicting intentions and interest is conscious insider intent. Keeping alignment with original intent will make lack of coherence between original intent and actual manifestation immediately visible. Realizing lack of coherence creates the possibility for expressing discontent and creating other possibilities.

Part III: A New Paradigm for Open Development

For Yochai Benkler, as he writes in the foreword to this book, open development is about freedom: "for development in particular, open models provide an important counterweight to the neoliberal Washington consensus, as well as later efforts to soften it. In particular, open models offer a degree of freedom, in the engineering sense, for designing development-oriented interventions without strong dependencies on either markets or states." This idea is echoed again and again with reference to the Internet: it is about free sharing, not hampered by control of code, property rights, or the market. It is about creating open and free spaces where actors can express, connect, and share to the degree they want and with whom they want. As is stated on the Mozilla website, "We believe that the internet should be public, open and accessible."[39] The concept of openness may have been a translation of freedom at a certain time, to escape the "ideological and confrontational connotations of the term 'free software.'"[40] But the fact remains that in exercising freedom of expression and sharing, the conceptual constellations of freedom and openness intersect and collide, and become markers that guide as well as give meaning to what is happening in the real world.

For *Time* magazine editor Levv Grosman, open development is about connection: "It's a story about community and collaboration on a scale never seen before. It's about the cosmic compendium of knowledge Wikipedia and the million-channel people's network YouTube and the online metropolis MySpace. It's about the many wresting power from the few and helping one another for nothing and how that will not only change the world, but also change the way the world changes."[41] If economic value were equated with monetary value, there is not much of an economy happening in the work these organizations undertake. But in the open, virtual, global spaces they create, a lot is happening that contributes directly to human freedom and—through enhancing the choices that people have—to human progress and development. And even though money still plays a role—journals like *Truthout* and activist organizations like Avaaz need funding to keep functioning—separating nonprofit organizations like Wikipedia and Mozilla from *Truthout* and other online journals would not enhance our understanding of the global focus and scope of these enterprises. It is about "people to people . . . that was what the Web was supposed to be all along," as Tim Berners-Lee stated.[42]

Through their actions open development thinkers and doers have aligned themselves with enabling and enhancing equity, sharing, and connectedness. It is obvious that their contributions are not driven primarily by greed or competition but by the intrinsic human needs to make useful and meaningful contributions, share openly and collaborate freely. Open development could thus be framed as a critique on the existing utilitarian, growth-driven, econocentric mainstream worldview.

The most significant characteristic of open development, albeit not expressed in words, but in actions, is individual, personal intent. The most important and most powerful driver of development and hence also of open development, is human intent, the intent of all the human beings who are part of development processes. It is human intention that keeps a project aligned to a purpose. But in open development individual human intent is undeniably key to everything: most of the work is self-initiated and unpaid. This makes it all the more imperative to give human intent a prominent and explicit place in the concepts, measures, and strategies that aim to do justice to open development initiatives, whether it refers to design, research, practice, or participation. But I also think that creating an explicit place for human intent in processes of initiating, reflecting, and communicating will go a long way in assisting open development initiatives as conceptual constellations to withstand co-option or colonization by the mainstream econocentric worldview.[43]

In the Zimbabwean and Zambian case studies, the research participants realized the disjuncture between their intent and the eventual manifestation when they were reminded of their original intent. This learning can be transferred to efforts in open development in general. Dialoguing about the relationship between intent, conceptualizations, activities, outcomes, and manifestation or impact will open up the tautological feedback loop that so many conceptual constellations set up. In such dialogues, the concepts will be taken out of their explanatory field of justification and explanation and held up to their promise and the individual human intentionalities that inspired their design and use.

Furthermore, acknowledging each other's human intentionality in line with the shared purpose will create a field for meaningful dialogue and interaction between actors. A focus on intent rather than on objectives and outcomes will keep the process and product development aligned with the project purpose but will also allow a flexible and fluid unfolding of unexpected and maybe even unintended positive effects. Additionally, such a development or research process will do justice to the dream and nature of open development.

It is argued, therefore, that it might be good to create an alternative paradigmatic space for open development as a field of human action and knowledge construction. Although it is always a delicate matter to speak for others—and definitely dangerous to speak for a whole collective or set of collectives of people investing much of their open mind and free time to collaboration on open development ventures—it would be dangerous to leave open development in a conceptual void. I aimed to make clear in part I and part II of this chapter why it would be dangerous to do so: the chance that the dominant world view which obviously runs counter to the thinking and doing in open development could colonize and co-opt open initiatives and spaces is very real. Furthermore, as knowledge construction processes in open development evolve in a particular way, any research, monitoring, and evaluation that aims to make worthwhile contributions to open development would have to do justice to that; failing to do this would not only create dissonance and incoherence in terms of process but also to distortion of knowledge content. Therefore, leaving a conceptual constellation such as open development in a methodological void is not rational in the current force field of conflicting conceptual constellations and power differentials. If we do not explicate the intentions for open development as they present themselves, then we risk having its potential and the time and energy of its contributors co-opted by other visions of development.

The paradigmatic contours of ontological, epistemological, axiological, and methodological dimensions are emerging in the concepts, the discourses, the explanations, and most importantly in the actions of the humans co-creating the open development efforts. Paradigm recognition work should be a collaborative effort, and definitely when it refers to open development! In presenting a very brief outline of a paradigm for open development, I hope it will be perceived as I intended: as a temporary place-holder that aims to stimulate future methodological action and reflection. So although it cannot be conclusively stated what open development is (and I argue that it needs to stay that way) in order for open development to stay open, it needs its own conceptual framework with shared understandings regarding the conceptualization of these entities:

- International development and human development.
- A human being.
- Knowledge.
- What a society is or should be.
- The human values in use.

With this in mind, the intention of open development as a paradigm includes the following "definitions":

Progress as Human Development. Progress is defined as enhancing well-being for humans and human community. *Development* is defined as freedom. Important indicators are the Human Development Index, the Inequality-adjusted Human Development Index, the Gender Inequality Index, and the Multidimensional Poverty Index.[44]

Human Beings. Human beings are intentional, emancipatory, and creative actors. These qualities refer to developers and researchers and also to participants and beneficiaries.

Knowledge. Knowledge should be agile, fluid, and openly accessible. Knowledge should lend itself for sharing and co-creating. Processes of learning, sharing and collaboration, and networking are important fields of study. All research approaches are valued as far as they give insight into particular phenomena.

Society. A society should stimulate open spaces for human interaction and sharing in horizontal ways. The main thrust of economic systems should be to stimulate conscious human evolution and more freedom.

Values. Caring, sharing, and collaboration are rational values. Human progress is defined by real freedom for all people. The human capacity for sharing, creating and giving is infinite. Humans living together can create a non zero-sum state.[45]

This outline could guide insiders as well as external agents dealing with open development in choosing concepts, measures, and accountability strategies that could do justice to the specific nature of open development initiatives.[46] They also serve as a balance sheet of intentionality for open development initiatives. Where the project does not meet these intentions in practice, then the process has become closed to the agency of its participants.

The thinkers and doers in open development have shown, more through their actions than through their reflections on their actions, what their paradigm for design, research, action, and action research in open development could look like. They are offering an egalitarian space that is an alternative to the hegemony of the mainstream econocentric worldview and that challenges the existing mainstream research paradigm that focuses on knowledge and action for control and prediction instead of change, expression, sharing, and creativity.

Acknowledging the importance of human intent will allow open development initiatives to remain open and yet participate in accountability discourses. To strengthen human intent and hence human agency is also coherent with the project of open development itself that is so grounded in the freedom of connection, sharing, and expressing. Open development may be a freedom song in more ways than we can imagine even now; the field is still expanding and creating new horizons. It has made our world already a more free, caring, and sharing place. We have much to look forward to. As well, in fostering the field of open development, we would do well in honoring the intent of the human beings that are thinking and creating it into existence. Honoring this intent means revealing it and freeing its power.

Notes

1. See introduction to this volume.

2. P. Moddel, "Intent and the Process of Becoming Conscious: A Phenomenological View. Society for Scientific Exploration," 2009, http://www.scientificexploration .org/talks/27th_annual/27th_annual_moddel_p_phenomenology_intent.html.

3. M. Smith and L. Elder, "Open ICT Ecosystems Transforming the Developing World," *Journal of Information Technology and International Development* 6, no. 1 (Special Issue on open development, 2010): 65–71.

4. It opens up at the same time the realization of the intentionality of the people thinking and reflecting on open development.

5. In gratitude to Amartya Sen for opening up the perspective on human agency in international development with his thinking on wealth, functioning, capability, voice, and critical agency. A. Sen, *Development as Freedom* (Oxford: Oxford University Press, 1999); A. Blunden, "Amartya Sen on Well-being and Critical Voice," August, 2004, http://home.mira.net/~andy/works/sen-critical-voice.htm.

6. The last two concepts were the focus of research projects that took place under the umbrella of GRACE (Gender Research in Africa and the Middle East into ICT for Empowerment). GRACE is an IDRC-funded research network comprising twenty-one teams in fourteen countries.

7. Willis Harman has passed away.

8. S. van Gelder, "The Transformation of Business," Summer, 1995, http://www.context.org/iclib/ic41/harman.

9. Ibid.

10. See J. E. Stiglitz, "Moral Bankruptcy," *Mother Jones*, 2010, http://www.motherjones.com/politics/2010/01/joseph-stiglitz-wall-street-morals.

11. D. Kleine, "'None but ourselves can free our minds'—Development, Technological Change and Escaping the Tyranny of Direct Impact," paper presented at the IFIP 9.4 Workshop "Theorising Development and Technological Change," London School of Economics, May 26, 2010.

12. UNRISD Gender Report, *Gender Equality: Striving for Justice in an Unequal World*, Occasional Paper 15 (Geneva: United Nations Research Institute for Social Development/UN, 2005).

13. M. Molyneux and S. Razavi, *Beijing Plus 10: An Ambivalent Record on Gender Justice*, Occasional Paper 15 (Geneva: United Nations Research Institute for Social Development/UN, 2006).

14. A. Sen, *Development as Freedom*, 1999; M. C. Nussbaum, *Women and Human Development: The Capabilities Approach* (Cambridge: Cambridge University Press, 2000); M. C. Nussbaum, "Capabilities as Fundamental Entitlements: Sen and Social Justice," *Feminist Economics* 9, no. 2–3 (2003): 33–59.

15. Furthermore, the successes the developed world has enjoyed in the area of health and education were not developed from within an economic business model.

16. See K. Gwynne, "Visionary Nurses Confront Wall Street and Advocate for their Patients in Rollicking Wall Street Rally," *AlterNet,* June 22, 2011, http://www .alternet.org/story/151398/thousands_of_visionary_nurses_confront_wall_street_ and_advocate_for_their_patients_in_rollicking_wall_street_rally.

17. One single world currency, as Stiglitz has been advocating since the 2008 financial crisis, may eliminate financial trade in currencies but it will not address the systemic problems of this economic system. See J. Detrixhe and S. Elsen, "Stiglitz Calls for New Global Reserve Currency to Prevent Trade Imbalances," *Bloomberg,* April 10, 2011, http://www.bloomberg.com/news/2011-04-10/stiglitz-calls-for-new-global -reserve-currency-to-prevent-trade-imbalances.html.

18. See interview with Milton Friedman where he asserts that greed is needed to drive the economy and where he attributes even emergence of human genius to capitalism and greed, "Milton Friedman on Greed," Phil Donahue Show, 1979, http://www.youtube.com/watch?v=RWsx1X8PV_A.

19. "Jacques Fresco," http://en.wikipedia.org/wiki/Jacque_Fresco.

20. Furthermore, if we take our clue of what a human being is from economists, what do we have all the other disciplines for? The impasse we experience in thinking through alternatives about a different economic global system is exactly located in this dynamic: that we have allowed a subsystem that ideally should regulate some areas of human behavior to become disproportionately important and dominant. From a historical and cultural perspective there is nothing natural or inevitable about this choice: we can evaluate the effects of this choice and choose another constellation.

21. The Technium, "Why the Impossible Happens More Often," August 26, 2011, http://www.kk.org/thetechnium/archives/2011/08/why_the_impossi.php?utm _source=feedburner&utm_medium=feed&utm_campaign=Feed%3A+thetechnium+ %28The+Technium%29.

22. van Gelder, "The Transformation," 1995.

23. The empirical-analytical paradigm (also called positivist research) still finds more favor with policymakers and academia than research done according to the thinking in the interpretive-hermeneutic and critical-emancipatory paradigms. For an overview of these three paradigms see: J. Habermas, *Theorie des kommunikativen Handelns* (Frankfurt am Main: Suhrkamp Verlag, 1981); A. Smaling, "The Pragmatic Dimension: Paradigmatic and Pragmatic Aspects of Choosing a Qualitative or Quantitative Method" *Quality and Quantity* 28, no. 3 (1994), 233–249; A. Smaling, Qualitative Research Summer Schools, organized by the Center for Research Methodology, Human Sciences Research Council (Pretoria, South Africa: 1993–1994).

24. I. Buskens, "Agency and Reflexivity in ICT4D Research: Questioning Women's Options, Poverty and Human Development," *Information Technologies & International*

Development 6, (Special Edition, 2010): 19–24; M. C. Nussbaum, *Women and Human Development*, 2000; M. C. Nussbaum, "Capabilities as Fundamental Entitlements," 33–59; A. Sen, *Development as Freedom*, 1999.

25. M. L. Smith, L. Elder, and H. Emdon, "Open Development: A New Theory for ICT4D," *Journal of Information Technology and International Development* 7, no. 1, (Special Issue, 2011): iii—ix.

26. The thinking in action research and participatory research resonates with the critical-emancipatory paradigm as understood by Habermas. For a sample of approaches relevant to research in open development see: J. Ludema, D. L. Cooperrider and F. J. Barrett, "Appreciative Inquiry: The Power of the Unconditional Positive Question," in *Handbook of Action Research: Participative Inquiry and Practice*, ed. P. Reason and H. Bradbury, (London: Sage, 2001), 187–199; P. Senge and O. Scharmer, "Community Action Research: Learning as a Community of Practitioners, Consultants and Researchers," in *Handbook of Action Research: Participative Inquiry and Practice*, ed. P. Reason and H. Bradbury (London: Sage, 2001), 238–249; A. Smaling, "Open-Mindedness, Open-Heartedness and Dialogical Openness: The Dialectics of Openings and Closures," in *Openness in Research: The Tension Between Self and Other*, ed. I. Maso, P. A. Atkinson, S. Delamont, and J. C. Verhoeven (Assen, NL: Van Gorcum, 1995), 21–32; A. Smaling, "Dialogical Partnership: The Relationship Between the Researcher and the Researched in Action Research," in *The Complexity of Relationships in Action Research*, ed. B. Boog, H. Coenen, and R. Lammerts (Tilburg, Netherlands: Tilburg University Press), 1–15.

27. While the GNP looks at the income of the people in a country, GDP looks at the output within a country; http://8020vision.com/2009/06/22/nobel-laureate-joseph -stiglitz-on-sustainability-and-growth.

28. M. Leone, "Stiglitz: GDP Blinded Us to the Crisis," *CFO*, September 29, 2009, http://www.cfo.com/article.cfm/14443847/?f=rsspage.

29. J. Stiglitz, A. Sen and J.-P. Fitoussi, *Report by the Commission on the Measurement of Economic Performance and Social Progress*, Executive Summary, point 3. (Paris: Commission on the Measurement of Economic Performance and Social Progress, 2009), http://www.stiglitz-sen-fitoussi.fr/documents/rapport_anglais.pdf.

30. M. Leone, "Stiglitz," 2009.

31. "Genuine Progress Indicator," http://en.wikipedia.org/wiki/Genuine_progress _indicator.

32. UNDP Human Development Report, *The Real Wealth of Nations: Pathways to Human Development: 20th Anniversary Edition* (New York: United Nations Development Programme, 2010).

33. See I. Buskens, "The Importance of Intent: Reflecting on Open Development for Women Empowerment," *Information Technologies & International Development* 7, no. 1 (Spring 2011): 71–76, http://itidjournal.org/itid/article/view/698/296.

34. B. Mbambo-Thata, E. Mlambo, and P. Mwatsyia, "When a Gender Blind Policy Results in Discrimination: Realities and Perceptions of Female Students at the University of Zimbabwe," in *African Women and ICTs: Investigating Technology, Gender and Empowerment*, ed. I. Buskens and A. Webb (London; Ottawa: Zed Books; IDRC, 2009), 67–76.

35. K. B. Abraham, "The Names in Your Address Book: Are Mobile Phone Networks Effective in Advocating Women's Rights in Zambia?," in *African Women and ICTs: Investigating Technology, Gender and Empowerment*, ed. I. Buskens and A. Webb (London; Ottawa: Zed Books; IDRC), 97–104.

36. A. Gurumurthy, "From Social Enterprises to Mobiles—Seeking a Peg to Hang a Premeditated ICTD Theory," *Information Technologies & International Development* 6, (Special Edition, 2010), 57–63.

37. For the concept of adaptive preference, see M. C. Nussbaum (2000).

38. M. Hill, "Development as Empowerment," *Feminist Economics* 9, no. 2–3 (2003): 130.

39. See https://wiki.mozilla.org/Website/Mozilla.org/Archive/HomepageRedesign/Content_Notes.

40. "Open Source," http://en.wikipedia.org/wiki/Main_Pagehttp://en.wikipedia.org/wiki/Open_source.

41. "You (*Time* Person of the Year)," http://en.wikipedia.org/wiki/You_(Time_Person_of_the_Year).

42. "Web 2.0," http://en.wikipedia.org/wiki/Web_2.0.

43. It can be argued that this happened with Google: various people have suggested that Google as it grew into the impressive commercial entity it has become, it lost its initial idealistic perspective as expressed in their slogan "Don't be evil," http://en.wikipedia.org/wiki/Don%27t_be_evil.

44. UNDP Human Development Report, *The Real Wealth of Nations*, 2010.

45. M. Smith, personal communication, sharing and collaboration represent a non-zero-sum proposition as opposed to the worldview of competition and greed.

46. Outcome Mapping Methodology, an approach toward planning, monitoring, and evaluating, developed by the Evaluation Unit of the International Development Research Centre has given "human intent" a foundational and fundamental place. See S. Earl, F. Carden, and T. Smutylo, *Outcome Mapping: Building Learning and Reflection into Development Programs* (Ottawa: IDRC, 2001). It can be combined with research processes such as those in emancipatory action research. See I. Buskens and S. Earl, "Research for Change—Outcome Mapping's Contribution to Emancipatory Research in Africa," *Action Research* 6, no. 2 (2008): 173–194.

Bibliography

Abraham, K. B. "The Names in Your Address Book: Are Mobile Phone Networks Effective in Advocating Women's Rights in Zambia?" In *African Women and ICTs: Investigating Technology, Gender and Empowerment*, ed. I. Buskens and A. Webb, 97–104. London; Ottawa: Zed Books; IDRC, 2009.

Blunden, A. "Amarta Sen on Well-being and Critical Voice." August, 2004. http://home.mira.net/~andy/works/sen-critical-voice.htm.

Buskens, I. "Agency and Reflexivity in ICT4D Research: Questioning Women's Options, Poverty and Human Development." *Information Technologies & International Development* 6, (Special Edition, 2010): 19–24.

Buskens, I. "The Importance of Intent: Reflecting on Open Development for Women Empowerment." *Information Technologies & International Development* 7 (1) (Spring 2011): 71–76.

Buskens, I., and S. Earl. "Research for Change—Outcome Mapping's Contribution to Emancipatory Research in Africa." *Action Research* 6 (2) (June 2008): 173–192.

Earl, S., F. Carden, and T. Smutylo. *Outcome Mapping: Building Learning and Reflection into Development Programs*. Ottawa: International Development Research Centre, 2001.

Elder, L., H. Emdon, B. Petrazzini, M. Smith,. "Open Development: A New Theory for ICD4T." *Information Technology & International Development* 7, (1) (Special Issue, 2011): iii–ix.

Gurumurthy, A. "From Social Enterprises to Mobiles-Seeking a Peg to Hang a Premeditated ICTD Theory." *Information Technologies & International Development* 6, (Special Edition, 2010): 57–63.

Habermas, J. *Theorie des kommunikativen Handelns*. Frankfurt am Main: Suhrkamp Verlag, 1981.

Hill, M. "Development as Empowerment." *Feminist Economics* 9 (2–3) (2003): 117–135.

Kleine, D. "'None but Ourselves Can Free Our Minds'—Development, Technological Change and Escaping the Tyranny of Direct Impact." Paper presented at the IFIP 9.4 Workshop "Theorising Development and Technological Change. London: London School of Economics, May 26, 2010.

Leone, M. "Stiglitz: GDP Blinded Us to the Crisis," *CFO*, September 29, 2009. http://www.cfo.com/article.cfm/14443847/?f=rsspage.

Ludema, J., D. L. Cooperrider, and F. J. Barrett. Appreciative Inquiry: The Power of the Unconditional Positive Question. In *Handbook of Action research: Participative Inquiry and Practice*, ed. P. Reason and H. Bradbury, 187–199. London: Sage, 2001.

Mbambo-Thata, B., E. Mlambo, and P. Mwatsyia. "When a Gender Blind Policy Results in Discrimination: Realities and Perceptions of Female Students at the University of Zimbabwe." In *African Women and ICTs: Investigating Technology, Gender and Empowerment*, ed. I. Buskens and A. Webb, 67–76. Ottawa: Zed Books, IDRC, 2009.

Molyneux, M., and S. Razavi. *Beijing Plus 10: An Ambivalent Record on Gender Justice*, Occasional Paper 15. Geneva: United Nations Research Institute for Social, 2006.

Moddel, P. "Intent and the Process of Becoming Conscious: A Phenomenological View. Society for Scientific Exploration." 2009, http://www.scientificexploration .org/talks/27th_annual/27th_annual_moddel_p_phenomenology_intent.html.

Nussbaum, M. C. *Women and Human Development: The Capabilities Approach*. Cambridge: Cambridge University Press, 2000.

Nussbaum, M. C. "Capabilities as Fundamental Entitlements: Sen and Social Justice." *Feminist Economics* 9 (2–3) (2003): 33–59.

Sen, A. *Development as Freedom*. Oxford: Oxford University Press, 1999.

Senge, P., and O. Scharmer. "Community Action Research: Learning as a Community of Practitioners, Consultants and Researchers." In *Handbook of Action Research: Participative Inquiry and Practice*, ed. P. Reason and H. Bradbury, 238–249. London: Sage, 2001.

Smaling, A. "The pragmatic dimension: Paradigmatic and Pragmatic Aspects of Choosing a Qualitative or Quantitative Method." *Quality & Quantity* 28 (3) (1994): 233–249.

Smaling, A. "Open-mindedness, Open-heartedness and Dialogical Openness: The Dialectics of Openings and Closures." In *Openness in Research: The Tension Between Self and Othe,*. eds. I. Maso, P. A. Atkinson, S. Delamont, and J. C. Verhoeven eds. Assen, Netherlands: Van Gorcum, 1995, 21–32.

Smaling, A. Dialogical Partnership: The Relationship Between the Researcher and the Researched in Action Research. In *The Complexity of Relationships in Action Research*, ed. B. Boog, H. Coenen, and R. Lammerts, 1–15. Tilburg, Netherlands: Tilburg University Press, 1998.

Smaling, A. Qualitative Research Summer Schools, organized by the Center for Research Methdology, Human Sciences Research Council, Pretoria, South Africa, 1993–1994.

Smith, M., and L. Elder, "Open ICT Ecosystems Transforming the Developing World," *Journal of Information Technology and International Development* 6 (1) (Special Issue on Open Development, 2010): 65–71.

Stiglitz, J., A. Sen, and J. P. Fitoussi. *Report by the Commission on the Measurement of Economic Performance and Social Progress, Executive Summary, point 3*. Paris: Commission of the Measurement of Economic Performance and Social Progress, 2009.

UNDP Human Development Report. The Real Wealth of Nations: Pathways to Human Development: 20th Anniversary Edition. 2010. New York: United Nations Development Programme.

U.N.R.I.S.D. *Gender Equality: Striving for Justice in an Unequal World*, Occasional Paper. Geneva: United Nations Research Institute for Social Development; UN, 2005.

Contributors

Yochai Benkler, Jack N. and Lillian R. Berkman Professor for Entrepreneurial Legal Studies, Faculty Co-Director, Berkman Center for Internet and Society, Cambridge, Massachusetts

Carla M. Bonina, Research Fellow, Department of Management, London School of Economics and Political Science, London, United Kingdom

Ineke Buskens, Executive Director GRACE, Research for the Future and Facilitating the Future, Grabouw, South Africa

Leslie Chan, Director, Bioline International; Associate Director, Centre for Critical Development Studies, University of Toronto Scarborough, Toronto, Canada

Abdallah S. Daar, Professor of Public Health Sciences and Surgery, University of Toronto Sandra Rotman Centre, Toronto, Canada; and Stellenbosch Institute for Advanced Study, Stellenbosch, South Africa

Jeremy de Beer, Associate Professor, Faculty of Law, University of Ottawa, Ottawa, Canada

Mark Graham, Director of Research,, Oxford Internet Institute, University of Oxford, Oxford, United Kingdom

Eve Gray, Honorary Research Associate, Centre for Educational Technology, and Senior Research Associate, IP Law and Policy Research Unit, University of Cape Town, Cape Town, South Africa

Anita Gurumurthy, Executive Director, IT for Change, Bangalore, India

Håvard Haarstad, Postdoctoral Research Fellow, Department of Geography, University of Bergen, Bergen, Norway

Blane Harvey, Senior Program Officer, International Development Research Centre, Ottawa, Canada

Myra Khan, Graduate Student, London School of Economics and Political Science, London, United Kingdom

Melissa Loudon, Doctoral Student, University of Southern California, Annenberg School for Communication and Journalism, Los Angeles, United States

Aaron K. Martin, Policy Analyst, Organisation for Economic Co-operation and Development, Paris, France

Hassan Masum, Researcher, Waterloo Institute for Complexity and Innovation, Waterloo, Toronto, Canada

Chidi Oguamanam, Associate Professor, Faculty of Law, University of Ottawa, Ottawa, Canada

Katherine M. A. Reilly, Assistant Professor, School of Communication, Simon Fraser University, Vancouver, Canada

Ulrike Rivett, Associate Professor, Department of Civil Engineering, University of Cape Town, Cape Town, South Africa

Karl Schroeder, Writer and Futurist, Toronto, Canada

Parminder Jeet Singh, Director, IT for Change, Bangalore, India

Matthew L. Smith, Senior Program Officer, International Development Research Centre, Ottawa, Canada

Marshall S. Smith, Former Under-Secretary, United States Department of Education, Former Dean and Professor, Stanford University School of Education, Palo Alto, California

Index